Transitions Towards Sustainable Mobility

Jo A.E.E. van Nunen • Paul Huijbregts •
Piet Rietveld
Editors

Transitions Towards Sustainable Mobility

New Solutions and Approaches for Sustainable Transport Systems

Springer

Editors
Jo A.E.E. van Nunen † 2010
Professor of Logistic and Information
Systems
Erasmus University Rotterdam
Rotterdam
The Netherlands

Dr. Paul Huijbregts
DINALOG
Princenhagelaan 13
4813 DA Breda
The Netherlands
huijbregts@dinalog.nl

Prof.Dr. Piet Rietveld
VU University
Department of Spatial Economics
De Boelelaan 1105
1081 HV Amsterdam
The Netherlands
p.rietveld@vu.nl

ISBN 978-3-642-44688-7 ISBN 978-3-642-21192-8 (eBook)
DOI 10.1007/978-3-642-21192-8
Springer Heidelberg Dordrecht London New York

Printed on acid-free paper

Springer is part of Springer Science+Business Media (www.springer.com)

Preface

One of the challenges for the coming decades is to arrive at a decoupling of economic growth and emissions of various pollutions and CO_2. Transport is one of the sectors confronted with this ambitious goal. Some 25–30% of world energy consumption is related to transport and its share in total energy use is increasing, making it a main factor in the global problems of energy scarcity and greenhouse gas emissions. Present developments do not show a clear tendency towards a decoupling of developments in transport-related energy use and GDP. Hence, it is no surprise that transport has been identified as one of the main sectors that need a transition. At the same time, transport systems in many countries are subject to other problems, including lack of quality and reliability and high costs. The relevant dimensions can be represented by means of the well-known triangle of 'people', 'planet' and 'profit'. Clearly, the challenges that the transport system is facing call for a broad approach, and a wide range of interlinked changes in various domains such as technology, institutions, land use and behaviour. The aim of the present book is to address a number of dimensions in such a transition.

This volume contains a selection of the results from the Transumo (TRANsition SUstainable MObility) programme carried out between 2004 and 2010. Transumo was a large Dutch innovation programme in which hundreds of private companies, governments and knowledge institutes cooperated in the development of knowledge on transitions towards sustainable mobility and a mobility system that is more efficient, more economically competitive, of higher quality and having less negative impacts on the environment. More information on the programme can be found on the website www.transumofootprint.nl.

Outputs of the Transumo programme have been published in a wide range of journals in the scientific and applied field. This can easily lead to a fragmented treatment of the broad theme of sustainable transport. Therefore, we considered it time to bring together some of its results in one volume to illustrate the broad scope of the theme.

We would like to thank many colleagues who have contributed to this volume: authors, reviewers, and the support staff who have made this project possible, in particular Ineke Spaans (Transumo) and Ellen Woudstra (editor, Spatial Economics, VU University, Amsterdam).

It was a great shock to us that Jo van Nunen, who was the initiator of this book and a source of inspiration of Transumo, unexpectedly passed away on May 12, 2010. Jo was scientific director of Transumo since 2004 and he has been of decisive importance for the successful completion of the programme. He was close to his official retirement in September 2010, and he had many plans to remain active in his fields of interest: innovations in logistics, sustainable transport, optimisations of port operations, and several more.

This book is just a small part of Jo van Nunen's heritage. We hope that it will inspire a next generation of researchers to be active in this field of transitions towards sustainable mobility.

March 2011 Paul Huijbregts
Breda/Amsterdam Piet Rietveld

Contents

1 **Introduction to Transitions Towards Sustainable Mobility** 1
Jo van Nunen, Paul Huijbregts, and Piet Rietveld

Part A Integrating Transport Infrastructure and Land Use Planning

2 **A Transition Towards Sustainable Strategy Making: Integrating Land Use and Transport Knowledge Types** 19
Marco te Brömmelstroet and Luca Bertolini

3 **The Impact of Accessibility on the Value of Offices** 41
Ghebreegziabiher Debrezion, Thomas de Graaff, and Piet Rietveld

4 **Funding Transport Infrastructure Development Through Value Capturing: A Game Theoretical Analysis** 59
Ary Samsura and Erwin van der Krabben

5 **NETLIPSE: Managing Large Infrastructure Projects** 81
Marcel Hertogh and Eddy Westerveld

Part B Experiments with Dynamic Transport Optimization

6 **Rewarding Peak Avoidance: The Dutch 'Spitsmijden' Projects** 101
Jasper Knockaert, Jessie Bakens, Dick Ettema, and Erik Verhoef

7 **Managing Supply Chains: Transport Optimization and Chain Synchronization** 119
Tom van Woensel, Said Dabia, and Ton de Kok

8 Real-Time Coordination in Container Trucking – Prototyping and Evaluating a Multi-agent System for Real-Time Container Truck Planning at Post-Kogeko 139
Hans Moonen and Jos van Hillegersberg

9 Demand Management in Transportation and Logistics 161
Niels Agatz and Jo van Nunen

Part C Towards Reliable Transport Systems

10 Beyond Punctuality: Appropriate Measures for Unreliability in Rail Passenger Transport 175
Martijn Brons and Piet Rietveld

11 Algorithmic Support for Railway Disruption Management 193
Leo Kroon and Dennis Huisman

Part D Sustainable Logistics and Traffic Management

12 Customized Solutions for Sustainable City Logistics: The Viability of Urban Freight Consolidation Centres 213
Hans Quak and Lori Tavasszy

13 Closing the Global Supply Chain: The Gateway Towards Sustainability 235
Erwin van der Laan

14 Transitions Towards Sustainable Dynamic Traffic Management: A Living Systems Approach 247
Ben Immers and Rien van der Knaap

15 Advanced Traffic Monitoring (ATMO) for Sustainable Traffic Management 267
Hans van Lint, Albert Valkenberg, and Arjan van Binsbergen

16 Dynamic Traffic Management Measures to Optimize Air Quality, Climate, Noise, Traffic Safety and Congestion: Effects of a Single Objective Optimization 297
Luc Wismans, Eric van Berkum, and Michiel Bliemer

List of Contributors 315

About the Authors

Jo van Nunen received his Master's and Ph.D. degree in applied Mathematics from the Technical University Eindhoven. Van Nunen was professor of Logistics and Information Systems at the Rotterdam School of Management, Erasmus University Rotterdam. His research on e-commerce, closed-loop supply chain management, and multi-modal transportation was published in 6 books and over 150 articles in (inter)national (top) journals. Until 2010, Van Nunen was chairman of the Department of Decision and Information Sciences of the Rotterdam School of Management, Erasmus University. Jo van Nunen unexpectedly passed away in May of 2010.

Paul Huijbregts got his Master's degree in 1993 in Logistics, Transport Planning and Management from the University of Westminster in London. He works at the Dutch Institute of Advanced Logistics in Breda, the Netherlands, as programme manager within the national innovation programme for logistics and supply chain management. His previous work experience include positions such as programme manager at Transumo – the Dutch innovation programme on the TRANsition to SUstainable MObility – and Senior Researcher at the Transport Research Centre of the Dutch Ministry of Transport, where he is involved in research on the impact of logistics and transport on infrastructure. He has also conducted many different research projects as a Senior Scientific Researcher at NEA Transport Research in many different national and international/EU projects on multimodal transport, retail logistics, supply chain management and logistics.

Piet Rietveld studied econometrics at Erasmus University, Rotterdam (cum laude degree) and received his Ph.D. in economics at Vrije Universiteit, Amsterdam. He worked at the International Institute of Applied Systems Analysis (Austria) and was research co-ordinator at Universitas Kristen Satya Wacana in Salatiga, Indonesia. Since 1990 he has been professor in Transport Economics at the Faculty of Economics, VU University, Amsterdam. He is a fellow at the Tinbergen Institute.

Marco te Brömmelstroet is a researcher at the Amsterdam Institute for Metropolitan and International Development Studies (AMIDSt) of the University of

Amsterdam. His main academic interests are the implementation gap of Planning Support Systems, the use of transportation models in decision making and the integration of transport and land use strategy making.

Luca Bertolini is professor of Urban and Regional Planning at the University of Amsterdam. His main interests are the integration of transport and land use planning, methods for supporting the option-generation phase of the planning process, concepts for coping with uncertainty in planning, and ways of enhancing theory-practice interaction.

Ghebreegziabiher Debrezion received his Bachelor's degree in Business Management in 1998 from the University of Asmara, Eritrea. In 2001, he received Masters of Science degree in the fields of Operations Research-Econometrics from the University of Groningen. After joining the department of Spatial Economics at the VU University Amsterdam and Tinbergen Institute Amsterdam in 2002, he received his Ph.D. in 2006. Since January of 2007, he is working as a Postdoc researcher in the same department. His studies focus on the economic impacts of transportation infrastructure, more specifically on the impact of railway accessibility on real estate values.

Thomas de Graaff is currently an assistant professor in the Department of Spatial Economics at the VU University, Amsterdam. He holds a Master's degree in business econometrics from the VU University in Amsterdam in 1997 and a Ph.D. in economics from the Department of Spatial Economics at the Free University, Amsterdam. After obtaining his Ph.D. in 2001, he continued working at the department of Spatial Economics as a researcher and subsequently as an assistant professor. He also has been a quest researcher at the Netherlands Bureau for Economic Policy Analysis (CPB) and the Netherlands Environmental Assessment Agency (PBL). Spatial location patterns of households and firms, spatial econometrics, and migration theory are among his main research interests.

Ary Samsura is a Ph.D. researcher at the Department of Spatial Planning at Radboud University Nijmegen. He received his bachelor degree in Regional and Urban Planning from Institute Technology of Bandung in Indonesia and graduated from TU Delft with M.Sc. in Engineering and Policy Analysis. Before coming to the Netherlands, he has worked as a planner at the Directorate of Technology Policy for Regional Development and as a researcher at Urban and Regional Development Institute, all in Indonesia. His interests include urban management, policy analysis and decision-making modelling in urban planning, also game theory and institutional approach for urban planning.

Erwin van der Krabben started working in the Institute of Management Research (IMR), Radboud University Nijmegen, Department of Spatial Planning in 2006, where he holds a position as professor of spatial planning (since 2010). His expertise is in the areas of land and property development, greenfield and brownfield developments, integrated infrastructure and location development projects and land policy. He coordinates various research projects, including research into industrial estates development, inner-city redevelopment, climate-proof area development and negotiation processes related to land and property development. In an international context, he participates in various research projects related to land management strategies. Next to his scientific research Erwin van der Krabben is frequently invited to advise ministries, provinces and municipalities.

Marcel Hertogh studied civil engineering at the Delft University of Technology, Civil Engineering and at the Erasmus University, Economics. Together with Eddy Westerveld he completed his Ph.D. 'Playing with Complexity' on management of large infrastructure projects, Currently he is a member of the board of AT Osborne. Since the initiation in 2005, he is the programme director of NETLIPSE. Marcel has been involved as senior consultant with several large projects: infrastructure, urban development, water and environmental projects. He is a professional trainer and a frequent speaker at congresses. He is the (co-)author of eight management books.

Eddy Westerveld studied business administration at the University of Groningen. Together with Marcel Hertogh he completed his Ph.D. 'Playing with Complexity' on management of large infrastructure projects. Eddy works as a consultant, researcher and project manager in large infrastructure and urban renewal projects, such as the Westerscheldetunnel, HSL-South, Rijnboog Arnhem and the Amsterdam North South Metroline. For NETLIPSE he co-ordinated the research on 15; large infrastructure projects in Europe. Eddy specializes in project management. He is lead assessor for the IPMA excellence award. He is regularly involved in training and international classes relating to project management for clients and for students.

Jasper Knockaert is affiliated as a postdoc researcher in Spatial Economics at the VU University. His research focuses on analysing and modelling behavioural aspects of transport users. This study involves the design and implementation of large scale experiments to collect extended observation datasets which are analysed using econometrical models (discrete choice theory). The collected insights are used to underpin first best and second best transport regulating schemes. The experiments and the consolidation of the obtained results are established in a series of research projects both at EU and national level.

Jessie Bakens is currently affiliated as a Ph.D. student in Spatial Economics at the VU University. Her research focuses on the impact of international migration on regional growth in Europe, and in particular on urban regions in the Netherlands. Previous to this position, Jessie worked as a researcher in Spatial Economics at the VU University on a project studying behavioural decisions of public transport users.

Dick Ettema is associate professor at the department of Human Geography and Planning of the Utrecht University. He has published extensively on activity-based travel analysis and modelling, time use analysis, application of reward measures in travel demand management, and the effect of travel and activity participation on well-being. He is director of education of the Netherlands Graduate School of Urban and Regional Research (NETHUR), elected member of the Committee of Travel Behaviour and Values of TRB and chairman of the WCTR Special Interest Group on travel and ICT.

Erik Verhoef is affiliated as a full professor in Spatial Economics at the VU university, and is a research fellow at the Tinbergen Institute. His research focuses on efficiency and equity aspects of spatial externalities and their economic regulation, in particular in transport, urban and spatial systems. Important research themes include second-best regulation, network- and spatial analysis and methodological development, dynamic modelling, efficiency aspects versus equity and social acceptability, and policy evaluation. His research is at the interface of welfare-, micro-, transport-, urban-, spatial- and environmental economics. He has published various books and numerous articles on these topics.

Tom Van Woensel is associate professor of Operations Management and Logistics at the Technische Universiteit Eindhoven in the Netherlands. He holds an M.Sc. in Applied Economics and a Ph.D. in Operations Management from the University of Antwerp (Belgium). After the completion of his Ph.D., he moved to the Eindhoven University of Technology where he started as Assistant Professor (2003–2010) with a specialization in Retail Operations, distribution logistics and the analysis of manufacturing systems. Today, his research is mainly focused on transportation planning under uncertainty and retail operations. He published over 30 papers in academic journals (including Management Science, Production and Operations Management, Computers and Operations Research, Transportation Research, European Journal of Operational Research, Journal of Mathematical Modeling and Analysis, and International Journal of Production Economics) and several chapters in international books.

Said Dabia is a Ph.D. candidate at the School of Industrial Engineering at Eindhoven University of Technology. He started his Ph.D. studies in May 2007. Said has a Bachelor degree in Mathematics and Physics, and Master degree in Operations Management and Logistics. In April 2007, he graduated with a project on Capacitated Inventory Systems. Now, Said conducts research on exact methods and approximation algorithms for multi-objective time-dependent optimization problems, specifically vehicle routing problems and knapsack problems.

Ton de Kok graduated at the Rijksuniversiteit Leiden, The Netherlands in Mathematics and Economics in 1981 and attained his Ph.D. degree in 1985 from the VU University of Amsterdam. Thereafter he joined the Centre for Quantitative Methods (CQM) of Philips Electronics in Eindhoven, The Netherlands as consultant in Operations Research. In 1990 he became Certified Fellow in Production and Inventory Management (CFPIM) of the American Production and Inventory Control Society (APICS). From 1990–1992 he was a teaching professor at Boston University Brussels. In 1990 he was appointed Manager Logistics Innovation of Philips Consumer Electronics. Since 1991 he is a parttime professor Industrial Mathematics at the Eindhoven University of Technology and since 1992 full time professor Operations Management at the same university. He is the director of the

European Forum on Global Supply Chain Management at Eindhoven University of Technology. His main research areas are Production Management and Supply Chain Management with emphasis on quantitative analysis. In this area he published over 40 papers in international and national journals.

Hans Moonen splits his time between consulting and academia. At Logica he works in the transport & logistics domain, whereas at the University of Twente Hans works in the Information Systems & Change Management department as an assistant professor. The past ten years, Hans has always operated on the interplay between supply chain management, process change and innovative software solutions. Before his current positions, Hans studied Industrial Engineering & Management Science at Eindhoven University of Technology, worked at enterprise software vendor Baan, followed by a position at Erasmus University, where he obtained his Ph.D. The research reported on in this chapter was performed while Hans was with Erasmus.

Jos van Hillegersberg is a full professor at the University of Twente, where he is heading the department of Information Systems & Change Management since 2005. Jos has a background in Computer Science from Leiden University, worked at IBM on artificial intelligence and expert systems, and then did his Ph.D. at Erasmus University Rotterdam. After his Ph.D. Jos worked two years with Aegon, setting up Aegon's internet banking, and then returned to Erasmus to continue his career as an associate professor. His research interests include component based software systems, IT management, global outsourcing and multi agent systems for supply chains.

Niels Agatz is an assistant professor at the Rotterdam School of Management, Erasmus University. He obtained his M.Sc. in Industrial Engineering from the Eindhoven University of Technology and his Ph.D. from the Rotterdam School of Management, Erasmus University. In December 2008, Niels was rewarded a Rubicon fellowship from the Netherlands Organization for Scientific Research (NWO) which enabled him to spend 12 months as a postdoctoral researcher at the School of Industrial Engineering of the Georgia Institute of Technology in Atlanta, USA. His research interests are in demand management and pricing, sustainable transportation and the interface between marketing and operations, specifically in B2C Internet retailing.

Martijn Brons received his master's degree in economics at the Vrije Universiteit Amsterdam in 2001. In 2006, at the same university, he successfully defended his Ph.D. thesis entitled "Meta-Analytical Studies in Transport Economics. Methodology and Applications." Afterwards, he worked for three years as a post-doctoral researcher in the field of transport economics at the Spatial Economics department of the Vrije Universiteit. Since 2009 he works as a research fellow at the Institute for Prospective Technological Studies, one of the Joint Research Centres of the European Commission, where his work focuses on model-based impact analysis of transport policy scenarios.

Piet Rietveld studied econometrics at Erasmus University, Rotterdam (cum laude degree) and received his Ph.D. in economics at Vrije Universiteit, Amsterdam. He worked at the International Institute of Applied Systems Analysis (Austria) and was research co-ordinator at Universitas Kristen Satya Wacana in Salatiga, Indonesia. Since 1990 he has been professor in Transport Economics at the Faculty of Economics, VU University, Amsterdam. He is a fellow at the Tinbergen Institute.

Leo Kroon studied mathematics at the VU University in Amsterdam. In 1990, he received his Ph.D. from Erasmus University Rotterdam. Currently, he is a part-time professor in Quantitative Logistics at the Rotterdam School of Management of that same university. He also holds a part-time position as a logistic consultant at Netherlands Railways. His research focuses on the development of decision support tools for the planning and real-time operations control of public transport systems. Dennis Huisman studied Econometrics at Erasmus University Rotterdam, and in 2004 he received his Ph.D. from the same university. Currently, he is a part-time associate professor in Logistics and Management Science at the Econometric Institute of Erasmus University. In addition, he works parttime as an Operations Research consultant at Netherlands Railways. Finally, he is co-founder and director of the Erasmus Center for Optimization in Public Transport. In 2008, both authors participated in the team of Netherlands Railways that won the 2008 Franz Edelman Award of INFORMS (also known as the Super Bowl of Operations Research).

Hans Quak, Ph.D., is logistics advisor at TNO (Mobility and Logistics) in Delft. He studied Business Administration at the RSM Erasmus University and completed a Ph.D. study on the sustainability of urban freight transport. He moved to TNO in 2007. Quak has experience in research in the area of city logistics; he was project manager of the Transumo-project 'Transition towards sustainable urban freight. He has been involved in several research projects on sustainable logistics, influences of external factors on the logistics organization, and logistic collaboration. He (co) authored several reports and papers on freight transport, (city) logistics and (local) policy. Quak is also appointed as assistant professor for one day a week at the Delft University of Technology.

Lori Tavasszy is senior advisor at TNO in Delft, the Netherlands. He studied Civil Engineering at the Delft University of Technology and completed a Ph.D. study on the effects of European integration on international freight transport flows within Europe. He moved to TNO in 1996 and has headed the departments of Mobility, Infrastructure and Spatial Development. He started as part time professor in Freight Transport & Logistics at the University of Nijmegen from 2006 till 2009. Since 2009 he is appointed in this position at the Delft University of Technology. Tavasszy has abundant experience in research in the area of transportation and spatial economic systems. He carried out many advisory projects for national and European government which included scenario building, freight system analysis, model development, guidelines for project evaluation and policy analysis.

Erwin A. van der Laan is an associate professor at RSM Erasmus University, where he teaches operations management and logistics. His research interests include reverse logistics, operations of sustainable supply chains and humanitarian supply chains. Acting as project leader of DINALOG-ECO (2005–2009) and "Value Creation by Closing the Loop" under the Dinalog umbrella (2011–2013) he has ample experience in bringing together theory and practice of closed loop supply chain management. His work has been published in *Management Science*, *Operations Research*, *European Journal of Operational Research and Production* and *Operations Management*, among others.

Ben Immers graduated as civil engineer at the Technical University of Delft. He started his professional career as research fellow at the Netherlands Institute for Transport Research. He was lecturer and associate professor in Transportation Planning and Transportation Modelling at the Technical University of Delft. He was secretary-director of the Delft research school for Transport, Infrastructure and Logistics (TRAIL) and worked as senior research fellow at the Netherlands Organisation for Applied Scientific Research (TNO). At present he is part-time university professor in transportation planning and highway engineering at the Catholic University of Leuven (Belgium), works at the Centre for Expertise on Traffic Management. He combines these jobs with a professorship in Traffic, Infrastructure and Logistics at the Technical University of Delft. He is also scientific director of TRAIL research school.

Rien van der Knaap is co-founder of management consultancy firm Organizational Coaching BV (1989) in Eindhoven. He is specialized in innovations, transformation and transition processes on the edge of human factors and technique with traffic and transport as a special field of interest. He has been involved in many innovations in traffic and transport, advised many of the top 100 companies in the Netherlands as well as public parties. A main focus is on projects and processes where public and private organizations need to co-operate. He has a BSC degree in Social Geography and master degrees in Spatial Planning and Business Economics. He worked for the KUN in Nijmegen and the EUR in Rotterdam and for several major consultancy firms before he became a private consultant.

Hans van Lint received his M.Sc. (in Civil Engineering) and his Ph.D. degree (in Traffic modelling and prediction) at Delft University of Technology. At present, he is associate professor at the Transport & Planning Department at Civil Engineering, and director of education of the Transport, Infrastructure and Logistics M.Sc. program, both at Delft University of Technology. His expertise areas include traffic flow theory, modelling and prediction, traffic management, and ITS. He is member of several international platforms and is associate editor of the IEEE Transactions on ITS. Van Lint acquired and managed various large research projects, received a personal 4-year NSF (Veni) grant in 2007 ("reversing the traffic jam") and has (co-) authored 20 ISI rated journal articles, eight book(part)s and over 70 peer reviewed international conference papers.

Albert Valkenberg studied Mechanical Engineering at Delft University of Technology, with a specific focus on Industrial Organisation. During his study he took a two-year leave to set up a project-based learning. After graduation, he worked in the supply chain of the Albert Heijn supermarkets. Later, he returned to Delft University of Technology as a Project secretary of the ATMO Project, led by the faculty of Civil Engineering, department of Transport and Planning. Currently, he is lecturer at the Faculty of Mechanical Engineering at Delft University of Technology.

Arjan van Binsbergen studied civil engineering at the Delft University of Technology, graduated in 1992 on intermodal transfer facilities for passenger transport and received his Ph.D. on urban distribution systems in 2001. He is associate professor at the department of Transport & Planning and programme manager at Valorisation Centre TU Delft. Previously, he was member of the management team of the Transumo research programme (transition to sustainable mobility) with a focus on the traffic management part thereof. His fields of expertise include long-term transport scenario studies, freight transport, and transition and implementation studies.

Luc Wismans received a M.Sc. degree in Civil Engineering in 1999 from the University of Twente, The Netherlands. He works as a consultant for Goudappel Coffeng BV, which is the largest independent Dutch traffic and transport consultancy of the Netherlands and is involved in studies related to dynamic network modelling, dynamic traffic management, evaluation studies and research and development, in particular concerning traffic and external effects. In 2008 Luc started as a part time Ph.D. student at the University of Twente, focussing on the multi-objective optimization of traffic systems.

Eric van Berkum received his M.Sc. in Applied Mathematics at the University of Twente. After a relatively short career as a software engineer at Cap Gemini he moved in 1988 to Goudappel Coffeng BV, where he worked for 21 years and had several positions. His main research interests cover transport modeling, networks, travel behaviour and traffic management. In 1998 he became a part-time professor in traffic management at the Centre for Transport Studies. In 2009 he left Goudappel Coffeng and became full professor and head of the Centre for Transport Studies.

Michiel Bliemer obtained his M.Sc. degree in Econometrics (with honours) in 1996 from the University of Groningen in the Netherlands and received his Ph.D. from Delft University of Technology in traffic engineering in 2001. He currently holds a position as associate professor in Delft, and is also consultant at Goudappel Coffeng BV, the largest transport and traffic consultancy in the Netherlands. Michiel's main research interests cover dynamic network modelling, road pricing, dynamic traffic management and travel behaviour. Research on experimental design for stated choice studies is conducted in cooperation with the University of Sydney, where Michiel works as an assistant professor.

Chapter 1
Introduction to Transitions Towards Sustainable Mobility

Jo van Nunen, Paul Huijbregts, and Piet Rietveld

1.1 Sustainable Transport

Transport plays a major role in the world economy, both within countries and between countries. Button (2010) mentions several basic reasons why transport is needed. First, the *heterogeneity* of the earth's surface means that resources available at one place have to be transported to other places. Second, as already indicated by Adam Smith, *specialization* strongly contributes to productivity and quality, but inevitably leads to transport flows. This holds even more because of the existence of *economies of scale*. In addition to these production-related reasons, there are reasons related to personal travel. Trips are needed for *social interaction* with friends and relatives, for activities such as *recreation, culture and sports*, and also for *work* (commuting), given the desire to separate work and residential activities. These reasons make clear that transport demand has become increasingly fragmented in space as well as in time, and that transport serves a broad range of needs of people and companies. Hence, transport is strongly linked to activities in other domains of consumption, production, and land use, implying that solutions of transport problems not only have to be sought in the transport domain itself, but also in these other domains. This need for a broad orientation makes transport such a fascinating field of research.

J. van Nunen
Rotterdam School of Management, Erasmus University of Rotterdam, Rotterdam, The Netherlands

P. Huijbregts (✉)
Dutch Institute for Advanced Logistics, Princenhagelaan 13, Breda 4813 DA, The Netherlands
e-mail: huijbregts@dinalog.nl

P. Rietveld
Department of Spatial Economics, VU University Amsterdam, De Boelelaan 1105, Amsterdam 1081 HV, The Netherlands
e-mail: p.rietveld@vu.nl

J.A.E.E. van Nunen et al. (eds.), *Transitions Towards Sustainable Mobility*,
DOI 10.1007/978-3-642-21192-8_1, © Springer-Verlag Berlin Heidelberg 2011

The problems that transport systems are facing have been summarized in many ways, ranging from congestion, high costs, high energy use, local pollution, greenhouse gas emissions, to traffic accidents, and lack of supply of services at certain places or for certain groups. The term 'sustainable transport' has been introduced to represent a transport system where these problems have been reduced to much lower levels such that they do not threaten the long-term welfare of people in a broad sense. In the context of this volume we will discuss the notion of sustainability by means of the well-known triangle of the three P's: people, planet and profit (European Council of Ministers for Transport 2002).

1.1.1 People

As already noted above, transport is essential to satisfy the demands of people for all kinds of consumption goods, and for various types of activities. Despite the problems mentioned above, transport has been remarkably successful in achieving these goals during the past centuries. The low cost of long-distance freight transport makes it possible to import products from everywhere in the world against very low prices so that people have access to a broad variety of products. Also in terms of activity patterns, there is now a very large range of mixtures of activities in which people can be involved. These broad varieties of material goods and of activities are important, because as people get richer, they tend to attach higher priority to quality and variety in their consumption activities and activity patterns, than to quantities per se (Button 2010).

This demand for quality also applies to people's transport activities themselves. Thus, increasingly, passengers demand travel alternatives that are affordable, reliable, non-delayed, convenient, comfortable, accompanied by high level services, and that have experiential value. These trends cannot only be observed in the developments of the private car, but also in collective forms of transport, where public transport operators do their best to try and follow the developments of the private car. One of the trajectories followed to improve the quality of travel is the increasing use of ICT as an accompanying element of trip making. Another dimension of the 'people' element in transport is traffic safety. Here too, we observe that in many countries the overall tendency is to make the transport system safer, resulting in an absolute decrease of casualties, even when traffic volumes continue to grow.

Technological and economic developments have strongly contributed to improvements of the 'people' component of sustainable transport. Many people have become richer so that motorized transport has become affordable for a large share of the world population. And technological developments have led to many quality and safety improvements in transport systems. At the same time, the transport system is threatened by its own success, as witnessed by severe congestion problems in virtually all dynamic economies in the world.

A final dimension of the 'people' component in transport concerns the theme of social exclusion: certain groups in society have less opportunities to participate in social networks due to handicaps, lack of income, etc. Part of this exclusion may be due to lack of access to transport, for example in the case of citizens without driving license who live at places where public transport is poor (see for example Church et al. 2000; Preston and Raje 2007). Social exclusion is among the main reasons for public transport subsidies.

1.1.2 Planet

One way to address the planet level of sustainable transport is to consider the notion of decoupling. Is it possible to realize an increase in total transport volumes and at the same time have a reduction in certain emissions such as NOx or CO_2? The experiences are clearly mixed. For certain types of emissions the transport sector has been very successful in reducing the environmental burden. For example, the introduction of the catalytic converter has led to a strong decrease of NOx, and the introduction of unleaded fuels has strongly reduced Pb emissions in transport. Clearly, in parts of the environmental spectrum, a clever mixture of technological improvement and fiscal measures led to successful examples of decoupling. Thus, transport provides in some respects a nice example of the Environmental Kuznetz curve, which says that for many emission types, a phase of increasing emissions is followed by a phase with decreasing emissions (Mills and Waite 2009).

However, it appears difficult to achieve this decoupling for some key elements of transport related emissions – just like the environmental Kuznetz curve is not unchallenged. In particular, use of fossil fuels and the related CO_2 emissions do not show a decoupling tendency in transport yet (Rothengatter 2003; Rietveld 2006). Long-run trends in global transport indicate that energy use is about proportional to gross domestic product (GDP). Several decades of efforts to improve the energy efficiency in transport did not yield substantial results in terms of reductions in CO_2 emissions. Among the countervailing mechanisms are the increasing tendency towards using faster – and more energy-intensive – transport modes such as aviation, and the use of more comfortable and safer and hence heavier cars. It is notable that where in the safety domain it appeared relatively easy to convert the increasing trend in casualties into a decreasing one, this appears to be a much more difficult challenge in the field of CO_2 emissions.

One of the reasons why the decoupling of transport and its greenhouse gas emissions is so much more difficult compared with traffic safety must be the so-called social dilemma. Individuals benefit themselves considerably from a safe vehicle and safe driving style. With CO_2 emissions this direct benefit does not exist since global warming is a global phenomenon. This will stimulate free rider behaviour, implying that many individuals will not change their behaviour in a direction that would be good for the society and the planet at large.

1.1.3 Profit

The third dimension of sustainability refers to efficiency. In a competitive setting, suppliers in the transport sector will operate in an efficient manner so that they provide services to their clients – other firms, consumers – against the lowest possible prices. The mechanism is that a strong degree of competition in transport would in most transport markets drive profits of transport firms down towards zero. Low-cost transportation has in a way enabled companies to concentrate their production and distribution activities in fewer, but larger (often specialized) facilities to reap the benefits of economies of scale. This means that the benefits of efficient transport systems are not so much reaped within the transport system itself, but by the clients, implying a maximum benefit in the broader economy. Indeed, most transport sectors are characterized by high degrees of competition leading to very low profit margins. The aviation and trucking sectors are telling examples (Button 2010) of transport sectors with structurally low profits, thus contributing to the efficiency of national economies. Market imperfections like market power due to natural monopolies and asymmetric information may, however, have adverse effects on efficiency in some transport markets, such as the rail and taxi market.

In well-functioning markets the aim of entrepreneurs to maximize profits leads to the remarkable result of profits close to zero and the supply of services against lowest possible costs for the customers. Also in the domain of transport innovations and hence that of dynamic efficiency, the profit motive will have beneficial effects, although in this context the emergence of firms with monopoly power has a higher probability. Such a trend can be clearly seen in the ICT domain where some firms have been extremely successful in making large monopoly profits (Shapiro and Varian 1999), but in the transport domain this situation has been much less the case thus far, with the possible exception of aircraft manufacturing where the degree of competition is very low. An important motive for R&D efforts of firms in this sector is that a major technological breakthrough leading to large-scale market adoption, may lead to high profits in the earlier stages of adoption.

1.1.4 Conflicts Within the Sustainability Concept

It is clear that autonomous forces in transport sectors have favourable impacts on several dimensions of the sustainable transport concept. Technological development, income growth and increased competition between suppliers have led to substantial improvements of the quality of transport systems and their efficiency. There are however, several problems that are not solved so easily. Among these problems are congestion in urban areas, equity in the provision of transport services and in particular also greenhouse gas emissions.

The various dimensions of the sustainability concept may be both complementary and conflicting. For example, successful policies to improve load factors in transport will have a positive impact on both efficiency (costs and profits), energy use and emissions. However, optimization within the sector will gradually make these quick wins more and more difficult so that at a certain stage the conflicts between the dimensions will start to dominate, such as the insight that more advanced technology will make transport more energy efficient, but also more expensive. Optimizing transport systems so that the trade-offs involved between the people, planet and profit domain are properly addressed, requires major efforts.

However useful these strategies may be, in the long run they will probably not be able to address the main challenges related to energy use of fossil fuels and climate change. This calls for an even broader approach.

1.2 Transition Towards Sustainable Transport

Arriving at a sustainable transport system is not just a matter of developing and adopting a number of technological innovations. A broader structural and societal transition is needed in technology, the economy, culture, behavioural patterns and institutions. Transitions usually take one generation or even longer to materialize because they involve putting aside barriers and routines that often are strong and persistent. Also new infrastructures have to be developed. Among the relevant barriers are technological, administrative, legal, political, socio-cultural, psychological and institutional factors.

Major institutional changes and regulatory reform took place in transport during the past several decades in many parts of the world. The stronger orientation on market forces led to a strong increase in efficiency and consumer welfare in aviation, whereas regulatory reform in the railway sector had mixed effects, ranging from positive in the USA – where freight dominates rail transport – to mainly negative in the EU – where railways are predominantly used for passenger transport. Similarly, in the field of eliminating trade restrictions at borders (NAFTA, EU, etc.) we observe substantial welfare increases or benefits since transport and trade have become cheaper. It is important to observe that these institutional changes had a beneficial impact on the people and profit dimension of sustainability, but most probably not on the planet side, because it meant a strong increase in transport-related pollution. This example illustrates that it is not easy to favourably affect all three dimensions of the sustainability concept. It also illustrates that it is probably more difficult to achieve major improvements in the planet domain compared with the two other domains. The changes in transport systems due to these institutional changes have been substantial, but even bigger will be the changes in a transition towards a sustainable transport system where energy and climate change problems are adequately addressed.

The question is how such a transition can be realized. Free markets will not solve the problems of sustainable transport given the market failures related to external effects, free riding, market power or information asymmetries (Gravelle and Rees

2004). The traditional solution of these failures is to activate the public sector to correct for these market failures. Typical tools proposed are financial instruments such as taxes, charges and subsidies, and command and control instruments such as emission standards and physical restraint of traffic.

One of the reasons why this economic way of addressing market failures does not always work is that also governments often fail (Mueller 1989). The public sector usually does not stand out in terms of efficiency of service provision, given the lack of stimuli from the market. Governments are subject to the temptations related to market power and free-riding. Democratic mechanisms do not guarantee that governments do what is best for the overall benefit. Mechanisms exist that governments systematically underestimate the costs of projects they want to implement (Flyvbjerg et al. 2003). Governments may go for projects with a high 'visibility' rather than for less spectacular but more useful projects. 'Trees don't vote', so there is no guarantee that governments pay sufficient attention to environmental aspects. And the temptation to give priority to the present generation above future generations does not only hold for firms, but also for governments. Finally, it appears that in some cases governments who have solid ideas to counter congestion, for example, by means of congestion pricing, do not get sufficient political support from voters. Thus, the classical hierarchical model, where the public sector takes the lead to achieve a sustainable transport system would be a serious simplification of empirical realities.

There is a strong need for a broader view in which neither the free market, nor the public sector provide the unique key driving forces for the transition towards a sustainable transport system. Nevertheless, market forces and government regulation will continue to play an important role in this transition. Elements of such a broader view are among others a multi-actor approach, where also multiple spatial scales and multiple domains are connected. The orientation would not exclusively be on system optimization, but on system innovation. Complexity and uncertainty are essential ingredients. This implies among others that learning by doing is an important ingredient of this approach (Rotmans and Loorbach 2009).

One of the features of a system-wide approach to adaptation is also that rebound effects are properly addressed (van den Bergh 2011). Not only may innovations and policies adopted in various domains reinforce each other, they may also conflict with each other, and the gains achieved in one domain may well lead to unintended losses elsewhere in the system. For example, a possible rebound effect of increasing opportunities of telework by reducing the frequency of commuting may be that in the long run workers reconsider their choice of residence location implying a partial or full cancelling of the reduction in commuting distances travelled by the workers concerned. A more general phenomenon of this is the so-called law of constant travel times formulated by Zahavi (1979) (see also van Wee et al. 2006). This empirical finding indicates that innovations such as faster transport or lower frequencies of commuting travel would lead to broader behavioural adjustments so that the initial saving of travel time would in the end lead to longer travel distances, keeping total travel time more or less constant. It is essential to incorporate such effects because otherwise one runs a serious risk of overly optimistic views on future transport systems.

1.3 Transumo

Transumo (TRANsition SUstainable MObility) was a Dutch innovation programme in which over 300 private companies, governments and knowledge institutes cooperated in the development of knowledge with regard to a transition towards sustainable mobility and a mobility system that is more efficient, more economically competitive, with better quality and less negative impacts on the environment.

The activities of Transumo started in 2005 and continued until the end of 2009. Over 35 projects have been conducted within Transumo. Research and knowledge development activities in these projects focused on sustainable transport and mobility concepts as well as on new organizational and governance concepts which were intended to promote the development and implementation of sustainable mobility systems.

The transition approach outlined above implies that the Transumo programme has adopted a broad multi-disciplinary approach including disciplines like traffic engineering, logistics, economics, physical planning and policy science. An essential element is the involvement of both the private and public sector in the various projects carried out. Also the domains involved have been broad. For example, land use and transport have been studied in an integrated manner. And mobility management of firms has been connected to facility management and human resource management in order to break routines that hamper innovations. More information on the Transumo programme and the outputs can be found on the website www.transumofootprint.nl.

Most of the applications within the Transumo programme took place in the Netherlands. This book gives a sample of outputs in the various domains of the programme, most of them with a focus on this country, but also relevant for other countries facing transition challenges. In the present book we have clustered the various contributions of the Transumo programme according to four themes:

1. Integrating transport infrastructure and land use planning
2. Experiments with dynamic transport optimization
3. Towards reliable transport systems
4. Sustainable logistics and traffic management

Integrating transport infrastructure and land use planning is a field that needs important transitions. The two fields are rather unconnected, both in the realities of the professional routines, and in academic research. Transport planning is strongly model oriented, whereas land use planning is mainly a creative activity. A challenge is how to reinforce the link between the two domains in such a way that policies in one field can reinforce developments in the other. This theme is a nice example of the broadening of the scope of transport policy and research.

Dynamic transport optimization can be improved by means of the application of more efficient algorithms, but a major step forward would be a stronger involvement of a client perspective by taking into account the willingness to pay for the services provided. Since social acceptance of users of these services may be a bottleneck against large scale adoption, it is important to carry out pilot projects to test the viability of such transitions. Examples of such pilots will be reported both in the public and private domain.

Improving the reliability of transport systems: from a supply-driven towards a demand-driven approach. Making transport systems more reliable by achieving pre-defined reliability standards has been a dominant aim for transport service suppliers. However, reliability was mainly approached from a supply perspective (trains arriving in time versus travellers arriving in time). The paradigm shift from the supplier to the user leads to questions such as: what is the best indicator contributing to customer satisfaction: delays of 3 min or standard deviations of arrival times?

Sustainable logistics and traffic management: In these fields many improvements have been made, but it is by no means clear whether they have been broad enough to improve the planet dimension of sustainability. In this part, again examples of pilots are discussed carried out at both the local level of city distribution and the global level of closed supply chain loops. Also, conditions under which improved information and communication technologies will contribute to sustainability improvements are analyzed.

1.4 Outline of the Book

Part A addresses the integration of land use and transport infrastructure domains. The message is that by stronger links between the two, the planning of transport infrastructure can be improved. For this purpose, new model types are needed, as well as new planning approaches in order to adequately address the complexity of spatial planning.

In Chap. 2, Marco Te Brömmelstroet and Luca Bertolini discuss transitions towards sustainable strategy making by integrating knowledge from land use and transport domains. Empirical evidence shows that such integration is hard to achieve in daily planning practice, due to many institutional barriers and substantial differences. More specifically, the tools developed to support land use transport strategy development have very low implementation rates in daily planning practice. A transition is needed. This chapter introduces the concept of 'knowledge generation' as a potentially useful mechanism for closing the gap between support tools and planning practice. Through two specific planning cases, the authors analyze the applicability of this concept in supporting integrated land use- and transport (LUT) strategy development. The focus in this chapter is on the developed strategies, how these differ from current practice, and how knowledge generation supported their development. They argue that socialization produces shared strategies, and that effective socialization needs to be supported by efficient mutual exchange between tacit and explicit knowledge. Such a way of working is a transition compared to the current practice of knowledge use. The chapter is concluded by a discussion on the implications of this argument for the wider practice of LUT planning integration.

Another aspect of the integration of land use and transport is addressed in Chap. 3 by Ghebreegziabiher Debrezion, Thomas de Graaff and Piet Rietveld. They focus on the impacts of accessibility on the value of office buildings. This is an important theme, since it sheds light on the possibility to mobilize new financial resources to finance transport infrastructure. Although the impact of accessibility on the Dutch housing market has been examined extensively, the impact of accessibility on the office market remains a relatively unexplored area. This study, therefore, analyses the impact of accessibility on office property values, making use of nationwide data on office rental records. The study also makes use of additional data on the quality of railway stations, travel times on the road between zip code areas where the office is located and the residential areas of the Dutch workforce. In addition, this study considers the broader concept of accessibility in relation to offices with respect to proximity and service quality of a railway station, the location relative to the workforce and proximity to the international airport Schiphol. Controlling for all other variables, all accessibility components appear to influence the value of office buildings. The influence of railway stations appears – although large – to be mainly local.

In Chap. 4, Ary Samsura and Erwin Van der Krabben further discuss the issue of financing transport infrastructure by applying a game theoretical analysis. In the Netherlands, mobility problems and the reduced accessibility of larger cities have led to a strong call for increased public capital investments in local infrastructure. Traditionally, such investments are based on tax revenues. Alternatively, value capturing methods offer an additional opportunity to achieve those goals. The increment in land and property values to be captured can be considered as positive externalities generated from public goods provision. Externality problems can also be seen as a failure of defining and assigning property rights. Therefore, the implementation of value capturing should consider the clarification and assignment of property rights. Moreover, it also suggests the importance of interdependency and cooperation among stakeholders involved. This chapter presents the discussion of implementing value capturing as internalization mechanisms for the externalities by relying on concepts and notions drawn from game theory. A game theoretical approach provides a way to formulize the interdependency and cooperation among stakeholders (infrastructure provider, land owners, property developers) in complex decision-making projects, as well as to examine the structure of individual decisions with regard to the implementation of value capturing. This approach is elaborated in this chapter to provide arguments for efficient ways of implementing value capturing methods. To observe the applicability of the arguments, a game theoretical model based on the Dutch context will be constructed.

The broader context of managing large infrastructure projects is analysed in Chap. 5 by Marcel Hertogh and Eddy Westerveld. They carry out a systematic comparison of large European infrastructure projects from the viewpoint of success of implementation in terms of delays and cost overruns. Whereas in the past one organization – that is, the government – was involved, the current situation is characterised by numerous stakeholders that all have some kind of influence: 'No one is in charge.' At the same time, there are more requirements to be met, for instance, because of the tightening of legislation and the attitude towards failure. From numerous complexity scans at projects, we conclude that social complexity is most prominent. Social complexity is high when the following elements are observed: conflicts of interest, different meanings and perceptions, as well as large impacts. Contrarily, legal complexity proved to be of less importance. Based on experiences in various countries, the authors propose dynamic management as most appropriate to address the complexities. Dynamic management involves finding the appropriate balance between control and interaction, and between top–down and bottom–up elements. This will have positive effects on the quality of project outputs, reduce costs or speed up the project delivery.

Part B addresses dynamic transport optimization with a stronger client orientation, in particular on the possibilities to differentiate between users of transport services with a high willingness-to-pay, and those with a low willingness-to-pay. This is no doubt an essential element of policies to keep transport infrastructure investments at reasonable levels, while at the same time distributing the scarce capacities in the congested situations in a reasonable way. This approach can be used not only for road pricing, but also in pricing strategies of logistics service providers.

In Chap. 6, Jasper Knockaert, Jessie Bakens, Dick Ettema and Erik Verhoef discuss the results of some pilots with price instruments in the Netherlands. 'Spitsmijden' (peak traffic avoidance) is a new concept developed to mitigate the increasing congestion on the Dutch road network. Spitsmijden entails the rewarding of car drivers or train passengers if they avoid the peak period, either by choosing other modes of transport, or by travelling at different times. As part of the Transumo project, a series of projects was carried out to gain experience with this concept. This chapter summarizes the organization and results of these projects. Issues such as recruitment of participants, reward strategy, detection and administration of travel behaviour and communication are discussed for each project. Key findings of the projects are that Spitsmijden may lead to a reduction of peak travel by participants of about 50%. This reduction is primarily achieved by adjustments of trip timing, mostly by shifting trips to the pre-peak period or choosing other routes. Changing travel mode or working at home occur much less frequently. However, participants in the voluntary Spitsmijden project represent only a limited segment of the total population, in particular, those without strong constraints at work or in the household. An important issue in the further development of Spitsmijden is how to motivate a larger share of road users to participate in Spitsmijden initiatives.

Transport optimization and chain synchronization are addressed by Tom van Woensel, Said Dabia and Ton de Kok in Chap. 7. They describe new concepts for transport optimization and chain synchronization based on real-life cases. With regard to transport optimization, due to the real-life complexities, coping with real-life dynamic and stochastic environments is a critical and difficult problem to handle. The authors demonstrate both theory and practice in the area of routing trucks into a congested road network. Second, they also describe innovative concepts with regard to supply chain synchronization from retailer to manufacturer. More specifically, the goods flows are optimized in such a way, that the complete chain from retailer to manufacturer is more synchronized. The overall challenge they consider is moving inventory as much and as soon as possible downstream the supply chain. Furthermore, they demonstrate that transport in the largest possible quantities – full pallets, full truck loads – has many large advantages. Throughout the chapter, examples are used to illustrate the various concepts.

Chapter 8 is on real-time coordination in container trucking, written by Hans van Moonen and Jos van Hillegersberg. Multi-agent systems (MAS) are a relatively new approach to constructing information systems that have the potential to improve (logistical) operations and therewith contribute to a more sustainable society. Key herein is the combination of real-time information utilization and chain coordination as primary planning instruments. This chapter discusses the development and evaluation of a MAS prototype for the planning of road-container transport at a logistics service provider in The Netherlands. This (design) research is one of the first real-life try-outs of MAS in logistics. A prototype is developed which is evaluated through four evaluation approaches, with different levels of evaluation, levels of control and different rigor/relevance balances. The approaches utilized are system development, simulation, expert evaluation and an in-company field test. The use of multiple evaluation methods provides a balanced insight in the aspects surrounding future application. The authors conclude that multi-agent systems are a promising instrument for planning and coordination in logistics operations that deal with dynamism, distributed information, and coordination between multiple parties, such as the planning of road-container transport. MAS can be a useful building block for applications for network orchestration, city logistics, or demand management, to name three neighbouring examples. An important next step is real implementation – this research provides several handles to help in making this step.

In Chap. 9, Niels Agatz and Jo van Nunen further look into demand management in transportation and logistics from the perspective of revenue management. The key lesson from revenue management is that a company should try to use its scarce capacity for its most valuable customers in terms of willingness-to-pay. Instead of accepting demand first-come, first-serve, it may be beneficial to reserve capacity for more valuable customers that may still arrive in the future. Modern ICT technology and Internet retailing make revenue management applications available beyond these traditional sectors. In transportation and logistics, however, the variable operating costs often play an important role and demand management has to take both revenues and costs into account. Delivery time windows and locations are key input parameters for the optimization, thus determining the efficiency of the resulting solutions. Instead of taking demand (i.e. time windows) as a given, the Internet enables companies to dynamically manage time windows and their corresponding prices in order to increase revenues and cost-efficiency. Demand management may focus on other criteria than profitability alone. Global environmental concern has increased the interest in more sustainable ways to do business. Transportation and logistics activities have a direct impact on environmental and social performance criteria, such as CO_2 emissions, pollution and traffic congestion. The authors introduce several research projects that consider the application of demand management ideas in transportation and logistics, including the home delivery of groceries, automotive logistics and the supply of retailers in the city.

Part C is on the theme of reliability in transport systems. Reliability becomes more and more important. First, congestion in networks, such as road, air and rail, has become increasingly severe, and this makes the systems vulnerable from a reliability perspective. Furthermore, the clients of transport services are gradually becoming more demanding on the quality of the services delivered, one of the backgrounds being the long-run increase in income. The emphasis in this part is on a transition from a supply driven to a demand driven approach to reliability.

In Chap. 10, Martijn Brons and Piet Rietveld examine the issue of adopting the appropriate measure of reliability in rail transport. Point of departure is that the Dutch Railways are held accountable by the Ministry of Transport for the so-called 'punctuality' of trains, measured at 35 important rail interchange points in the Netherlands. A train is considered to be punctual if it arrives within 3 min of delay. It is questionable whether such a process-oriented approach of reliability corresponds very well to the customer-oriented ambitions of the Dutch Railways. The punctuality indicator does not account for the size of the delay, nor for the travel time variation. Furthermore, unreliability on departure is ignored. This chapter addresses these issues by identifying and comparing six different indicators and specifications. Based on a correlation analysis, two clusters of indicators could be identified: those that place specific weight on extreme delays and those that do not. Results from a series of regression and correlation analyses indicate that the two indicators in the latter cluster, i.e. the punctuality indicator as used by Dutch Railways, and an alternative indicator based on the average size of the delay, are most closely related to the customer experience of travel time unreliability, in particular, when an arrival-based specification of unreliability is used. For the other four indicators, which do place specific weight on extreme delays, a departure-based specification leads to better results.

The follow-up of this chapter is presented by Leo Kroon and Dennis Huisman, who analyse decision support systems for railway disruption management in Chap. 11. A disruption of a railway system usually leads to longer travel times and much discomfort and uncertainty for the passengers. The authors argue that a stronger passenger orientation in the disruption management process – facilitated by powerful algorithmic support – will lead to a mitigation of these adverse effects for the passengers. The latter will contribute to an increased service quality provided by the railway system in terms of a higher seating probability and less cancelled trains. This will be instrumental in increasing the market share of the public transport system in the mobility market, and thereby the sustainability of mobility. Since disruptions of railway systems are inevitable, such systems must be prepared to deal with them effectively. However, in case of a disruption, rescheduling the timetable, the rolling stock circulation, and the crew duties is usually so complex, that solving these problems manually is too time consuming in a time critical situation, where every minute counts. This may lead to unnecessarily cancelled trains. Therefore, algorithmic support in such situations is badly needed. To that end, models and algorithms for real-time rolling stock and real-time crew rescheduling are currently being developed in close cooperation with Netherlands Railways (NS). These models and algorithms are to be used as the kernel of decision support tools for disruption management.

Part D of the book is on sustainable logistics and traffic management. The Transumo theme 'Transition towards Sustainable Mobility' asks for inspiration and the dare to come with stimulating, new ideas. The sustainability challenge ahead of us will need such input.

In Chap. 12, Hans Quak and Lori Tavasszy discuss the theme of sustainable city logistics from an empirical perspective, using a case study. Urban freight transport is well known for its negative sustainability impacts. To organize urban freight transport in a more sustainable way, customized solutions – based on logistics, policy and technological innovations – are necessary that take all actors' stakes in account. An example of such a solution is Binnenstadservice (BSS), operating since 2008 in Nijmegen. The clients of these urban consolidation centres are local shop-owners, who receive the basic service (receiving goods and bundled delivery) for free. After 1 year, a slight decrease in the amount of truck kilometres in the city centre was observed, as well as a nuisance reduction. BSS extends to other Dutch cities; carriers can save considerably on costs and CO_2 emissions, due to the growth of BSS branches in Dutch cities. Cost savings of over 60% per delivery are within reach if goods are no longer delivered directly, but via a BSS branch. The main challenge is to secure the positive effects of BSS for the future, by creating a business model that will be self-supporting in time. This requires that BSS also receives incomes from carriers, since these actors profit most from BSS. This asks for a behavioural transition of carriers; they have to share their savings with BSS, so that this sustainable urban freight transport solution will become a win-win situation for both the carrier and BSS.

In Chap. 13 – on 'Closing the Global Supply Chain' – Erwin van der Laan aims at empirically identifying the main barriers and facilitators for efficient and effective global (that is cross-border) recovery supply chains. The bundling of waste streams and the successful recovery and integration of these flows in the forward supply chain contributes to sustainability in the reduction of emissions, energy use and demand for material need. In this chapter, first a framework for possible barriers is built from various literature sources and subsequently validated through the analysis of a number of case studies. Based on empirical findings, the author suggests a number of actions that may remove the identified barriers to succeed in a transition towards a truly sustainable system of freight transport.

In Chap. 14, Ben Immers and Rien van der Knaap discuss the transition towards sustainable dynamic traffic management. They argue that several paradigm shifts in the field of traffic management are inevitable and necessary. One of them is to recognize that the traffic system needs to be seen and treated as a 'living system'. This has far-reaching implications for current thoughts on how a traffic system should be 'managed and controlled' and might be of fundamental importance in the search for sustainable mobility. In this contribution, the authors explore some of these implications, more specifically, those that deal with the relationship between the degree of complexity and the type of management and control that should apply.

The basic question explored in this contribution is when and how interventions in the traffic system should take place, under what conditions, and in such a way that the quality of the system improves in terms of traffic performance, sustainability, safety, comfort for the end users, etc.

Hans van Lint, Albert Valkenberg and Arjan van Binsbergen give an analysis of advanced traffic monitoring for sustainable traffic management in Chap. 15. In the context of sustainability, traffic monitoring entails not just observing or estimating 'classic' traffic data and information such as average speed, volume, or delay and travel time – but also more diffuse concepts – such as travel time reliability, traffic safety and environmentally related quantities. This requires the development of new hybrid methods and models for traffic and travel time prediction, online traffic simulation models, and new travel time reliability measures, to mention a few. The authors argue that bridging the gap between science and practice in the field of traffic monitoring requires entrepreneurial academics, sharing of data and results, and tailor-made post-graduate courses and education. In this chapter, special attention is paid to three areas where progress is made: travel time prediction; travel time reliability; and real-time monitoring of vehicle emissions.

The last chapter, written by Luc Wismans, Eric van Berkum and Michiel Bliemer is on the optimization of air quality, noise and other aspects of the planet dimension of sustainable transport. The optimization of traffic systems by expanding or improving an existing network is often referred to as a Network Design Problem. The optimization of dynamic traffic management measures can be seen as a variant of this network design problem. Traditionally, this type of optimization is focussed on improving accessibility, given particular boundary conditions for traffic safety and liveability (set by law). Yet, the quality of traffic systems is not only a matter of accessibility, but also of externalities such as traffic safety, air quality and climate. This chapter describes the results of research on optimization of dynamic traffic assignment measures to improve externalities. The formulation and calculation of the objective functions are described, using a dynamic traffic assignment model and also three solution approaches are presented, using genetic algorithms and compared in a case study. Furthermore, the authors present an analysis of objectives being opposite or aligned when a traffic system is being optimized using these measures.

References

Button KJ (2010) Transport economics. Edward Elgar, Cheltenham

Church A, Frost M, Sullivan K (2000) Transport and social exclusion in London. Transp Policy 7:195–205

European Council of Ministers of Transport (2002) Implementing sustainable urban travel policies. OECD, Paris

Flyvbjerg B, Bruzelius N, Rothengatter W (2003) Megaprojects and risk; an anatomy of ambition. Cambridge University Press, Cambridge

Gravelle H, Rees R (2004) Microeconomics. Prentice Hall, London

Mills JH, Waite TA (2009) Economic prosperity, biodiversity conservation, and the environmental Kuznets curve. Ecol Econ 68(7):2087–2095
Mueller DC (1989) Public choice II. Cambridge University Press, Cambridge
Preston J, Raje F (2007) Accessibility, mobility and transport related social exclusion. J Transp Geogr 15:151–160
Rietveld P (2006) Transport and the environment. In: Tietenberg T, Folmer H (eds) The international yearbook of environmental and resource economics 2006/2007. Edward Elgar, Cheltenham, pp 208–254
Rothengatter W (2003) Environmental concepts – physical and economic. In: Hensher DA, Button KJ (eds) Handbook of transport and the environment. Elsevier, Oxford, pp 9–35
Rotmans J, Loorbach D (2009) Complexity and transition management. J Ind Ecol 13:184–196
Shapiro C, Varian HR (1999) Information rules. Harvard Business School Press, Boston
van den Bergh JCJM (2011) Energy conservation more effective with rebound policy. Environ Resour Econ 48(1):43–58
van Wee B, Rietveld P, Meurs H (2006) Is average daily travel time expenditure constant? In search of explanations for an increase in average travel time. J Transp Geogr 14:109–122
Zahavi Y (1979) The UMOT-project. US Department of Transportation, Report DOT-RSPA-DPB-2-79-3, Washington, DC

Part A
Integrating Transport Infrastructure and Land Use Planning

Chapter 2
A Transition Towards Sustainable Strategy Making: Integrating Land Use and Transport Knowledge Types

Marco te Brömmelstroet and Luca Bertolini

2.1 The Struggle for Land Use and Transport Integration

As extensively discussed by other scholars, there is a growing awareness that the integration of land use and transport (LUT) planning is a crucial prerequisite for the transition towards more sustainable transport patterns and urban development that foster interaction between people, support a sustainable business climate and reduces negative effects on the environment and climate (see, for example, Banister 2002, 2005; Cervero 1998; Meyer and Miller 2001; TRB 2004). However, in the Netherlands (and in other countries), such integration is scarcely present in daily planning practice (see, for instance, Hull and Tricker 2006). If anything, one can speak of policy coordination rather than 'integration'; i.e. it is dialogue or information exchange which is geared at avoiding conflicts between projects, but does not seek to establish similar policy goals (Stead et al. 2004). Achieving integration in earlier phases of planning (for example, strategy development, goal orientation or visioning) can potentially produce shared policy goals, which would promote mutually reinforcing (instead of obstructing) land use and transport measures. However, for this to happen, a transition on its own is needed.

A wide variety of barriers block such early integration, for example: distinctive budgets, different procedures, weak/contradictory incentives for cooperation, reluctant departmental culture or the lack of efficient management mechanisms (see Cabinet Office 2000; Hull and Tricker 2006; TRB 2004). Besides these institutional barriers there are large substantive differences between the domains of land use and transport planning in: planning objects (places vs. networks/flows); tools and instruments (e.g. spatial GIS vs. mathematical transport models); operational

---

This chapter is based on an earlier article by Te Brömmelstroet and Bertolini (2009)

M. te Brömmelstroet (✉) • L. Bertolini
AMIDSt – Amsterdam institute for Metropolitan and International Development Studies, University of Amsterdam, Nieuwe Prinsengracht 130, Amsterdam 1018 VZ, The Netherlands
e-mail: marco@transport-planning.eu; L.Bertolini@uva.nl

J.A.E.E. van Nunen et al. (eds.), *Transitions Towards Sustainable Mobility*,

DOI 10.1007/978-3-642-21192-8_2,

modes (holistic visioning vs. optimizing problem solving); and educational carriers. Hence, the two professions speak different professional languages (a point further elaborated in Te Brömmelstroet and Bertolini 2008; see also van der Bijl and Witsen 2000; Wachs 1985). In early planning phases, focusing on the development of new (and shared) knowledge and group learning, this lack of a common lexicon is particularly problematic (Couclelis 2005; Jones and Lucas 2005; Klosterman 2007). Tennøy recently used the concept of conflicting reference frames (Schön and Rein 1994) to analyze the conflicting views of different parties (e.g. land use and transport planners) on the issue of sustainability (Tennøy 2009). These conflicting views result in two different sets of planning languages, which are hard to integrate. Although we recognize the great importance of institutional barriers to LUT integration, in this chapter we focus on these substantive barriers, which have been addressed much less extensively in the literature.

Many (computer-based) tools and instruments have been developed to try and provide such a common LUT language for integrated visioning or strategy development, for example, UrbanSim (Waddell 2002) and MARS (Emberger et al. 2006) (for extensive overviews see Wegener 2005; Wilson 1998). However, these instruments face serious implementation problems. Recent research shows that the gap between instrument development (by consultants and/or universities) and daily planning practice creates the main implementation bottlenecks. The present technology- rather than user-focus produces unsuitable instruments: focused only on scientific rigour rather than also on practical relevance; not adapted to the complex and dynamic planning context; not transparent; not user friendly, and inflexible. Therefore, such instruments cannot link up with the context specifics of early LUT integration (Te Brömmelstroet 2009). These findings mirror the wider academic debate on implementation bottlenecks of these so-called Planning Support Systems (PSS) (see for example Geertman 2006; Uran and Janssen 2003; Vonk et al. 2005) and on the role of transportation models in an increasingly communicative planning practice (see e.g. Timms 2008; Willson 2001). In the light of the potential importance of such tools from a sustainability perspective, we need to search for potential solution directions. A transition towards a different way of working for both PSS developers and their potential users seems necessary.

2.1.1 A Transition Towards Improved Support

Similar problems are addressed in the knowledge management literature. In recognition of the limited role of scientific and technical information in decision-making, it introduced concepts which addressed the personal and softer dimension of knowledge. In their seminal study on innovations in Japanese companies, Nonaka and Takeuchi (1995) introduced the concept of *knowledge generation*. Innovating companies designed enabling environments, in order to provide a confrontation between technical information and the personal dimensions of knowledge. Iteratively going through these confrontations produced new knowledge and thus innovative potential. This provides useful insights for successfully linking the technical information of LUT PSS with personal knowledge.

To assess this potential, we have used the concept of knowledge generation to structure two exploratory cases, where a group of planners engaged in integrated LUT strategy-making in the Netherlands on a regional (Amsterdam) and local scale (Breda). This chapter will (1) describe these applications, focusing on their divergence from existing practices, and (2) analyze the contributions of the knowledge generation concept.

Our research methodology followed the logic of realistic evaluation (Pawson and Tilley 1997), which seeks to identify a solution for a particular class of problems, or a 'technological rule'. A technological rule follows the general form: "if you have a context C, use an intervention type I, to achieve outcome O through the mechanisms M" (Denyer et al. 2008; Pawson and Tilley 1997). In Sect. 2.2, we will introduce a division of knowledge and elaborate on the concept of knowledge generation, exploring its possible applicability to LUT strategy-making. Sections 2.3 and 2.4 will provide detailed examinations of the two cases, including the context (LUT planners in LUT strategy design processes on the local/regional scale in the Netherlands), the intervention (the concept of knowledge generation) and the outcome (integrated strategies). Section 2.5 will further analyze the general relationship between the identified mechanisms and outcomes. Finally, we will present the conclusions, followed by a discussion of possible implications for wider planning practice and support.

2.2 Knowledge, Knowledge Generation and Planning Support

The differences in knowledge used in LUT planning are a substantive barrier, which hinders integrated LUT strategy-making. The academic domain of knowledge management offers useful insights for overcoming the gap between these professional languages.

2.2.1 *Explicit and Tacit Knowledge*

In the field of knowledge management, Polanyi (1967) introduced the distinction between explicit and tacit knowledge. Explicit types of knowledge are formal (e.g. data, scientific formulas and general/universal principles and theories) and are therefore easily codified with a wide validity. Explicit knowledge usually resides within certain (planning) disciplines, following institutionalized rules about: the manner of creating new knowledge, conducting analysis or surveys, and the validity of evidence or argumentation. Recently, Healey used the term *systematized* to refer to similar knowledge in strategy-making processes (Healey 2007). The second dimension is *tacit knowledge*, sometimes referred to as invisible knowledge. This is personal and hard to formalize, which makes it difficult to communicate or share with others (for example practical know-how, intuitions and hunches). In the words of Polanyi: "one can know more than one can tell" (1967, p. 138). Tacit knowledge and information are not necessarily related to particular disciplines, but rather to people's (e.g. planners) individual experiences (Gibbons et al. 1994). Nonaka and Konno asserted that, "tacit knowledge is deeply rooted in an individual's actions and experience as well as in the ideas, values, or emotions he or she embraces" (1998, p. 42). Polanyi introduced the concept of tacit knowledge to conceptualize the knowledge that (by definition) cannot be described or talked about (writing it down would make it explicit). Here, we will use the term less strictly to broadly conceptualize the experiential knowledge of planners in order to assess its relationship with the explicit (or systematized) knowledge of for instance transport models (an argument also made by Healey 2007).

Several authors (Gibbons et al. 1994; Innes 1998; Khakee et al. 2000; Scharmer and Kaufer 2000) emphasized that tacit knowledge plays an increasingly important role in formal decision-making, and should be duly recognized in planning processes. If planners want to address complex socio-economic planning problems (and thus cope with the many associated uncertainties), explicit knowledge and information should play an important role; however, it is pivotal to realise that the explicit should be combined and confronted with the tacit. If explicit information is not made understandable and more transparent, and if it remains disconnected from daily practice, the practitioners will not use it. In addition to satisfying academic rigour, scientific knowledge should thus also be relevant, useful and understandable for the planning actors. This was already one of the key elements of Friedmann's transactive planning (Friedmann 1973). Interestingly, instead of highlighting the 'democratic' motives for improving inclusiveness, "the argument for transactive planning is that expert knowledge should be wedded to experiential knowledge to achieve a greater rationality in decision-making" (Friedmann 1973, p. 378).

2.2.2 Knowledge Generation

At the end of the last century, Western and Japanese research on knowledge management arrived at similar insights concerning knowledge generation, describing it as a social process. Creating rigorous and relevant knowledge required linking the explicit with the tacit through interaction (Gibbons et al. 1994; Nowotny et al. 2001). In their seminal work on knowledge creation in Japanese companies, Nonaka and Takeuchi conceptualized four key modes of knowledge conversion in their SECI model (Nonaka and Takeuchi 1995, pp. 61–71):

- *Socialization* (tacit with tacit) – sharing experiences to create new tacit knowledge, observing other participants, brainstorming without criticism;
- *Externalization* (tacit with explicit) – articulating tacit knowledge explicitly, writing it down, creating metaphors, indicators and models;

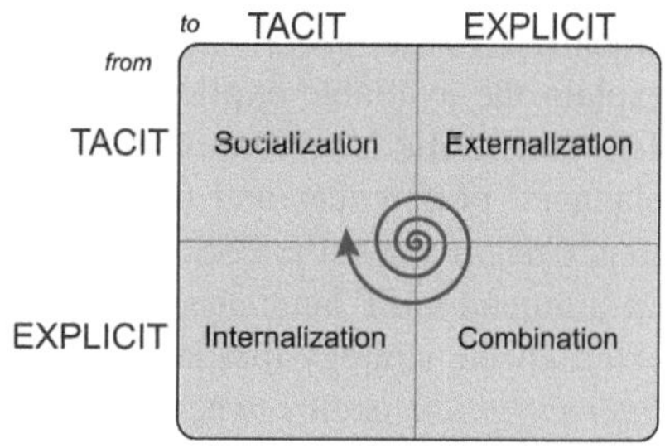

Fig. 2.1 The SECI model of knowledge generation (Adapted from Nonaka and Takeuchi 1995, p. 61)

- *Combination* (explicit with explicit) – manipulating explicit knowledge by sorting, adding, combining, looking to best practices; and
- *Internalization* (explicit with tacit) – learning by doing, developing shared mental models, goal-based training.

Figure 2.1 shows the resulting matrix of knowledge generation. The spiral represents a process of knowledge generation within a group, iteratively acting in all four modes of knowledge conversion.

Various authors criticized the model due to its methodological inconsistency (tacit knowledge *per definition* cannot be made explicit) (Tsoukas 2003) and the limited empirical support for the model (Gourlay 2006). In spite of these shortcomings (also recognized by Nonaka et al. [2006]), the SECI model has enjoyed enthusiastic acceptance in organizational science and practice, and also has a paradigmatic status in the field of knowledge management. We use it to provide a conceptual framework for linking different kinds of explicit scientific knowledge with strategic urban planning processes.

2.2.3 *Knowledge Management to Support Strategy-Making*

LUT strategy-making is a social learning process, in which actors use not only explicit information but also earlier experiences, concepts from their educational careers and personal feelings (Healey 2007; Mintzberg and Waters 1985; Simon 1993). The concept of knowledge generation can be a useful guiding principle for improving this learning process in integrated LUT strategy-making. In this, it links to, and attempts to further articulate the concept of the reflective practitioner, as originally developed by Donald Schön (1983).

By experiencing the four knowledge conversion modes, planners can develop a shared explicit language and use it to develop integrated strategies. S*ocialization* provides a platform where people can interact and learn from each others' concepts of reality, views of the planning object, working modes and professional languages. In this first important step, the participants build a common understanding of each others' tacit foundations. In Step 2, *Externalization*, the planners are challenged to formalize this in a shared working process (including a planning problem, planning steps and a preferred outcome) and in a shared set of indicators, information and models. Externalization takes place in dialogue with PSS developers, who can explain the available explicit LUT knowledge and its possibilities/shortcomings. The end result is a contextualized professional LUT language, combining the planners' preferences and the available PSS. In the third knowledge conversion step, *Combination,* the PSS developers link different models and indicators (based on a mutual LUT language), which provide support for the different steps of the externalized strategy-making process (e.g. designing or choosing alternatives). *Internalization* occurs when the PSS output is presented to the planners (e.g., demonstrating the effects of alternative strategies). In order for this explicit LUT knowledge to be useful for the planners, it has to be explained and discussed. The PSS developers have to provide transparency by explaining the assumptions and uncertainties in the modelling, thus enabling the planners to internalize these results and to discern their cause-effect relationship. After these four steps, the planners have a mutually understandable and applicable set of explicit knowledge. Through the use of this language, some of their tacit knowledge has changed (land use planners incorporate new transport insights and vice versa), thus adding value to other strategy-making processes. Also, new shared LUT strategies have been developed. After the four steps are finished a new round can start, when the planners use the internalized knowledge to discuss new interventions.

This knowledge management approach to planning support shares elements of other normative methods that aim to support the use of explicit knowledge in collaborative working. Joint Fact Finding aims to facilitate the use of technical or scientific knowledge in a contested environment (Ehrmann and Stinson 1999, p. 2). However, its aim is to fill information gaps and explore uncertainties and does not explicitly give guidelines for the use of this information and the iterative (and reciprocal) exchange with the tacit knowledge of participants. Group Model Building facilitates the development of a shared view on reality, often a conceptual framework of a problem (Vennix 1996). This important first step in many collaborative endeavours does still not mention how to organize the full circle of knowledge generation. The SECI model emphasizes – in addition to these methods – the importance of going through at least one full circle of tacit-explicit-tacit. It identifies four specific phases of knowledge transition with unique dynamics and thereby adds to our understanding of how such processes work and can work.

To explore if and how the SECI model can support real-life integrated LUT strategy-making processes, we applied it in two Dutch cases: the Amsterdam region and the city of Breda. In both cases, planners from the municipality approached the University of Amsterdam to guide them in a process of integrated land use – transport strategy making. Together with these planners, potentially relevant providers of explicit planning support knowledge were selected and asked to support this process. The authors of this chapter were involved in both cases as organizers and chairs of the sessions. Both experiences were made possible by the Dutch national government sponsored research programme TRANSUMO ("Transition to Sustainable Mobility"). While addressing real-world issues with real-world stakeholders, they had no formal relationship with the political decision-making process.

From a methodological point of view, we followed the realistic evaluation approach of (Pawson and Tilley 1997) as described above. Following this approach, below we will describe the context, intervention and outcome of both cases and how these differ from existing practices. Based on data obtained from direct observations, questionnaires and in-depth interviews, we will then explore the link between the outcome and the concept of knowledge generation (the hypothesized mechanism).

2.3 Facilitating Growth in the Amsterdam Metropolitan Area

2.3.1 Context: Substantive and Institutional

The Amsterdam metropolitan area (Fig. 2.2) is facing substantial land use and transport challenges in the coming decades. As one of the few Dutch regions where economic and population growth is foreseen in all future scenarios, the region has to plan for a large number of new high quality jobs and houses (both around 150,000 until 2030). However, mainly due to nature preservation and airport noise regulations, space for new urban development is scarce. In addition, the region is facing dramatic growth in traffic flows and congestion in the near future. Instead of seeing these as separate challenges needing separate strategies, the municipal (and regional) land use and transport planners are looking for ways to develop integrated strategies.

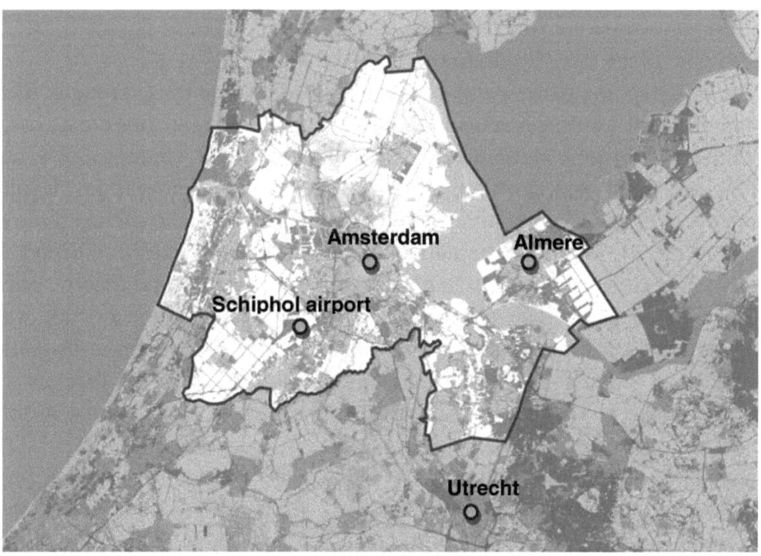

Fig. 2.2 The Amsterdam metropolitan area (Adapted from Noordvleugel 2008)

Many planners (especially in Amsterdam) already work together in several (thematic or geographical) project teams. The Municipality of Amsterdam is also known for its strong strategic capacity and close collaboration with the university (Healey 2007). However, the planners experienced that it was sometimes difficult to develop strategies together. In this case, not so much due to separated institutions, but because of difficulties in using information that was understandable and meaningful in both planning domains.

Since the 1980s, Amsterdam has been using its own in-house transportation model (GenMod), a static and multimodal four-step transportation model based on household surveys and mobility counts. GenMod is capable of calculating transportation impacts for both land use and transport developments in the Amsterdam metropolitan area. Despite the fact that it is considered one of the best transportation models in the Netherlands, it is not being used to support strategic planning processes in early phases (let alone integrated land use and transport planning endeavours), but only to assess and detail already developed strategies. This is felt as a missed opportunity to develop more LUT integrated strategies.

2.3.2 Intervention: The Sessions

In 2006 and 2007, six sessions were held in the Amsterdam region. In these sessions, land use and transport planners from the Municipality of Amsterdam and the Amsterdam Metropolitan Area (*Stadsregio Amsterdam*), transport modellers and a strategic planner from the Dutch Railways set out to develop integrated LUT strategies for the region up to 2030. We used GenMod to support this effort. The sessions were designed to allow the different phases of the SECI model to take place (see discussion in Sect. 2.3.4).

In the first step, the participants discussed and agreed on the framing of the LUT planning problem – to foster economic growth up to 2030 (and thus create space for 150,000 additional jobs and houses) with supporting LUT strategies. The second step involved a discussion on how to shape the planning process for developing integrated strategies. The iterative strategy-making process chosen had three steps: first diverging (developing alternative urbanization and [later] transport interventions), then converging (assessing and comparing effects) and, finally, selecting (identifying strategies). The participants also agreed that they did not want to develop a 'final LUT plan', but rather wanted to develop common insights into 'no regret', or 'robust' strategies (strategies that can work in different future scenarios) and in LUT interdependencies ("if… then…" statements, improving the understanding of the implications of the options available). In the third step, the PSS developers introduced information deemed useful for this planning process. The participants discussed it and consequently selected: (for diverging strategies) spatial accessibility and sustainability maps, based on cumulative opportunity measures and measured in travel time and distance; (for converging strategies) network maps of the effects of strategies on the road and transit networks; and a number of indicators for the effects of strategies (overall accessibility indicators for the region). By using it, the information was also transformed, namely made more simple and transparent. In the fourth step, spanning three separate sessions, they developed shared LUT strategies. After two design sessions, the effects on the indicators of the developed strategies were presented. They supported the final step, the selection of 'no regret' strategies (using different sets of assumptions on future conditions in the region) and interdependencies ("if we do A.....than we should be aware of effects such as B"). All the steps are synthesized in Fig. 2.3 below:

2.3.3 Outcome: Integrated LUT Strategies

Through the steps discussed above (extensively described in Te Brömmelstroet and Bertolini 2008), the group of participants developed a list of 'no regret' strategies and LUT interdependencies. These are specific outcomes of this groups' learning exercise and should be interpreted solely in this context. The following examples of 'no regret' LUT strategies highlight how they differ from current practices:

- Land use choices, due to their marginal influence on accessibility, can and should be based on existing accessibility characteristics (instead of trying to influence accessibility characteristics through land use choices). Land use planners reported gaining new insight that the influence of the existing regional urban fabric on the cumulative opportunity measures is very strong and minimizes the effects of new land use strategies.
- A polycentric 'network city' (centred on multiple public transport nodes) is not less accessible or less sustainable than a 'compact city'. One of the alternative urbanization strategies based on this concept scored high (or even higher than the other alternatives) on sustainability indicators, which was a surprise for many of participants.
- Spatial programs should be developed in existing transit corridors. During the exercise, it was discovered that some of the existing transit corridors offer

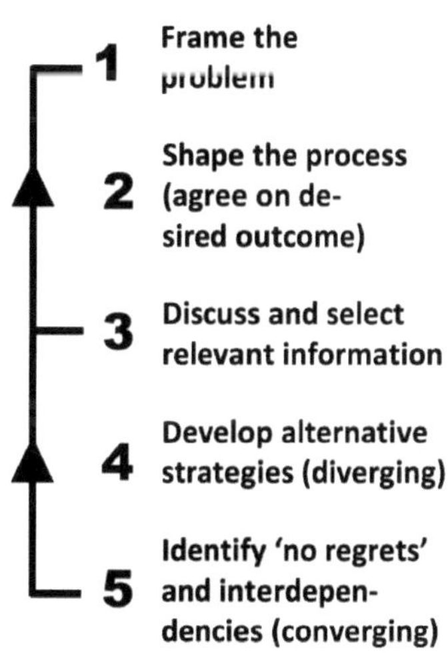

Fig. 2.3 Intervention steps to support integrated LUT strategy-making

additional opportunities for developing new station areas (notwithstanding existing restrictions, such as nature reservation).

- The orbital bus rapid transit system should be extended to link several existing/ upcoming housing developments with working areas. This is not a new idea, but during the exercise it was more widely shared and supported by explicit information.
- Once the currently planned extensions are completed, development of the highway network should stop. This highly controversial idea was supported by the indicators which showed that by implementing demand related interventions (i.e. road pricing) the current road network will retain sufficient capacity, even with increases in houses and jobs.
- Transit travel speeds towards the new town of Almere and capacity towards the airport Schiphol should be increased. The planners learned that job accessibility for Almere was contingent on reducing the travel time to Amsterdam within acceptable limits (in addition to direct job creation in Almere). On the other hand, Schiphol is already close to other important locations (also in travel time), but the number of tracks will become a bottleneck in the (near) future.

Based on the strategy design process and the effects shown in maps and indicators, the participants identified three important LUT interdependencies:

- *If* more housing is developed in and around Almere, *then* it has to be on the west side and a direct and fast transit link to Amsterdam (south and central) is crucial.
- *If* there is development around transit stations, *then* especially working (rather than housing) functions can have a significant effect on the modal split. Based on their research, the Dutch Railway planner explained that people are more likely to commute by train, if the transit nodes are close to their destination. There is a sufficient number of acceptable travel options to the station on the origin side (including own bike or car); however, opportunities are lacking on the destination side. Many of the participants had not explicitly recognized this issue before the sessions.
- *If* the housing targets in the western part of the region (Bollenstreek) cannot be met, *then* regional growth figures have to be reduced. One of the land use planners emphasized the crucial position of this area, a completely new notion for the other participants.

Overall, the outcomes were not entirely new to the planners. However, the participants did find the concepts more thought-out, jointly deliberated, and supported by relevant information. On the individual level, some planners gained more confidence and insight into the use of the supporting model. As a result, participants stated that there is an increased chance that such similar integrated strategy development processes will be used in the Amsterdam metropolitan area in the future. The questionnaires revealed that most planners felt that they had a more constructive attitude towards the need and possibility of strategy integration, due to the focus on collectively accepted explicit knowledge. This made it possible to discuss land use impacts of – at first sight – irrelevant transport strategies and vice versa. Especially the platform, provided by the accessibility maps, seemed to allow a free, and yet structured flow of tacit knowledge.

2.3.4 *Mechanism: Knowledge Generation*

The organized sessions helped the LUT planners to develop integrated strategies. The participants considered that process as an improvement to existing practices, especially in its enhanced sharing of insights and its providing improved support for concepts. To illustrate the mechanism behind this improvement, below we will discuss the four components of the SECI spiral of knowledge generation, and how these supported the development of integrated strategies.

2.3.4.1 Socialization

In the first step (see Fig. 2.3), defining a shared LUT planning problem, the planners had to link together the specific issues of their domain, and to arrive at a definition of the overarching shared problem – how to facilitate growth in the region. Also, during the first step of designing alternatives, they exchanged tacit knowledge; experience and personal knowledge about the area. In turn, they increased their understanding of its strengths/weaknesses and produced individual strategies for intervention.

In the second step, the participants discussed their view of current planning processes and how to improve them through integration. This resulted in a shared view on the reasons why it is difficult to develop an integrated LUT strategy in practice, and how to organize a process bridging these difficulties. Although one land use planner stated that, "with the current area-based approach [...] there is already an integral way or working," another land use planner addressed that this open start, "without a presumption about which planning domain is leading," was a positive change compared to common practices.

Finally, socialization occurred when the participants identified and shared their viewpoints regarding 'no regret' strategies and LUT interdependencies (in the words of one transport planner, "especially the interactive way of working was positive").

2.3.4.2 Externalization

In the third step, participants translated their tacit into explicit knowledge, discussing different indicators suitable for the defined planning issue and thereby describing the issue in terms of explicit information. In the fourth step, designing scenarios, the planners externalized their strategies in concrete interventions on the map. This was a crucial trigger for dialogue between land use and transport planners; they had to explain to each other their preferred choices and the LUT strategy suitability of the particular choice.

2.3.4.3 Combination

Sometimes planners used a combination of different forms of model outputs to assess the effects of specific planning interventions in the fourth and fifth steps. The planners preferred having a large number of impact maps at their disposal, categorized in a digital environment. Such a system enabled them to access and combine several maps and indicators, thus articulating complex trends in multiple comprehensible maps.

2.3.4.4 Internalization

The participation of the modellers during all of the steps was crucial for *internalization*; they formed the essential bridge between the explicit information of GenMod and the tacit knowledge of the planners. In the last two steps, where the effects of certain interventions were presented, the planners asked the modellers many questions about the assumptions behind the information and the meaning of the presented indicators. Through dialogue, they could use the information to first optimize their own strategies and later to develop shared strategies. One transport planner emphasized the importance of making the indicators useful by providing "good explanation and clarification". Simple (understandable) explicit information provided a necessary platform for exchanging tacit information. At first, the modellers provided information (distance decay, competition and congestion effects) that was too complicated to be internalized and used, but through dialogue the information and its understanding were improved.

Due to this well-supported internalization, the planners could start a second knowledge generation cycle aimed at further strategy development. The participants' questionnaire responses highlighted the value of socialization, for example: "as a land use planner, I am now more aware of the different ways of using accessibility measures than before" and "although the information is often not exactly what you want, you are more aware of the information that is used."

2.4 Integrating Station Development and Land Use Plans in Breda

2.4.1 Context: Substantive and Institutional

The city of Breda aims to develop a peripheral railway station on an existing railway line, located between its urban centre and the neighbouring city of Tilburg. The station should function as a Park and Ride facility (located near the A27 highway) and it should create opportunities for more public transport oriented development in the future (see top of Fig. 2.4). This idea fits in the regional

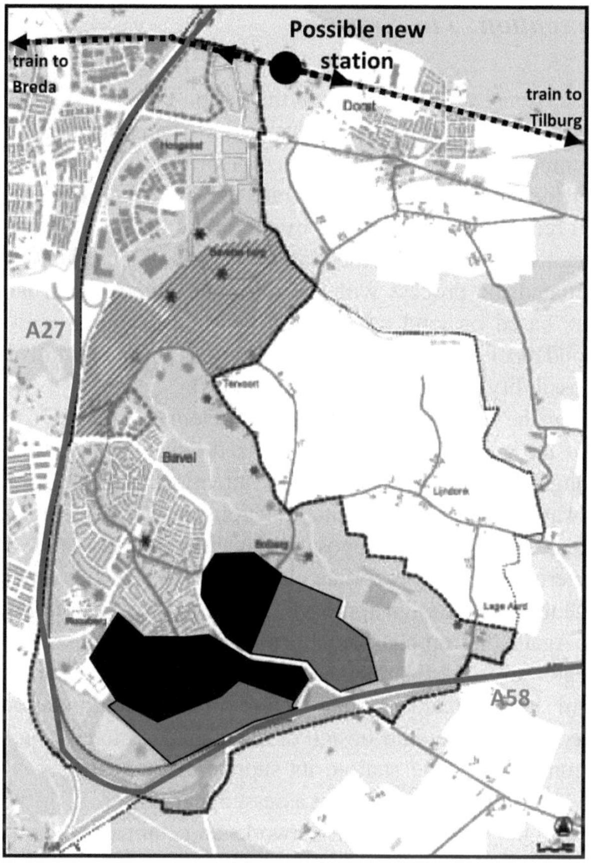

Fig. 2.4 Spatial structural plan of Breda and the new railway station; *black* for housing, *grey* for working functions and shaded for a leisure centre (Adapted from Gemeente Breda 2005, p. 4)

perspective of an intensified regional railway network (Brabantstad 2003). Parallel to this transport concept, Breda developed a strategic land use plan for the eastern part of the city as an extension of the existing urban fabric, illustrated in Fig. 2.3. The distance between the proposed railway station and the leisure centre (projecting two million visitors a year) is about 1½ km. The distance to the new housing and working areas is over 3 km (while the A58 highway is only 500 m away!). This evidently disjointed land use and transport thinking inspired a group of planners to approach us to explore the scope for an improved integrated strategy for this area.

Basically, this group of planners was less used to work across disciplinary boundaries than the Amsterdam group. In interviews prior to the sessions, the planners stated that overall there is limited cooperation between the land use and transport planning domain and that, in contrast to Amsterdam, they have very limited in-house modelling capacity (relying instead on input from consultancy firms hired for specific projects).

2.4.2 Intervention: The Sessions

In Breda, four sessions were facilitated in the period between April and November 2007. Land use and transport planners from the municipality of Breda and the neighbouring municipality of Oosterhout (potentially affected by the proposed railway station) deliberated how to integrate the train station with land use proposals that had recently been approved by the municipality. As a key stakeholder who determines the feasibility of the station, two strategic planners of the Dutch Railways facilitated the process with their Circalex model (calculating potential new train users based on land use around the station), along with the transport consultant Goudappel Coffeng (who calculated the cumulative opportunity measures [accessibility] for different travel modes).

In the first step, the framing of the planning problem (see Fig. 2.3), the participants decided to split the group, because they realized that there were two (related but distinct) planning issues which needed specific attention: (1) how to optimize the user base of the railway station by maximizing functions in its catchment area and (2) how to integrate the recent land use proposals into the public transport system. In the second step, determining the appropriate planning process, both teams chose to work according to the three step design approach used in Amsterdam (diverging, converging, selecting). Again, they emphasized that the preferred outcomes were shared LUT insights ('no regret' or 'robust' strategies and LUT interdependencies) and not a LUT plan. In the third step, the teams chose different supporting information. The railway station team decided to base their design on the Circalex model; considering development opportunities near the station, its support for train use was optimized by adding jobs and housing. The other team assessed and optimized the public transport strategies by using maps of the current networks and comparing them with sophisticated accessibility maps (which show the most accessible locations for car, transit, slow modes and combinations based on a cumulative opportunity measure). These maps illustrated the potential for a specific strategy to effectively change the accessibility of an area from car-oriented to public-transport oriented. Thanks to the preparatory interviews, these three steps could all be performed in one morning session. The fourth step, using the information to develop strategies, took place in the second and third sessions, during which the group also developed a list of 'no regret' strategies and LUT interdependencies (the final step). These steps follow the ordering presented in Fig. 2.3.

2.4.3 Outcome: Integrated Strategies

Examples of 'no regret' LUT strategies in Breda were:

- Even if the new station is unlikely to be feasible at present, future spatial plans should always keep the option to develop high-end offices or housing near the proposed station open, and thus realize emerging opportunities. For example, if the region decides to invest in a regional rail network, the possibility of locating high-density developments at the station would be very beneficial.

- Basic public transport (a regular bus travelling to the city centre every half hour) has to be provided in the new housing and working areas. It would significantly increase the accessibility by public transport, although it would not make Breda-Oost a top public transport location. In the present context, the latter is not a realistic option (an important point to be communicated to the municipal councilpersons).
- Do not develop a Bus Rapid Transit system only for this area, as there are insufficient numbers of inhabitants and jobs to support it. Despite the politicians' drive to develop Breda-Oost into a top public transport location, the strategies demonstrate that it would be an expensive investment yielding weak results. Such an analysis increases the politicians' awareness of costs and benefits.
- As the new areas in Breda-Oost will not become a top public transport location, it is necessary to also plan for car accessibility. If this is neglected, the area will probably face problems in the housing market and in the realm of mobility.
- Developing mixed living and working areas would increase employment opportunities in the near vicinity of housing and would encourage a more balanced use of (public transport) infrastructure. The accessibility maps showed that accessibility is not only improved by mobility, but also by such land use measures.

Besides these strategies, the group learned about LUT interdependencies:

- *If* all the spatial opportunities in the vicinity are filled, *then* the railway station is feasible (for construction and exploitation by Dutch Railways); however, given the rural character of its surroundings this is hardly realistic.
- *If* there is no clarity about the exact spatial program, *then* the station should not be developed. All of the available land use potential needs to be developed in order for the station to be viable; therefore, uncertainty about the surrounding developments is not acceptable;
- *If* public transport is going to play a big role in this area, *then* it should focus on improving access to shopping activities in the city centre (in combination with a 'Park and Ride' near the leisure centre and pricing incentives for inner city parking). The additional volume of users would make an enhanced bus service to Breda-Oost feasible.
- *If* the leisure centre focuses on big single national events and on young people (rock concerts) *then* the station can play an important role. *If* the focus is on regional/local events, on mixed public and on continuous visitors (e.g. skiing hall) *then* the train will play only a marginal role.

The participants acknowledged that they gained new insights into LUT interdependencies and recognized that such an integrated process "should have been included in the development process of the land use plans." They also agreed that similar processes "should have taken place in early stages of future projects." Especially the exchange of the previously one-directional land use or transport views of an area was seen as an added value (i.e., the exchange of tacit knowledge). Similar to the Amsterdam case, the initial discussion and agreement on what was relevant explicit knowledge for the issues at hand, proved a starting point for a structured substantive exchange with more depth than usual. In the words of one transport planner: "although it makes the process more complex at the start, it will show its advantages in the end." On an individual level, the participants stated that they learned more about the useful applications of explicit information in providing support to LUT projects.

2.4.4 *Mechanism: Knowledge Generation*

Below, we will again review the four elements of the SECI spiral and analyze how they supported the process of LUT strategy development.

2.4.4.1 Socialization

Even though socialization was included too late in the planning process; it did provide valuable insights for future projects in the case of Oost-Breda. The interaction with planners of the Dutch Railways was of particular significance, as the planners could better understand the company's position regarding the financing of new railway stations. By explaining and openly discussing their line of thinking, the Dutch Railways planners could link up with the knowledge and planning processes of the land use and transport planners and vice versa.

In the fourth step, designing strategies, the planners discussed the balance between the ideal and the feasible development around the station. The land use planners explained their concerns regarding nature preservation in the area to the transport planner.

2.4.4.2 Externalization

Selecting and discussing an appropriate process and indicators (Steps 2 and 3) were a crucial part of the first session. Due to a lack of modelling capacity in Breda, primarily the railway planners and the consultant provided the information; this involved a greater leap for all planners as they had no significant prior experience with this type of information. For instance, the Circalex model was not seen as useful at the start; however, while using information later to develop strategies (Step 4), the model was seen as more appropriate and had a central place in designing the interventions (a 'learning by doing' mechanism). Again, the evident difficulty of bridging tacit and explicit knowledge surfaced in the perception of the accessibility indicators as too complicated and insufficiently detailed. It seemed that the absence of the PSS developer (who did not attend all workshops) was an important barrier hampering the effective use of the information. In a following workshop, this was overcome through a dialogue between planners and the PSS developer in between workshops, which clarified the information demand.

2.4.4.3 Combination

Clear examples of combinations are found in the maps showing the current plans and possible intervention effects. The municipality provided the former, while the latter came from the Dutch Railways (in the station team) and the consultant (in the public transport team). As a result, the inconsistencies and (missed) integration opportunities were clearly identified.

2.4.4.4 Internalization

As in Amsterdam, the importance of modeller participation during the entire process was crucial. In the fifth step (during the third session), with the consultant absent, there was little internalization of the results, and the public transport group was unable to develop a shared list of strategies. A fourth session was prepared, where the consultant could present and clarify the assumptions and reasoning behind the accessibility maps. Only then, the group was able to compose a full and shared list of strategies.

2.5 Conclusions

The chapter started by introducing the difficulties of integrated LUT strategy development and the low implementation rates of associated planning support tools. We presented knowledge (specifically through the process of knowledge generation) as an important mechanism, which can bridge the substantial differences between land use planners and transport planners. The cases of Amsterdam and Breda analyzed *if* and *how* knowledge generation (through socialization, externalization, combination and internalization) can support integrated LUT strategy-making. Based on the results, we can conclude that (1) integrated LUT strategy-making is still not commonplace practice in the Netherlands; (2) land use planners and transport planners have different sets of tacit and explicit knowledge; this gap hampers providing support with explicit knowledge; (3) the concept of knowledge generation and its application in a step-by-step iterative planning support development process offers useful guidelines for improving the link between tacit and explicit knowledge through a process of knowledge interactions; (4) through such a process, planners can develop shared knowledge and ultimately integrated strategies; and (5) this means a transition for the working approach of PSS developers and their potential users.

We set out in this chapter to explore the functioning of the mechanisms behind the intervention (knowledge generation) and its outcomes (shared LUT strategies) in a specific context (land use and transport planners participating in strategy-making processes at the local/regional scale in the Netherlands). Based on a literature study and on observations, questionnaires and interviews of two exploratory cases, we can conclude that:

- Both cases showed that accessibility measures are a central part of the professional lexicon that both land use and transport planners can relate to.
- From knowledge management literature, it can be concluded that socialization is an important process which creates shared LUT knowledge, because it increases insight into the working methods and the underlying assumptions in both domains.
- From knowledge management literature, we learn that for socialization to be constructive, both processes of externalization and internalization are crucial. The planners are stimulated to express their tacit knowledge in a shared explicit language of indicators and information. The socialization process is steered beyond mere discussion into designing and testing of alternatives.
- Our cases confirmed these general findings. In addition, they emphasized that both the planning problem and the supporting information (content of the PSS) have to be discussed and selected in an open dialogue between planners and PSS developers. The result is a contextualized PSS connected to the planner's specific needs and sets of tacit knowledge. It also takes into account what PSS developers can deliver in practice.
- The cases also indicated that PSS developers (modellers) need to be present throughout the process (from problem definition to strategy selection) to support externalization and internalization of the explicit LUT knowledge provided by their tools.
- Finally, the cases seem to show that for such an integrated strategy-making process to be useful for the planners, it has to be set up as an environment in which they can *learn* about important LUT relations. The absence of an immediate link to the formal political decision process seems part of this (for instance, when at one point in Breda an attempt was made to capitalize on the unfolding dialogue with the railways and elicit a deal, the free exchange of knowledge abruptly stopped). The goal is not to develop a final LUT plan or vision, but rather to develop shared insights (in robust measures [no regret] and tradeoffs [LUT interdependencies]). This common knowledge can be used in future situations and can be communicated to politicians and other actors.

2.6 Reflection and Discussion

This study shows that socialization of knowledge might be an important element in integrated LUT strategy-making. However, simply placing the practitioners in one room will not produce the desired results; communication alone is not enough. To bridge this substantial barrier (linking their different sorts of tacit knowledge), they have to be systematically supported with relevant explicit LUT knowledge through processes of externalization and internalization. On the one hand, these processes provide structure and content for debate, enabling learning effects; while on the other hand, they trigger participants to share tacit knowledge, develop new combinations of explicit knowledge and internalize a common language. When we compare this with other research about the caveats of collaborative planning (Innes and Gruber 2005), we see that in our cases, there was more distance between the meetings and actual decision making. Also, the meetings comprised mainly what Innes and Gruber call 'staff'. This distance and composition allowed for more focus on learning instead of negotiation, although this focus had to be made clear from the beginning, and re-established on occasions. Innes and Gruber see conflicting planning styles as a major reason for the failure of collaboration. In our cases, the styles of planners differ somewhat, but they all seem more or less to employ a technical/bureaucratic style. This is of course related to the closed composition with only limited involvement of external stakeholders. The lack of conflict also has to do with the history of cooperation among the planners. Although in Breda there were two municipalities involved, the focus on a relatively abstract level of strategy making prevented a focus on conflict.

The two cases seem to show that full benefits of acquiring new shared knowledge can be obtained only by going through the entire knowledge generation cycle. The research methodology of practice-oriented experiments does not allow for a control group; however, the examples of 'normal' daily planning practices where at best just socialization takes place (little or no systematic externalization, combination and internalization of knowledge) show that these processes do not generate new LUT knowledge or strategies most of the time. This point was also confirmed by the participants. The same argument could be made for processes of simple combination; i.e. scientists or PSS developers building new models and instruments, based on combinations of scientific insight and without interaction with planners' tacit knowledge (and thus no internalization).

Although the concept of knowledge generation provides a useful analytic framework for analyzing new learning by artificially dividing the process in categories, in the real world the four modes of knowledge conversion overlap and dynamic shortcuts occur (see also Gourlay 2003). In both cases, there were moments where several (or even all) four steps were taken at the same time (simultaneous internalization and externalization during design steps). Also, some steps occurred more often than others and in different sequences. Thus, although all steps are important, the framework should be applied with some flexibility.

A social learning process seems important for successful LUT strategy-making (or other strategy-making which concerns separate planning and/or knowledge domains). The planners face complex planning environments, in which they are only one of many actors who try to shape the future of a city or region. They are involved in planning processes, marked by many uncertainties and the unpredictability of shifting conditions in daily practice. For them, it seems much more useful to develop better, and more shared knowledge about crucial relationships, than to develop a final vision or plan. Also, if the participants realize that it is a learning process, they are more open to sharing their tacit knowledge and discussing their assumptions. In Breda, one participant explicitly stated that he only joined the process because it did not aim at negotiation, which would have hampered learning. At least for the initial, strategy identification phases of planning processes, the prevalence of a learning mode seems essential.

The research described here, is based on observations, (qualitative) questionnaires, and interviews. However, more detailed analysis of the exact nature of what tacit knowledge was exchanged between the participants and how this impacted on the practical outcomes is still underway. This has to do with the different time scales of different kinds of outcomes. Direct learning effects can be analysed on the spot (accurately measuring them is a whole different matter), but the translation of these learning effects in concrete plans or other follow up (e.g. more regular interaction between land use and transport planners in the organization) can take some time.

This idea of strategy-making as social learning also has an impact on the development of relevant planning support. As the cases show, in the early phases of planning, the selection and contextualization of a common language is a crucial part of knowledge generation; PSS which are developed on the basis of generic views of planning and models are therefore difficult to apply. For a PSS to be relevant, it seems that the developers (modellers) have to be open to engage in the learning process as well and be open for implementing changes in their instruments (even if this implies sacrificing some scientific rigour for the benefit of practical relevance). In the world of land use and transport planning, this would imply a different way of using transport models (more as communicative instead of predictive devices), and recognizing their limitations and subjectivity (as also argued by Timms 2008). This chapter focused on developing support for planners from two domains; however, more research is needed specifically on the position of the PSS developer (modeller) in this process.

References

Banister D (2002) Transport planning. Spon Press, New York

Banister D (2005) Unsustainable transport: city transport in the new century. Routledge, London

Brabantstad (2003) Verkenning OV-netwerk Brabantstad: Samen investeren. Brabantstad, Den Bosch

Cabinet Office (2000) Wiring it up. Whitehall's management of cross-cutting policies and services. A performance and innovation unit report. The Stationery Office, London

Cervero R (1998) The transit metropolis: a global inquiry. Island Press, Washington

Couclelis H (2005) Where has the future gone? Rethinking the role of integrated land-use models in spatial planning. Environ Plann A 37:1353–1371

Denyer D, Tranfield D, Van Aken JE (2008) Developing design propositions through research synthesis. Organ Stud 29(3):393–413

Ehrmann J, Stinson B (1999) Joint fact-finding and the use of technical experts. In: Susskind L, McKearnan S, Thomas-Larmer J (eds) The consensus building handbook. Sage, Thousand Oaks
Emberger G, Ibesich N, Pfaffenbichler P (2006) Can decision making processes benefit from a user friendly land use and transport interaction model? In: 8th international conference on design & decision support systems in architecture and urban planning, Eindhoven, The Netherlands
Friedmann J (1973) Retracking America, a theory of transactive planning. Anchor Press/ Doubleday, Garden City
Geertman S (2006) Potentials for planning support: a planning-conceptual approach. Environ Plann B 33(6):863–880
Gemeente Breda (2005) Bavel, Beek en Berg: Voorontwerp Structuurplan Breda-Oost. Breda
Gibbons M, Limoges C, Nowotny H, Schwartzman S, Scott P, Trow P (1994) The new production of knowledge: the dynamics of science and research in contemporary societies. Sage, London
Gourlay S (2003) The SECI model of knowledge creation: some empirical shortcomings. In: McGrath F, Remenyi D (eds) Fourth European conference on knowledge management, Oxford, pp 377–385, 18–19 Sept 2003
Gourlay S (2006) Conceptualizing knowledge creation: a critique of Nonaka's theory. J Manage Stud 43(7):1415–1436
Healey P (2007) Urban complexity an spatial strategies: towards a relational planning for our times. Routledge, London
Hull A, Tricker R (2006) Findings of the 'phase 1' survey on the barriers to the delivery of sustainable transport solutions. UWE, Bristol
Innes JE (1998) Information in communicative planning. J Am Plann Assoc 64(1):52–63
Innes JE, Gruber J (2005) Planning styles in conflict: the metropolitan transportation commission. J Am Plann Assoc 71(2):177–188
Jones P, Lucas K (2005) Option generation: literature review. UCL, London
Khakee A, Barbanente A, Borri D (2000) Expert and experiential knowledge in planning. J Oper Res Soc 51(7):776–788
Klosterman RE (2007) Deliberating about the future. In: Hopkins LD, Zapata MA (eds) Engaging the future: forecasts, scenarios, plans and projects. Lincoln Institute of land policy, Cambridge, pp 199–219
Meyer MD, Miller EJ (2001) Urban transportation planning: a decision-oriented approach. McGraw-Hill, New York
Mintzberg H, Waters JA (1985) Of strategies, deliberate and emergent. Strategic Manage J 6:257–272
Nonaka I, Konno N (1998) The concept of 'Ba': building a foundation for knowledge creation. Calif Manage Rev 40(3):40–54
Nonaka I, Takeuchi H (1995) The knowledge-creating company: how Japanese companies create the dynamics of innovation. Oxford University Press, New York
Nonaka I, von Krogh G, Voelpel S (2006) Organizational knowledge creation theory: evolutionary paths and future advances. Organ Stud 27(8):1179–1208
Noordvleugel (2008) Metropoolregio Amsterdam: Ontwikkelingsbeeld Noordvleugel 2040. Metropoolregio Amsterda, Amsterdam
Nowotny H, Scott P, Gibbons M (2001) Re-thinking science: knowledge and the public in an age of uncertainty. Polity, Cambridge
Pawson R, Tilley N (1997) Realistic evaluation. Sage, London
Polanyi M (1967) The tacit dimension. Doubleday, New York
Scharmer CO, Kaufer K (2000) Universities as the birthplace for the entrepreneurial human being. reflections. http://www.ottoscharmer.com/docs/articles/2000_Uni21us.pdf
Schön D (1983) The reflective practitioner: how professionals think in action. Temple Smith, London
Schön D, Rein M (1994) Frame reflection: toward the resolution of intractable policy controversies. Basic Books, New York

Simon HA (1993) Strategy and organizational evolution. Strategic Manage J 14:131–142
Stead D, Geerlings H, Meijers E (2004) Policy integration in practice. The integration of land use planning, transport and environmental policy-making in Denmark, England and Germany. Delft University Press, Delft
Te Brömmelstroet MCG (2009) Equip the warrior instead of manning the equipment: state of practice of land use and transport planning support in the Netherlands. J Transp Land Use 3 (1):25–41
Te Brömmelstroet MCG, Bertolini L (2008) Developing land use and transport PSS: meaningful information through a dialogue between modelers and planners. Transp Policy 15(4):251–259
Te Brömmelstroet M, Bertolini L (2009) Integrating land use and transport knowledge in strategy-making. Transportation 37(5):85–104
Tennøy A (2009) Why we fail to reduce urban road traffic volumes: does it matter how planners frame the problem? Transp Policy 17(4):216–223
Timms P (2008) Transport models, philosophy and language. Transportation 35(3):395–410
TRB (2004) A new vision for mobility: guidance to foster collaborative multimodal decision making. Transportation Research Board, Washington, DC
Tsoukas H (2003) Do we really understand tacit knowledge? In: Easterby-Smith M, Lyles MA (eds) Organizational learning and knowledge management. Blackwell, Oxford, pp 410–425
Uran O, Janssen R (2003) Why are spatial decision support systems not used? Some experiences from the Netherlands. Comput Environ Urban Syst 27:511–526
Van der Bijl R, Witsen PP (2000) Probleemoplossers versus toekomstdenkers. Blauwe Kamer 4:28–36
Vennix JAM (1996) Group model building: facilitating team learning using system dynamics. Wiley, Chichester
Vonk G, Geertman S, Schot P (2005) Bottlenecks blocking widespread usage of planning support systems. Environ Plann A 37:909–924
Wachs M (1985) When planners lie with numbers. J Am Plann Assoc 55:476–479
Waddell P (2002) UrbanSim: modeling urban development for land use, transportation and environmental planning. J Am Plann Assoc 68(3):297–314
Wegener M (2005) Overview of land-use and transport models. In: Henscher DA, Button K (eds) Transport geography and spatial systems. Pergamon/Elsevier Science, Kidlington, pp 127–146
Willson R (2001) Assessing communicative rationality as a transportation planning paradigm. Transportation 28:1–31
Wilson AG (1998) Land-use/transport interaction models, past and future. J Transp Econ 32 (1):3–26

Chapter 3
The Impact of Accessibility on the Value of Offices

Ghebreegziabiher Debrezion, Thomas de Graaff, and Piet Rietveld

3.1 Introduction

Accessibility is becoming an increasingly important issue in the Netherlands, not only for policymakers but also for daily workers on the road and employers, who have to deal with a growing uncertainty of their staff being on time. Not only the access via roads is important; but also the unreliability of public transport (as experienced by passengers), and the lack of parking areas in many places contribute to the importance of accessibility in society.

The above indicates that accessibility is not a clearly defined concept. Accessibility depends on mode of transport, destination, and the travellers themselves. Thus, the experience of accessibility for people who are shopping in the centre of Amsterdam can be different from people who work there. Similarly, the value of the accessibility of Schiphol is different for people who go on a holiday, people who are visiting friends and family, and business travellers. Furthermore, research shows that congestion in public transport is clearly a different experience than congestion on the road.

Geurs and Ritsema van Eck (2001) distinguish four different components of transport that play an important role in the value of accessibility (see Bos 2005). These are: (1) a transport component that describes the travel time, travel cost and travel inconvenience; (2) a spatial component that relates to the size and spatial distribution of activities; (3) a time component that relates to the time constraints of activities (e.g., opening hours and working hours); and (4) an individual component that reflects individual needs, capacities and capabilities. All the components can be seen from different angles for example, from an economic utility maximization or infrastructure optimization point of view.

G. Debrezion (✉) • T. de Graaff • P. Rietveld
Department of Spatial Economics, VU University Amsterdam, De Boelelaan 1105, Amsterdam 1081 HV, The Netherlands
e-mail: g.debrezion@vu.nl; t.de.graaff@vu.nl; p.rietveld@vu.nl

J.A.E.E. van Nunen et al. (eds.), *Transitions Towards Sustainable Mobility*,
DOI 10.1007/978-3-642-21192-8_3,

Due to these different components, it becomes difficult to assign a value to accessibility. As a result, many studies focus on special cases, such as uncertainty in the public transport and road congestion. However, we can measure the value of all different aspects of accessibility collectively by assuming that the monetary impact of accessibility is capitalized on property values. Specific examples include housing near railway stations, which are typically valued higher than similar houses away and highly esteemed locations of offices near the highway ramps.

In the Netherlands, however, this has never been done exclusively for office buildings (for housing, see e.g. Debrezion Andom 2006 and Visser and van Dam 2006). This study focuses on the value of office buildings, where we focus on the (monetary) values that we can assign to the different forms of accessibility. Does it matter if such an office is located close to Schiphol Airport or a train station? Answers to this type of question can be used to improve the benefits of infrastructural projects, to identify where costs can be better distributed over the interested parties, etc.

While in the present paper we focus on the accessibility via various transport modes (in particular road versus rail), it is clear that this is closely related to notions of *sustainable* transport with its underlying dimensions of people, profit and planet. The '*people*' aspect is covered since accessibility is defined in terms of activity patterns of individuals, who try to make use of transport networks in order to achieve their aims. The '*profit*' aspect is addressed, among others, via the impacts of transport networks on real estate values. In this way, our paper sheds light on the profitability of real estate developments on various locations. The '*planet*' dimension receives less explicit attention in the present study, although there are clear links. In particular, our study can be used to mobilise resources for improvements in rail transport systems in terms of speed, frequency and number of stations. These quality aspects of public transport services have a direct impact on accessibility values and our contribution is to compute the implications for real estate values. This can then be used to determine the potential contribution of real estate owners near railway stations to covering the costs of the additional railway services and the associated reduction of environmental pollution. This chapter is therefore closely linked to two other chapters in the present book. The first one is the chapter on *Integrating Land Use and Transport Knowledge in Strategy-Making* (Chap. 2). The present paper clearly contributes to this chapter by informing decision makers on the potential changes in prices of real estate under various network configurations. The second one is the chapter on *Funding Transport Infrastructure Development through Value Capturing: A Game Theoretical Analysis* (Chap. 4). Here the participants in the games can improve their strategies when they are well informed on how the real estate market will respond to changes in transport infrastructure networks.

This chapter is organized as follows. In the next section, we start with a brief literature review – nationally and internationally – about what is already known regarding the relationship between accessibility and property values. Then, we discuss the methodology for measuring the different types of accessibility. Section 3.4 contains the description on the data used, and the operationalization of the results. The final section presents the conclusion.

3.2 Literature Review

3.2.1 Value of Accessibility in an International Context

In general, in the international (mainly American) literature, we see two approaches in assessing the impacts of accessibility, namely examining effects accessibility on land use changes, and examining the impacts of accessibility on property values. In this respect, we review some of the studies on the effect of railway stations on commercial properties from the perspective of both approaches.

In one of the earliest studies, Quackenbush et al. (1987) studied the impact of the Red Line in Boston on land use. He found that the largest effect was on commercial properties, with a slight increase on residential properties. In addition, Weinstein and Clower (1999) indicated that, due to the announcement of Dallas Area Rapid Transit (DART), the occupancy rate of commercial properties within one quarter of a mile of the station increased on average by 5%.

In the literature, various studies have been undertaken on the effect of railway station on commercial property value. The study on the effect of proximity to metro station on commercial property value in Washington D.C. was among the early studies in this regard (Damm et al. 1980). The study found that the value of commercial properties declines with distance. Proximity to a metro station results in a steeper effect on commercial property value as compared with the effect of proximity on residential property value. The elasticity of proximity to the railway station on property value was around four times higher for commercial properties than residential properties. This shows that in the immediate neighbourhood the premium of closeness to a station is greater on commercial properties.

Commercial land value premiums were also found by Fejarang (1994). They found that commercial spaces in Los Angeles city that are located within half a mile of a rail transit station, had an additional $31 increase in mean sales price over comparable parcels outside the corridor. In addition to the land use changes as a result of the announcement of the opening of DART, Weinstein and Clower (1999) observed an increase in the rent of three classes of offices within one quarter of a mile of a station ranging from 20.9 to 47.4 compared to similar offices outside that range. Similarly, the study conducted by Hickling Lewis Brod, Inc. indicates the price per square foot of commercial space decreases by about $2.3 for every 1,000 ft further from a railway station. This value accounts for approximately 2% of the value (Hickling Lewis Brod 2002). Furthermore, Nelson (1998) found that the price per square metre in Atlanta falls by $75 for every metre away from a transit station.

In an effort to present background information against the lawsuit brought by private property owners in Santa Clara County, claiming a burden due to the existence of light rail transit (LRT), Weinberger (2001) tested several hedonic price models on the rental rates of commercial property. The finding reveals that commercial properties within one quarter of a mile of the station are rented 10% higher than commercial properties beyond three quarters of a mile of a light rail station. When controlling for highway access, the rail proximity benefit was maintained, and it was shown that highway coverage in the county is so dense, that there are no particular locational advantages associated with highway coverage.

A similar study was also undertaken by Cervero and Duncan (2001) in the same county. They found that commercial properties within one quarter of a mile of a light railway station were sold 23% higher than commercial properties outside this range. The capitalization on property values even becomes even pronounced in the case of proximity to commuter railway station. Commercial properties within one quarter of a mile of the commuter railway station sell more than 120% above commercial properties outside this range.

Contrary to the above positive effects of proximity to railway stations, Cervero and Duncan (2001–2002a,b) found a mixed effect of proximity to railway stations on commercial property values. The study in Los Angeles county shows that, for commercial properties located within one quarter of a mile of a station, the impact of different stations range from a negative effect as big as 30% to a positive effect of 16% compared to the values of properties outside the one quarter mile range. Similarly, the study in San Diego County reveals the impact of proximity to a railway station within one quarter of a mile on commercial property value ranges from a negative effect of 10% to a positive effect as big as 90%. Landis et al. (1995) found no premium for commercial land. However, the lack of finding a positive impact is attributed to a data and methodological problem, instead of the lack of a real value premium.

3.2.2 Location Factors in the Netherlands

The price of real estate depends on the attractiveness for decision makers to choose a site for their activities. Besides hedonic price models, different types of studies can be distinguished that aim to identify and rate the location factors that underlie the attractiveness of locations. Most common studies are economic-geographic surveys, in which an importance ranking of location factors is provided, based on questionnaires. These surveys typically take account of a large number of location factors and are, therefore, very well suitable to attain an overview of the field. For the Netherlands, a great number of researches of this type have been conducted (see e.g. Pellenbarg 1985; Jansen and Hanemaayer 1991; Sloterdijk and Van Steen 1994; and see Healey and Baker 1996 for an international study that includes the Netherlands). Besides questionnaires, other more advanced quantitative methods can also be used. Examples in the Netherlands include stated choice studies (e.g. Rietveld and Bruinsma 1998) and advanced rating studies (Berkhout and Hop 2002). The number of location factors in these studies is normally smaller.

Little uniformity exists in the specification of location factors. Still, when examining these studies four general categories of location factors can be distinguished:

- *Accessibility-related*: includes proximity to actors or infrastructure, and the availability of personnel;
- *Properties of the building*: availability, representativeness, possibilities for expansion;
- *Properties of the surroundings*: type of environment, representativeness;
- *Other regional factors*: working mentality, quality of life, investment subsidies.

The analysis in this study looks into the effect of the first three factors on the rent levels of office spaces in the Netherlands. However, the discussions focus on accessibility-related factors, which are of main interest in this study. Accessibility-related aspects are among the most important location factors. Aspects of accessibility in location studies are, on the one hand, the connectivity to the network (access distance or travel time to a network node, or the level-of-service of this node) and, on the other hand, potential accessibility (relates to the possibility to reach destinations, e.g. the availability of potential personnel). In general, accessibility by car can be seen to be more important than accessibility by public transport (e.g. Jansen and Hanemaayer 1991).

However, the link with the value of real estate is not always clear. Therefore, this study focuses on the effects of accessibility of both railway and highway on the values of real estate.

3.3 The Effect of Accessibility on Property Value: Theory

This section consists of two parts. The first part deals with the theoretical framework for a price analysis of property values. The second part focuses on how to measure accessibility in the Netherlands effectively.

3.3.1 Hedonic Price Analysis

The real estate market is characterized by similar but heterogeneous products. This means that, although properties may look similar, they are not exactly identical, so they are imperfect substitutes for each other. This market can also be seen as a form of 'monopolistic competition': the providers of properties are in competition with each other, but each provider of a specific variant has a monopoly on that exact version. This means that suppliers have a form of market power and thus the opportunity to set their prices individually. They could not do so indefinitely, because the properties, in this case the offices, are to a certain extent, substitutes for each other, allowing tenants of high-priced office buildings to seek an alternative landlord.

Because the offices are not exactly identical, it is difficult to compare the prices of these firms directly. An alternative is to valuate the separate components of these offices, and then to compare the offices, based on the number and type of components that they consist of. This form of price analysis is called hedonic price analysis.[1]

Suppose that each office in the Netherlands can be described by a fixed number of features, let's call it X; one can think of the most diverse characteristics such as age of the office, number of elevators, location of the office, image of the surrounding area, etc.. Let us suppose that – according to the classification in Sect. 3.2.2 – we can divide the characteristics into four distinct groups, namely:

- *Accessibility factors* ($\mathbf{X}_a$): How close is the office building at a railway station, bus station or highway? Are there parking areas nearby? Is the area hard to reach by congestion?
- *Characteristics of the property/tenant* ($\mathbf{X}_k$): does the building have a cafeteria, elevator, similar equipment? When was it built? What is the size of the property? Etc.
- *Environmental factors* ($\mathbf{X}_e$): Where is the property located? How is the environment used (business area or city centre)? What is the surrounding of facilities for employees? And so on.
- *Regional factors* ($\mathbf{X}_r$): What are the regional characteristics? How open or closed is the regional economy? What is the average education level of the region and what is its image?

An essential assumption of the hedonic price analysis is that the value of an office building is a function of these characteristics and thus, we can compare office buildings based on these characteristics. Therefore, if tenants' average accessibility by car is important, then office buildings that are easy to reach are higher priced than office buildings that are difficult to access by car, ceteris paribus. We can also write this relationship in a mathematical form as:

$$\ln p = f(\mathbf{X}_a, \mathbf{X}_k, \mathbf{X}_e, \mathbf{X}_r), \tag{3.1}$$

where p is the rent of the office property and *ln* is the natural logarithm.

An important underlying assumption is that the market price correctly reflects the real value of the office building, but this is not always the case. Although this theory works in practice, the data must meet some conditions. First, the office market must be in equilibrium to allow the price p to reflect the proper value for an office. With a real estate market that requires a long time from planning to building, this is often not the case. Furthermore, it is important that the market is not segmented, so there is a price p for each combination of characteristics.[2]

---

[1]Rosen (1974) is probably the first to publish this theory in an economically fully developed manner and, therefore, can be taken as a good starting point for the interested reader.

[2]Good, but somewhat technical, papers on the latest situation in hedonic price modeling can be found in, for example, Palmquist (2003) en Bajari and Benkard (2005).

The formulation of (3.1) does almost automatically remind us of a regression-based approach, where different features are additional, but have different weights. This is a usual practice in the bigger part of hedonic price literature (Malpezzi 2002).

3.3.2 Accessibility

Accessibility by itself is a difficult concept to operationalize. In any case, it does not mean that the areas with the least congestion have high accessibility. Accessibility for a given site can be defined as the potential interaction with sites in the vicinity. This interaction increases with the volume of activities in different locations, and decreases the cost of interaction. Accessibility is specific to a particular activity (e.g. work).

In general, accessibility can be divided into accessibility by road and accessibility by public transport. In this study, public transport is mainly represented by railway. Road accessibility can further be enriched by looking at the access to the potential employees and business clients.

In this study, we are mainly interested in three types of accessibility:

- Access to potential employees on the road during peak and non-peak hours
- Access to potential employees by public transport, particularly travelling by train
- Access to Schiphol airport as a measure of accessibility to foreign destinations

In addition, the accessibility by road can also be divided into trips and parking. Namely, to many people the effort needed to park a car appears to be a major component of accessibility. However, because of the lack of correct information, we could not include parking in the analysis of this paper.

The main scientific contribution of this paper is the coverage of the accessibility dimensions and the detailed way in which accessibility has been measured. In particular, we pay attention to the level of services on the railway system. This aspect has not been taken into account in the literature thus far. Our approach allows us to study the consequences of changes in the level of service on certain links for the accessibility and the real estate prices near stations at the link, or further away in the network. This implies that the paper makes an important step forward by appropriately linking land use to transport systems. It also makes the model we have estimated of high relevance for the assessment of policy proposals.

3.4 The Effect of Accessibility on the Rents of Office Buildings

The previous section dealt with a theoretical and methodological framework for measuring the value of accessibility on property values. It also gave a breakdown of the various forms of accessibility that are potentially relevant for property values, or, in our specific case, for office buildings.

This section shows that the above described importance of accessibility by an explicit attaching value to these forms. We do this as follows. The next subsection first describes the data used for this the estimation used in this paper. Then we implement our accessibility variables, as measured by ($\mathbf{X}_a$), namely: accessibility by road (during peak and non-peak hours), accessibility by railway, accessibility to Schiphol airport and accessibility to other offices. Then we find the real effect of measurement, as described above, hedonic price analysis. We conclude this section with a brief discussion of the results.

3.4.1 Description of the Data

The most important variable for a hedonic price analysis is the (transaction) price of an office building. As the measure of price, we use the rent of office areas per m^2 the Netherlands since 1983. These rental record data are collected by DTZ real estate broker. DTZ processes the larger part of the office rental transaction in the Netherlands, and can, therefore, be considered fairly representative of the national real estate market. In addition to information on the rent level, the records include postcode address (4–6 digits), size of the rental area (in m^2), time of the rental agreement, type of contract, building status, and business characteristics of the tenant. Information on the type of contract relates to whether the contract is a first hand contract between the owner and the tenant, an extension of previous contract, or a sublease. The information on the status of the building relates to whether the office area occupied by the tenant is in a new building, the office area has been occupied previously, the office area has just undergone renovation, the office area is under construction, or the building has yet to be built.

The postcode data are important, because we use them to link to other databases. The data, which relate to the characteristics of office buildings (as measured by $\mathbf{X}_k$), are taken from the DTZ rental contract records, other features stem mainly from other databases. As mentioned in this paper, subsequently we will discuss the three main accessibility characteristics (accessibility by rail, accessibility by road and accessibility to the airport).

3.4.1.1 Accessibility by Rail

For many firms it is important to locate close to a railway station. Especially for haulage firms, it is important to locate within walking distance of a railway station. Furthermore, the service quality of a station is of interest. Especially the number of routes, frequency and number of stops prove to be of great interest to railway passengers. That is why we introduced a Rail Service Quality Index (RSQI) for each railway station as a measure of the important level of a railway station (as a destination station).

We consider the station from the destination point of view. The RSQI of a station j as an arrival station depends on three components:

- **O_i**: The size of departure station i, i.e. the total number of departures from station i. This shows how important the connections to other stations.
- **GTJ_{ij}**: This is the generalized journey time between each origin station i and destination station j. The generalized journey time depends on the average waiting time, the actual travel time by train, transfer time, and a "punishment" for the number of steps.
- **GTJ_{ij}/d_{ij}**: This gives the ratio of the generalized journey time and distance for each origin station i and destination station j. If the value for the ratio is high, this indicates that the train takes a considerable detour and, therefore, in many cases, it can be more attractive to use other alternative transport modes, like the car.

Details on the exact way of measuring RSQI are given in the appendix.

The stations with the highest RSQ indices lie in the Randstad, close to the big cities. The first ten railway station with the highest values for RSQI as arrival stations are: Utrecht Centraal (RSQI = 1.46), Leiden Centraal (RSQI = 1.29), Duivendrecht (RSQI = 1.27), Den Haag HS (RSQI = 1.12), Amsterdam Centraal (RSQI = 1.06), Amsterdam Sloterdijk (RSQI = 1.06), Schiphol (RSQI = 1.05), Rotterdam Centraal (RSQI = 1.04), Dordrecht (RSQI = 0.96), en's Hertogenbosch (RSQI = 0.95). A complete list of RSQI for the stations in the Dutch railway network is found in Debrezion Andom (2006).

3.4.1.2 Accessibility by Road

We interpret the accessibility to the workforce (20–65 years) by road as the accessibility of a firm occupying an office location to (potential) employees. Indeed, one can assume that an office location will be worth more, if the potential for workforce in the immediate vicinity is high. Therefore, we construct a variable, b_i, for each office location i that defines the aggregate working population in the vicinity (weighted by travel time by road) from this office location:

$$b_i = \sum_{j=1}^{R} \left[\text{WorkingPop}_j \times f\left(t_{ij}\right) \right], \tag{3.2}$$

where R is the total number of postcode areas in the Netherlands and $f(t_{ij})$ is the so-called distance decay function. The latter indicates that the influence of postcode areas located further away is less important compared with those, which are close to the office location. However, an assumption has to be made on the shape of the decay function. In this paper, we use the following specification[3]:

[3]This specification was suggested by the simulation results of Goudappel-Coffeng (see www.bereikbaarheidskaart.nl).

$$f\left(t_{ij}\right) = \frac{1}{e^{2t_{ij}^{3}}}. \tag{3.3}$$

t_{ij} is here measured in hours. Compared with the more common specification,, t_{ij}^{-1}, this specification places more emphasis on nearby locations.

3.4.1.3 Distance to Schiphol Airport

From previous studies (see e.g. Debrezion Andom 2006) and expert interviews, wc know that office locations are more expensive as they are located closer (in kilometers) to Schiphol airport. In fact, office locations at the airport are among the most expensive locations in the Netherlands (together with those of the Amsterdam South Axis). Therefore, we include an explicit measure of distance to the airport in our specification.

3.5 Estimation Results

Table 3.1 gives the estimated results using linear regression for the hedonic price model (given by [3.1]) for the main variables, namely the accessibility variables, characteristics of the building and environment characteristics.

The accessibility characteristics give intuitively plausible coefficient values. First, if the accessibility by road (as measured in [3.3]) of the workforce is increased by 100%, then the rental level of the office location increases by about 1.5%. This effect, although statistically significant, is rather small. However, it could explain the differences in rent levels between the major cities.[4]

The distance from a railway station to an office location appears to be very important. To illustrate this, the coefficients from Table 3.1 are converted into Fig. 3.1.

The biggest effect of proximity on a railway station is found to be for offices located within 500 m of a station. This is not surprising since at the egress side, workers and visitors often depend on foot for access the offices. Table 3.1 and Fig. 3.1 assume that the RSQI is exactly one. The line in Fig. 3.1 indicates the increase or decrease in the percentage of office rent for the same percentage increase or decrease in the RSQI.

The final accessibility measure – the distance to the airport – appears to have, as expected, a negative sign and statistically significant effect on office rent level. The value of −0.06 in this case indicates that doubling the distance between the office

[4]This is mainly due to the specific log-sum approach used to measure accessibility by road. This makes a direct interpretation difficult.

Table 3.1 Estimation results: hedonic price analysis on *ln* (rent) per m^2 (number of observations = 11.298)

Variables	Coefficient	T-value
Constant	4.912	75.643
Total surface area	0.000	1.822
Accessibility		
Distance to *NS station (reference category: distance > 7,000 m)*		
Distance to NS station < 250 m	0.159	8.988
Distance to NS station 250–500 m	0.171	10.714
Distance to NS station 500–1,000 m	0.118	8.580
Distance to NS station 1,000–2,000 m	0.068	5.157
Distance to NS station 2,000–4,000 m	0.072	4.996
Distance to NS station 4,000–7,000 m	0.036	1.588
Log (road accessibility) (b_i)	0.015	8.447
Log (distance to Schiphol airport [km])	−0.069	−16.516
Building status (*reference category: first user*)		
Second user	−0.132	−15.969
Renovation	−0.075	−4.818
Under construction	0.022	0.579
Yet to be built	−0.017	−0.296
Type of contract (*reference category: rent*)		
Rent extension	0.036	1.265
Sublease	0.050	2.548
Sector tenant (*reference category: industries and public works*)		
Building and civil engineering	−0.042	−1.993
Trade and repairing companies	−0.081	−5.044
Transportation and storage	−0.029	−1.431
Communication companies	0.002	0.098
Credit and insurance services	0.092	5.392
Financial business services	0.054	3.428
Other business services	0.005	0.382
Computer companies	−0.006	−0.400
Public administration, defence or social security	−0.010	−0.619
Education and health care	−0.105	−6.703
Other institutions and companies	−0.089	−6.536
Land use (*reference category: agricultural sites*)		
Residential area-high density	0.018	0.893
Residential area-high/medium density	−0.042	−2.528
Residential area-medium density	0.103	3.913
Residential area-medium/low density	−0.328	−5.101
Residential area-low density	0.067	0.465
Firm sites	−0.152	−7.144
Social-cultural sites	0.004	0.067
Seaport	−0.537	−10.049
Recreational sites	0.240	7.928
Nature areas	0.125	3.536
Other	−0.004	−0.086

(continued)

Table 3.1 (continued)

Variables	Coefficient	T-value
Infrastructure	0.181	3.046
Water	−0.156	−2.902
remaining land use	0.020	1.352
Cities (*reference category: rest of the Netherlands*)		
Amsterdam	0.229	18.901
Rotterdam	0.099	9.084
Utrecht	0.104	7.921
Den Haag	0.138	10.502
Eindhoven	0.072	5.376
$\mathbf{R^2}$		**0.360**

Year dummies are not reported

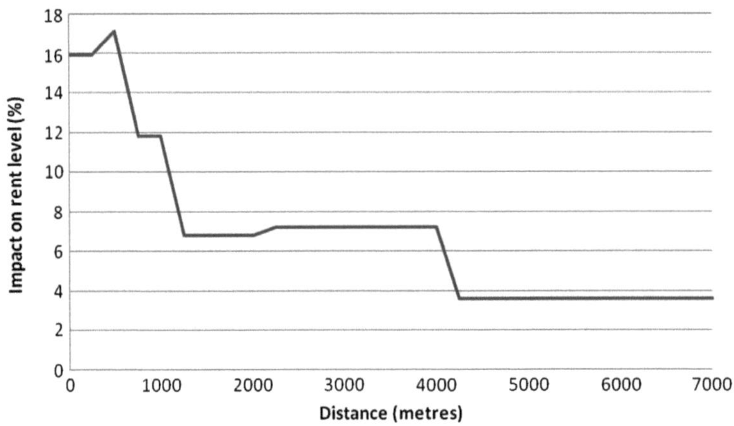

Fig. 3.1 The relationship between rent levels of office locations and distance to nearest railway station

location and Schiphol decreases the rent of the office location by 6%, while the other factors are held constant.

The effects of the remaining variables also correspond to the literature and many are statistically significant. User type, contract type, status of the building and surrounding land are all characteristics of interest.[5] Striking example is the high coefficient for infrastructure of surrounding land use. Offices that are located close to highways are valued higher, which may indicate the importance of office sight from the highway lines. Furthermore, office locations in Amsterdam and The Hague are structurally valued higher, compared to other locations in the Netherlands. This probably indicates the presence of image effects.

[5]Land use is defined here as the percentage of a particular land use type in a four-digit postcode area. They are based on a grid size of 25 by 25 m.

3.6 Conclusion

Accessibility in all its facets is becoming an increasingly important issue in the Netherlands. Not only the increasing congestion on the road plays is of key importance in policy making, but also other accessibility issues play a role, such as the uncertainty in the public transport, the increasing importance of (international) nodes such as Schiphol, the growing cluster of companies in business services and parking issues.

However, little is known about the (monetary) value of these different forms of accessibility. How important are train stations to office buildings? Do employers attach importance to accessibility to the potential labour force? How important is it for offices to be located near Schiphol? This study gives answers to these questions by linking measurable aspects of accessibility statistics to property value of offices.

Indeed, accessibility has a significant impact on the value of real estate offices. However, the impacts of the effects differ for the different forms of accessibility:

- The location of an office in relation to Schiphol airport plays a major role. Each doubling of the distance between a firm and Schiphol decreases the property value of that office by 6%.
- The average distance to the surrounding working population also plays a significant role. Even though the parameter specification used for this variable makes it difficult to give a summary of the effects, our research shows clearly that, the availability of a large potential employees nearby increases the property value of an office.
- If an office is located within 500 m from a railway station, then the value is about 16% higher compared to similar offices located more than 7 km from the stations. This effect is clearly smaller as an office is located more than 1 km from a train station. The latter can be explained by the fact that egress to the office location is usually done by foot.

Besides the accessibility factors, we also examined the effects of factors associated with the region, the specific office, or the tenant. Most results are consistent with the results found in the literature. However, it is important to point out the fact that values of offices in cities like The Hague and Amsterdam seem to be structurally valued higher than comparable firms elsewhere are. This fact points to image effects. Apparently, many companies attach much value to a particular postcode on their business card.

The present study has taken its point of departure in the accessibility concept. This means that it is based on behavioural parameters on spatial interactions of commuters in labour markets. This is a reflection of the 'people aspect' of the broad sustainability concept. The 'profit' aspect has been addressed via the profit making of real estate developers in the office market. They find that office values are positively affected by proximity to railway stations, and by the level of railway services. The 'planet' aspect has not received explicit attention, but is directly related to environmental effects since office developments near railway stations would have effects on modal choice, and hence on environmental pollution.

The major contribution of the present paper in terms of transitions towards sustainable mobility is, that it offers convincing insights into new ways of mobilising funds for the financing of transport projects. The findings enable public actors to better understand the potential value of a property after improvements of infrastructure. This provides them with a motive for a portion of the costs to be recovered from developers active in the neighbourhood (for example by a so-called 'value capture' scheme). The model developed here provides an operational tool for public actors that want to be active in mobilising additional financial resources to finance infrastructure projects.

Appendix A

The estimation of the Rail Service Quality Index (RSQI) of a station is based on the doubly constrained spatial interaction model, given as follows:

$$T_{ij} = A_i O_i B_j D_j f(GJT_{ij}) g(GJT_{ij}/d_{ij}) \exp(\xi_{ij}) \tag{A1}$$

$$O_i = \sum\nolimits_j T_{ij} \tag{A2}$$

$$D_j = \sum_i T_{ij} \tag{A3}$$

where T_{ij} is the number of trips between stations i and j; O_i is the total number of trips originated in station i; D_j is the total number of trips attracted by station j. A_i and B_j are the balancing factors which ensure that the constraints on origins and destinations (given by [2] and [3A3]) are met; GJT_{ij} is the generalized journey time between origin station i and destination station j; d_{ij} is the Euclidian distance between origin station $i$and destination station j; and ξ_{ij} is the error component of the model which follows an independently and identically normal distribution. We specify the functions f and g as follows:

$$f(GJT_{ij}) = \exp\left(\sum_{c=1}^{C} \beta_c DGJT_c^{\ ij}\right) \tag{A4}$$

$$g(GJT_{ij}/d_{ij}) = \left(GJT_{ij}/d_{ij}\right)^{\gamma} \tag{A5}$$

where, $DGJT_c^{\ ij}$ is a dummy variable, which is equal to 1, if GJT_{ij} falls in the generalized journey time category $c$and 0 otherwise. Thus, the doubly constrained gravity model we estimated is given by:

$$T_{ij} = A_i O_i B_j D_j \exp\left(\sum_{c=1}^{C} \beta_c DGJT_c{}^{ij}\right) \left(GJT_{ij}/d_{ij}\right)^{\gamma} \exp(\xi_{ij}) \tag{A6}$$

This equation can be linearized by taking the natural logarithm of both sides:

$$\ln\left(T_{ij}/O_i D_j\right) = \ln A_i + \ln B_j + \left(\sum_{c=1}^{C} \beta_c DGJT_c{}^{ij}\right) + \gamma \ln\left(GJT_{ij}/d_{ij}\right) + \xi_{ij} \tag{A7}$$

The coefficient of the generalized journey time categories, the ratio of generalized journey time, and the balancing factors will be estimated from the above equation. Thus, in the estimation, the logs of the balancing factors in the equation represent the coefficients to be estimated. This requires that the logs of the balancing factors are multiplied by the dummy variable for the corresponding station. Therefore, the equation for the estimation is given as:

$$\ln\left(\frac{T_{ij}}{O_i D_j}\right) = \sum_{\tilde{i}=1}^{N} \ln A_{\tilde{i}} S_{\tilde{i}} + \sum_{\tilde{j}=1}^{N-1} \ln B_{\tilde{j}} S_{\tilde{j}} + \ln\left(\sum_{c=1}^{C} \beta_c DGJT_c{}^{ij}\right) + \gamma \ln\left(\frac{GJT_{ij}}{d_{ij}}\right) + \xi_{ij}. \tag{A8}$$

where, N is the number of railway stations in the railway network; and $S_{\tilde{i}}$ and $S_{\tilde{j}}$ are dummy variables for departure station $\tilde{i}$ and destination station $\tilde{j}$. They assume the value 1 when $i = \tilde{i}$ and $j = \tilde{j}$, respectively, and 0 otherwise. Given the assumption on the error components above, (8) can be estimated using ordinary least squares (OLS). The estimated coefficients are then used in determining the Rail Service Quality Indices (RSQIs) for each station. The RSQI of any departure station i is determined as the aggregation sum of the quality measures over all the destination stations (j's). Thus, the RSQI of a given departure station is given by:

$$RSQI_i = \sum_j \hat{B}_j D_j \hat{f}(GJT_{ij}) \hat{f}(\frac{GJT_{ij}}{d_{ij}}) = \sum_j \hat{B}_j D_j \exp\left(\sum_{c=1}^{C} \hat{\beta}_c DGJT_c{}^{ij}\right) \left(\frac{GJT_{ij}}{d_{ij}}\right)^{\hat{\gamma}}; \tag{A9}$$

References

Bajari P, Benkard CL (2005) Demand estimation with heterogeneous consumers and unobserved product characteristics: a hedonic approach. J Polit Econ 113:1239–1276

Berkhout PHG, Hop JP (2002) Een prijskaartje aan kwaliteitskenmerken van kantoren. In opdracht van DTZ Zadelhoff en Twynstra Gudde. Amsterdam: Stichting voor Economisch Onderzoek der Universiteit van Amsterdam

Bos I (2005) Knooppuntontwikkeling en bereikbaarheid: state of the art. Working paper, Nijmegen, Mimeo

Cervero R, Duncan M (2001) Rail transit's value added: effect of proximity to light and commuter rail transit on commercial land values in Santa Clara county California. Paper prepared for National Association of Realtors Urban Land Institute

Cervero R, Duncan M (2001–2002a) Land value impact of rail transit services in Los Angeles County. Report prepared for National Association of Realtors Urban Land Institute

Cervero R, Duncan M (2001–2002b) Land value impact of rail transit services in San Diego County. Report prepared for National Association of Realtors Urban Land Institute

Damm D, Lerman SR, Lerner-Lam E, Young J (1980) Response of urban real estate values in anticipation of the Washington metro. J Transp Econ Policy 14:315–336

Debrezion Andom G (2006) Railway impacts on real estate prices. Thela Thesis, Amsterdam

Fejarang RA (1994) Impact on property values: a study of the Los Angeles metro rail. Preprint prepared for Transportation Research Board 73rd annual meeting, Washington, DC, 9–13 Jan 1994

Geurs KT, Ritsema van Eck JR (2001) Accessibility measure: review and applications. Evaluation of accessibility impacts on land-use transport scenarios, and related social and economic impacts. RIVM Report 408505006. National Institute for Public Health and the Environment, Bilthoven

Healey & Baker (1996) European real estate monitor. Healey & Baker, London

Hickling Lewis Brod (2002) Commercial property benefits of transit: final report. Federal Transit Administration, Washington, DC

Jansen A, Hanemaayer D (1991) Eisen aan de bedrijfsomgeving in de Randstad, NSS Beleidsonderzoek & Beleidsadvies, Den Haag

Landis J, Cervero R, Guhathukurta S, Loutzenheiser D, Zhang M (1995) Rail transit investments, real estate values, and land use change: a comparative analysis of five California rail transit systems. Monograph 48, Institute of Urban and Regional Studies, University of California at Berkeley

Malpezzi S (2002) Hedonic pricing models: a selective and applied review. The Center for Urban Land Economics Research, the University of Wisconsin, Madison

Nelson AC (1998) Transit stations and commercial property values: case study with policy and land use implications. Paper presented at Transportation Research Board 77th annual meeting, Washington, DC

Palmquist RB (2005) Property value models. In: Karl-Göran M, Jefferey V (eds) Handbook of environmental economics, vol II, Valuing environmental changes. Elsevier North Holland, Amsterdam, pp 763–819

Pellenbarg PH (1985) Bedrijfsrelokatie en ruimtelijke kognitie; onderzoekingen naar bedrijfsverplaatsingsprocessen en de subjektieve waardering van vestigingsplaatsen door ondernemers in Nederland. Dissertation R.U. Groningen, Sociaal-Geografische Reeks no. 33, Geografisch Instituut R.U. Groningen

Quackenbush KH, Holst-Roness E, Humphrey TJ, Slater G (1987) Red line extension to alewife: before/after study – appendices. Central Transportation Planning Staff for the Massachusetts Bay Transportation Authority, Boston

Rietveld P, Bruinsma F (1998) Is transport infrastructure effective? transport infrastructure and accessibility impacts on the space economy. In: Advances in spatial science. Springer, Berlin

Rosen S (1974) Hedonic prices and implicit markets: product differentiation in pure competition. J Polit Econ 82:34–55

Sloterdijk MS, van Steen PJM (1994) Ruimtegebruik en ruimtelijk gedrag van ondernemingen: economisch-demografische bouwstenen. Groningen: Rijksuniversiteit Groningen, Faculteit der Ruimtelijke Wetenschappen

Visser P, van Dam F (2006) De Prijs van de Plek. NAi uitgevers, Rotterdam

Weinberger R (2001) Light rail proximity: benefit or detriment. The case of Santa Clara County California. Paper presented at the Transportation Research Board 80th annual meeting, Washington, DC, 7–11 Jan 2001

Weinstein BL, Clower TL (1999) The initial economic impact of the DART LRT system. Unpublished manuscript

Chapter 4
Funding Transport Infrastructure Development Through Value Capturing: A Game Theoretical Analysis

Ary Samsura and Erwin van der Krabben

4.1 Introduction

As already mentioned in Chap. 2 of this book, the development of major transportation infrastructure and location development (i.e. residential areas, industrial estates, office and retail parks) increasingly takes place in an integrated way. An integrated approach may not only contribute to a better, more sustainable spatial outcome of the development process (from the society's point of view), but it might also be more efficient, although the increased complexity may have an unintended counter effect on efficiency as well (Van der Krabben et al. 2007). Moreover, in financial terms, the integrated approach also provides new opportunities. Traditionally, the public investments in transportation infrastructure are based on tax revenues. Usually, the according budgets available for transportation infrastructure development are limited and – almost by definition – not sufficient to develop all desired infrastructure. In looking for alternative funding for transportation infrastructure development, governments should try to find a way that allows for efficient economic performance, financial justice, and social facility. When transportation infrastructure and location development are combined, value capturing methods may, to a certain extent, offer an opportunity to achieve those goals (Banister and Berechman 2000; Batt 2001). Here, we define value capturing as a process by which all or a portion of increments in land value, that resulted from the installation of special public improvements or any other actions attributed to the 'public effort', are recouped by the public sector and used for public purposes (Smolka 2000; Smith and Gihring 2006). In Chap. 3, Debrezion et al. paid attention to the issue of value capturing especially on how to calculate the increment in property values caused by the infrastructure development, or to be specific a train

A. Samsura (✉) • E. van der Krabben
Department of Spatial Planning, Institute for Mangement Research, 9108, 6500 HK, Nijmegen, The Netherlands
e-mail: d.samsura@fm.ru.nl; e.vanderkrabben@fm.ru.nl

J.A.E.E. van Nunen et al. (eds.), *Transitions Towards Sustainable Mobility*,
DOI 10.1007/978-3-642-21192-8_4, © Springer-Verlag Berlin Heidelberg 2011

station. However, there are still questions about whether value capturing might be a feasible method to finance infrastructure development projects and also about the explanation of decision-making process with respect to the implementation of value capturing methods.

The increment in land and property values can be considered as positive externalities, generated by public goods provision, that should be internalized (Webster and Lai 2003; Van der Krabben and Needham 2009). Referring to the new institutional economics framework, externalities problems are generated by a 'failure' in the definition and assignment of property rights (see e.g. Coase 1960; Barzel 1997). Therefore, the implementation of value capturing should take into account the clarification and assignment of property rights, which suggests the importance of interdependency and cooperation among stakeholders involved. From the new institutional economics perspective, there are some difficulties in implementing value capturing. One of the problems is the difficulty of capturing the increasing land value, especially when the land owners refuse to give it up, because the property rights over the increment in land value had been assigned to them initially. As mentioned by Barzel (1997), property rights of individuals over assets consist of the rights or power to consume, obtain income or benefit from, and alienate their assets. It means that land owners have the right to enjoy the increment in value themselves without any obligation to give it back to the community. Therefore, in a situation where the property rights are well assigned – i.e. to the land owner in the Netherlands, who will receive the increment in land value (Munoz-Gielen 2008) – it will be problematic to apply value capturing unless the institutional arrangements with respect to the assignment of property rights over the increment in land value will be changed, or the parties involved will start a bargaining process to reallocate the increment in land values among them.

Real-life bargaining processes to reach a consensus and agreement between a transportation infrastructure developer and a location developer are often muddy and obscure. In this chapter, we offer an analysis of bargaining processes in the implementation of value capturing methods as internalization mechanism for the externalities, by relying on concepts and approaches drawn from game theory.

A game theoretical approach provides a way to formulize the interdependency and cooperation among stakeholders (infrastructure provider, land owners, property developers) in complex decision-making projects. Moreover, it can be used to examine the structure of individual decisions (Samsura et al. 2010; Te Brömmelstoet and Bertolini 2009, and Chap. 2 of this book by the same authors). This approach is elaborated in this chapter to provide an analysis in implementing value capturing methods. The institutional setting of land development related to infrastructure development and funding in the Netherlands will be used to provide an empirical context to the analysis. The transition that we analyze in this chapter is the integration of infrastructure and location development and the related financial opportunities of value capturing. Thus, we aim to contribute to the development of a new generation of financial tools for integrated infrastructure and area development.

The structure of this chapter is as follows. In Sect. 4.2, we will discuss value capturing and externalities problems in detail. Section 4.3 provides an introduction to game theory and a discussion of the supposed advantages as well as limitations of applying this approach to analyse the bargaining process in implementing value capturing methods. Section 4.4 presents a brief description of issues related to value capturing within the context of location and infrastructure development processes and its funding mechanisms in the Netherlands. In this section, the stakeholders involved will be introduced along with their strategies and the institutional context in which they operate. In Sect. 4.5, the bargaining model, based on a game theoretical approach will be constructed with respect to the implementation of value capturing methods in the Netherlands. Finally, Sect. 4.6 discusses the usefulness of bargaining game theory for modelling the implementation of value capturing processes and suggests the next steps for further analysis.

4.2 Value Capturing and Externalities Problems

As mentioned above, the increment in land and property values to be captured can be considered as positive externalities generated from public goods provision. From an economic perspective, attempts should be made to solve the externalities problem (see e.g. Webster and Lai 2003; Van der Krabben and Needham 2009). Therefore, value capturing can be considered as a set of tools to internalize the increment in land and property values and thus as the solution for externalities problems.

In any economics textbook, the discussion about solving externalities problems almost always refers to the works of Pigou (1920) and Coase (1960). Pigou's approach on externalities focuses on the market equilibrium outcome, which has to be Pareto efficient. The presence of externalities will break down this equilibrium, because the externalities will make the private marginal costs diverge from the social marginal costs associated with each party's actions. The result is that parties will face the 'wrong' price, which will lead to an inefficient allocation of resources. Pigou's solution for this situation is to levy taxes, to force private marginal costs to meet social marginal costs. However, this solution will raise some problems. First, it requires an omniscient and also benevolent tax authority, because it should know the exact tax level to reach marginal social costs. Moreover, this tax authority will be insensitive to rent-seeking behaviour. Second, there is a problem of fairness with the Pigouvian tax concept, because it does not necessarily consider the damage done to parties when they are being taxed and induced to produce at social optimum efficiency.

Coase's approach tries to deal with these problems. He argues that the market itself is able to solve the problem of externalities: when property rights are well-assigned and transaction costs are zero, resource allocation is efficient and independent of the pattern of ownership (Coase 1960). This principle is well known as the Coase Theorem. Based on this principle, the producers of negative externalities or the receivers of positive externalities should not be taxed, instead they should bargain to decide how and to what extent the externalities could be reduced (see among others Calabresi 1968; Dahlman 1979; Varian 1994).

Considering value capturing, taxes, fees, and regulatory instruments are often used as its main tools (see e.g. Smolka 2000; Batt 2001; de Wolff 2007). However, using Coase's terminology, land and property owners have the right to enjoy the increment in values of their land and properties, while at the same time the infrastructure developers also have the right to take benefit from it. Therefore, bargaining and negotiation should take place among the parties involved to arrive at the agreement upon the efficient allocation of the increment in land value as well as the compensations to reach such agreement. In this chapter, the cooperative game theoretic approach is applied to analyse the implementation of value capturing based on the Coase Theorem. The main assumption in cooperative games is that the parties can make binding agreements about the distribution of payoffs without any cost and the solution will be the most desirable coalition structure for all parties involved.

However, Coase's approach goes not without problems, especially, because the prerequisite of zero transaction costs is a very strict one, which is often not fulfilled in real situations.[1] Moreover, the ability of parties to make a commitment upon the ex-ante agreement to share the outcome in the end is doubtful (Samuelson 1995). In this kind of situations, the non-cooperative game theoretical approach should be taken into account. The main assumption in this approach is that the parties involved choose strategies separately to get the most desirable outcomes of bargaining for each of them. However, in this chapter, we make use of the cooperative game, because we have reasons to believe that in the case of spatial planning in general and infrastructure and location development decisions in particular the parties involved will be able to make a commitment.

4.3 Bargaining Game: A Brief Description

In general terms, bargaining can be defined as a process to reach mutual agreement or a contract between two (or more) parties upon a choice of one specific alternative from a given set of alternatives available to them. Bargaining also involves the exchange of consideration among the parties involved. Problems in bargaining arise when the parties involved have conflicting interests over the available set of alternatives. Hence, the main issue that confronts the parties in a bargaining situation is the need to reach an agreement. A main focus of any theory of bargaining is on two intertwined properties, namely, efficiency and distribution. Efficiency

[1]Coase was fully aware of this, when he defined the theorem. In fact, what Coase wanted to show is the reverse of the Coase Theorem: "when transaction costs are positive it *does* matter how we have defined an attributed our property rights" (Buitelaar 2007, p. 22).

relates to the possibility that the agreement can be reached by the parties involved after some costly delay, while distribution relates to the issue of how the gains from the outcome of the agreement are divided among the players.

Our main tool in analyzing bargaining situations is game theory, or, to be specific, cooperative game theory. Game theory has been applied widely to analyze collective decision-making situations in which the decision makers involved – or, in game theoretical terms, the players – have conflicting preferences or interests (Samsura et al. 2010). It provides a bag of analytical concepts to study the situations in which the conflicting decision-makers interact. Game theory uses mathematics as its main language, although the theory itself is not necessarily mathematical (Myerson 1991). A game is called cooperative, if the players are able to form binding commitments, and are called non-cooperative, if otherwise. In general, the cooperative game theory approach is used to analyse situations in which the players find and implement the solution jointly or by forming a coalition. There are two main focuses in a cooperative approach. The first is to find out the coalition structure which gives most benefit to all players. And the second is to observe how the members of a coalition will distribute the outcome or revenues available to the coalition among themselves. In game theoretical terms, this is called the *payoffs*. One of the basic questions in the cooperative approach is "*How will the payoff be distributed among the players?*" There are many solution concepts for this problem, among which is *the core* concept. A core payoff vector is a payoff distribution among the players that can not be improved by any coalition. That is, no other coalition can be formed in which the individuals gain more payoffs. Clearly, the core is a strong equilibrium concept and, as such, a powerful predictor for games in coalition form. Note that the core may consist of many core payoff vectors and hence need not be unique. However, there is also a possibility that a game has an empty core. In fact, any constant-sum game, in which the sum of the payoffs to the players is a constant, always has an empty core. Therefore, other solution concepts have been developed to predict the payoff distributions for this kind of game such as *stable set* and *Shapley value* (see e.g. Kahan and Rapoport 1984; Owen 1995; we will discuss it in more detail in the next section). Mainly, cooperative game theory uses the *characteristic function form* as its descriptive frameworks. In *characteristic function form*, a game is given as a pair (N,v), where N denotes a set of players and $v: 2^N \rightarrow \boldsymbol{R}$ is a characteristic function in which a value is assigned to each coalition (called the value of the coalition). The basic idea in coalition making is that each player can gain more payoffs; hence arrive at a better outcome, by forming or joining a coalition.

In the case of value capturing implementation, cooperative game theory is applied to analyse the situation in which infrastructure developers and location developers agree to cooperate in pursuing their development goals by forming a joint venture, but it is still not clear for them how they are going to cooperate. Value capturing implementation in the form of distribution of increment in value is one of the considerations that all the parties involved will take into account in deciding the form of cooperation. Therefore, this formulation will reflect the bargaining situation among the parties involved in the infrastructure and location development process, especially in relation to how they are going to divide the increment in land and property value when they want to make a partnership or a joint venture.

However, like any modelling exercise, inescapably, game theoretical modelling indeed implies a simplification and abstraction from the real world. Moreover, the game theory approach is usually claimed to be too abstract and its underlying assumptions too unrealistic, including complete information, rational behaviour of players, and the unitary character of players. One might claim that these assumptions are violated in real-life situations. With regard to complete knowledge, stakeholders might not know exactly in which game they are playing and moreover, they might lack information on the preferences of their opponents. The assumption of rationality has also met criticisms. First, are stakeholders able to make a consistent ranking of their preference? And secondly, if stakeholders are capable of defining their preferences, do they indeed act in an optimal way? Another question is whether stakeholders are indeed unitary actors, or whether they them selves are a collection of decision making actors who cannot speak with one voice. Several authors have discussed problems with these assumptions (see e.g. Aumann 1990; Hargreaves-Heap and Varoufakis 2004). Also, experimental evidence shows how people might make different choices than theory would predict (e.g. Goeree and Holt 2001; Plous 1993).

However, as discussed by Aumann (1985), the assumptions in game theory should not be attacked, but instead the theorems and conclusion resulting from the modelling. A complete rejection of the assumptions in game theory is indeed not useful, but repairing several assumptions in particular setting of the game can make the theory better applicable and more relevant. In addition, game theory has been capable of developing more realistic solutions in the last decades for several of the assumptions that are discussed above (Camerer 1991; Goeree and Holt 2001). Incomplete information has been modelled in Bayesian games (Harsanyi 1967). Myerson (1998) developed a general theory of cooperation under uncertainty and Aumann and Mascheler (1995) also worked on the issue of incomplete information. A reply to the rationality assumption has been the idea of bounded rationality (Simon 1978). Although no formal version of Simon's idea has been developed, Aumann (1997) reviews some of the approaches that game theory has used to deal with rationality, such as evolutionary dynamics and the use of computer simulations.

However, here we stick to the more traditional game-theoretical methods with the underlying expected utility maximising model and rational behaviour. The advantage of this approach is that it structures the situations to be studied in a simple and clear way. As a first step, it therefore provides insight into the decision problems at stake, which in a later stage may be refined and extended into a more sophisticated or realistic model. As we shall see, even the classical methodology of game theory creates useful insights into the case of value capturing implementation.

4.4 Spatial Development Process and Value Capturing in the Netherlands

From a policy perspective, the main concern of this study is the possibilities for value capturing in cases that the development of infrastructure is integrated with property development. In those cases, it is assumed that property developers benefit financially from the increased accessibility of the location as a result of the public investments in infrastructure: end users (companies or households that will buy or rent the property) will accept higher prices or rents, because they prefer locations with high accessibility. On the other hand, the public authorities that are responsible for the infrastructure development are often confronted with substantial gaps in the available public budgets for infrastructure development. In such situations, there seems to be room for negotiation or bargaining: when property developers benefit in financial terms from the public investments in infrastructure, it makes sense that the public sector asks the private sector for a financial contribution to the necessary investments.

The next section presents a game theoretical model focusing exactly on these negotiations for value capturing. In the present section we pay attention to the context in which those negotiations take place. What is the rationale for value capturing? How much value can be captured? And how is the development process for those integrated developments organised?

4.4.1 Rationale for Value Capturing

The Dutch national government aims to reduce mobility problems by, among other things, large public investments in new road infrastructure and public transport, but struggles to find the resources to finance these plans. To resolve the financial problems, innovative financial arrangements with respect to both road infrastructure and public transport development are being investigated. The *Raad voor Verkeer en Waterstaat* (RVW), the advisory board to the Minister of Transport, has suggested to implement improved instruments for value capturing in projects that combine large infrastructure development with location development (RVW 2004). This proposal is supported by another influential advisory board, the VROM Raad, which advises the Minister of Spatial Planning (VROM Raad 2004). The assumption underlying those proposals is, that the public investments in infrastructure and/or public transport will improve the accessibility of (development) locations connected to the new infrastructure or public transport link, which will result in higher property prices and rents (Van der Krabben et al. 2007). The RVW defines *value capturing* as:

> A group of instruments that enable capturing, directly or indirectly, the increased value of land and property as a result of public investments in transport infrastructure, and to use it for financing the activities that are responsible for the increased values. (RVW 2004, p. 47; translation by the authors)

It is clear that financing infrastructure projects or public transport plans would be made easier, if the government body involved could capture value increases. One of the issues here is, however, what the rationale is for value capturing. For a better understanding of this issue, we refer to the distinction, made by Van der Krabben and Needham (2009), between the concepts of *cost recovery*, *creaming off development games*, and *value capturing*. 'Cost recovery' refers to a situation where the costs of public works in a plan area are recovered from the property owners in that area. In the Netherlands, the municipalities' legal powers for the enforcement of cost recovery have improved considerably since July 2008 through the introduction of a new Spatial Planning Act that involves new legislation on planning processes as well as on cost recovery (Tweede Kamer der Staten Generaal 2008). The second concept concerns 'creaming off' the development gain (or: betterment), caused by changes in the land-use plan (in the sense of the 1942 Uthwatt Report on compensation and betterment for the UK). The supposed development gain is based on increased property values in the area. Internationally, there is much discussion on the legitimacy and the feasibility of this. The other reason why property values might increase is public works – in particular, transport infrastructure, but new open space also might have a similar effect – which enhance the value of properties near to them. In those situations, 'value capturing' may be considered. Van der Krabben and Needham (2009) state that: "*when a project includes both changing the land-use plan and improving infrastructure, it can be difficult to distinguish between the value increase caused by betterment and that caused by improved services*". In the Netherlands, both instruments for creaming off development gains and value capturing are missing. However, the contribution of property owners to the financing of plan-related costs of public works – based on cost recovery by the government body responsible for the plan – usually involves part of their development gains. And moreover, the government body involved and the property developers may still come to a voluntary agreement regarding capturing the increased value of land and property as a result of public investments in transport infrastructure.

4.4.2 How Much Value Can be Captured?

A substantial body of literature exists discussing value capturing. Many studies, mainly based on US-based experiences, have demonstrated the positive impact of public sector infrastructure investments on property prices (e.g. Church 1990; Batt 2001; Riley 2001; Enoch 2002; Rybeck 2004). To illustrate how much value can be captured, we refer to a recent study by Van der Krabben et al. (2007) in which the potential for value capturing has been calculated in Dutch station areas. The value to be captured in those cases concerned the (expected) value increase of new properties in the station areas, as a result of public investments in the railway stations and the rail connections (upgrading to high speed train rail services). For each of the areas, it was estimated how high the office rents would be in the vicinity of the station both *without* the (new) transport infrastructure and *with* the new infrastructure. The difference can be attributed to the investment in transport infrastructure. These estimates were made, using a property value model that was discussed extensively in Chapter 3 by Debrezion et al. The case study analysis for three Dutch station area redevelopment projects shows that between 15% and 20%

Table 4.1 Increase in office rents, based on estimations from the property value model[a] (van der Krabben et al. 2007)

	Office rents in station areas		
	Breda	Arnhem	Schiedam
Present situation (without positive impact station area)[a]			
Annual office rents per m^2	181.52 €	178.91 €	205.14 €
Present situation (before station area redevelopment)[a]			
Annual office rents per m^2	208.39 € (+14.8%)	208.79 € (+16.7%)	240.22 € (+17.1%)
Improved situation (after station area redevelopment)			
Annual office rents per m^2	210.56 € (+16.0%)	210.04 € (+17.4%)	240.83 € (+17.4%)

[a]The rents predicted by the model under 'present situation' are not necessarily equal to the actual rents in the 'present situation', due to the fact that the variables related to the characteristics of the building/tenant are left aside. This means that the model predicts rents for 'average' office space, specified for the locations involved

of the rents for office space in the vicinity of a railway station can be ascribed to the accessibility by public transport (Table 4.1). It means that in the case of a new railway or light rail station, the infrastructure developer could in principle claim 15–20% of the values of the properties that will be developed in the station area.

4.4.3 Development Model

Finally, the (outcome of) negotiation processes about value capturing will depend on both the project type and the development model that has been applied to the integrated development of both new infrastructure and property. We distinguish between two project types: line infrastructure development (for instance, a new motorway combined with the development of industrial estates near the motorway) and node development (for instance, station area development combined with public transport development). Usually a national (or provincial) government body is responsible for the infrastructure development, while municipalities together with property developers take care of the location development. Until recently, separated financial schemes were used for both the infrastructure and the location development project. Consequently, the national government body responsible for the infrastructure development did not negotiate with the location developers for a financial contribution.

So, until recently the national infrastructure developer used to have almost no bargaining powers to negotiate about value capturing. However, the above mentioned introduction of a new Spatial Planning Act in 2008 also changed this status quo. Under the former Spatial Planning Act, provincial and national government bodies were not allowed to develop land use plans, which led to the situation that has been explained above (municipalities were responsible for location development). Under the new Spatial Planning Act, however, national and provincial government bodies may develop land use plans and can decide to take charge of the location development as well. It is assumed that national and provincial government bodies will make use of this right in case of supra-local projects (like line infrastructure projects). This will bring them in a much better position to negotiate directly with the location developers for value capturing.

4.5 Bargaining Game for Value Capturing

The bargaining game presented in this study models part of the decision-making process with regard to the integrated development of both new infrastructure and property, in the Dutch planning context (under the new Spatial Planning Act).[2] The part of the decision-making process that will be simulated in our game concerns the negotiations about value capturing between the infrastructure developer (usually a government institution) and the property developer(s). The model excludes other parts of the decision-making process, including decisions regarding for instance location choice, the desired accessibility profile of the location, the real estate programme and the partnership construction.

4.5.1 Cooperative Game Model

As mentioned earlier, in this study we have restricted ourselves to the analysis of a game in cooperative approach, more specifically, in characteristic function form, in analyzing the bargaining process regarding the implementation of value capturing, as well as its solution concept. By applying this approach, we aim to analyse the bargaining process between the infrastructure developer and the location developer, assuming that there is an increment in value of land and properties caused by the development of infrastructure to be captured. The solution concept for the game is utilised to find the equilibrium for the payoffs disbursement, i.e. the distribution of the increment in value among players involved. This will allow us to analyse the amount of increment in value that can be captured by the infrastructure development from the bargaining process. In this experimental game, we consider

[2]The national planning context probably influences for a great deal the outcome of the bargaining processes. When we would model a similar bargaining game for instance within the context of the British planning system, the outcome would be influenced by the concept of planning obligation in the Town and Country Planning Act. The concept of planning obligation means that the local authority grants permission only, if the developer pays for related works, like infrastructure and open spaces (Cullingworth and Nadin 2002).

a situation with three players: one Infrastructure Developer (ID) and two Location Developers (LD1 and LD2). This provides us with a basic situation for analyzing the games with an infinite number of players which are often called as n-person games (Luce and Raiffa 1957). These three players bargain to form a deal about the contribution of the location developers to financing the costs of the infrastructure development. The deal is, in game theoretical terms, to agree on how to divide the outcome of a coalition.

The game is based on a number of assumptions regarding the strategies of the players, their bargaining powers and the planning context. Those assumptions are mainly derived from development practice in the Netherlands, as explained in the previous section.

1. First, we assume that there is no institutional restriction for the infrastructure developer to capture the increment in land value throughout the formation of a joint venture or coalition with the location developer(s). This is related to the new legal powers for national and provincial government bodies to develop land use plans under the new Spatial Planning Act. On the other hand, the infrastructure developer does have legal powers for the enforcement of cost recovery, but does not possess any legal powers to enforce value capturing. It is assumed that full cost recovery takes place, but that the development gains for the location developers exceed the costs that are recovered.
2. The second assumption is that the existing land use plan allows both the planned infrastructure and planned location development project.
3. The infrastructure developer holds the land for infrastructure development; the location developers own all the land that is available for location development. It implies that land owners are not involved in the game.[3] And, since the infrastructure developer will be responsible for the land use plan, the municipality is also not involved in the game.
4. In the game we distinguish between situations in which the bargaining process takes place before the infrastructure development process has actually started and situations in which bargaining starts after the infrastructure has been developed (see below).
5. The game concerns new infrastructure development, because the increment in land and property values will be more substantial in this kind of projects compared with projects intended to improve the existing infrastructure.
6. In line with the empirical evidence of the amount of value that can be captured in station area development projects we found in Van der Krabben et al. (2007), we assume in our game that the development of new infrastructure will increase land and property values by 20%. Suppose each LD has 100 units of land and

[3]A different game can be played when the game starts at an earlier point in time, before the location developers had acquired the land. In that case, the (original) landowners should be involved in the game as well. However, in Dutch planning practice, the bargaining about value capturing will usually take place between ID and LD's.

properties, and each unit will be worth 1,000 €. Then, *ceteris paribus*, the value or profit of LD's land and property development without infrastructure will be 100,000 € and the development of infrastructure will add as much as 20,000 €. The analysis is focused on how to divide these outcomes among the three players involved.

7. It is also assumed, in addition to the previous point, that location development will still be profitable, in case the maximum of 120,000 € will be captured (in that case: profit will be low, but still acceptable for the location developer).
8. Finally, like in any kind of game in game theory, the solution for this game will be focused on the determination of the outcome which can be expected to occur if the game is played by rational players.

In cooperative games, the concept of rationality diverges into *individual rationality* and *collective rationality*. The concept of individual rationality implies that a player in a coalition will not accept any payoffs less than what he could obtain, if he acts alone or without forming any coalition with anyone and without making any bargaining at all. Formally, this concept is given by the inequality:

$$x_i \geq v(\bar{i}) \qquad (i = players\,involved = 1, 2, \ldots, n) \tag{4.1}$$

The concept of group rationality, on the other hand, implies that no subset of players should get less than they can get by joining a coalition or in a formal way:

$$v(S) \leq \sum\nolimits_{i \in S} x_i \quad for\ all\ S\ \ (S = coalition) \tag{4.2}$$

We also might say:

$$\sum\nolimits_{i=1}^{n} x_i = v(N) \quad (N = grand\ coalition) \tag{4.3}$$

When these two rationalities apply, or in another words, those three equations are fulfilled in a set of payoff structure, then that particular payoff structure is called the core of the game: the equilibrium of the coalition. The core is a very appealing solution concept, because it is relatively easy to apply.

As mentioned earlier, the core of the game might be empty. Basically, the non-emptiness of the core can be investigated from the characteristic function of the game. As discussed by Kahan and Rapoport (1984), for N = 1, 2, 3, the core is not empty only, if $v(123) \geq \frac{1}{2}\,[v(12) + v(13) + v(23)]$ Furthermore, this condition also implies that the game must be superadditive and the core will always be found in the coalition structure {123} or the grand coalition. The core solutions for the grand coalition can also be visualized in a geometrical representation (see below).

For this game, we consider three situations in which the players can form a coalition:

1. ID will build the infrastructure only, if it can form a coalition with LD. Along with that, LD will not be able to build the land and properties, if there is no infrastructure to be built by ID. The bargaining process is assumed to take place before the infrastructure development process has started.

2. Similar to Situation 1, ID will only build the infrastructure, if it is able to form a coalition with LD. However, unlike in Situation 1, LDs are able to develop the land and properties even, if the infrastructure is not provided by ID. However, the new infrastructure will increase the value of LD's land and properties. In this situation, the bargaining process is also assumed to take place before the development process has started.
3. ID is able to build the infrastructure without making any coalition with LD. However, a coalition would provide more benefit to ID. In this situation, the bargaining process will take place after the infrastructure has been developed.

Based on the assumptions and concepts above, we are able now to analyze the bargaining process in the implementation of value capturing, for each situation where ID, LD1 and LD2 can form a coalition. Each location development can create a value of 100,000 € (without infrastructure development) or 120,000 € (with infrastructure development). Infrastructure development can also create a value of 20,000 €, without location development. The costs of the infrastructure and location development are left outside the game, because they are not part of the bargaining process.

4.5.1.1 The Game for Situation 1

Under the first situation, no player alone can realize a profit, so $v(\mathrm{ID}) = v(\mathrm{LD1}) = v(\mathrm{LD2}) = 0$. ID and LD1 together will create a value of 120,000 €, if they form a coalition, because LD1 can create 100,000 € and the extra 20,000 € will be added to it as the increment in value caused by the infrastructure development. It will be also the case for a coalition between ID and LD2. However, the coalition between LD1 and LD2 alone will be worth nothing, because both developers cannot build their land and properties if the infrastructure is not provided. The grand coalition, consisting of ID, LD1 and LD2, will create a value of 240,000 €, because LD1 and LD2 will each create 100,000 €, while for both of them 20,000 € will be added because of the infrastructure development. For ID = 1; LD1 = 2, and LD2 = 3, we summarized this information by the characteristic function.

$$\left\{\begin{array}{l} v(1) = v(2) = v(3) = 0; \\ v(12) = v(13) = 120{,}000; \\ v(23) = 0; \\ v(123) = 240{,}000 \end{array}\right\}$$

In this game, there are several payoff divisions which satisfy both individual and group rationality, i.e. the core. One such division is (80,000; 80,000; 80,000). We can see in this structure that ID, LD1 and LD2 get more than they would have received, if they would have acted alone. Therefore, it satisfies the individual rationality. It is also obvious that in this payoff structure, each pair gets more than they would have received in a coalition and all three get as much as they can

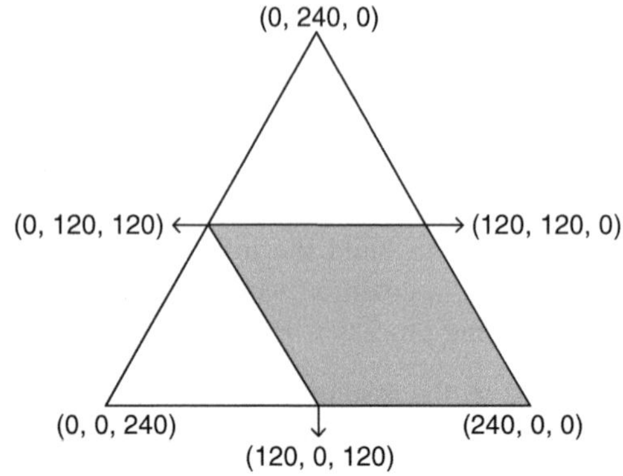

Fig. 4.1 The core of the game for the first situation

in this game, which means that the requirement for group rationality has been fulfilled. However, this payoff structure is not the only one that satisfies the two concepts of rationality. Figure 4.1 shows all the cores of the game for the first situation.

Figure 4.1 shows that the core payoffs (all points in the shaded area) are within a convex polygon bounded by four points: (120, 120, 0); (120, 0, 120); (0, 120, 120); and (240, 0, 0).[4]

Although these boundary points satisfy the two concepts of rationality and hence can be considered as the core, these particular payoff structures may still seem to be unfair. The fact that the core in this situation might not be unique and fair, makes it difficult to apply as a predictive tool. The best outcome of the game would be to find a solution concept, that predicts a unique expected payoff allocation for the players. Shapley (1953) approached this problem axiomatically. He was looking for properties we might expect to satisfy such a solution concept. For that purpose, he characterized the mappings φ that satisfy these properties.

In the game, assuming the players to be rational, the players can foresee that the grand coalition will eventually form, since all three players can get more by working together than in any partition into a separate coalition. The question that each player is then considering, is how to bargain as the grand coalition will be formed.

In this game, suppose ID approaches LD1 with the proposition to form a coalition. At the most, ID could ask 120,000 from LD1, because the joint venture between ID and LD1 will exceed LD1's prospects when acting alone (LD1 gets nothing if it acts alone). It will be the same if ID approaches LD2. Of course, ID cannot expect that LD1 or LD2 will immediately agree to this proposition. In fact, the same proposition can also be brought forward by LD1 to ID or LD2 to ID. The other possibility for ID is to approach LD1 and LD2 together at the same time. ID could ask, at the most, 240,000, because the coalition of LD1 and LD2 only would

[4]To calculate the boundary points, consult Kahan and Rapoport (1984).

get nothing at all. Therefore, ID is worth 240,000 to them as the third member of the coalition. Here we can see that the players' bargaining power depends on which coalition he or she is about to join.

To generalize the situation, let us suppose that the grand coalition will eventually be formed by increasing from one to two to three members. Without any specific information on the order in which the members will join, let us suppose that all orders are equal. Therefore, the following orders of joining may arise with the probabilities as noted:

(ID, LD1, LD2) with probability 1/6
(ID, LD2, LD1) with probability 1/6
(LD1, ID, LD2) with probability 1/6
(LD1, LD2, ID) with probability 1/6
(LD2, ID, LD1) with probability 1/6
(LD2, LD1, ID) with probability 1/6

It is clear that each player – when he took the initiative – was not approached by anyone in two of the six circumstances. In that case, the value will be zero. Therefore, with a probability of 1/6 + 1/6 = 1/3, each player can expect to get 0. Let us continue to analyze ID. With a probability of 1/6, ID can expect to get 120,000 from LD1 or from LD2. Then there are two circumstances that ID is approached by the coalition of LD1 and LD2. In this case, with the probability of 1/3, ID can expect to receive 240,000. In sum, ID's expected prospect is:

$$\varphi_{ID} = 1/3^{*}0 + 1/6^{*}120,000 + 1/6 * 120,000 + 1/3^{*}240,000 = 120,000$$

This expectation is called the *Shapley value* of the games to ID. This value does not only represent the expectation, but also the bargaining power of ID in the coalition. In general, by designating the Shapley values by φ_i (in which i is the players involved) and for ID = 1; LD1 = 2, and LD2 = 3, we have:

$$\varphi_1 = \frac{1}{3}[v(\overline{123})] - [v(\overline{23})] + \frac{1}{6}[v(\overline{12})] - [v(\bar{2})] + \frac{1}{6}[v(\overline{13})] - [v(\bar{3})] + \frac{1}{3}[v(\bar{1})] - [v(\bar{\phi})] \quad (4.4)$$

$$\varphi_2 = \frac{1}{3}[v(\overline{123})] - [v(13)] + \frac{1}{6}[v(\overline{12})] - [v(\bar{1})] + \frac{1}{6}[v(\overline{23})] - [v(\bar{3})] + \frac{1}{3}[v(\bar{2})] - [v(\bar{\phi})] \quad (4.5)$$

$$\varphi_3 = \frac{1}{3}[v(\overline{123})] - [v(\overline{12})] + \frac{1}{6}[v(\overline{13})] - [v(\bar{1})] + \frac{1}{6}[v(\overline{23})] - [v(\bar{2})] + \frac{1}{3}[v(\bar{3})] - [v(\bar{\phi})] \quad (4.6)$$

We can then calculate the expected prospects of LD1 and LD2:

$$\varphi_{LD1} = 60,000$$

$$\varphi_{LD2} = 60,000$$

It is obvious that the summation of the expected prospects of all players is equal to the value of the grand coalition.

4.5.1.2 The Game for Situation 2

In Situation 2, ID alone cannot build the infrastructure and create any profit, while LD1 and LD2 still can develop their land and property and create 100,000 € each, if they act alone. Like in the first situation, if either LD1 or LD2 agrees to create a coalition with ID, the pair (LD1,ID or LD2,ID) will create a value of 120,000 €, because the infrastructure will then be developed creating an extra value of 20,000 € for LD1's or LD2's initial value. However, unlike in the first situation, here the coalition between LD1 and LD2 will create a value of 200,000 €, because it will combine their initial value. The value of the grand coalition will be the same as in the first situation, because it will combine the value of the coalition of ID and LD1 and also ID and LD2. Then, for ID = 1, LD1 = 2 and LD2 = 3; this information can be summarized by the characteristic function as follows:

$$\left\{\begin{array}{l} v(1) = 0; \\ v(2) = v(3) = 100,000; \\ v(12) = v(13) = 120,000; \\ v(23) = 200,000; \\ v(123) = 240,000 \end{array}\right\}$$

Using the same method that has been applied for the first situation, we can also conclude that the core for the game in the second situation is non-empty and it can be drawn using the geometrical representation as shown in Fig. 4.2.

Here we found that the core is lying within a convex polygon bounded by three points: (0, 120, 120); (20, 120, 100); and (20, 100, 120). Similar to Situation 1, these core structures also seem to be unfair. Therefore, again, we look for the solution concept that predicts a fair and unique expected payoff allocation for the players, i.e. the Shapley value. Using the (4.4), (4.5), and (4.6) we can find the Shaply Values for ID, LD1 and LD2 in Situation 2. They are:

$$\varphi_{ID} = 20,000$$

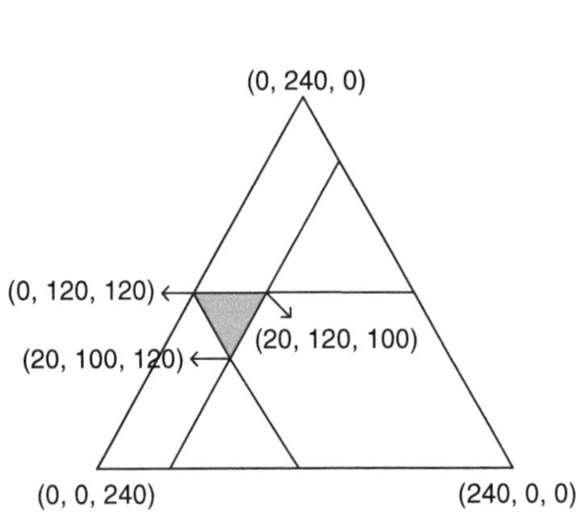

Fig. 4.2 The core of the game for the second situation

$$\varphi_{LD1} = 110,000$$

$$\varphi_{LD2} = 110,000$$

4.5.1.3 The Game for Situation 3

In Situation 3, ID can build the infrastructure without making any coalition with LD1 or LD2. Then, when ID develops the infrastructure alone, this development will increase the value of LD's land and property 'automatically' by 20%. Using the same figures as in the first and second situation, both LD1 and LD2 will have a value of 120,000 € due to this development. Suppose ID and LD1 agree to form a coalition. The value they create will also be 120,000 €, because there is no additional value brought into the coalition by ID due to the fact that this has already been delivered to LD1. The coalition of ID and LD2, consequently, will also give the same outcome. While the coalition of LD1 and LD2, in this situation, will create a value of 240,000 €, as the summation of their initial values. And the grand coalition will also create a value of 240,000 €, again, because ID gives no additional value to the coalition. This information can be summarized by the characteristic function as follows for ID = 1; LD1 = 2, and LD2 = 3:

$$\left\{ \begin{array}{l} v(1) = 0; \\ v(2) = v(3) = 120,000; \\ v(12) = v(13) = 120,000; \\ v(23) = 240,0000; \\ v(123) = 240,000 \end{array} \right\}$$

Unlike in the first and the second situation, we found here that the core is in a single point (0, 120, 120). The geometrical representation of this core is given in Fig. 4.3.

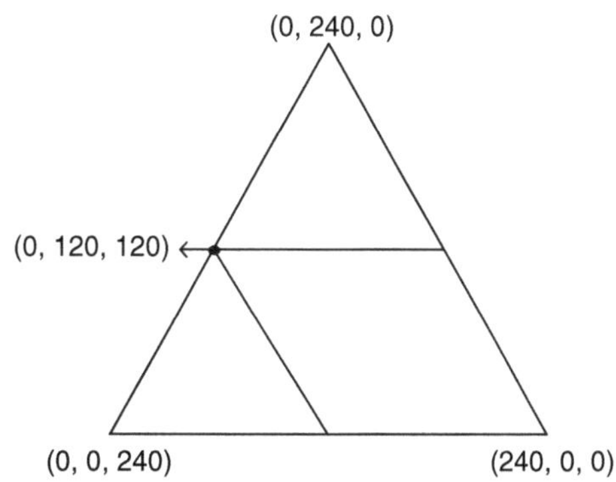

Fig. 4.3 The core of the game for Situation 3

Interestingly, using the analysis of Shapley value, we also found the same result:

$$\varphi_{ID} = 0$$

$$\varphi_{LD1} = 120,000$$

$$\varphi_{LD2} = 120,000$$

4.5.2 Discussion

Based on the analysis of the bargaining process for capturing increment in land value as performed above, we found three different outcomes for three different situations in which the players can form a coalition. Based on these outcomes we can investigate how much value can be captured, if the players involved can bargain to divide the increment in value of land and property within the process of coalition formation. In Situation 1, the infrastructure developer could obtain 120,000 € based on its bargaining power. It means that the value that can be captured by the infrastructure developer is more than the increment in value it creates from the development of the infrastructure. Using our experimental figures, the increment in value caused by the infrastructure development for one location developer is 20,000 €. Since in our experimental game there are two location developers, the total increment in land and properties value will be 40,000 €. The infrastructure developer might be able to obtain 120,000 €, because its bargaining power is very strong in this situation due to the fact that the location developers cannot develop their land unless the infrastructure is developed. The increment in values of location developers' property caused by the infrastructure development in this situation is therefore not 40,000 € but 120,000 €.

In Situation 2, the infrastructure developer can expect a result of 20,000 € from the bargaining process in the coalition formation with location developers. It means that the value to be captured by the infrastructure developer is lower than the total increment in values it creates. Here the bargaining power of the infrastructure developer is not as strong as in the previous situation, because the location developers still can develop their land even though the infrastructure developer does not build the infrastructure.

And for Situation 3, the bargaining power of the infrastructure developer is even lower than in the second situation. The expected payoff in forming a coalition is zero for the infrastructure developer. This situation can be explained as follows: the fact that the infrastructure developer can build the infrastructure without forming a coalition with the location developers, makes the option of forming a coalition become unattractive for the location developer. The location developer can get the increment in value automatically when the infrastructure is built by the infrastructure developer. Based on the concept of rationality, forming a coalition is only attractive if it brings added values for the coalition member. In this case, the attractiveness of forming a coalition is related to the possibility of acquiring the increment in land and property value. In this situation, the infrastructure developer has therefore no bargaining power, because there is no added value for the location developers to form a coalition with the infrastructure developer. The coalition that will be formed will then only have a payoff distribution that is equal to the initial value of its member.

From the analysis above, we found that the equilibrium amount of increment in value caused by infrastructure development that can be captured varies from one situation to another. Therefore, we can learn that the policy of value capturing that endorses the infrastructure developer to recoup the increment in land and property values, without any consideration of the situation in which the infrastructure development process interacts with the land development process, will be problematic because it may result in an inefficient allocation of resources.

4.6 Conclusion

In this chapter, we analysed the bargaining process between the infrastructure developer and the location developer(s) regarding the implementation of value capturing, by making use of a cooperative game theory approach. We have argued that bargaining is a 'natural process' to solve externality problems. We have also brought forward that, like in everyday life, bargaining quite often plays a decisive role in decision-making processes for spatial development. The outcome depends, of course, to a large extent on the institutional planning context in which those decisions are made. Negotiations about contributions to plan-related costs, creaming off development gains and value capturing almost always involve a process of bargaining. Modelling those bargaining processes may help to improve our understanding of the outcome of it. In this study, we aimed to demonstrate the usefulness of game theoretical modelling for this purpose.

The games show how game theory can be used to increase our understanding of bargaining processes. We found from the analysis, that the amount of increment in land and property values caused by the infrastructure development – which can be captured from the bargaining process – varies. This is due to the situation or context, in which the players can form a coalition which will affect the bargaining power of the players involved. We also found from the analysis that the Infrastructure Developers' bargaining power is stronger when the Location Developer is dependent on the infrastructure to be built and also when the decision to build the infrastructure can only be taken by the Infrastructure Developer, if the Location Developer agrees to cooperate beforehand. Our advice to the Infrastructure Developer in the game would be to wait with infrastructure development until (one of) the Location Developers is willing to make a coalition. To convince the Location Developers to form a coalition, it will help when the success (or: profitability) of the location development heavily depends on the infrastructure development (for example, in case of the development of a new transport node). Contrarily, our advice to the Location Developers would be to start location development (and even acquiring land) only after the infrastructure has been completed (though they probably would have to pay more for the land). The recent changes in Dutch planning law and the possibility for the national government body, that is responsible for the infrastructure development to develop its own plans and enter the negotiations about value capturing directly – as we did in our game – is believed to influence the (outcome of the) bargaining process. Because the experiences with the new planning law and the changing roles for national and provincial government bodies are still very limited, we do not know yet how the status quo will change.

We are aware of the analytical problems of this approach. Since every model is a simplification of the real world, its reliability depends on basic assumptions that are used as the basis for its construction. In the games that we have constructed in this article we have assumed that the transaction costs of the bargaining process and the coalition process are zero. We referred to the Coase theorem to explain that a situation of zero transactions costs cannot easily be fulfilled in the real world. Therefore, the next step for this research should be an analysis that takes transaction costs in forming a coalition into account. It means that we must bring in the institutional context into the model, which is in fact the argument made by Coase. We believe that – as the next steps in the construction of the model – at least part of this complexity can be brought into the model. Second, the figures regarding the value of the coalition still should be validated empirically, although we use the results of earlier studies to draw those experimental figures. This can be done as well, for instance by surveys amongst all stakeholders. Moreover, the outcomes of the games and the equilibriums that we have found must be tested. For this purpose, the games can be 'played' in a laboratory situation by real stakeholders. Another aspect that must be analyzed is, in the case of value capturing, the impact of the 'captured value' on both the financial budgets of the infrastructure developer and the location developers. In our game, the profits of the location developers will drop with 20%, which is quite substantial. However, in case of a major infrastructure development, the value captured most likely only adds a small percentage to the financing scheme of the infrastructure developers. Finally, the model we developed in this study does not take into account the possibility of the free-rider problem. Here we consider that free rider behaviour gives no benefit to all players involved. The reality may not be like that. However, in the case where the free rider problem may occur, the model can be extended into the so-called *partition function form* which is the generalization of the *characteristic function* form that we employed in this study.

References

Aumann RJ (1985) What is game theory trying to accomplish? In: Arrow K, Honkapohja S (eds) Frontiers of economics. Basil Blackwell, Oxford

Aumann RJ (1990) Nash equilibria are not self enforcing. In: Gabszewewicz JJ, Richard JF, Wolsey L (eds) Economic decision making: games, econometrics, and optimisation (essays in honor of Jacques Dreze). Elsevier, Amsterdam

Aumann RJ (1997) Rationality and bounded rationality. Game econ behav 22:2–14
Aumann RJ, Mascheler M (1995) Repeated games with incomplete information. MIT Press, Cambridge
Banister D, Berechman J (2000) Transport investment and economic development. UCL Press, London
Barzel Y (1997) Economic analysis of property rights. Cambridge University Press, New York
Batt HW (2001) Value capture as a policy tool in transportation economics: an exploration in public finance in the tradition of Henry George. Am J Econ Sociol 60(1):195–228
Buitelaar E (2007) The cost of land use decisions. Applying transaction cost economics to planning and development. Wiley-Blackwell, Oxford
Calabresi G (1968) Transaction costs, resource allocation and liability rules – a comment. J Law Econ 11(1):67–73
Camerer C (1991) Does strategy research need game theory? Strategic Manage J 12:137–152
Church A (1990) Transport and urban regeneration in London Docklands: a victim of success or a failure to plan? Cities 7(4):289–303
Coase RH (1960) The problem of social cost. J Law Econ 3:1–44
Cullingworth B, Nadin V (2002) Town and country planning in the UK. Routledge, Oxford
Dahlman CJ (1979) The problem of externality. J Law Econ 22(1):141–162
de Wolff H (2007) The new Dutch land development act as a tool for value capturing. Paper presented in the ENHR international conference on 'sustainable urban areas', Rotterdam, 25–28 June 2007
Enoch MP (2002) Recouping public transport costs from gains in land values: the cases of Hong Kong and Copenhagen. Traffic Eng Control 43(9):336–340
Goeree J, Holt C (2001) Ten little treasures of game theory and ten intuitive contradictions. Am Econ Rev 91(5):1401–1422
Hargreaves-Heap S, Varoufakis Y (2004) Game theory: a critical text. Routledge, London
Harsanyi J (1967) Games with incomplete information played "Bayesian' players", part I-III. Manage Sci 14(3):159–182
Kahan JP, Rapoport A (1984) Theories of coalition formation. Psychology Press, New York
Luce RD, Raiffa H (1957) Games and decisions: introduction and critical survey. Wiley, New York
Munoz-Gielen DM (2008) Public value capturing and the financing of public infrastructure in England, Valencia, and the Netherlands. Paper presented in the international seminar on planning, law, and property rights, Warsaw, 14–15 Feb 2008
Myerson (1998) Population uncertainty and Poisson Games. Int Jnl of Game Theory 27:375–392
Owen G (1995) Values of games with a priori unions. In: Henn R, Moeschlin O (eds) Essays in mathematical economics and game theory. Springer, Berlin, pp 76–88
Pigou AC (1920) The economics of welfare. Macmillan, London
Plous S (1993) The psychology of judgment and decision making. McGraw-Hill, London
Riley D (2001) Taken for a ride: trains, taxpayers and the treasury. Centre for Land Policy Studies, London
RVW (2004) Ieder zijn deel: Locatiebereikbaarheid anders aanpakken. Raad voor Verkeer en Waterstaat, Den Haag
Rybeck R (2004) Using value capture to finance infrastructure and encourage compact development. Public Works Manage Policy 8(4):249–260
Samsura DA, van der Krabben E, van Deemen A (2010) A game theory approach to the analysis of land and property development processes. Land Use Policy 27(2):564–578
Samuelson PA (1995) Some uneasiness with the Coase theorem. Jpn World Econ 7:1–7
Shapley LS (1953) A value for n-person games. In: Kuhn H, Tucker A (eds) Contributions to the theory of games volume II (Annals of mathematical studies, 28). Princeton University Press, Princeton, pp 307–317
Simon H (1978) Rationality as process and product of thought. Am Econ Rev 68(2):1–16

Smith JJ, Gihring TA (2006) Financing transit systems through value capture. Am J Econ Sociol 65(3):751

Smolka MO (2000) Value capture for Urban development: an Inter-American comparison. Research paper of the Lincoln Institute of Land Policy

Te Brömmelstoet M, Bertolini L (2009) Een gestructureerde dialoog tussen planologen en PPS ontwikkelaars. Planningsondersteuning voor integrale ruimte-mobiliteit strategie ontwikkeling; een toepassing in Breda. Tijdschr Vervoerwetenschappen 45(1):33–42

Tweede Kamer der Staten Generaal (2008) Wijziging van de WRO wat betreft grondexploitatie. The Hague, document no. 30218

van der Krabben E, Needham B (2009) Land readjustment for value capturing: a new planning tool for urban redevelopment. Town Plann Rev 79(6):651–672

van der Krabben E, Martens K, De Graaff Th, Rietveld P (2007) How to define the optimal level of public-sector infrastructure development. A conceptual model for decision-making in infrastructure projects. Plan Pract Res 23:363–383

Varian HR (1994) A solution to the problem of externalities when agents are well-informed. Am Econ Rev 84(5):1278–1293

VROM RAAD (2004) Gereedschap voor Ruimtelijke Ontwikkelingspolitiek. Vrom Raad, Den Haag

Webster CJ, Lai LWC (2003) Property rights, planning and markets: managing spontaneous cities. Edward Elgar, Cheltenham

Chapter 5
NETLIPSE: Managing Large Infrastructure Projects

Marcel Hertogh and Eddy Westerveld

5.1 Large Infrastructure Projects: Introduction

5.1.1 European Ambition

Transport networks are needed for modern economies to create wealth and employment. But the current networks of infrastructure are not considered to be sufficient. To meet rising and changing demands for interregional and international mobility, infrastructure projects are being developed, for example, High Speed Links, Rail Freight Lines and motorways. On a European scale, 30 trans-national axes have been identified by the European Commission which cross the borders of the European Union. In 2005, the total remaining investment required to complete the 30 priority projects and axes in 2020 was estimated to be 252 € billion. If all the other projects of so-called common interest are included that are not on the priority list, the total cost of completing and modernising are much higher. Mr Barrot, Vice President of the European Commission, and responsible for transport, wrote in 2005 (European Commission 2005): "*In view of growth in traffic between Member States the investment required to complete and modernise a true trans-European network in the enlarged EU amounts to some € 600 billion.*"

NETLIPSE is a Network for the dissemination of knowledge on the management and organisation of Large Infrastructure Projects in Europe, started in 2006. Currently 25 countries are active in the network.

M. Hertogh (✉) • E. Westerveld
AT Osborne, J.F. Kennedylaan 100, 3741 EH, Baarn, The Netherlands
e-mail: mhe@osborne.nl; ewe@osborne.nl

J.A.E.E. van Nunen et al. (eds.), *Transitions Towards Sustainable Mobility*, 81
DOI 10.1007/978-3-642-21192-8_5, © Springer-Verlag Berlin Heidelberg 2011

5.1.2 Insufficient Performance

The implementation of transport networks and infrastructure projects is an enormous task. This becomes visible when we look at activities necessary to design and construct the new infrastructure: Often, for construction, participants rely on different kinds of new technology, which can be very complex. Also stakeholder networks active within large infrastructure projects (hereafter abbreviatied as LIPs) is a complicating factor: Often with lengths of hundreds of kilometres, these projects have a big impact on the landscape, environment and, generally, on the numerous stakeholders that are involved. This challenge seems to be a difficult task, since the performance is disappointing. The performance fails to meet the expectations in terms of (1) time, (2) costs and (3) stakeholder satisfaction.

In 1994, the European Commission initiated 14 priority projects (since 2005 this number has been increased to 30). What were the results after 10 years of priority projects? Mr. Jacques Barrot, reflected on the progress made so far in 2005 (European Commission 2005): *"After 10 years, however, it is clear that the results fall short of the overall ambitions. In 2003, barely one third of the network had been built. And only 3 of the 14 specific projects endorsed by the European Council at Essen in 1994 has been completed"*.

Projects are not only failing in terms of time performance. Flyvbjerg studied 258 transportation infrastructure projects worth US$ 90 billion (Flyvbjerg et al. 2003; Flyvbjerg 2007). Using his database, he studied the reliability of cost estimations and found that:

- Cost overruns of 50–100% in real terms are common in mega projects, overruns of more than 100% are not uncommon;
- Inaccuracy in cost forecasts is on average 45% for rail, 34% for bridges and tunnels, and 20% for roads (see Table 5.1).

Apart from the disappointing performance in terms of money and time, we notice general dissatisfaction of involved stakeholders with the development and realisation of large infrastructure projects (Teisman 1992; WRR 1994, and more recently, Hertogh et al. 2008).

In the Netherlands, cost overruns of two big projects were the immediate cause for the parliamentary enquiry, executed by the Temporary Committee for Infrastructure (TCI) that carried out a thorough investigation into the decision-making process concerning the Betuweroute and the High Speed Line South, two projects that also are part of the TEN-T priority axes and projects (TCI 2004). One of the conclusions the TCI reported was that LIPs generally fail to meet the demands of

Table 5.1 Inaccuracy of transportation cost estimates by type of project

Type of project	Number of cases	Average cost overrun (%)	Standard deviation
Rail	58	44.7	38.4
Bridges and tunnels	33	33.8	62.4
Road	167	20.4	29.9

society, not only regarding the delays and overruns, but also in other areas, where stakeholders involved are often not satisfied with the final results of a project in terms of the added value (benefits) and with the way of dealing with the protection of 'negative interests'. LIPs often seem to be 'out of fit', causing a democratic deficit (Nijssen 2006).

5.1.3 *Rising Demands*

Whereas in the past one organisation – that is, the government – was dominant and able to implement a project, using their own planning, the current situation is characterised by numerous stakeholders that all have some kind of influence, but not one has decisive power. In short: 'No one is in charge.' At the same time, legislation has become tighter. The big influence of all kinds of stakeholders and the diminishing acceptance of flaws, result in a severe challenge for the project delivery organisation that tries to realise a large infrastructure project, but also for the other stakeholders involved. What was considered 'good' 10 or 20 years ago, is not good enough anymore.

5.1.4 *Enormous Challenge*

The demands for and expectations of LIPs have increased rapidly during the past two decades. Ambitions are high and the performance is disappointing. It is now time to address the challenge we are facing. The TCI (2004) reported that the development of new infrastructure projects is greatly hampered by inadequate policy-making, as well as by the management of the projects. Are management and administration able to cope with these challenges? Or is it a 'mission impossible'? We are convinced that it is possible, as long as the management and administration improve their performance in line with the added requirements (Fig. 5.1).

5.1.5 *Transition Towards Sustainable Mobility*

The need to increase management performance of LIPs means the following in terms of People, Planet and Profit:

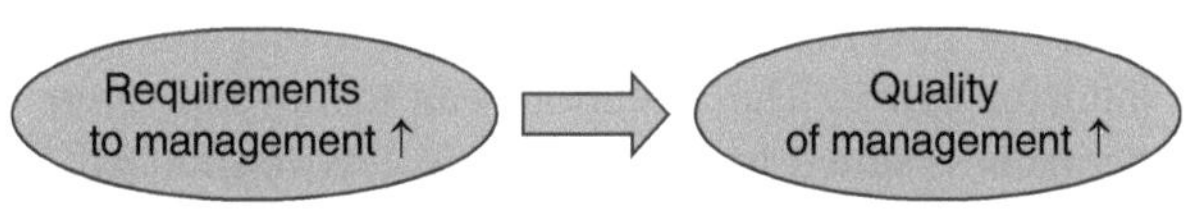

Fig. 5.1 The requirements to the management of LIPs

People

People have great need of mobility. This is illustrated by the enormous growth of recreational traffic to which society has to respond. By increasing the opportunities for mobility, infrastructure projects indirectly contribute to the development of people (talents, abilities). It will lead to shorter travel times and, at the same time, to a higher service level. This will increase customer satisfaction. On the other hand, by adding competences to project managers, the quality of the solutions will improve. For example, this could mean less inconveniences for neighbouring people along the line, and a higher safety level with the participation of fire brigades.

Planet

The last decade, there has been a further increase in environmental requirements nationally, as well as internationally from the EU, Kyoto, habitat legislation, fauna legislation (e.g. birds), compensation rules, the Malta agreement on archaeology, and so on. These regulations are an expression of the concern about the environment, but also make the development of infrastructure more difficult and complex. The challenge for project managers and decision makers of infrastructure projects is to meet these environmental requirements as formulated in the great many new rules and laws.

Many of the projects under research were aimed at the improvement of the environment (e.g. transition from car or airplane towards public transport, as is the case at West Coast Mainline and Gotthard and Lötschberg) (Schalcher et al. 2007 and Hertogh et al. 2008). By improving the management, themes like sustainability and environment, can be better incorporated in the projects, and moreover, take an important role in the initiation of these projects.

Profit

Infrastructure is very expensive. We suppose that a more advanced way of management and organisation will reduce the costs and, by this, also consumer fees. By decreasing the costs of mobility, the economic sector spends less money, leading to a rise in productivity. The European Union and her members have stressed, that the quality of mobility is important for the social and economic development of Europe, and that this quality doesn't fit our needs today. In other words, if we do not succeed in improving mobility, Europe will lose its competitive position. The costs of traffic jams for the economy amount to billions of euros. These costs will rise if we are not able to realise high-quality infrastructure.

Looking at sustainability, the added value of the PhD study is largely indirect, as will be clear when looking at the results of the study and the description of the three P's. This indirect relationship is illustrated in Fig. 5.2.

Figure 5.2 shows that the ambitions in terms of sustainability can only be realised by effectively combining measures (i.e. 80%) and increasing management capability (i.e. 20%) or governance. The developed management approaches contribute to the latter category. The intention was to develop more sophisticated management approaches, suited to meet the demands formulated, in such a way that interests (for example, environmental) are better incorporated in the

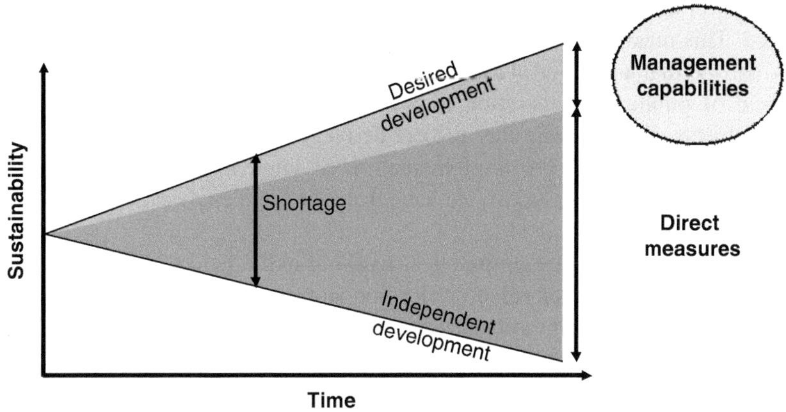

Fig. 5.2 Role of management capability in stimulating sustainability

implementation and operational phase of LIPs. And, thus, to contribute to a sustainable society.

5.2 Methodology

The challenge described in Sect. 5.1, was tackled by setting up two related studies:

1. PhD research on the management of complexity
2. NETLIPSE programme for the European Commission

The results shown in this chapter are a summary and selection of the conclusions of both these studies. Please note that not all references in the list at the end of this chapter are referred to in this chapter.

5.2.1 PhD Research on the Management of Complexity

In 2004, two practitioners started a PhD study to find suitable ways to improve the management of the implementation process of LIPs (Hertogh and Westerveld 2010). The main question of the thesis was:

How does the implementation process of large infrastructure projects in Europe evolve, how are the characteristics of complexity visible in the implementation of large infrastructure projects, how is this process managed and what are suitable ways to improve the management of the implementation process?

To answer the research question, the viewpoint of methodological pluralism was adopted. This means that the methodology was specifically tailored to answer this question, and that no universal methodology was applied. The research relates to of the field of public administration as well as management science, because the central objects of study were the 'project delivery organisations' and stakeholders that are concerned with the implementation of large infrastructure projects. In addition to studying these issues, we have described and analysed the implementation processes of LIPs.

Since the researchers are, in practice, working in the field of LIPs, the research was a specific case of action research (Reason and Bradbury 2001). This means that the researchers are an important part of the studied subject. The researchers operated as 'reflective practitioners'. The aim of this study was both practical and scientific. The goal was to develop 'substantial theory'. The theory developed can be helpful in solving practical dilemmas in the management of complexity in large infrastructure projects. This means that the developed theory consists of heuristics to be used by stakeholders in the field of LIPs, which are based on the analysis of empirical data.

In this thesis comparative case studies were used, combined with some of the principles of grounded theory (Glaser and Strauss 1967) as the primary research strategy. This research contained an explanatory approach to generate theory. This means that the study is performed in the context of discovery, where the aim is to construct new theory from practice, with a mainly qualitative focus.

For this research a case study protocol was used to structure the research. This protocol contained the conceptual model and the research design. The conceptual model contained the theoretical framework used to collect and analyse the case study data. In order to answer the primary research question, six cases were studied: The Betuweroute, HSL-South, RW73-South, Gotthard, Lötschberg and West Coast Mainline.

5.2.2 NETLIPSE Program for the European Commission

In 2006, the European Commission financed the initiative NETLIPSE, in which 15 large projects have been studied by a consortium of eight organisations throughout Europe (ministries, knowledge institutes/universities and private companies) (Hertogh et al. 2008). NETLIPSE and the PhD study are closely related. In fact, NETLIPSE originated when the Commission showed their interest in the outcome of the PhD study and challenged the involved scientists to write a proposal fitting their sixth framework proposal.

The NETLIPSE project was to set up an interactive and dynamic network for LIPs in Europe for the dissemination of experience and knowledge, specifically focussed on the management and organisational aspects of these projects. At the core of the project is a knowledge capturing methodology that has been used to assess the quality of 15 LIPs (see Fig. 5.3) that have been reviewed in order to

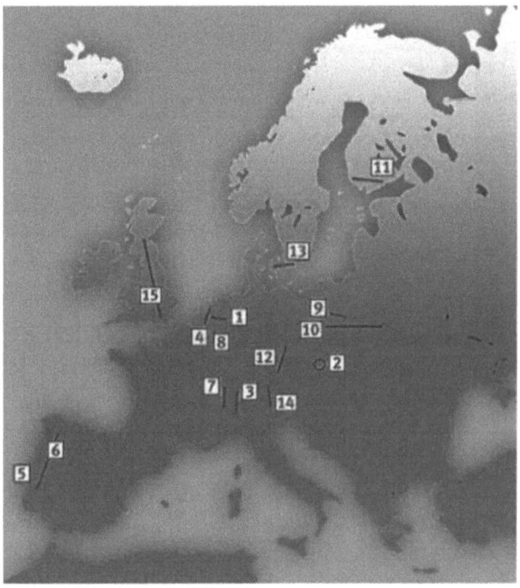

Projects (mode):

1. Betuweroute (rail)
2. Ring road Bratislava (road)
3. Gotthard Base Tunnel (rail)
4. HSL-South (rail)
5. Lezíria Bridge (road)
6. Lisbon - Porto (rail)
7. Lötschberg Base Tunnel (rail)
8. Maaswerken (water)
9. Motorway A2 (road)
10. Motorway A4 (road)
11. Motorway E18 (road)
12. Nuremberg - Ingolstadt (rail)
13. Øresund bridge (road & rail)
14. Unterinntalbahn (rail)
15. West Coast Main Line (rail)

Fig. 5.3 The 15 projects studied by NETLIPSE

identify best practices for other projects. Through the network, partners can benefit from the experiences of other LIPs by sharing the knowledge gained.

5.3 Main Findings

5.3.1 What is Complex in the Management of LIPs?

In (1) the PhD thesis we developed a complexity scan, and (2) in NETLIPSE research programme we looked at management themes.

5.3.1.1 Complexity Scan

To answer the question 'What is complex in the management of LIPs?' for the PhD thesis, we developed a complexity scan. In this scan we distinguished six types of complexity:

- Technical complexity
- Social complexity
- Financial complexity
- Legal complexity
- Organisational complexity
- Time complexity

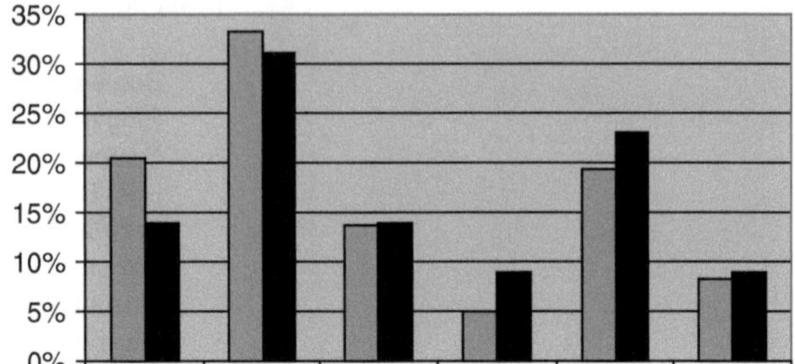

	Techn.	Social	Financ.	Legisl.	Organis.	Time
■ Average Interviews	20%	33%	14%	5%	19%	8%
■ Average Events	14%	31%	14%	9%	23%	9%

Fig. 5.4 Results complexity scan

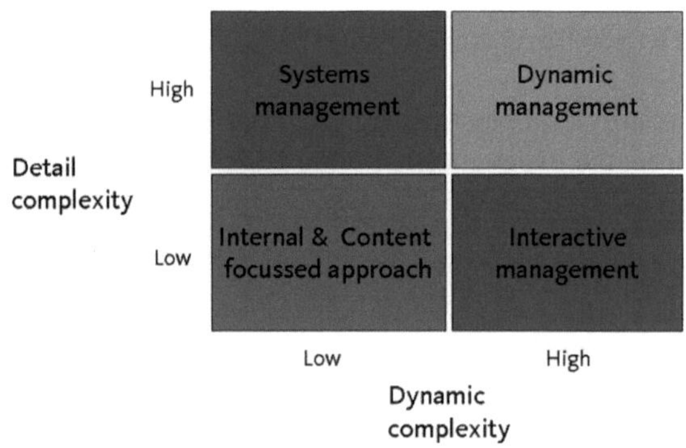

Fig. 5.5 Four approaches to complexity management

We used the complexity scan in two ways, first, by analysing the answers of interviewees on the question: "What makes your project complex?" (direct approach: blue columns) and also by analysing 14 crucial events in the six projects (indirect approach: red columns). The results are shown in Fig. 5.4. The figure shows the relative importance of each complexity: the total of the six complexities for each project is 100%.

By looking at the answers from respondents and analysing our cases, we conclude that the most dominant form of complexity experienced by practitioners is social. Social complexity is high when we observe the following elements: conflicts of interest, different meanings and perceptions, as well as large impact. Dealing with social complexity can be done by applying the strategies from 'interactive management' (Fig. 5.5).

Legal complexity proved to be of less importance. This is interesting, because many recent initiatives trying to stimulate the successful implementation of LIPs have focussed on legal aspects.

Organisational complexity was mainly visible in the relationship between the project delivery organisation and its parent and principal organisation. Two main examples of technical complexity are: dealing with new innovative technology; and technological uncertainty. Financial complexity is, for example, related to the distribution of costs and benefits, the perception of cost developments; different perceptions about definitions and agreements; optimism bias and pessimism bias etc. We found that the Betuweroute was a best practise in dealing with financial complexity in the realisation phase (Flyvbjerg and Westerveld 2007).

In our analysis, time complexity turned out to be the exceptional dimension, since it is heavily related to the nature of change which affects the other five elements of our framework. Each project has a unique history and is strongly influenced by unique events. As a result, the implementation of LIPs can often be characterised as a non-linear implementation process. For managers, this type of complexity means that a unique, tailor-made approach needs to be developed in order to meet the challenges faced by a specific LIP.

5.3.1.2 Eight Management Themes

The NETLIPSE research focused on eight themes: Objectives and scope; Stakeholders; Financial Management; Organisation and management processes; Risks (threats and opportunities); Contracting; Legal consents; Knowledge and technology. For each of these themes, many best practises and lessons learnt have been found.

From a quantitative analysis, we have drawn the following main conclusions for the 15 projects researched:

1. In general, Scope & Objectives, Finance and Legal consents are organised best.
2. In general, Stakeholder Management lacks measurement, Knowledge & Technology are less organised, and Human Resource matters appear to be neglected.
3. The 'hard factors' are better organised than the 'soft factors'.
4. The 'control' part is better organised than the 'interactive' parts.
5. The projects are not very open to optimisations, opportunities and new ways.
6. Projects are open to research, knowledge management and new technologies only to a limited extent.

In both the PhD study and the NETLIPSE research, the question was asked to what degree the conclusions on the management of LIPs are valid in each country. At first, it appeared that national context and culture would be a key factor, which would make drawing general conclusions on an international level highly difficult. But, throughout the studies, it quickly became clear that management themes and challenges faced in projects are highly similar across the studied projects. So there is a sufficient basis for knowledge exchange. On the other hand, it was also concluded that simply copying best practice from one case to another, without paying attention to the local context, could lead to disappointing results. So, while management themes are similar, project managers always need to take the local context into account when developing their own, customised, practices.

5.3.2 Management Approaches

5.3.2.1 Four Approaches

'How can managers responsible for the implementation of LIPs manage the complexity inherent in these projects?'. In our answer to this question, we have developed a framework of four management approaches, that are graphically presented in Fig. 5.5.

Detail complexity can be seen as the traditional view, in which the number of elements and relationships form the basis. Dynamic complexity, on the other hand, can be linked to a perspective where the relationship between cause and effect is diffuse, and coincidences play an important role. This dynamic complexity has broken with the traditional view on systems as being knowable and predictable. According to Senge (1994), dynamic complexity occurs when the same action has totally different effects in the short and the long run; when an action has one set of consequences locally and a different set of consequences in another part of the system; when obvious interventions produce non-obvious consequences.

5.3.2.2 Content Focused Approach

The first approach is the internal and content-focussed approach (Hertogh 1997). In our case analysis, it quickly became clear, that there was a frequently used approach which was not a part of our theoretical framework. We labelled this 'the internal & content focussed approach' because it involves a lack of clear management strategies, but relies on a pure focus on finding a technical solution to a perceived problem, without paying too much attention to strategies of control and interaction. The approach is highly internal: the satisfaction of involved stakeholders is not regarded a major concern.

It was striking that we often observed the content-focussed approach. We found that the success rate of this approach in the management of complexity is very low. Factors that we have observed that proved to be a stimulus for the content-focussed approach are:

- Lack of attention and low priority;
- Experts in the role of project manager with an underlying focus on content;
- Financial tensions and 'imperatives', e.g. budget or cost overruns, that may lead to decisions unpopular with (main) stakeholders, without (sufficient) interaction with them;
- Organisations that are unfamiliar with each other's characteristics, causing decisions to be made without sufficient attention being paid.
- A limited internally focused group in charge leading to 'groupthink'.

The content-based approach may lead to premature convergence, which removes the possibility of exploring other, possibly promising, alternatives. This proves the extreme importance of the starting conditions. In addition, the negative impact of the approach, animosity, may last long after the approach has been changed to a more control- and/or interaction focussed approach.

While the content-focussed approach might possibly be successful in situations of low complexity, the likelihood of success of this approach in situations of high detail and dynamic complexity turns out to be fairly low. Overall, the approach has very limited scope for dealing with both detail and dynamic complexity. In addition, it may lead to dissatisfaction amongst stakeholders.

5.3.2.3 Systems Management

Detail complexity is linked to strategies of systems management, in which strategies are focussed on control. Systems management can be classified as an approach based on a 'deterministic' perspective: tight monitoring and steering of costs, time and scope (Turner 1997). The aim of this approach is to make sure that the project will be delivered according to the set specifications, and within the set boundaries of costs and time. Tools and techniques have been developed to structure the collection of information so as to minimise the chances of unpleasant surprises (Westerveld and Gayá Walters 2001).

From our research, we conclude that, although systems management is often regarded a hygiene factor in the management of LIPs, its application is certainly not a given. Systems management within LIPs is a time-consuming task, often supported by sophisticated tools, that requires continuous attention in the set-up and use of appropriate instruments of project control.

5.3.2.4 Interactive Management

The strategies control described in the previous section has proved to be less suitable in dealing with dynamic complexity, especially the dynamic development of the stakeholder system in LIPs, but this is where our third approach, 'interactive management' comes into play (Teisman 1992; Hertogh 1997 and de Bruijn et al. 1998). Interactive management was originally developed as an alternative or supplement to systems management. Traditional systems management strategies turned out to be not capable of dealing with the dynamics of (local) stakeholders, often found in LIPs. Interactive management essentially focuses on interests of all stakeholders, so as to improve their support of the project. But interactive management goes further than creating support for a decision that already has been made: it also covers joint initiatives, co-production and co-financing. The strategies of interactive management have an external focus – looking at stakeholder satisfaction – and also focus on the flexibility required to deal with the many changes within LIPs. This makes these strategies better suitable for dealing with dynamic complexity.

The case analysis proved convincingly that interaction pays off. It can improve satisfaction for both the civil principal, project delivery organisation, and the external stakeholders. An open approach towards stakeholders has more chances of success in the management of high complexity than an internal approach.

But be careful. An over-application of interaction might lead to false expectations and time- consuming processes that, in the end, offer no benefits to those involved. So, interactive management is not the only necessary condition.

5.3.2.5 Dynamic Management

The fourth and final approach is called 'dynamic management'. This approach is based on a synthesis of our findings in the successful management of complexity. It is our answer to the question: 'How to manage complexity in LIPs'. Dynamic management is based on: (1) Balancing control and interaction and (2) Doing the extraordinary.

Balancing Control and Interaction

In major projects, there is a fine balance to be drawn between the need for control (with the use of traditional systems management techniques) and constructive interaction between the parties. Strong control helps to prevent purpose and scope 'creep'. Constructive interaction can help projects to accept new, and often external, changes or delivery methodologies. These changes might potentially improve the project outputs, reduce costs or speed up the project delivery.

De Bruijn et al. (2004) concluded that control and interaction are complementary. Both are needed. The challenge is to balance both approaches. Because LIPs show both the characteristics of high detail and high dynamic complexity, strategies of control and interaction need to be balanced in order to be successful (Fig. 5.6).

Doing the Extraordinary

We saw that one key to successful management in LIPs is clearly the effective combination of the strategies of control and of interaction. But is that all there is?

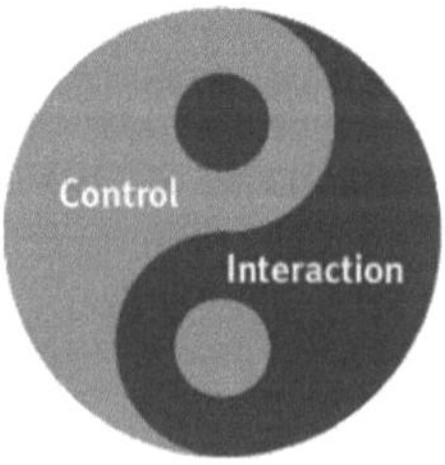

Fig. 5.6 Balancing control and interaction

When looking at our case material, we found that, in order to be truly successful in the management of complexity, we need 'extraordinary efforts'. This is the second element of our dynamic management approach.

These extraordinary efforts can be made at the following levels:

1. Stakeholders system – achieving a higher degree of cooperation
2. Level of the 'actor' or 'player' – going the extra mile, the project delivery organisation working as project champion
3. Personal level – competent people making a difference

Apart from working at these levels we also need:

4. Extraordinary new management solutions
5. Participants in LIPs to recognise and use momentum in projects. They need to use the apparent windows of opportunity that occur within the lifespan of LIPs. Many times events perceived as threats may lead to 'golden opportunities'.

An illustration of the elements of the dynamic management approach was observed at the West Coast Mainline.

Case West Coast Mainline

The West Coast Main Line (WCML) (Hertogh et al. 2006; and Teisman et al. 2009) is Europe's busiest mixed-use railway (see Fig. 5.7 for an illustration). It connects London with major urban areas in the northwest. More than 2,000 trains a day use the line, transporting both passengers and freight. The train services consist of long-distance, regional and local (short-distance) commuter trains, along with substantial freight traffic. The latter represents around 40% of the total rail freight traffic movements in the UK. The WCML relates to the 650 km main line between London Euston and Glasgow, which also serves the West Midlands (Birmingham), the North West (including Manchester amd Liverpool) and North Wales (with connections to and from Ireland). Presently, there are some 22 million passenger-train km a year and six million freight-train km a year.

Until 1993, the WCML was totally located within the public monopoly of British Rail (BR). Due to the inability of BR to innovate the line, a new approach was adopted, mainly based on private interference and private, market-oriented decision making. Government officials thought that they were relieved from the burden of improving the WCML. The private approach, however, led to huge cost overruns and, finally, to the bankruptcy of Railtrack, the private successor to BR. The Rail Administration took the responsibility back (2001) and a new combined arrangement on the edge of public and private domain was developed. Even though this institutional dynamic is exceptional, the shifts between public and private stage setting and direction is not unique at all. WCML can be seen as a large-scale reproduction of the difficult combination of public and private interferences with large infrastructure projects. WCML shows, better than any other case probably

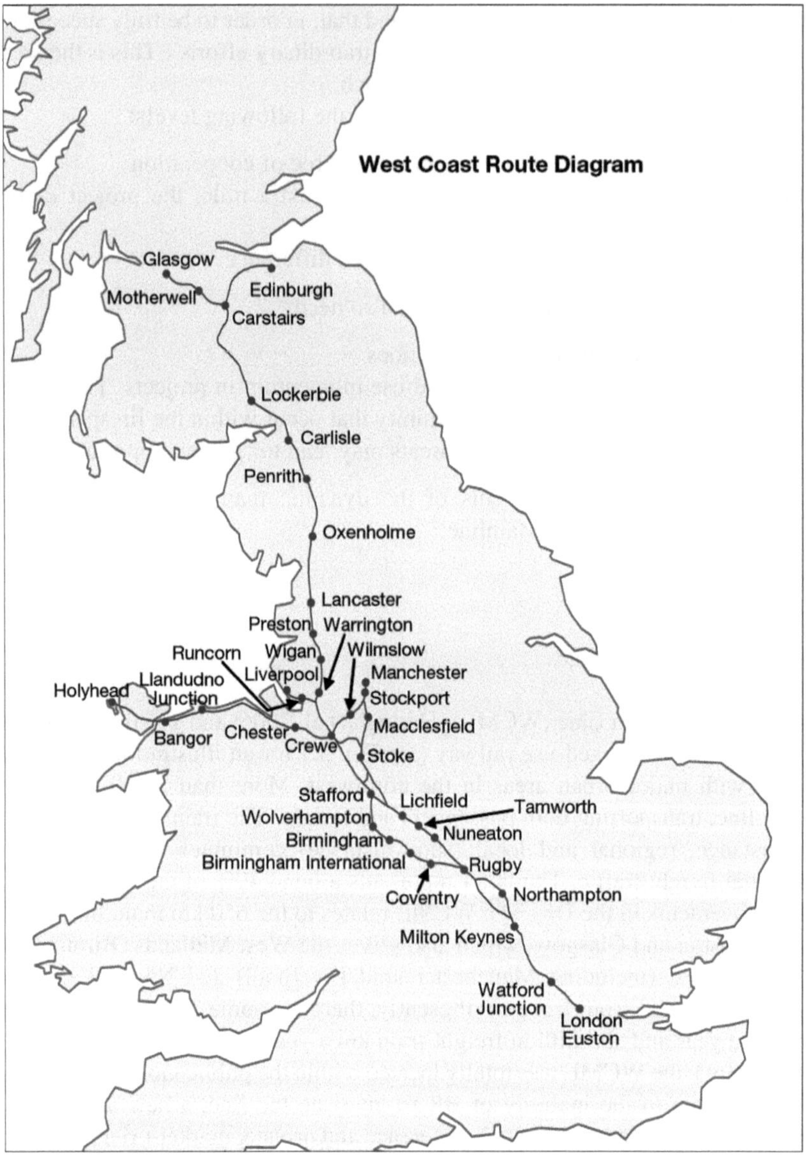

Fig. 5.7 West coast mainline

could do, *that neither the pure private responsibility, nor the pure public responsibility leads to a successful implementation.*

In the BR period, the renovation was neglected, and in the RT period the reality of the existing assets of a highly integrated and complex rail system was neglected. In the last period of joint responsibility between public and private partners, a new balance between public leadership and private realisation power was found. This hybrid management context is needed for high-quality upgrading, but also requires really high-quality management, able to deal with two quite different value systems. It was one of our striking insights that some managers in the area of WCML mainly dealt with public values, some with private values and at least two dealing with public values but understanding private values or the other way around. This chain of managers seems to be an important part of mature management of large infrastructure projects.

Furthermore, it is fascinating to see that there seems to be a clear formal distinction between public (DfT, Office of Rail Regulation) and private domain (Network Rail, Virgin and other operators) but that, in fact, the whole rail industry is operating as a network of partners. The degree of maturity does more depend on the quality of the network of managers, than on the formal structures themselves.

As in every formal structure unable to deal with the complexity of a project like WCML, there are tensions between participating formal bodies like DfT, ORR and NR, and between Virgin and NR and so on, but since the network management and the network of management has developed, for instance in terms of joint sessions and joint documents, the parties involved act with more knowledge about the reality of the rail systems as well as the possibilities for renovation, innovation and return on investment. The parties have also been brought together by the common objective of achievement: it was clear to the whole industry that the £5.6 billion that the UK Treasury was willing to donate in 2002 – on top of the £2.5 billion already spent – was a last chance for the whole industry to demonstrate its ability to achieve strong results from investment. Many observers felt that if the project had failed again, the whole network would be starved of investment.

5.3.3 The Level of Shared Perceptions

We identied four levels in conceiving, managing and operating LIPs. The first level represents the design and realisation of a physical project. The second level describes this project within the stakeholder network of cities, NGO's etc. The third level is the project fulfilment of the needs of the transport network. And, finally, the fourth level is reached when a project meets the requirements of society (see Fig. 5.8).

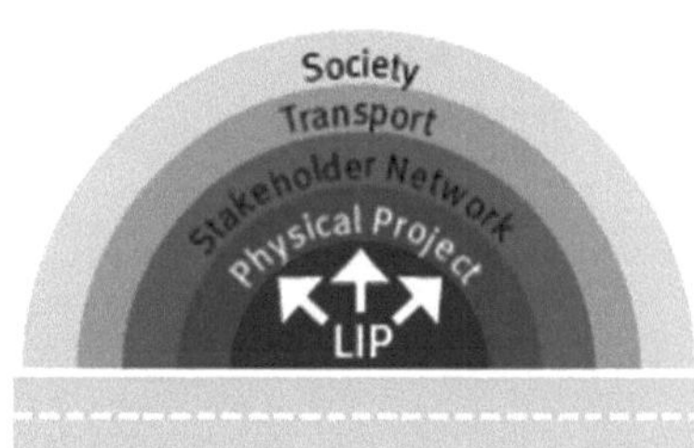

Fig. 5.8 Four distinctive levels of goals of LIPs

From the NETLIPSE research, we concluded that too many projects remained on the lower levels. We recommended that projects must be managed as an integrated whole, with the prime purpose being the user, social and economic benefits derived from a new or improved transport link, rather than the completion of a physical project as an end in itself. Because the success of the outputs depends on operational interfaces as well as on infrastructure construction, they must be managed from the outset and integrated into the programme management of the whole project. The case of the Øresund Crossing illustrates this finding.

5.3.3.1 Øresund Crossing

The construction of the Øresund Crossing is aimed at enhancing economic and cultural cooperation in the Øresund Region, which comprises Zealand, the smaller island of Lolland-Falster and Bornholm in Denmark, and Scania in Southern Sweden (Westerveld et al. 2007). The region has 3.6 million inhabitants. The location of the crossing is shown in Fig. 5.9.

An agreement for the crossing was set out in the Treaty between Denmark and Sweden signed in 1991. This treaty defined the strategic economic, cultural and social objectives for the scheme, on a national and regional basis. This was a key step. It provided the formal legal framework for the scheme; the vehicle for political support; assurance in relation to financing; the mandate for ØSK and; the vision for the public and stakeholders. The focus solely on high-level objectives and outcomes at this early stage, with better transport links seen as a driver for these, also provided ØSK with greater freedom to develop the optimum scope and

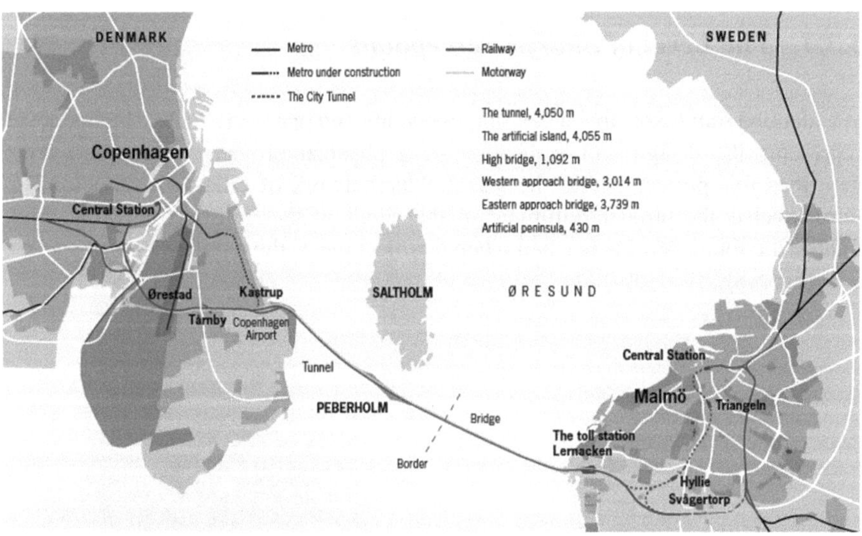

Fig. 5.9 Location of the Øresund crossing

delivery plans for the crossing. Overall, success was founded on a clarity of objectives, roles and responsibilities – within governments, within the project and with the wider stakeholders, from a societal point of view, right from the start and throughout the project.

During the project, citizens from both sides discovered the mutual advantages of Denmark and Sweden. In Skane, house prices are lower than in the Copenhagen region, taxes for cars are lower, and there is more natural habitat around the houses. In Denmark, wages are higher and there is more demand for employees. This combination of facts makes people willing to commute. The Swedish people tend to use the train, and the Danish people who have moved to Sweden tend to use their car.

Some examples of the benefits of the project are: a GDP increase – increases in Skåne have been higher than anywhere else in Sweden and it was lagging until then. Unemployment changes – dropping unemployment from 1999 to 2007 due to new employment in Skåne and movement to Denmark. The area is being established as a logistics distribution centre. There have been large increases in location of Nordic headquarters in the Malmö area, some of which have been new. Göteborg, Copenhagen or Stockholm to Malmö transfers have been the main changes of location.

5.4 Conclusions

The main objective of the NETLIPSE project was to set up an interactive and dynamic network for LIPs in Europe for the dissemination of experience and knowledge, specifically focussed on the management and organisational aspects of these projects. In January 2010, more than 15 countries are involved. Partners in the network come from the member states of the European Union and other European countries. The group of participants consists of clients/sponsors, project delivery organisations, specialists, politicians, civil servants, academics and consultants.

The NETLIPSE research shows unambiguously that knowledge exchange in Europe is scarce. When comparing the projects, we found that often similar challenges are faced. The chance to learn from other projects is a field yet to be developed. Dissemination of results was the key of NETLIPSE. We are proud that organisations in almost every country of the EU are involved in the network.

Through the network, we found that partners do benefit from the experience of other LIPs and scientific developments, and from knowledge institutes – such as infrastructure research and project management organisations – by sharing their knowledge and experience.

The development of the NETLIPSE network will be an ongoing and evolving process. One of the key objectives is to link organisations and stakeholders responsible for developing and introducing new transport policies. This should be done both locally and internationally in Europe for the dissemination of experience and knowledge, specifically focussed on the management and organisational aspects of Large Infrastructure Projects (LIPs).

References

Commission E (2005) Trans-European transport network, TEN-T priority axes, projects. European Commission, Brussels
de Bruijn JA, ten Heuvelhof EF, in't Veld RJ (1998) Process management. Academic Service, Schoonhoven
de Bruijn JA, Hertogh MJCM, Kastelein N (2004) Balanceren tussen belangen. Procesmanagement dynamisch complement van projectmanagement. Projectie 12:25–29
Flyvbjerg B (2007) Truth, lies about megaprojects, faculty of technology, policy, management. Delft University of Technology, Delft
Flyvbjerg B, Westerveld E (2007) Betuweroute als best practice, NRC (newspaper in the Netherlands) Handelsblad 16-07-2007
Flyvbjerg B, Bruzelius N, Rothengatter W (2003) Megaprojects risk: an anatomy of ambition. Cambridge University Press, Cambridge
Glaser BG, Strauss AL (1967) The discovery of grounded theory. Aldine, Chicago
Hertogh MJCM (1997) Belangen bij complexe infrastructurele projecten. Elsevier, Amsterdam
Hertogh MJCM, Westerveld E (2010) Playing with complexity – management and organisation of large infrastructure projects, Erasmus University Rotterdam, AT Osborne
Hertogh MJCM, Teisman GR, van Geest M (2006) Case study report west coast mainline, NETLIPSE
Hertogh MJCM, Baker SK, Staal PL, Westerveld E (2008) Managing large infrastructure projects, Netlipse
Nijssen B (2006) Process guidance at the Charles, Erasmus Universiteit Rotterdam
Reason R, Bradbury B (2001) Handbook of action research. Sage, London
Schalcher HR, Wadenpohl F, Hertogh M (2007) Case study report Gotthard base tunnel and Lötschberg base tunnel, NETLIPSE
Senge PM (1994) The fifth discipline. Currency Doubleday, New York
TCI, Tijdelijke Commissie Infrastructuurprojecten (2004) Onderzoek naar infrastructuurprojecten. Sdu Uitgevers, Den Haag
Teisman GR (1992) Complexe besluitvorming, een pluricentrisch perspectief op besluitvorming over ruimtelijke investeringen. VUGA, Den Haag
Teisman GR, Westerveld E, Hertogh M (2009) Appearances and sources of process dynamics: the case of infrastructure development in the UK and the Netherlands. In: Teisman GR, van Buuren MW, Gerrits L (eds) Managing complex governance systems. Dynamics, self-organisation and coevolution in public investments. Routledge, London, pp 56–75
Turner JR (1997) The handbook of project-based management. McGraw-Hill, New York
Westerveld E, Gayá Walters D (2001) Het verbeteren van uw projectorganisatie. Kluwer, Dordrecht
Westerveld E, Baker SK, Teisman GR (2007) Case study report Øresund, NETLIPSE
WRR (1994) Besluite*n over grote projecten*, WRR rapport nr. 46, Sdu Uitgeverij, Den Haag

Part B
Experiments with Dynamic Transport Optimization

Chapter 6
Rewarding Peak Avoidance: The Dutch 'Spitsmijden' Projects

Jasper Knockaert, Jessie Bakens, Dick Ettema, and Erik Verhoef

6.1 Introduction

The Dutch road network is becoming increasingly congested. In late 2006, a group of companies, universities and government institutions established the Spitsmijden project. 'Spitsmijden' is the Dutch term for 'avoiding the peak'. This joint initiative aimed to identify and assess a short-term solution that could extend the portfolio of transport policy instruments that may be used to manage temporal peaks in transport demand.

A first evidence-based Spitsmijden experiment was conducted in the autumn of 2007, as part of research into demand management concepts within the framework of the national transport research programme Transumo. This reward trial on the A12 motorway between Zoetermeer and The Hague proved the effectiveness of positive financial stimuli: the 340 participants reduced their number of morning peak trips by half. The results of this first Spitsmijden experiment demonstrated the concept to be innovative and promising, which made it eligible for further development.

In the international arena, there are relatively few comparable evidence-based experiments or experiences. With this in mind, the second Spitsmijden trial was developed. The aim of this experiment was to test the durability of rewards as an effective transport demand management tool over a longer time period. The reward trial was conducted from September 2008 to May 2009, on the A12 motorway

J. Knockaert (✉) • J. Bakens • E. Verhoef
Department of Spatial Economics, VU University Amsterdam, De Boelelaan 1105, Amsterdam, HV 1081, The Netherlands
e-mail: j.knockaert@vu.nl; j.bakens@vu.nl; e.t.verhoef@vu.nl

D. Ettema
Urban and Regional Research Centre Utrecht, Utrecht University, 80115, Utrecht, TC 3508, The Netherlands
e-mail: d.ettema@geog.uu.nl

J.A.E.E. van Nunen et al. (eds.), *Transitions Towards Sustainable Mobility*,
DOI 10.1007/978-3-642-21192-8_6,

stretch between Gouda and Den Haag. About 750 regular morning rush hour drivers participated in this experiment.

The phenomenon of peak demands for infrastructure capacity is, however, not limited to road transport. Also in public transport a morning and evening travel peak is usually observed. A question that arose was to what extent the Spitsmijden concept is effective in managing public transport demand. A third experiment was designed to answer this question. This public transport reward trial focused on the Utrecht-The Hague rail link, where travellers were offered an off-peak travel pass which allowed them to realise a reward by travelling off-peak. The experiment was held during the spring of 2009, and was extended by a country-wide survey conducted with regular peak hour train travellers.

This chapter presents these three experiments, and discusses the choice behaviour of rush hour travellers under different reward schemes. The focus of the analysis concerns the temporal, modal and spatial travel preferences. Furthermore, we study if (and how) travel behaviour evolves over time. Through their very nature, experiments are at the heart of the Transumo research on demand steering. Both in terms of the design of the instrument – tailored to reduce peak demand by seducing travellers to seek alternatives – and in terms of the research priorities set out for these projects – in which demand analysis is central – the projects have primarily contributed to this line of research in Transumo. In a broader sense, the Spitsmijden projects contribute to the objective of the Transumo programme to attain progress toward more sustainable forms of transportation. Spitsmijden includes the three dimensions (people, planet, profit) of sustainability central to the Transumo programme. The focus on behavioural change and stimulating individuals to explore behavioural alternatives to avoid congestion addresses the 'people' component. The project adds to the 'planet' component through stimulating the use of more sustainable travel modes and more fuel efficient ways of driving (i.e. at uncongested time). Also, the final objective of reducing congestion improves accessibility, which has positive economic effects (the 'profit' component). The Spitsmijden project is unique in that attention is given to the development of the concept as such, including embedding it in an open consortium of governmental, commercial and academic partners who exchange knowledge and experiences about the concept. At the end of this chapter, we briefly discuss some lessons from simulation models that were designed on the basis of behavioural analysis.

6.2 Contribution to Existing Literature

With the rapid growth of traffic congestion in most modern societies, and the emergence of technologies that allow the implementation of electronic road pricing, transport pricing is receiving increasing attention both in policy circles and in academic research. This academic literature started with seminal contributions by Pigou (1920), Walters (1961), Vickrey (1963, 1969) and Beckmann et al. (1956), all of whom emphasized, from different angles, the economic inefficiency inherently present in unpriced traffic congestion. The inefficiency stems from the existence of an unpriced external cost of travelling, which arises because an additional trip raises transport costs for other road users as a result of increased travel times. A massive body of literature has emerged afterwards, building on these fundamental insights, addressing various aspects of transport pricing.

One line of literature that is relevant for a better understanding of the pro's and con's of using rewards rather than taxes in the regulation of traffic congestion, concerns studies into second-best aspects of road pricing. This can be loosely defined as the study of pricing schedules that are designed so as to optimally satisfy certain constraints – on the tolling instrument itself, or on prices on related markets – that prevent theoretically optimal pricing from being possible. In the case of Spitsmijden, an important constraint is that 'prices' be negative; so subsidies, where taxes would be optimal given that congestion entails an external cost (not a benefit). This literature on second-best pricing is reviewed in Small and Verhoef (2007), and includes – among many other topics – contributions on pricing on just a part of the network (e.g., Lévy-Lambert 1968; Marchand 1968); and contributions on 'step tolling' where continuously varying tolls would be optimal (Arnott et al. 1993). Because this chapter deals with the behavioural impacts of Spitsmijden, we will not address the second-best aspects of the policy here; the interested reader is referred to Rouwendal et al. (2010).

A second line of literature concerns studies into the (behavioural and traffic) impacts of transport pricing. Various reviews have appeared over the past decades, all off which typically report potentially strong behavioural impacts of transport pricing, depending on the exact design of the policy, the level of the prices, and local circumstances. Some reviews can be found, among many others, in Small and Gómez-Ibáñez (1998), Santos (2004), Small and Verhoef (2007), and Jensen-Butler et al. (2008). These reviews cover examples from all around the globe, including well-known cases in Singapore, London, Stockholm, California, and Norway. Despite the originality of the Spitsmijden projects, focussing on rewards, the experiments thus fit in a much wider international trend in experimenting and working with price incentives to reduce peak congestion.

A third line of literature concerns the behavioural effects of rewarding versus tolling or punishment. Since rewarding measures are new in transport policy, this literature addresses a variety of other domains such as education, health etc. Psychological literature on voluntary behaviour stresses incentives such as rewards or punishments. However, also socialization factors (e.g. communication, influence, conformity, persuasion and identification) are mentioned to play a role. Cognitive response theory asserts that individuals are most likely to respond to a reward if they recognize they have personal stakes in the matter, information provided is precise and triggers concordant thinking (Petty and Caciappo 1986). Literature on voluntary travel behaviour change has also reported that providing exact information influences the probability of change (Ampt 2003; Stopher 2004). For example, Eriksson et al. (2008) and Jakobsson et al. (2002) note that habit, plan formation, normative and motivational issues, but also economic (dis)incentives play a role in structural behavioural change.

The contribution of this paper in the context of the existing literature is that it provides empirical insight in the effects of rewarding in the specific domain of travel behaviour. In particular, it describes how travellers' activity scheduling decisions (departure time choice) and mode choice are affected by various reward schemes, and what (potential) consequences this bears on traffic flows and congestion patterns. These empirical results provide a first insight in the effects of rewarding relative to the effects obtained from pricing policies.

6.3 Methodology

The Spitsmijden experiments study the travel behaviour of the individual commuter and how this behaviour changes after a reward is offered to avoid the morning peak hour.

The methodology applied in the different experiments described in this chapter is to a large extent identical. Central to each Spitsmijden iteration is a field experiment where a group of commuters is selected, based on their reference travel behaviour. The participants to the different experiment are then offered a reward that correlates to their change in rush hour travel behaviour.

In each experiment, the observation of rush hour travel behaviour is to a large extent automated. For the road experiments, cameras with licence plate recognition technology are installed, whereas for the rail experiment, a customised e-ticket is developed. Additional information on travel behaviour, such as trip motive and use of other modes, is logged using a web based travel diary.

Travel behaviour is registered in a period before the experiment, during the experiment and in a period after the reward ends. This leads to a set of observations that covers both rewarded and unrewarded behaviour of the same group of individuals.

The information on travel behaviour is supplemented with one or more surveys, in order to be able to answer specific research questions that are important to study our experiment. A specialised survey format is the conjoint choice experiment in which participants are presented with a series of fictitious choice sets. The participant indicates for each choice set his or her preferred alternative. The conjoint experiment allows to collect choice information for situations which were absent in the field experiment.

The analysis of travel behaviour can be conducted by applying a myriad of methodologies, going from techniques as simple as frequency tables to estimating advanced mixed logit choice models.

A common theoretical framework in the analysis of travel behaviour is discrete choice theory. Discrete choice theory describes how in a choice situation the probabilities of each choice alternative are determined by an alternative specific utility representation. The utility U_i of each choice alternative i is the combination of a deterministic term V_i (function of observed variables) and a randomly distributed term ε_i (representing unobserved choice variables):

$$U_i = V_i + \varepsilon_i$$

The traveller then chooses the alternative providing him or her with the highest utility U_i. An in-depth discussion on discrete choice theory can be found in Ben-Akiva and Lerman (1985), Train (1986/1990), Anderson et al. (1992) and Train (2003).A common representation for utility in the study of peak hour travel decisions is based on the bottleneck model, where a traveller chooses between departure times (and potentially also between travel transport modes) by trading off schedule delay efforts for differences in travel time (congestion) and monetary stimuli (charges or rewards). Throughout the different experiments, this is the behavioural reference model used to analyse observed travel choices. For a discussion of the bottleneck model we refer to Arnott et al. (1993).

For the simulation of policy scenarios, two modelling frameworks are applied. A first one is that of the bottleneck model, which is a stylised representation of travel behaviour on a single congested road link. The advantage of this modelling approach is that it allows for optimisation of the reward specification under various policy constraints. A second modelling framework is that of the INDY model, which carries a network representation and hence allows to cover a broader scope of impact dimensions when simulating reward implementations.

6.4 The First Experiment: Spitsmijden A12 Zoetermeer-The Hague

This section introduces the first reward experiment that was carried out. For a more detailed discussion, we refer to the Spitsmijden project report (Knockaert et al. 2007).

6.4.1 Overview

The trial was launched on October 2, 2006. The test area was the Dutch A12 motorway corridor from Zoetermeer towards The Hague. On weekday mornings, this stretch of motorway is heavily congested with vehicles heading towards The Hague. There are relatively few alternative routes, and relatively few on- or off-ramps on this stretch of motorway, which made the trial relatively easy to control.

The morning rush-hour was defined as lasting from 07.30 to 09.30 a.m., since this period has the highest reported traffic densities. The participants in the trial could earn a reward for not travelling by car from Zoetermeer to The Hague during the morning rush hour.

Upon registration, the participants chose one of two types of reward. The first type of reward was an amount of money for each morning rush hour that the participant avoided. The second type comprised credits that, when a sufficient number were earned, allowed keeping a ('Yeti') smartphone at the end of the trial. This Yeti was available to the participants already during the peak, but with insufficient credits earned, it had to be returned.

The objective was to recruit 500 participants. To this end, we organised three recruitment waves. The first two waves were based on license plate observations, where we approached frequent rush hour travellers on the A12 motorway stretch (minimum three trips per week). These two rounds delivered 283 participants to the experiment. To further increase this number, a last recruitment wave was organised, using a *member get member* approach and a renewed invitation to vehicle owners that had not reacted in the first two waves. This resulted in a final sample of 341 participants, who completed the full experiment.

Before the start of the experiment, the participants had an electronic device installed in their cars, allowing for the registration of their car travel behaviour on the corridor under consideration. The registration system was further completed with licence plate recognition cameras in order to extend the coverage of the study area.

The trial lasted for 10 weeks. Observation in the 2 weeks preceding the trial as well as the week after the trial covered reference behaviour under unrewarded conditions. The participants had to complete a daily logbook providing additional morning commute information during the full period of the experiment.

6.4.2 Reward

Upon registration, the participants were asked which type of reward they preferred. There were two options. The first type of reward was an amount of money for each morning rush hour that the participant avoided. At the moment of registration the premium was indicated to amount to about 5 €; later it was explained how different reward levels would apply over the course of the trial.

The second type of reward was saving for a Yeti smartphone. These participants received a Yeti smartphone at the beginning of the trial. The Yeti provided them with traffic information during the trial. If the number of credits earned over the duration of the experiment exceeded a predefined number, the participant would be allowed to keep the Yeti at the end of the trial. If the participant failed to meet the threshold, he/she would have to return the smartphone at the end of the trial. Thus, it was an all-or-nothing scenario.

The majority of the participants chose a monetary reward. As the trial was set up to test both reward types, the remainder of the participants (including those who had said that they did not have a preference for one reward type over the other) were assigned to the Yeti variant. However, to prevent participants ending up with an unwanted and hence lowly valued reward type, we allowed them to switch to the other type until the start of the trial.

During the 10 weeks trial period, different levels of the reward were tested. The monetary reward amounted to 3 € or 7 € to avoid the entire morning peak interval (7.30–9.30 a.m.) and a more refined scheme made the participant receive 7 € to avoid the entire morning peak, which was reduced to 3 € if travelling in the shoulder periods (7.30–8.00 and 9.00–9.30 a.m.). For the Yeti reward, two schemes were tested, one scheme where the participant could save credits to obtain the smartphone, while in another period no credits could be earned but traffic information was still provided via the smartphone; this allows the researcher to distinguish the effects of information from the effects of the reward. All users faced each of the different schemes corresponding to their preferred reward option for the same amount of time, but in a randomised order to minimise possible biases.

Although we recruited among frequent rush hour car travellers, the observations from the unrewarded pre-trial weeks revealed differences in trip frequencies. To bring overall reward levels in line with reference behaviour, we customised the reward conditions for each participant. For the monetary reward, this meant a weekly maximum number of rewards ranging from one to five, whereas for the Yeti reward the threshold level was set between 15 (infrequent travellers) and 25 (frequent travellers) credits over the 5 week reward period.

The unit of behaviour rewarded was the use of the participant's car (by the participant or someone else) in combination with the place and time of driving. In the *logbook* (an online travel diary), the participant could indicate if the registered car was exceptionally used by someone else, or the converse situation, where the participant used a different car. We did not include this information in the reward algorithm, in order to remove any stimulus for the participant to provide incorrect information in the logbook.[1]

To calculate reward levels, the observation data were checked for peak hour travel (by the respondent's own car), applying a 5 min tolerance. For days on which no observation was available in the 6.00–11.00 a.m. period, the logbook information was used for verification, in order to correct for any possible failures in the observation technology. In case of ambiguities, the available data, together with any comments by the participants, were processed manually.

6.4.3 The Participants

The participants of the experiment had to complete a number of compulsory surveys. Most surveys were conducted before the experiment. In this section, we will provide a summary overview of selected results; for an in-depth discussion we refer to the project report (Knockaert et al. 2007).

[1]Upon recruitment the participants were also asked for the licence plate of any other cars in the household. The camera recognition technology allowed to track these cars as well. Together with the logbook information we periodically checked during the trial for participants who are too eager to receive rewards for using another car rather than avoid car travel during the rush hour, in order to exclude them from further participation.

Upon recruitment, the participant completed a first survey about their daily commute, followed by another survey on socio-demographic characteristics and the organisation of work and household.

Of the participants, 64.7% were male. About half of all participants were aged between 35 and 49. About 25% were younger than 35, while 25% were older than 49. The majority of the participants held a higher professional education certificate or a university degree. Most of the participants were married or cohabiting; most had children.

Of the participants, 98% lived in Zoetermeer; the remaining participants lived in the surrounding municipalities (e.g. Benthuizen, Berkel en Rodenrijs, Bleiswijk). Most of the participants worked in The Hague, although some worked in Delft, Leidschendam, Rijswijk or Voorburg.

Asked for the motivations for participation, the most frequent raised reason was the reward itself, although the majority of the participants also had at least one other motivation. Both the contribution to more insight into congestion and experimentation with alternative travel options were relevant motivations.

Of the participants, 62% commuted at least five times per week towards The Hague, using the A12 motorway; 26% commuted four times per week.

6.4.4 Behavioural Analysis

The first, and probably most important, source of behavioural observations concerns the *vehicle passages* registered by automated roadside equipment. Two networked observation systems were installed. A first system used license plate recognition cameras. A second system used Electronic Vehicle Identification (EVI) beacons that were connected with an on-board unit (OBU) installed in the participant's car. Both the EVI beacons and recognition cameras were installed at the exit of Zoetermeer on all roads belonging to the corridor studied.

Although the dual setup introduces redundancy, both systems have specific advantages. The EVI/OBU system proved to have an extraordinary reliability of 99.99%, but is, of course, limited to equipped vehicles. The reliability of the camera system is in the 94–98% range, but the camera system is more tamper-proof (no OBU in the participant's car) and allowed to follow up the use of other cars available to the participant (as far as they were registered in our database). For our analysis, we use – in the merged table of both observation systems – the observation (if any on a specific day) that is closest to 8.30 a.m. as an indication of the participant's behaviour during the morning rush hour.

A second source of behavioural information is the *logbook* (a travel diary). The participants completed for every working day (Monday-Friday) a web form presented on a personal webpage. The form collected information on trip motive (commute or other), transport mode used (or telework), and possibly the use of the participant's car by a different driver, or the participant using a different car. The data were automatically coded and saved in a database.

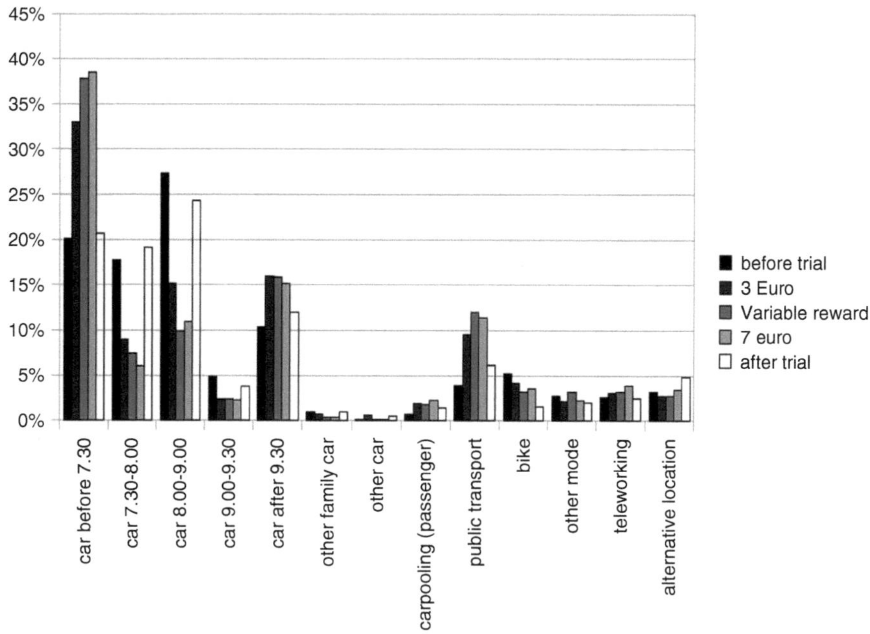

Fig. 6.1 Travel decisions for commuting trips as a function of monetary reward scheme

In our study of travel behaviour we focus on commuting behaviour. Figure 6.1 presents the travel decisions made by participants that opted for a monetary reward stimulus. The number of rush hour trips is roughly cut by half. As an alternative, most trips were rescheduled to take place before the rush hour or, to a lesser extent, after the rush hour.

Figure 6.2 provides more details on the share of different departure times. There is a clear shift away from the rush hour mainly towards time intervals immediately before or after the rush hour.

The main conclusion from the first experiment is that there is a group of flexible car travellers who, when offered rewards, whether monetary or in the form of a Yeti, can substantially decrease the number of car trips during the rush hour. Both variants result in a decrease of 50 per cent of the total number of car trips. The most important behavioural adjustment is departure time adjustment. Next comes the use of public transport, the use of which doubles as indicated by the respondents, but remains small, given the low reference value.

Another important observation is that a relatively low reward (3 €) results in a significant effect in avoiding traffic. The additional value of higher rewards is relatively small.

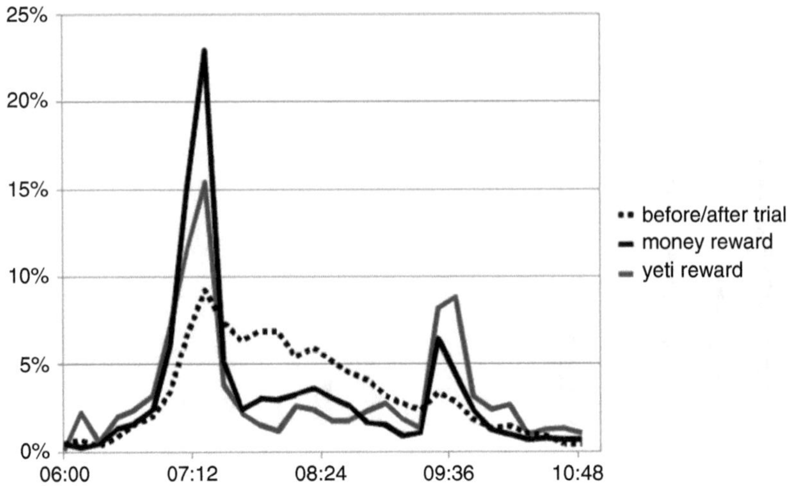

Fig. 6.2 Share of departure times

6.5 Spitsmijden 2A: A12 Gouda-Den Haag

A second reward experiment was conducted in order to study behavioural effects over a longer period of time. The route on which rewards were offered was the section of the A12 between Gouda and The Hague (Fig. 6.3). For the trial, the route was divided into two separate zones, with Oostweg in Zoetermeer (exit 7) marking the boundary between them. The peak period was determined before the commencement of the trial, again based on travel times measured in both zones. The peak period determined for the Gouda-The Hague trial is 06.30–09.30 a.m. for zone 1 (Gouda-Zoetermeer) and 07.00–09.30 a.m. for zone 2 (Zoetermeer-Gouda).

A total of 567 drivers participated in the experiment on the Gouda-Zoetermeer route. On the Zoetermeer- The Hague route, 705 drivers took part. Of these, 505 participated on both routes. Most participants had a baseline level of three trips per week or more. As in the first experiment, financial rewards were used as a positive incentive to encourage drivers to avoid the morning peak period. This reward was based on the behaviour of participants measured during the reference measurements (April to June 2008), prior to the trial. The participants were rewarded with 4 € per zone for each 'avoidance' compared to their reference rush hour travel frequency.

In analysing changes in travel behaviour, we look at how behaviour during the trial differs from when there are no rewards. We also investigate whether behaviour changes during the trial itself: is there a difference between the short and the long term?

The main part of our analysis is based on the camera observation records. We selected the best measurement data (meaning the best 'days'), in order to effectively analyse behaviour. This selection is based on a comparison of the intensity data

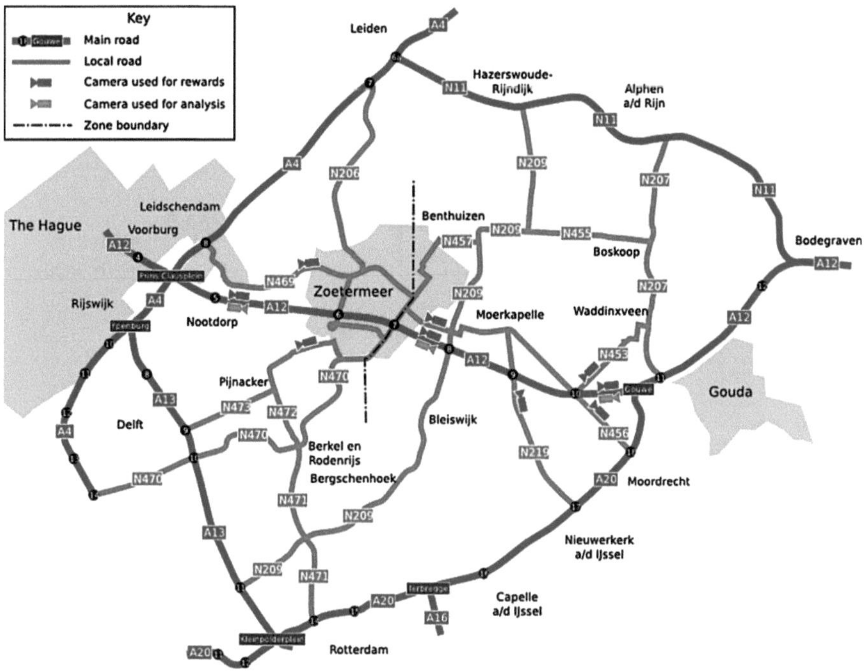

Fig. 6.3 The Spitsmijden area (the first experiment was limited to the western zone)

from the cameras on the A12 with the observation data from the induction loops built into the road.

A first examination concerns the number of trips made by participants both inside and outside the morning rush hour. Figure 6.4 presents the count statistics at the Nootdorp observation point (zone 2).

We observe a sharp cut in the number of rush hour trips by roughly 50%, coinciding with the reward trial. During the reward period, behaviour is remarkably stable. Observations at other camera locations confirm this picture.

More details on the choice of departure time are presented in Fig. 6.5, covering a selection of weeks before and during the reward experiment. The behavioural response to the reward is similar to what we observed in the first experiment. Moreover, we found that the response was stable throughout the experiment.

As with the first experiment, participants were instructed to complete a web based travel diary (but now for a selection of weeks only). The picture revealed by this information is in line with the earlier experiment, and confirms that modal choice contributed only to a modest degree in avoiding the congested roads compared to the contribution of departure time adjustments.

The larger geographical scale of the second experiment enabled a spatial alternative that was practically unavailable for participants in the first experiment. By choosing for a detour on the main road network, participants could realise a reward without temporal or modal behavioural change. Lacking observations on parallel

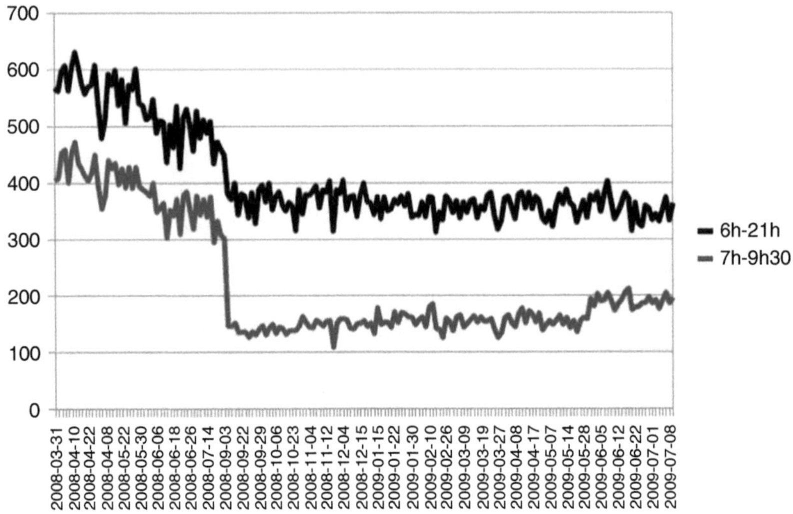

Fig. 6.4 Daily trip count at Nootdorp

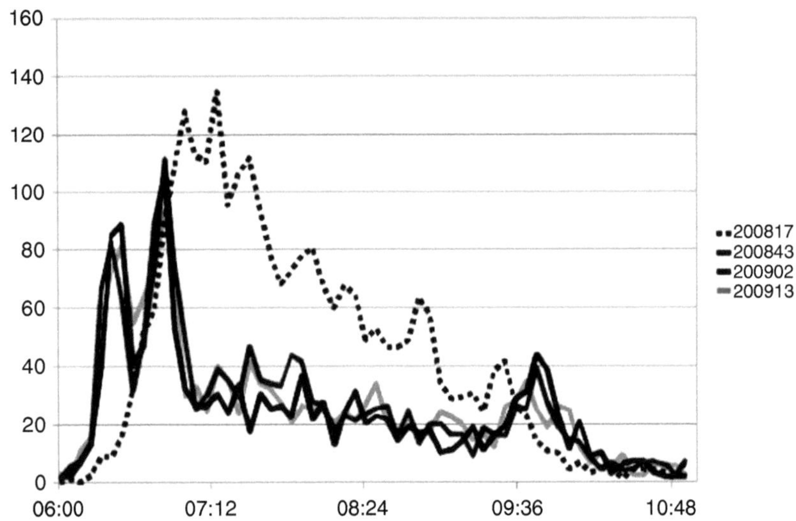

Fig. 6.5 Distribution of trips over the morning peak hour at Nootdorp (week 17 of 2008 is before the experiment, the other weeks are selected during the experiment)

main roads make it difficult to establish exact figures on the contribution of this travel alternative. But indirect derivations, based on return trips, provide us with an indication that detouring likely constituted a secondary alternative in abating A12 rush hour travel, with a contribution that may be about 20% of the avoided rush hour trips on the A12.

The second Spitsmijden experiment confirmed the results by the first one, and leads us to the conclusion that also over a longer time period Spitsmijden remains an effective transport demand management tool.

6.6 Spitsmijden 2 C: NS Utrecht-Den Haag

A third and final reward experiment in the framework of the TRANSUMO research programme focussed on public transport travellers.

Past research on behavioural aspects of transport infrastructure congestion traditionally focuses on demand for capacity on road networks. The reference behavioural paradigm is the *bottleneck model* introduced by Vickrey (1969), that describes how in a user equilibrium queuing occurs, when travellers trade off travel time for rescheduling efforts that come with less-than-ideal arrival (or departure) times.

The strictly scheduled nature of rail public transport results in minimal variation of travel times between peak versus off-peak. Therefore, for the study of preferences of rush hour train passengers, a different behavioural model needs to be developed. Moreover, with the train operator a new player enters the game, where travellers buy services from the operator, which in turn buys capacity from the infrastructure manager. The different nature of supply and demand for rail services was a key motivation in setting up a separate experiment to explore the opportunities for using a reward to manage temporal peaks in demand.

The study of rail travellers' behaviour is based on two sets of observations. A first set is obtained from a rail travellers panel based survey, and focused on the variables that determine passengers' choice for peak hour travel. A second set is obtained from a field experiment, where travellers were invited to trade in their travel pass for an off-peak one. For both experiments, the reward system considered concerns a discount on a season ticket (monthly or yearly pass), which turns it into an off-peak travel pass with the restriction that it is no longer valid during the peak, but that it is possible to buy a day specific upgrade to travel during the peak after all.

6.6.1 Panel Survey

The first part of the experiment consisted of a conjoint choice experiment. The choice experiment was developed to allow for the design and estimation of a quantitative behavioural model, to be used for the analysis of Spitsmijden as a public transport demand management tool. The conjoint choice experiment was included in a web based survey. The survey started out with registering usual travel behaviour of the respondent, after which the respondents were asked to assess a number of fictitious choice situation. Each choice situation presented the situation where an off-peak travel pass would be available, with its characteristics varying over the choice sets.

The different off-peak travel pass variables included in the choice sets, covered time of travel, rebate (compared to an unrestricted travel pass) and cost of a 1 day upgrade of the off-peak travel pass to allow for peak hour travel. If choosing for the off-peak travel pass, the respondent was asked to indicate how she/he would adapt the originally stated travel behaviour.

The respondents were sampled from the 100 k + passengers panel managed by the Dutch railways (NS). Sampling was limited to panel members having a travel pass covering a 30–70 km travel distance (one way). A 40% response rate was registered.

The dataset obtained by the conjoint choice experiment allowed for the estimation of a series of discrete choice model specifications. Analysis of the choice behaviour identifies a selection of travellers that are able to avoid peak hour travel, if there would be a financial stimulus to do so. Within the range of attribute levels presented in the choice experiment, about 20% of the choices made concerned the off-peak travel pass.

The model coefficients allow determining the trade-off that rail travellers make between different choice variables. Respondents to the survey indicated that they were willing to shift one trip an hour earlier or later in exchange for a 4 € rebate on the travel pass nominal tariff. At the same time, the same individual would accept to pay only 2.30 € for an upgrade that relieves the discomfort linked to a 1 h rescheduling of the trip. The difference in willingness-to-pay may well reflect the transaction costs associated with the purchase of an upgrade.

In a next step, the model was used for a serious of simulations, where the share of the off-peak travel pass as well as the amount of trip rescheduling, was studied as a function of attribute levels of the off-peak pass. The simulations revealed that the off-peak pass would potentially allow for a rescheduling of up to 5,8% of the original peak hour trips. On a 30–40 km trip this would cost the operator about 1.90 € per rescheduled trip (in lost revenue), or 0.05 € per seat kilometre. In the evaluation of a business case the operator would need to assess how this figure compares to peak hour production, assuming that off-peak marginal production costs are close to zero.

6.6.2 Field Experiment

A reward trial was conducted with travel pass holders on the Utrecht-The Hague railway line in the spring of 2009. 2,500 travel pass holders were approached using direct mail with the offer to exchange their traditional pass for an off-peak version. The off-peak pass came with a cash reimbursement amounting to roughly 20% of the nominal pass tariff. It would not be valid for peak-hour travel, defined as Monday to Friday between 7.30 and 9.00 a.m. Outside this period, the validity is identical to the original pass. The off-peak restriction applied to the rail part only in case of mixed bus-rail passes.

The participants had the option to upgrade the off-peak pass on a daily basis to match the validity of the original pass. The upgrade was priced such, that upgrading over the full period would result in an amount equal to the original reimbursement. As a result, the participant could never be worse off financially by participating. E-ticketing was used for the sale of the upgrades. An off-peak pass holder travelling during peak period and defaulting to produce a valid upgrade (or another valid transport title) upon inspection would be considered as travelling illegally and be eligible for a hefty charge (35 € plus regular ticket cost).

About 125 participants entered the experiment. One of the most obvious results (see Fig. 6.6) of the trial is that practically all trips by participants occurred in the off-peak period: only a very limited of upgrades was sold.

This behavioural observation can partly be explained by the travel behaviour before the trial started. Indeed: regular peak hour travel was not a requirement to enter the experiment, the proposition hence being very attractive for off-peak travellers whose only behavioural adaptation would be to cash the reimbursement.

Nevertheless, also the selection of peak hour travellers that entered the trial, nearly fully adapt the timing of their travel to avoid the defined peak period. It is observed that their regular time of travel was closer towards the start or end of the peak period, compared to what would be expected of the full population of peak hour travellers. For this group of peak shoulder travellers, a relatively small rescheduling effort suffices to time their entire trip outside the peak hour.

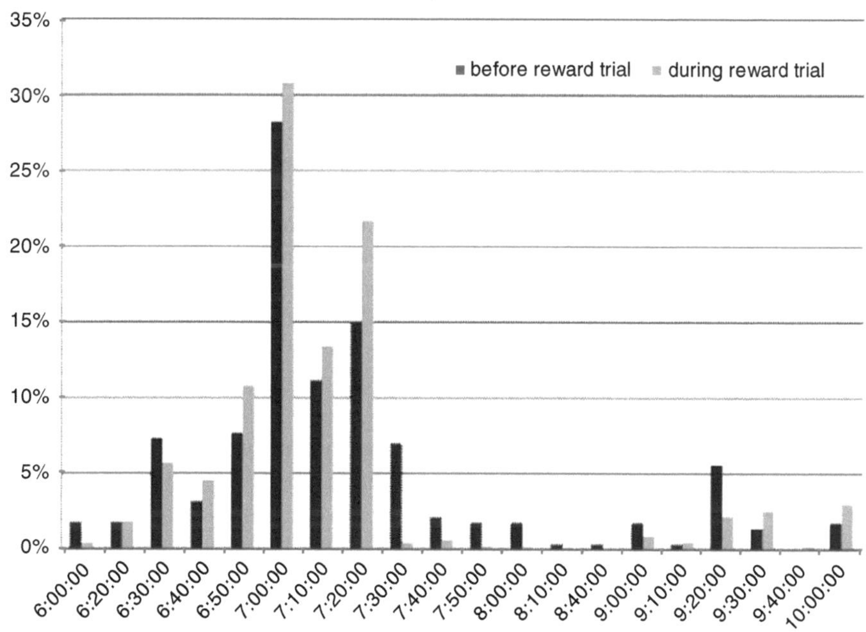

Fig. 6.6 Arrival at destination before and during the reward trial

The first public transport deployment of the Spitsmijden concept proved that there is a group of time-flexible rail travellers. A stated preference survey allowed for the qualitative assessment of responses by travellers to financial stimuli. A difficulty related to the rail application and that is unresolved in the first experiment, is the selection of regular peak travellers. Failing to do so risks the participation of travellers that already travel outside the peak and who cannot contribute to the goal of relieving peak demand levels.

6.7 Even More Spitsmijden: Lessons from Traffic Model Simulations

The conclusions of the first successful Spitsmijden experiment led to the decision to enhance and extend the understanding of the impact of rewards on transport demand by developing transport modelling tools. The experiment – limited both in time and space and with a limited focus on the congestion externality – had raised more questions than it answered. How would issues, related to scalability or geographical location, impact the tool's effectiveness? And how should the reward be positioned to abate different externalities?

A working group of different science institutes was established to conduct research and to develop and apply the required modelling tools. We will here only mention the main conclusions of the working group and refer to its report for the full story (Knockaert 2009). The different modelling exercises consistently identified the effectiveness of rewards as a transport policy tool. The transport models relate significant traffic impacts to a scaled up implementation of reward stimuli.

Comparing positive financial stimuli (rewards) to negative ones (charges), the models tell us that rewards are probably less effective and less efficient an instrument in taming transport demand. Differences in performance of both tools increase with the demand elasticity (here a measure for latent demand). But, obviously, one might prefer a reward as a policy instrument, in particular when acceptability or flexibility is an issue. Furthermore, the modelling exercises demonstrated that positive and negative stimuli can coexist when budget neutrality is a condition; the efficiency of such an arrangement naturally falls between that of pure rewards and pure charges.

The models provide us with an important understanding of edge impact that arise both in time and space. A key determinant of these effects is the definition of the peak period and the level of the corresponding reward. A peak period that is too small (compared to the original timing of congestion) may result in an ineffective instrument. A reward that is too high, results in congestion outside the defined peak period. The uniform character of the reward stimulus implies a rather small range beyond which the reward looses effectiveness and efficiency.

6.8 Conclusions

Within the framework of the TRANSUMO research programme, an extended series of Spitsmijden experiments was conducted. The different studies, applying both stated and revealed preference approaches, all focussed on the same objective of identifying the aspects of using positive financial stimuli to influence rush hour travel behaviour.

A key empirical lesson from the experiment is the identification of a group of flexible travellers who are able to reschedule their trips and are willing to do so in exchange for a relatively modest reward. In road applications, the observed reduction in peak hour trips amounted to roughly 50% when a reward was used.

The primary response to avoid rush hour travel is the rescheduling of trips. A secondary response may consist of rerouting trips conditional upon implementation variables (obviously the availability of parallel routes is a key variable here). Modal choice, in contrast, does not contribute significantly to the reduction of peak hour travel, an observation implying that modal shift should not be a primary focus of supporting measures that aim to increase the reduction in peak hour trips. The reward instrument proved to be relatively easy to implement, but the effective recruitment of participants in public transport applications is still an uncharted area of the concept.

The design and application of simulation modelling tools has extended the understanding of the reward instrument and revealed potential performance hits, when the scale of the reward passes beyond a threshold or when the reward conditions are poorly defined.

References

Ampt E (2003) Understanding voluntary travel behaviour change. Paper presented at 26th Australasian transport research forum, Wellington

Anderson SP, de Palma A, Thisse J-F (1992) Discrete choice theory of product differentiation. MIT Press, Cambridge

Arnott R, De Palma A, Lindsey R (1993) Economics of a bottleneck. J Urban Econ 27(1):111–130

Beckmann MJ, McGuire CB, Winsten CB (1956) Studies in the economics of transportation. Yale University Press, New Haven

Ben-Akiva M, Lerman SR (1985) Discrete choice analysis: theory and application to travel demand. MIT Press, Cambridge

Eriksson L, Garvill J, Nordlund AM (2008) Interrupting habitual car use: the importance of car habit strength and moral motivation for personal car use reduction. Transp Res F 11(1):10–23

Jakobsson C, Fuji S, Gärling T (2002) Effects of economic disincentives on private car use. Transportation 29(4):349–370

Jensen-Butler C, Sloth B, Larsen MM, Madsen B, Nielsen OA (2008) Road pricing, the economy and the environment. Springer, Berlin

Knockaert J (2009) Spitsmijden: het modelverhaal. Technical report, Rossum, The Netherlands

Knockaert J, Bliemer M, Ettema D, Joksimovic D, Mulder A, Rouwendal J, Amelsfort van D (2007) Experimental design and modelling. Technical report, Rossum, The Netherlands:

Spitsmijden Consortium. http://www.spitsmijden.nl/resultaten/Experimental_design_and_modelling_-_Spitsmijden.pdf. Accessed 1 Feb 2008

Lévy-Lambert H (1968) Tarification des services à qualité variable: application aux péages de circulation. Econometrica 36(3–4):564–574

Marchand M (1968) A note on optimal tolls in an imperfect environment. Econometrica 36 (3–4):575–581

Petty RE, Caciappo JT (1986) Elaboration likelihood model of persuasion. In: Berkovitz L (ed) Advances in experimental social psychology. Academic, New-York, pp 123–205

Pigou AC (1920) The economics of welfare, 1st edn. Macmillan, London. Chapter VIII: Divergences between marginal trade net product and marginal individual net product, pp 189–196

Rouwendal J, Verhoef ET, Knockaert J (2010) Give or take? Rewards vs. charges for a congested bottleneck. TI discussion papers series. Ext. rep. 10-062/3, Tinbergen Instituut (TI), Amsterdam

Santos G (2004) Road pricing: theory and evidence. Elsevier, Amsterdam

Small KA, Gómez-Ibáñez JA (1998) Road pricing for congestion management: the transition from theory to policy. In: Button KJ, Verhoef ET (eds) Road pricing, traffic congestion and the environment: issues of efficiency and social feasibility. Edward Elgar, Cheltenham, pp 213–246

Small KA, Verhoef ET (2007) The economics of urban transportation. Routledge, London

Stopher PR (2004) Reducing road congestion: a reality check. Transp Policy 11(2):117–131

Train K (1990) Qualitative choice analysis: theory, econometrics, and an application to automobile demand. MIT Press, Cambridge (Original work published 1986)

Train KE (2003) Discrete choice methods with simulation. Cambridge University Press, Cambridge

Vickrey WS (1963) Pricing in urban and suburban transport. Am Econ Rev 53:452–465

Vickrey WS (1969) Congestion theory and transport investment. Am Econ Rev 59:251–260

Walters AA (1961) The theory and measurement of private and social cost of highway congestion. Econometrica 29(4):676–697

Chapter 7
Managing Supply Chains: Transport Optimization and Chain Synchronization

Tom Van Woensel, Said Dabia, and Ton de Kok

7.1 Introduction

Transport optimization is part of the broad area of physical distribution and logistics management. Physical distribution involves the handling, movement, and storage of goods from the point of origin to their point of consumption or use, via various channels of distribution. Logistics management involves the management of these operations for efficient and cost effective physical distribution (Ghiani et al. 2004).

7.1.1 Inefficiencies

Coyle et al. (1996) report that approximately 40–50% of the total retail logistics costs are due to transportation. A UK study (McKinnon 1999) showed that almost one quarter of all road freight movements (measured in tonne-kms) are due to the retail sector and this share is still growing due to the increasing demands of the customers. Moreover in the same study, it was also shown that in 22% of all cases the trucks were running empty and the average truck utilization was only around 75%. All studies clearly demonstrate the potential operational improvements in transportation. A major reason for these inefficiencies is due to the inability to better represent real-life environments. In real life, accidents occur, travel times depend upon the moment one leaves the distribution center (and on many more factors), road networks are congested, demand varies, etc. All these dynamic and stochastic phenomena are rarely considered or are treated as deterministic and static in the transportation planning tools. Obviously, the world is dynamic and stochastic

T. Van Woensel (✉) • S. Dabia • T. de Kok
School of Industrial Engineering, Technische Universiteit Eindhoven, Den Dolech 2, 513, Eindhoven, MB 5600, 5612AZ, The Netherlands
e-mail: t.v.woensel@tue.nl; s.dabia@tue.nl; a.g.d.kok@tue.nl

J.A.E.E. van Nunen et al. (eds.), *Transitions Towards Sustainable Mobility*, 119
DOI 10.1007/978-3-642-21192-8_7, © Springer-Verlag Berlin Heidelberg 2011

and does not fit into a deterministic and static straitjacket. Moreover, any schedule built on these unrealistic assumptions is bound to be sub-optimal once realized. The impact of these dynamic components will be even more important when relating the approaches developed to urban contexts.

Furthermore, note that the last 50 m are becoming more and more dominant in the retail supply chains. On the other hand, we observe that this last link in the supply chain is also the weakest in terms of operational performance. Although manufacturers manage to deliver with over 99% reliability to the retailer's distribution centers or the stores, the on-shelf availability in many cases does not even reach 90%. One natural way to remain competitive is to reduce and/or manage costs in key areas, which is traditionally the key focus of supply chain management/operations management. Finally, we observed that the key player in physical distribution and logistics management is becoming more and more the shipper of the goods (e.g. retailers, manufacturers, etc.) rather than the transportation companies or the Logistics Service Providers (LSP).

7.1.2 The Road Ahead

We capture the real world complexities across their logistical processes and investigate how we can optimize those models separately, thereby taking into account the interactions between them. This chapter is organized along the different research lines we have been working on the past years for the TRAN-SUMO project. More specifically, we first focus on the research on transport optimization, including the vehicle routing work and secondly, on the supply chain synchronization issues.

7.2 Transport Optimization

Due to the real-life complexities, coping with these dynamic and stochastic environments is a critical and difficult problem, both in an offline and in an online setting. Offline means the generation of schedules beforehand (e.g. before the working day); Online refers to the actual realization of the schedule (e.g. during the working day). Typically, in the offline setting, one can plan either taking into account only deterministic and static information or one could take into account the stochasticity and the dynamics from real-life. Bertsimas and Simchi-Levi (1996) provide an interesting survey of static (i.e. time-independent) vs. dynamic (i.e. time-dependent) routing problems (e.g. the travel time being a function of the time of the day due to traffic congestion) as well as deterministic *vs.* stochastic routing problems (i.e. depending on whether some of the characteristics follow a certain probability distribution or not; typical examples are probabilistic demand quantities or probabilistic travel times).

The first situation (deterministic and static) has been the subject of research for decades. More and more, the literature is shifting towards considering some stochasticity and dynamics in the models. On a simultaneous track, some researchers immediately go to the online setting. In the online setting, we react to changes in the real-life environment during the execution of the prepared schedule. Decision makers typically try to repair the (off-line prepared) schedules considering the realizations so-far and some extra knowledge of the future. In these repair policies, stochastic or dynamic information about the remaining future time horizon is rarely considered. Similarly, from a governmental point of view, policy makers aim at an equal load on the road network. Offline, this implies that the road network configuration and the resulting traffic flows should be optimized (e.g. closing missing links, etc.). Online, this leads e.g. to the use of Dynamic Route Information Panels (DRIPs) to guide people through the network to ensure a better load balance.

Within TRANSUMO, we mainly worked on the offline side, looking at vehicle routes from a companies' perspective.

7.2.1 *Starting Point*

The main starting point of the research so far, is that a good schedule beforehand (offline) is better than to extensively repair during the realization of this schedule (online). Despite numerous publications dealing with efficient offline routing scheduling methods, very few addressed the inherent stochastic and dynamic nature of reality. Consequently, we mainly worked in the offline setting, with a strong focus on adding stochasticity and dynamics related to traffic congestion into the company's transportation decision problems, i.e. Vehicle Routing Problems (VRP). The objective of the VRP is to find the minimum cost vehicle routes such that every customer is visited exactly once by exactly one vehicle in its designated time window; all vehicle routes start and end at the depot; every vehicle is serving a total demand not exceeding the vehicle capacity; and every vehicle route has a length not exceeding a maximum length (Laporte 1992).

Traditionally, total transportation costs are calculated in terms of distances, i.e. overall distance traveled is minimized. The routes obtained as such are sub-optimal when applied in real-life. Clearly, if congestion occurs, the assumption of deterministic and static travel times is not valid anymore. Most traffic networks in Europe face high utilization levels, and consequently, congestion occurs. For a sufficiently high utilization, the smallest stochastic event causes waiting, which in the case of traffic systems, materialize in lower speeds. As speeds changes, travel times vary with time for a given distance. So all transportation problems which intend to minimize distance or time, are subject to these physical considerations of congestion. It is argued that routes should thus be constructed based on minimizing travel time rather than on minimizing distance.

7.2.2 Towards Time-Dependent Routing Problems

A time-dependent travel time component is added to the traditional vehicle routing formulation. The reasoning behind this is that leaving a customer a time x gives a different travel time compared to leaving at time $x + \delta$. This reasoning is added in the VRP and we developed specific meta-heuristics that deal with this time-dependent environment (i.e. a time-inflated graph). Note that the VRP is NP-hard (i.e. not likely to be solvable in polynomial time), as it can be reduced to a TSP which is shown to be NP-hard. The time-dependency significantly adds to this complexity of the VRP as then the solution space also grows exponentially with the number of time buckets considered. Theoretically, for every time bucket a different travel time distribution is needed to generate the relevant input data (e.g. expected travel time). The more information one can take into account of this travel time distribution, the more of the travel time stochasticity is considered.

In Van Woensel et al. (2005), both the static and the dynamic Vehicle Routing Problem (VRP) were solved using two heuristics (Tabu Search and Ant Colony Optimization). Results for a large number of datasets showed that the total travel times can be improved significantly when explicitly taking into account congestion during the optimization. Explicitly making use of the time-dependent congestion results in routes that are (considerably) shorter in terms of travel time. The average improvement achieved is 25.4% when looking at the Tabu Search heuristic and 22.2% when looking at the Ant Colony Optimization heuristic.

The analysis in Van Woensel et al. (2008) demonstrated the added value of adding the variance of the travel times in the optimization. Results showed that the variability of the routes significantly decreased depending on the weight given to the variance component in the objective function. Not taking into account travel time variability gave highly variable routes in all sets analyzed. A relatively small weight on the variance component yielded already significant gains in the planning process. Computational results suggested that in a dynamic environment, it is crucially important to explicitly consider the variability due to traffic congestion. The impact of these dynamic components will be even more important when relating the approach to urban contexts.

Kerbache and Van Woensel (2005) demonstrated a similar approach for small test sets for the vehicle routing problem with the addition of time windows. Preliminary results showed that the total lateness of the route can be improved significantly when explicitly taking into account congestion during the optimization. It is clear that using the information of dynamic travel times due to congestion, results in routes that are considerably better in terms of meeting the time window constraints imposed by the customers.

7.2.3 A multi-objective Time-Dependent Single Capacitated Vehicle Routing Problem with Time Windows

Consider the situation in which a vehicle is required to fill up money distributing machines located at different places from a central bank. For security reasons, it is not allowed to carry a large amount of money. Consequently, the vehicle is forced to make several short tours during its operating period (e.g. a working day) going back and forth to the central bank. Similarly, in the case of food home delivery, tours are relatively short as products are perishable (e.g. should remain warm) and thus need to be delivered as soon as possible to their destinations Azi et al. (2007). This again leads to multiple tours of the same vehicle. Clearly, a vehicle can make several tours during its designated operating time, respecting the vehicle's capacity for each tour. A logistics company we are currently working with, aims at scheduling its fleet such that a vehicle's total travel time is minimized, its capacity utilization is maximized and all customers get delivered in their specific time windows. This illustrates the importance to consider multiple dimensions for the objective function in the scheduling problem.

Formally, we consider a Multi-Objective Time-Dependent Single Capacitated Vehicle Routing Problem with Time Windows (denoted as MO-TD-SCVRP-TW). More specifically, a single vehicle departs from a central depot (denoted by 0), performs several tours to serve a set of geographically scattered customers and returns to the same depot. The vehicle routing problem at hand is capacitated on two dimensions: on the vehicle capacity (truckload) and on the time capacity. Time capacity means that the vehicle is only available for a limited amount of time, e.g. due to drivers' availability following the working regulations. Because of these vehicle and time capacity limitations, it might not be possible to serve all customers. Therefore, we need to decide on a subset of customers to be actually served. Finally, because of road congestion, travel times are time-dependent: depending on the specific departure time at a customer, a different travel time is incurred. Customers have time windows and these are considered to be hard. However, since customers are not directly harmed by possible waiting times, the vehicle is allowed to wait if it arrives early at a customer. Rather than using a single objective function in which each of the to be optimized dimensions is weighted, we consider a multi-objective cost function. Here, we minimize the total travel time including any waiting times (due to time windows), while the total quantity delivered by the vehicle is maximized.

In this work, we present an exact time-dependent Dynamic Programming (DP) algorithm (denoted as DP_{Exact}) which generates all feasible solutions in its in-between iterations, and keeps only the non-dominated ones in its final iteration. This rather primitive structure of DP_{Exact} is due to time-dependency of travel times. In fact, time-dependent travel times allow constructing non-dominated routes from dominated ones derived in earlier iterations. Therefore, optimizing the objective function in the in-between iterations may lead to dominated final solutions. By assuming travel costs to be positive integers, and imposing some structure on customers' time windows, we show that DP_{Exact} is pseudo-polynomial. However, solving large instances by means of DP_{Exact} is computationally hard. In practice, the assumed time windows' structure (e.g. non-overlapping time windows) may be encountered when, for example, delivery companies impose their own time windows on customers. To improve its efficiency, we make some additional assumptions concerning the structure of travel times and enhance the DP_{Exact} into two important directions:

1. By assuming travel time profiles that adhere to the FIFO assumption, we develop a modified exact DP based algorithm (denoted as DP_{Exact}^{FIFO}) based on the non-dominance principle. The FIFO assumption prevents constructing non-dominated routes from dominated ones. Hence, in each iteration of DP_{Exact}^{FIFO}, not all feasible solutions but only the set of non-dominated ones are kept. The complexity is considerably reduced.
2. By making one additional assumption regarding the structure of travel times, we develop an approximate time-dependent DP based algorithm (denoted as $DP_{Approx}^{\varepsilon}$), where ε is the approximation's worst case precision. We interfere with the execution of DP_{Exact}^{FIFO} by reducing, in each iteration, the set of non-dominated solutions by using a trimming method. Consequently, the complexity of DP_{Exact}^{FIFO} is reduced. The worst case performance of the approximate DP is guaranteed and its running time is polynomially bounded.

Vehicle routing problems are NP-hard. Hence, reasonably sized instances are unlikely to be solved to optimality in polynomial time. Consequently, these types of problems are usually dealt with using (meta-)heuristics, which deliver good solutions in reasonable computation times (see e.g. Braysy and Gendreau (2005a, b); Taillard et al. (1997) for some good reviews). Next to heuristics, many researchers have adopted exact approaches to handle VRPs. In Azi et al. (2007) and Gribkovskaia et al. (2008), a SVRP with time windows and multiple tours, and a SVRP with pickups and deliveries are optimized based on exact integer programming formulations. Other exact approaches (i.e. Branch-and-cut, cutting planes) have been applied to deal with VRPs (Kulkarni and Bhave 1985). In Malandraki and Dial (1996), a restricted DP heuristic is proposed to solve the time-dependent traveling salesman problem (TSP). In each iteration of the restricted DP, only a subset (hence "restricted") with a predefined size and consisting of the best solutions is kept and used to compute solutions in the next iteration. Time-dependency in dynamic programming was first introduced by Kostreva and Wiecek (1993) to solve a path-planning problem. In Klamroth and Wiecek (2000, 2001), time-dependent dynamic programming is used to deal with single machine scheduling and capital budgeting problems.

7.2.3.1 Overview of the Algorithms

We developed three algorithms based on a dynamic programming formulation: the DP_{Exact}, the DP_{Exact}^{FIFO} and the $DP_{Approx}^{\varepsilon}$. By assuming some structure on the common band, DP_{Exact} turns out to be pseudo-polynomial. It produces the Pareto-optimal front without assuming the FIFO property. Because of time-dependent travel times, DP_{Exact} generates and stores all distinct feasible solutions in its in-between iterations. By assuming the FIFO property, we formulated the DP_{Exact}^{FIFO}. The FIFO assumption prevents constructing Pareto-optimal routes based on dominated routes. Therefore, the DP_{Exact}^{FIFO} is designed in such a way that only distinct Pareto-optimal routes are kept in its in-between iterations. DP_{Exact}^{FIFO} is also pseudo-polynomial, it

Table 7.1 Overview of the different DP models

Algorithm	DP_{Exact}	DP^{FIFO}_{Exact}	$DP^{\varepsilon}_{Approx}$
Assumptions	1	1 and 2	1, 2 and 3
Structure	All distinct feasible generated and stored in the in-between iterations and distinct Pareto-optimal ones are kept in the final iteration	Only distinct Pareto-optimal solutions are generated and stored in all iterations	In each iteration not all Pareto-optimal solutions are stored but only those that are considerably distinct from each other
Complexity	$O(N^2TQ)$ Pseudo-polynomial	$O(N^2 min(T,Q))$ Pseudo-polynomial	$O(N^2L_1L_2)$ polynomial

produces the Pareto-optimal front and its complexity is lower compared to DP_{Exact}. However, to solve larger instances, the $DP^{\varepsilon}_{Approx}$ is developed. The $DP^{\varepsilon}_{Approx}$ has a provable worse case performance ε when an additional assumption is made with regard to the structure of travel times. Moreover, its complexity is polynomially bounded in the input size and in $\frac{1}{\varepsilon}$. Table 7.1 summarizes the presented algorithms and their complexities.

7.2.3.2 The Giant Tour Representation

When the vehicle capacity Q is the binding constraint, the time used up for the first tour might be less than the vehicle's total time availability T. Therefore, we can still use the vehicle for its remaining time to schedule a second tour (or more if time allows). One could use the one tour model for the remaining set of non-served customers and the remaining vehicle's time availability. This second tour will be non-dominated with regard to the new instance. However, because of time dependency, the schedule consisting of both tours might be sub-optimal. Therefore, this greedy approach will not be performing good. In what follows, we explain how we adapt the *giant tour* representation to our problem. Using the *giant tour* representation introduced by Funke et al. (2005), we can reduce the multiple tour model to a single tour model. As such, all results derived for the single tour MO-TD-SCVRP-TW in the previous section can be applied.

A formal description of the *giant tour* representation can be found in Funke et al. (2005). Many other researchers adopted the idea of the *giant tour* representation to transform the m-TSP to a standard TSP (Laporte et al. 1988; GuoXing 1995). Therefore, the result from the standard TSP can be applied to an extended graph describing the *giant tour* representation of the m-TSP. In our case, the case of a multiple tour single VRP, the solution is a set of Pareto-optimal schedules. Each schedule is a collection of routes all starting and ending at the depot. The modeling idea is to add dummy depots representing duplications of the real depot to the existing graph. Routes of a given schedule can then be linked via the dummy nodes into a long (*giant*) tour. Figure 7.1 gives the schedule $\{0-3-6-4-0, 0-2-5-0,$

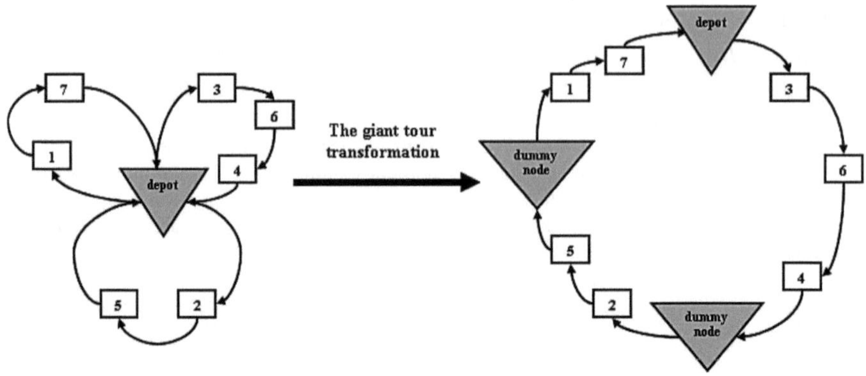

Fig. 7.1 The giant tour representation

$0-1-7-0\}$, after a *giant tour* transformation, as $\{0-3-6-4-0-2-5-0-1-7-0\}$ where 0 denotes the depot.

Funke et al. (2005) showed that the order of routes is not important. However, because of time-dependency, the order of routes is very important in our case. Since a schedule is equivalent to its *giant tour* representation, the results derived for the one tour SVRP can be directly applied to find the set of Pareto-optimal giant tours. The maximum amount of dummy nodes that can be added to the existing graph is $N-1$. This is the case when all N customers are served and during every tour only one customer is served. Moreover, when a schedule consists of $N-1$ tour, the total quantity delivered is bounded by $(N-1)Q$. Therefore, the complexity of DP_{Exact} in case of the Multiple Tour Model is proportional to: $O((N-1)(2N-1)^2T^2Q) = O(N^3TQ)$.

7.2.4 Some Results

We consider three different classes of instances depending on the geographic location of customers (R: random; C: clustered; RC: randomly clustered). The customers' location as well as their demand are taken from Solomon's data sets. However, time windows are modified in such a way that the common band structure is satisfied. Furthermore, congestion is taken into account. This is achieved by assuming that the speed on each link is time-dependent and derive the travel time profile by using the relation $tt_{ij}(t) = \frac{d_{ij}}{v_{ij}(t)}$ where d_{ij}, distance between customers i and j, are computed based on Solomon's data sets. The resulting travel times satisfy both the FIFO assumption and assumption 3, and have the profile illustrated in Fig. 7.2. Service times are included in travel times and always taken to be 90 min.

Furthermore, we consider the following experimental design: Instances = $\{C101, C201, R101, R201, RC101, RC201\}$

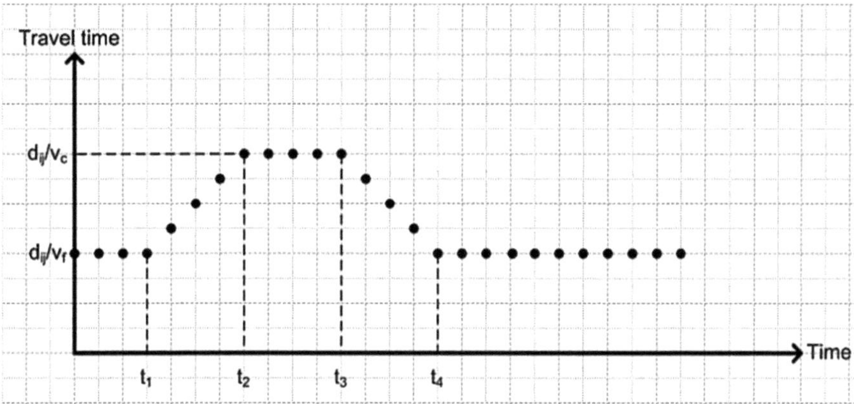

Fig. 7.2 Travel time profile

$v_c = 50$ km/hr, $v_f = 100$ km/hr
$N = \{50, 100\}$
$T = \{800, 1{,}550, 3{,}050\}$
$Q = \{100, 200\}$
$CB = \{20, 60\}$
This results in 144 experiments. A larger T allows for more tours and a larger Q allows for including more customers in a tour.

To compare the different Pareto fronts generated, we define two measures introduced by Zitzler: the two-set coverage metric and the average distance metric. The choice of the metrics is motivated by their intuitive explanation.

The *two-set coverage* metric is defined as:

$$C(X \succ Y) = \frac{|\{y \in Y;\ \exists x \in X : x \,\text{dominates}\, y\}|}{|Y|} \tag{7.1}$$

in which X and Y are two Pareto curves. The two-set coverage metric calculates the fraction of solutions in Y that are dominated by a solution in X. $C(X \succ Y)$ has values between 0 and 1. For example, $C(X \succ Y) = 1$ (respectively $C(X \succ Y) = 0$) means that every (respectively no) solution of Y is dominated by a solution of X. Both $C(X \succ Y)$ and $C(Y \succ X)$ should be reported since $C(X \succ Y)$ does not necessarily equal $1 - C(Y \succ X)$. However, since X corresponds to the optimal Pareto-front, we always have $C(Y \succ X) = 0$. Therefore, only $C(X \succ Y)$ will be reported.

Secondly, the *average distance* metric is defined as:

$$M(X, Y) = \frac{1}{|X|} \sum_{x \in X} min\{||x - y||;\ y \in Y\} \tag{7.2}$$

in which ||.|| is a distance metric. In our case, we take the euclidian distance as a distance metric. The metric M reflects how far two Pareto curves are from each other.

The algorithms DP^{FIFO}_{Exact} and DP_{Approx} are implemented on a Intel(R) Core(TM) 2 CPU, 2.13 GHz, 3 GB of RAM computer, in a Matlab R2008b environment. All instances and software is available from the authors upon request. Based on the results from Tables 7.2, 7.3 and 7.4, we conclude that, as expected, the accuracy of $DP^{\varepsilon}_{Approx}$ is excellent. For all instances, on average no more than 8% of the solutions generated by $DP^{0.01}_{Approx}$ are dominated by any of DP^{FIFO}_{Exact} solutions. Moreover, on average less than 23% of the $DP^{0.01}_{Approx}$ solutions are dominated by a DP^{FIFO}_{Exact} solution. Furthermore, the distance of the 0.01-Pareto approximate front from the optimal one is negligible (less than two in most cases). Moreover, even the distance of the 0.1-Pareto approximate front from the optimal one can be considered as very small compared to the magnitude of T and Q. However, the fraction of $DP^{\varepsilon}_{Approx}$ solutions dominated by a DP^{FIFO}_{Exact} solution increases slightly when randomness is added to the location of customers.

To illustrate the different Pareto fronts, we plotted these corresponding to an instance with a relatively bad accuracy, namely the R201.50 instance with the input parameters $T = 3{,}050$, $Q = 200$, and $CB = 20$. As expected, smaller values of the worst case precision ε result in a better Pareto front, i.e. closer to the one of DP^{FIFO}_{Exact}. In fact, the 0.01-Pareto approximate front practically coincides with the optimal one. Moreover, it is more dense as more solutions are kept during the execution of the DP. Furthermore, the deviation of a ε-Pareto approximate front from the optimal one increases as we proceed with the DP execution. However, the deviation stays within the worst case precision ε. Nonetheless, for most $DP^{\varepsilon}_{Approx}$ solutions, their relative deviation is much less than ε from a Pareto-optimal solution.

7.3 Supply Chain Synchronization

Supply chains are difficult to manage within a single company, let alone when it is managed by several companies each pursuing their own goals, as is the case with a retail supply chain. Over the past years new concepts in the literature have appeared on managing supply chains. Supply chain synchronization is one of them. As the name indicates, this concept deals with coordination of supply chain members. The basic idea of supply chain synchronization is that if stock is available in the chain, the best place for this stock should be at the end of the chain. In practice, this means that the manufacturer pushes its inventory as much as possible towards the retailers and retailers should push as much as possible their inventory into the stores. Supply chain synchronization involves thus the redesign of a retail supply chain by synchronizing distribution to production. Right from production goods should move downstream the supply chain at low cost in full pallets and in full truckloads, in quantities large enough to cover the needs until the next production run. By extending both the Newsvendor- and the EOQ-formulae to a multi-echelon divergent network, it can be proved that such forward positioning of inventory indeed is optimal and that overall supply chain inventories will drop. The suppliers

Table 7.2 The metrics *C* and *M* for the *C* instances

Instances	T	Q	CB	A	B	C	D
C101.50	**800**	**100**	**20**	0	0.11	0	0.98
			60	0	0.1	0	1.69
		200	**20**	0	0.11	0	1.05
			60	0	0.05	0	2.11
	1,550	**100**	**20**	0	0.1	0	4.28
			60	0.05	0.07	0.07	7.01
		200	**20**	0	0.2	0	7.03
			60	0.02	0.16	0.04	8.76
	3,050	**100**	**20**	0.16	0.33	18.9	46.84
			60	0.18	0.4	0.48	22.57
		200	**20**	0.17	0.39	0.86	33.97
			60	0.16	0.39	0.29	33.81
C101.100 800	**800**	**100**	**20**	0	0.06	0	0.58
			60	0	0.05	0	2.4
		200	**20**	0	0.09	0	1.17
			60	0	0	0	3.55
	1,550	**100**	**20**	0	0	0	4.9
			60	0	0.12	0	8.57
		200	**20**	0	0	0	6.31
			60	0	0.11	0	6.04
	3,050	**100**	**20**	0	0.31	0	21.02
			60	0.15	0.2	0	30.62
		200	**20**	0	0.23	0	17.75
			60	0.12	0.32	0.26	23.56
C201.50 800	**800**	**100**	**20**	0	0.11	0	2.15
			60	0	0.15	0	1.9
		200	**20**	0	0.17	0	3.44
			60	0	0.05	0	1.94
	1,550	**100**	**20**	0	0.07	0	4.17
			60	0	0.04	0	5.96
		200	**20**	0.02	0.13	0	5.25
			60	0.03	0.26	0.03	8.9
	3,050	**100**	**20**	0.05	0.47	0.45	32.5
			60	0.09	0.28	0.79	21.96
		200	**20**	0.16	0.67	0.94	36.1
			60	0.21	0.37	4.48	28.17
C201.100 800	**800**	**100**	**20**	0	0.05	0	1.83
			60	0	0.13	0	2.45
		200	**20**	0	0	0	1.51
			60	0	0	0	3.69
	1,550	**100**	**20**	0	0.03	0	6.29
			60	0.04	0.16	0.04	9.51
		200	**20**	0	0	0	4.92
			60	0.04	0.14	0.04	7.21
	3,050	**100**	**20**	0	0,21	0	21.68
			60	0	0.35	0.38	27.69

(continued)

Table 7.2 (continued)

Instances	T	Q	CB	A	B	C	D
		200	**20**	0	0.23	0	16.36
			60	0	0.37	0	25.38
Total						**28.05**	**577.53**
Average				**0.03**	**0.17**		

A $C(DP^{FIFO}_{Exact} \succ DP^{0.01}_{Approx})$, *B* $C(DP^{FIFO}_{Exact} \succ DP^{0.1}_{Approx})$, *C* $M(DP^{FIFO}_{Exact}, DP^{0.01}_{Approx})$, *D* $M(DP^{FIFO}_{Exact}, DP^{0.1}_{Approx})$

warehouses become stockless cross docking points, where goods from the suppliers from various sourcing plants are brought together to consolidate them into full truckloads. Whenever suppliers deliver lower volumes, they should better bring these goods to the nearest retailers facility; thereafter the retailer himself should move these goods onward to the proper destination within the retailers network. And finally shop replenishment should be rationalized based on shelf coverage, so as to enhance the retailers warehouse operations. Van der Vlist (2007) describes these kind of chains in detail (Fig. 7.3).

From an integral supply chain perspective, once a manufacturer's batch has been produced, the costs of it are borne and one has to make this inventory effective as soon as possible, and to move this inventory along the supply chain in the cheapest possible way. Relating these two challenges to the phenomena mentioned above, two solutions could be provided: (1) to make inventory as effective as possible it should thus be moved downstream the supply chain as soon and as much as possible. As will be demonstrated later, inventory should be moved preferably immediately after production to achieve overall minimum costs. (2) in order to move inventory along the supply chain in the cheapest possible way it should be moved in the largest possible quantities, preferably in full pallets and full truckloads.

When applying supply chain synchronization concepts, it is shown that the inventory costs decrease, the transaction costs decrease and that the transportation costs are decreased: a reduction up to 30% on overall transaction and inventory costs is observed in simulations. Moreover, it is better to have more safety stock and move it all downstream the supply chain thereby reducing most stock points to cross dock operations, with possible additional savings. Of course this concept is not new and has been described and practiced in different forms. It is however, an interesting idea to push inventory all the way down the chain to the place where it meets the customer immediately: retail outlets, *etc.*

Implementing supply chain synchronization is however, not trivial; several barriers have to be faced when implementing the concept. One of the first issues that has to be raised when implementing supply chain synchronization is the positioning of inventory; a difficult and not trivial problem. Retailer and manufacturer need to be willing to collaborate and exchange information on inventory levels, demand forecasts and production schedules. Both retailer and manufacturer need to adapt their processes and install proper functionality on their IT systems.

Table 7.3 The metrics *C* and *M* for the *C* instances

Instances	T	Q	CB	A	B	C	D
R101.50	**800**	**100**	**20**	0	0.23	0	2.66
			60	0	0.21	0.05	5.07
		200	**20**	0	0.23	0	2.66
			60	0	0.13	0.05	3.92
	1,550	**100**	**20**	0.02	0.17	1.03	8.6
			60	0.14	0.19	0.47	7.44
		200	**20**	0.04	0.25	0.46	11.24
			60	0.02	0.31	0.16	13.56
	3,050	**100**	**20**	0.39	0.17	3.64	24.7
			60	0.13	0.18	1.91	17.5
		200	**20**	0.47	0.44	3.58	27.06
			60	0.27	0.51	1.13	24.85
R101.100 800	**800**	**100**	**20**	0	0.03	0.06	2.23
			60	0	0.23	0.07	3,82
		200	**20**	0.02	0.03	0.07	2.48
			60	0	0.17	0.14	6.08
	1,550	**100**	**20**	0	0.29	0	9.9
			60	0.01	0	0.18	11.5
		200	**20**	0	0.21	0.02	11.54
			60	0.01	0.3	0.17	12.95
	3,050	**100**	**20**	0	0.31	0	18.66
			60	0.17	0.33	1.5	24.34
		200	**20**	0.1	0.29	1.02	18.58
			60	0.11	0.3	0.74	26.13
R201.50	**800**	**100**	**20**	0	0.23	0	2.66
			60	0	0.21	0.05	5.07
		200	**20**	0	0.23	0	2.66
			60	0	0.13	0.05	3.92
	1,550	**100**	**20**	0.02	0.17	1.03	8.6
			60	0.14	0.19	0.47	7.44
		200	**20**	0.04	0.25	0.46	11.24
			60	0.02	0.31	0.16	13.56
	3,050	**100**	**20**	0.39	0.17	3.64	24.7
			60	0.13	0.18	1.91	17.5
		200	**20**	0.47	0.44	3.58	27.06
			60	0.27	0.51	1.13	24.85
R201.100	**800**	**100**	**20**	0	0.03	0.06	2.23
			60	0	0.23	0.07	3,82
		200	**20**	0.02	0.03	0.07	2.48
			60	0	0.17	0.14	6.08
	1,550	**100**	**20**	0	0.29	0	9.9
			60	0.01	0	0.18	1.5
		200	**20**	0	0.21	0.02	11.54
			60	0.01	0.3	0.17	12.95
	3,050	**100**	**20**	0	0.31	0	18.66
			60	0.17	0.33	1.5	24.34

(continued)

Table 7.3 (continued)

Instances	T	Q	CB	A	B	C	D
		200	**20**	0.1	0.29	1.02	18.58
			60	0.11	0.3	0.74	26.13
Total						**32.9**	**594.94**
Average				**0.08**	**0.23**		

A $C(DP^{FIFO}_{Exact} \succ DP^{0.01}_{Approx})$, *B* $C(DP^{FIFO}_{Exact} \succ DP^{0.1}_{Apprpx})$, *C* $M(DP^{FIFO}_{Exact}, DP^{0.01}_{Approx})$, *D* $M(DP^{FIFO}_{Exact}, DP^{0.1}_{Approx})$

And last but not least, the chain benefits need to be shared among the different partners.

Besides the above difficulties, some specific operational issues need to be solved: e.g. “Is there enough space at the retail distribution centers, in the retail stores (backroom and shelves) to accommodate the extra inventory due to this pushing downstream of stock?”; “Is the current inventory control adequate to support the pushing of inventory downstream?”; “Are there any gains in efficiency when pushing inventory downstream?”, etc. Clearly, all these questions concern the last part in the retail supply chain: from retail DC to the retail stores. Focusing on the chain from the retailer’s distribution center to the stores it is observed that retailers create a costly chain while trying to minimize downstream inventory and avoiding out-of-stock situations with short lead-times, high delivery frequency and small order sizes. For more information, see Van der Vlist (2007).

7.4 Steps to Transitions

The research carried out in the TRANSUMO programme has many links to the educational programs of the School of Industrial Engineering. Next to this, we also have been closely involved with many retail and distribution companies to apply the TRANSUMO research and assist companies in improving their performance.

7.4.1 Courses

Mainly two courses are directly linked to the research in TRANSUMO. We briefly outline each of the courses.

7.4.1.1 Retail Operations

In 2005, part of the TRANSUMO research efforts were consolidated into a five credits elective in the Master of Science programme of Operations Management &

Table 7.4 The metrics *C* and *M* for the RC instances

Instances	T	Q	CB	A	B	C	D
RC101.50	**800**	**100**	**20**	0.2	0.31	0.38	9.28
			60	0	0.11	0	1.84
		200	**20**	0	0.11	0	1.47
			60	0	0	0	1.71
	1,550	**100**	**20**	0	0.04	0	3.69
			60	0	0.18	0	6.52
		200	**20**	0	0	0	3.45
			60	0	0.11	0	5.81
	3,050	**100**	**20**	0.05	0.21	0.53	27.55
			60	0.01	0.29	0.25	22.89
		200	**20**	0.03	0.36	0.53	32.36
			60	0.07	0.35	0.36	26.8
RC101.100	**800**	**100**	**20**	0	0.14	0	3.28
			60	0	0.04	0.05	4.4
		200	**20**	0	0.17	0	2.67
			60	0	0.09	0.11	24.42
	1,550	**100**	**20**	0.02	0.18	0.19	14
			60	0	0.17	0.39	11.82
		200	**20**	0	0.04	0	9.86
			60	0	0.21	0.25	9.86
	3,050	**100**	**20**	0.13	0.39	1.96	12.21
			60	0.25	0.32	2.75	35.38
		200	**20**	0.22	0.19	2.81	39.15
			60	0.24	0.21	2.1	31.32
RC201.50	**800**	**100**	**20**	0.2	0.31	0.38	9.28
			60	0	0.11	0	1.84
		200	**20**	0	0.11	0	1.47
			60	0	0	0	1.71
	1,550	**100**	**20**	0	0.04	0	3.69
			60	0	0.18	0	6.52
		200	**20**	0	0	0	3.45
			60	0	0.11	0	5.81
	3,050	**100**	**20**	0.05	0.21	0.53	27.55
			60	0.01	0.29	0.25	22.89
		200	**20**	0.03	0.36	0.53	32.36
			60	0.07	0.35	0.36	26.8
RC201.100	**800**	**100**	**20**	0	0.14	0	3.28
			60	0	0.04	0.05	4.4
		200	**20**	0	0.17	0	2.67
			60	0	0.09	0.11	24.42
	1,550	**100**	**20**	0.02	0.18	0.19	14
			60	0	0.17	0.39	11.82
		200	**20**	0	0.04	0	9.86
			60	0	0.21	0.25	9.86
	3,050	**100**	**20**	0.13	0.39	1.96	12.21
			60	0.25	0.32	2.75	35.38

(continued)

Table 7.4 (continued)

Instances	T	Q	CB	A	B	C	D
		200	**20**	0.22	0.19	2.81	39.15
			60	0.24	0.21	2.1	31.32
Total						**25.32**	**683.48**
Average				**0.05**	**0.18**		

A $C(DP^{FIFO}_{Exact} \succ DP^{0.01}_{Approx})$, *B* $C(DP^{FIFO}_{Exact} \succ DP^{0.1}_{Approx})$, *C* $M(DP^{FIFO}_{Exact}, DP^{0.01}_{Approx})$, *D* $M(DP^{FIFO}_{Exact}, DP^{0.1}_{Approx})$

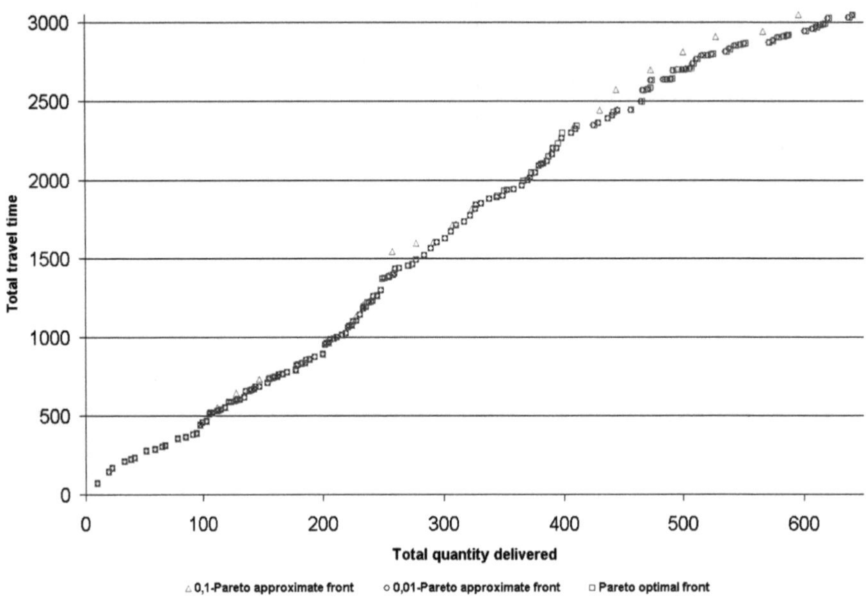

Fig. 7.3 Pareto-optimal front vs. Pareto-approximate fronts

Logistics (in the School of Industrial Engineering). Yearly, around 60 industrial engineering students attend the course. The faculty involved in the course are the same people as the ones involved in the retail operations research group. In total, we have a semester of 15 weeks in which we organize 10 weeks of contact sessions (2 h per week each).

The retail operations course aims to make the students acquainted with both the Dutch and international retail sector. We give an overview of the relevant research questions playing in the retail sector. The specific focus of the course is on the operational processes in retailing rather than on different marketing issues. The student is expected to be able to understand these processes in the retail sector and to model them. This will be possible by studying the most important papers in different decision areas of retailing (i.e. seminal papers on inventory control, distribution, store operations, *etc*.). Moreover, the student should be able to read and position retail operations management papers within the framework offered by this course. Throughout the course, we develop managerial insights for the retail sector and use quantitative and empirical modelling skills.

7.4.1.2 Strategic and Operational Decision Making in Transportation and Logistics

This advanced course describes the logistics industry, logistics systems, and the current trends in the development of advanced decision support systems. The course first discusses the logistics industry, markets and market developments in logistics and strategies of firms in the logistics industry. Second, emphasis is put on modeling and solving logistics problems using state-of-the-art approaches. The transportation, distribution and warehousing functions will be studied in detail through lectures and case studies.

At the end of the course, students should be able to:

- Understand the logistics industry, e.g. markets for transportation and logistics activities and the strategies of various firms that provide services in transport & logistics.
- Understand and master the strategic role, structure and functions of distribution systems (aiming at designing, operating and controlling the transportation, distribution and warehousing activities).
- Design the planning and control tasks of logistics systems and formulate, analyze and design solutions – using state-of-the-art and adequate methods – for logistics problems, especially in transportation & distribution. Logistics problems covered include network design, arc routing (e.g. garbage collection), node routing (e.g. parcel deliveries), *etc.*

7.4.2 Master Thesis Projects

Over the years, many master thesis projects within the Master of Science program of Operations Management & Logistics (at the School of Industrial Engineering) have been organized on the TRANSUMO project research lines. These projects are individual thesis work of 5 months full time, with preparatory period of 5–8 months during which the student is in partial contact with the company. Project focus is academic work within a specific industry context. More specifically, we did projects with Nabuurs, Jumbo Supermarkten, Metro, *etc.* assessing the value of the developed models and tools in real life. All projects were characterized by: thorough data analysis, quantitative modeling, extensive mapping of operational processes and solutions which are implementable and take account of the organizational circumstances.

Clearly, we have specific interest in problems that have a strong operational component, with an emphasis on in-store operations and its upstream supply chain.

Various types of projects are possible, although full access and usage of company data is essential in all projects. More information can be found on www.retailoperations.nl.

7.5 Conclusions and Future Outline

We described different different concepts for transport optimization and chain synchronization based on real-life cases coming from M.Sc students and company projects. Coping with real-life dynamic and stochastic environments is a critical and difficult problem to handle. In this chapter, we focussed on routing trucks into a congested road network and showed innovative concepts with regard to supply chain synchronization from retailer to manufacturer.

Given and based on the TRANSUMO research, a number of future research lines can be described. Without being exhaustive, the following topics can be considered:

- *Real life variants of the VRP* (tactical planning level): Many more variants of the VRP need to be considered in the same environment as we discussed earlier (dynamic and stochastic). In this research line, we focus on what is needed in real life, rather than tackling any possible variant in the VRP. This is related to the initial statement of being problem-motivated. Most of these variants come from M.Sc. projects carried out at different Logistics Service Providers (LSPs).
- *Green logistics* (strategic and tactical planning level): Obviously, the contemporary traffic prices do not reflect these external costs. In order to induce road users to make the correct decision, marginal external costs should be internalized.
- *Online repair policies and Consistent VRP* (operational planning level): The only certain thing is that any plan, once realized, goes wrong, even if the offline schedule is perfect. Moreover, not everything can or should be taken into account in the offline schedule. It is thus important, given the potential future realizations, to determine the right reaction or repair policies.

References

Azi N, Gendreau M, Potvin JY (2007) An exact algorithm for a single-vehicle routing problem with time windows and multiple routes. Eur J Oper Res 178:755–766

Braysy O, Gendreau M (2005a) Vehicle routing problem with time windows, part i: route construction and local search algorithms. Transportation Sci 39(1):104–118

Braysy O, Gendreau M (2005b) Vehicle routing problem with time windows, part ii: metaheuristics. Transportation Sci 39(1):119–139

Bertsimas DJ, Simchi-Levi D (1996) A new generation of vehicle routing research: robust algorithms, addressing uncertainty. Oper Res 44(2):286–304, March-April

Coyle JJ, Bardi EJ, Langley JJ Jr (1996) The management of business logistics. West Publishing, St. Paul

Funke B, Grünert T, Irnich S (2005) Local search for vehicle routing and scheduling problems: review and conceptual integration. Journal of heuristics 11:267–306

Ghiani G, Laporte G, Musmanno R (2004) Introduction to logistics systems planning & control. Wiley, Chichester, p 352

Gribkovskaia I, Laporte G, Aliaksandr S (2008) The single vehicle routing problem with deliveries and selective pickups. Comput Oper Res 35:2908–2924

GuoXing Y (1995) Transformation of multidepot multisalesmen problem to the standard travelling salesman problem. Eur J Oper Res 81:557–560

Kerbache L, Van Woensel T (2005) In: de Koster R, Delfmann W (eds) Planning and scheduling transportation vehicle fleet in a congested traffic Environment, supply chain management – European perspectives. CBS Press, Kopenhagen. ISBN ISBN 87–630–0148–9

Klamroth K, Wiecek MM (2000) Dynamic programming approaches to the multiple criteria knapsack problem. Nav Res Logist 135:4757–4776

Klamroth K, Wiecek MM (2001) A time-dependent multiple criteria single-machine scheduling problem. Eur J Oper Res 135:17–26

Kostreva MM, Wiecek MM (1993) Time dependency in multiple objective dynamic programming. J Math Anal Appl 173(1):28–307

Kulkarni RV, Bhave PR (1985) Integer programming formulations of vehicle routing problems. Eur J Oper Res 20:58–67

Laporte G, Nobert Y, Taillefer S (1988) Solving a family of multi-depot vehicle routing and location-routing problems. Transportation Sci 22(3):161–172

Laporte G (1992) The vehicle routing problem: an overview of exact and approximate algorithms. Eur J Oper Res 59(3):345–358

Malandraki C, Dial RB (1996) A restricted dynamic programming heuristic algorithm for the time dependent traveling salesman problem. Eur J Oper Res 90:45–55

McKinnon A (1999) Vehicle utilization and energy efficiency in the food supply chain, CSDF report, 46p

Taillard E, Badeau P, Gendreau M, Geurtin F, Potvin JY (1997) A tabu search heuristic for the vehicle routing problem with soft time windows. Transportation Sci 31(2):170–186

Van der Vlist P (2007) Synchronizing the retail supply chain, 90-5892–142–0, Phd Thesis ERIM, Rotterdam

Van Woensel TL, Kerbache H, Peremans N, Vandaele (2005) A vehicle routing problem with dynamic travel times. In: "Analysis of manufacturing systems – production management", ISBN 960–431–857, pp 141–150

Van Woensel T, Kerbache L, Peremans H, Vandaele N (2008) Vehicle routing with dynamic travel times: a queueing approach. Eur J Oper Res 186(3):990–1007

Chapter 8
Real-Time Coordination in Container Trucking – Prototyping and Evaluating a Multi-agent System for Real-Time Container Truck Planning at Post-Kogeko

Hans Moonen and Jos van Hillegersberg

8.1 Introduction

In a world that is fast becoming "Hot, Flat and Crowded" (Friedman 2008) our society and its systems have to become smarter than they currently are, and are in need of radical innovations. "*Instead of avoiding the unmanageable, we have to start managing the unavoidable*", as Friedman formulates it.

Multi-agent systems (MAS) have the potential to be one of the radical innovations that can help to organize (logistic) operations better (Fischer et al. 1996; Luck et al. 2004; Davidsson et al. 2005; Moyaux et al. 2006), and therewith contribute to a more sustainable society. Applied to logistics and transportation, MAS agents can improve efficiency, and therewith reduce the costs, pollution, and lead to more freedom for individual employees. Key herein is the utilization of real-time information in a planning process that primarily uses coordination in intra- and inter-organizational processes. Although logistics is often referred to as a potential candidate for the application of MAS, little research is done focused on (future) real implementation within logistics.

The research in this chapter is one of the first experiments with multi-agent systems in the real practice of logistics. The research case discussed here, covers the development and evaluation of a prototype MAS for the real-life planning problem of road-container transport at Post-Kogeko, a logistics service provider in The Netherlands. In Sect. 8.2 we will position MAS in the scientific literature, Sect. 8.3 then describes the application case at Post-Kogeko, the logistic service

H. Moonen (✉)
Logica Business Consulting, Postbus 159, Amstelveen, AD 1180, The Netherlands
e-mail: h.moonen@logica.com

J. van Hillegersberg
Department of Information Systems and Change Management, University of Twente, Capitool Building, Room C1-06, 217 Enschede, AE 7500, The Netherlands
e-mail: j.vanhillegersberg@utwente.nl

J.A.E.E. van Nunen et al. (eds.), *Transitions Towards Sustainable Mobility*,
DOI 10.1007/978-3-642-21192-8_8, © Springer-Verlag Berlin Heidelberg 2011

provider involved. In Sect. 8.4 the system design is covered, followed by an evaluation in Sect. 8.5. Finally, Sect. 8.6 presents the conclusion and discussion.

8.2 Multi-agent Systems in Logistics

The Enterprise Resource Planning (ERP) systems and Supply Chain Management (SCM) software nowadays utilized in logistics and transportation are typically of a centralized nature. Centralized information processing in supply chains results in a minimum amount of transactions, and one single point for optimization (Lewis and Talalayevsky 2004). However, this is not logic for operational-level decision-making in highly dynamic environments, where many factors are constantly changing (Singh et al. 2007). Centralized solutions have difficulties in coping with a high degree of complexity and change (Marik and McFarlane 2005). In fact, serious doubts exist about whether the current enterprise systems are suited for today's SCM challenges (Davenport and Brooks 2004).

Over the past two decades researchers have been working on a different type of information systems architecture, namely multi-agent systems (MAS) (Wooldridge and Jennings 1995). Other than centralized information systems, such as ERP, MAS consist of many autonomously interacting software agents. These interacting agents are small software programmes characterized by intelligence and individual behaviour (Schleiffer 2005). Communication and coordination (between agents) are the essential elements in such systems. Not all agents have to be equal: each agent may have unique capabilities and objectives, representing its real-world counterpart. The important characteristics of multi-agent systems are (Rudowsky 2004; Caridi and Cavalieri 2004; Moyaux et al. 2006): (1) agents need each other for completeness of information and problem solving; (2) there is no global control system; (3) data are decentralized; (4) asynchronous computation; (5) modularity; (6) multi-objective functions can be embedded; and (7) design can be a stepwise process. Application domains that are likely to benefit from multi-agent systems have the following characteristics (Sierra 2004): (1) very fast interactions; (2) interactions are repeated with either (a) high communication overheads, or (b) a limited domain so that learning done by the agent about user behaviour is effective; (3) each trade is of relatively small value; (4) the process is repeated over long periods of time; and (5) the product traded is relatively easy to specify.

Logistics and transportation are interesting domains for the application of multi-agent systems (Fischer et al. 1996; Luck et al. 2004; Davidsson et al. 2005; Moyaux et al. 2006). Not only do many logistic processes match with the characteristics listed above derived from Siera (2004), but especially the inter-organizational nature of the domain makes agents logical candidates, as the heavy interdependence on chain partners complicates the implementation and utilization of centralized systems. Decentralized solutions, of which multi-agent systems are an example, seem to be suitable in situations where a classical centralized solution is less suitable and where the distribution of information and decision-making is necessary. Marik and McFarlane (2005) specifically mention several characteristics that favour a decentralized solution approach. Fischer et al. (1996) show that MAS have the potential to perform similar to traditional centralized optimization mechanisms. Furthermore, MAS design may provide fundamental advantages such as increased flexibility, and real-time capabilities.

Nevertheless, MAS have not been widely adopted in logistics and transportation yet (Caridi and Cavalieri 2004; Davidsson et al. 2005). Even papers that describe "*practical applications*" (e.g. Adler and Blue 2002; Trappey et al. 2004; Lima et al. 2006; Moyaux et al. 2006) solely describe academic experiments without concrete implementations. In fact, these are theoretical design attempts that do not validate or test these designs, nor provide detailed plans on how to approach this – an observation shared by Wareham et al. (2005).

Little empirical or experimental research is done to really apply MAS in practice. The Dutch applied research institute TNO recently concluded, "*that many ideas on multi-agent systems exist, but applications and tests in the field of logistics are hard to find*" (Van Rijswijck and Davydenko 2007). Furthermore, they state, "*It appeared that the technology has not gone further than university research laboratories and some pilot projects*." Chmiel et al. (2005) conclude that most of the current multi-agent system research is far from realistic because the setting is oversimplified, and designs tend only to include a very limited number of agents. They plead to researchers to "*start designing and implementing large software systems, consisting of hundreds of agents, and study their behaviour*".

Therefore we choose to concentrate our research efforts on the application of multi-agent system to a real-life planning problem of sea-containers, as we believe that multi-agent systems can be an instrument to establish supply chain systems that focus on solving problems through (real-time) synchronization of activities – by means of communication and negotiation – rather than optimization in isolation, as tends to be the case in centralized architectures.

8.3 Application Case for Agents at Post-Kogeko

The empirical part of this research was performed at Post-Kogeko. Post-Kogeko is a Maasland, Netherlands, based logistics service provider active in distribution, forwarding and transport, which employs ±575 employees and operates ±500 trucks. The company is growing steadily, and is referenced by the Commissie Van Laarhoven (Van Laarhoven et al. 2006) as one of the industry's main innovators. Around 40 of its trucks and drivers are dedicated to the sea-container unit. Post-Kogeko is specialized in conditioned transport; 95% of the containers it transports are reefers. Reefers limit the dynamic reallocation of empty containers, as reefers have to be cleaned before re-entering the circuit of empty containers.

Transporting containers means interacting with terminals and customers. The interaction with the customers can be split in four different moments: (1) First, the order intake phase takes place, when Post-Kogeko receives its customers' orders.

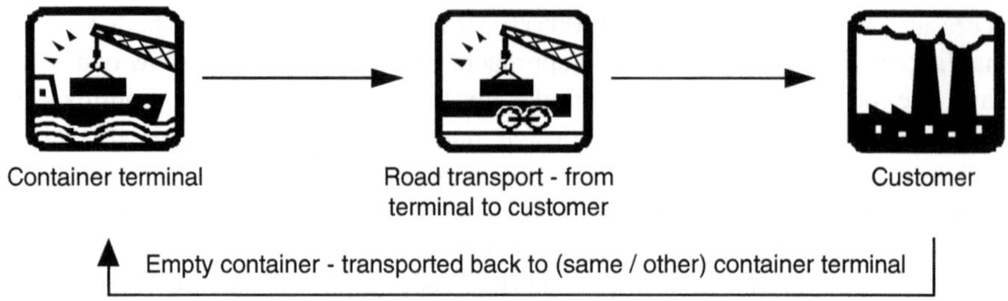

Fig. 8.1 Basic physical process flow in the transport of import sea-containers

Generally these orders specify the pickup of a container the next day. (2) During the execution day, contact about the order-status occurs. This type of contact generally takes place by phone, and is generally customer-initiated. (3) Then the actual delivery takes place: the driver delivers a full or empty container, and waits for unloading/loading of the container (see the physical process depicted in Fig. 8.1). (4) The invoicing occurs afterwards. An invoice is generally an accumulation of several orders processes over a longer period.

What complicates matters from an optimization perspective is that only around 50% of all containers are available at the start of operations early in the morning; either they have not physically left the ship yet, or they are delayed for administrative reasons – which can be due to non-settled payments or customs. Post-Kogeko can only transport released containers, which are allowed to leave the container terminal. As release times are unknown beforehand, doing the entire planning a-priori is not possible.

Potential savings in the container transportation where identified at the following three points (Oink 2005):

- Automation of the planning processes (assignment process as well as external information processing tasks) could result in a larger span of control for a planner, making it possible for the planner to plan more trucks.
- Better assignments, resulting in fewer mistakes, less unnecessary waiting, and less empty kilometres.
- Chain coordination – involving customers and terminals – enables a higher level of optimization. It no longer solely reacts upon (last-minute) orders, but has the potential to anticipate orders. This might result in shorter throughput times, less unnecessary waiting, lower costs (since one can further optimize resources and routes) and is likely to lead to more satisfied customers.

Container planning is an inter-organizational coordination problem. From interviews we heard back that technology to support this should be focused on coordination through communication, rather than on optimization alone. Preferably, this should be done through processes understandable to human planners, as Krauth (2008) showed: many companies in logistics (including our case company, Post-Kogeko) prefer a decision support system that, while automating most of the process, keeps the planner in final control, in this way increasing a planner's span of control.

8.4 System Design of the Multi-agent System

The multi-agent system designed is a real-time planning (support) system, which consists of different types of software agents monitoring their environments. This includes TruckAgents monitoring (real-time GPS based) truck movements and traffic jams, and OrderAgents monitoring container availability and customer preferences. Orders are assigned in real-time to trucks, based on a mechanism that considers the order details (minimizing lateness of orders), the movements of the fleet, reduce empty kilometres, and potential delays due to traffic jams. The way human planners currently work was taken as a starting point in the design. The planning processes were modelled as agent behaviours; making the system's decisions relatively human-understandable.

The agent system is developed in JADE, which is an efficient and scalable agent development platform (Chmiel et al. 2005). For more details about JADE, both technical and functional, we refer the reader to Bellifemine et al. (2007). The development of the multi-agent system was performed in Eclipse running under Windows XP. The engine gets its order data from the QFreight database, and the GPS location information from either the simulator or the CarrierWeb system database. Both databases are Microsoft SQL Servers. The SQL Servers (version 2005) contain the order information and run on Windows 2003 Servers, and the truck simulator on a RedHat Enterprise Linux Server. The LP-based route planning functionality covered Benelux countries only, and was provided by AND. The web-based user interface is developed with the Google Web Toolkit (GWT). It integrates a map, for which Google Maps was used. Both JADE and GWT lean on development in Java.

Four versions of the prototype system have been constructed (see Fig. 8.1). For pragmatic reasons we started off with the most extended (and perhaps most advanced) version, a fully automated version that runs on a simulator. Evolving from that version onwards, we first extended to a version with a UI, in fact an in-between, in order to visualize the working of the system, and to interact from a web interface with the multi-agent system and the simulator. This version runs on a web server (Apache Tomcat), and can be manually started and stopped, and furthermore set to simulate a certain day in a particular scenario. In turn, this version was the starting point for constructing a manually operated version that could run on the (same) simulator, and eventually a version without the simulator, which connected to the Post-Kogeko backend systems. The manual version was only developed in the last week before the field-test (as it was difficult to test with this version). The different versions, with their respective agents are listed in Table 8.1 – note that the two first versions (from Fig. 8.2) are bundled.

In the system, there are different types of agents; the two most important: TruckAgents, and OrderAgents. For each truck in the system a TruckAgent, and for each order an OrderAgent. The agents in the system process the information they receive – such as location changes, orders, order availability, customer preferences, and traffic jams. TruckAgents store all information of importance to

Table 8.1 Agents in the different versions of the prototype

Agents	Automatic assign./ simulator version (#1&2)	Manual assign./ simulator version (#3)	Manual assign./ field-test version (#4)
TruckAgent	X	X	X
OrderAgent	X	X	X
ManagementAgent	X	X	X
LogAgent	X	X	
TimeAgent	X	X	
SyncAgent	X	X	
SimAgent	X		

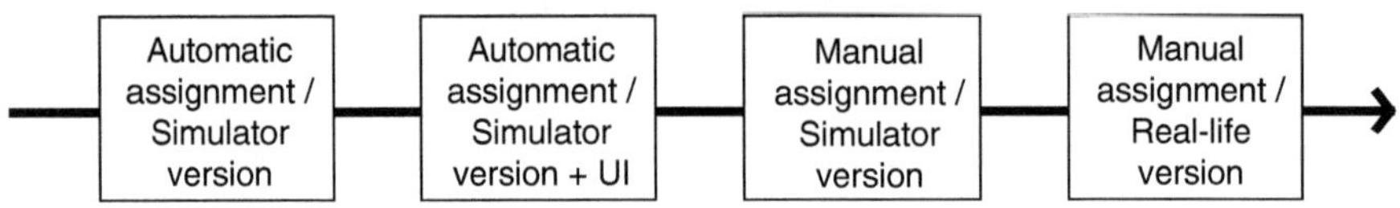

Fig. 8.2 Different versions of the prototype

that particular truck and the calculations that need to be made by the agent. With every status update, TruckAgents calculate their expected Estimated Time of Arrival (ETA), estimating the moment they will be free to execute their next order. OrderAgents encapsulate all details from an order that needs to be executed on the particular date. An order stores information on its preferred customer delivery time-window, the type of customer, the pickup, delivery and return locations, corresponding kilometres, and the availability of the order at the pickup terminal. An OrderAgent has behaviour to automatically check availability with the system from the terminal.

TruckAgents get their order assignments through real-time negotiation with the other agents in the system, hence that these decisions are based on the most up-to-date situation (and the interaction between agents illustrated in Fig. 8.3). As soon as a truck becomes available, its TruckAgent will notice and start actively negotiating for the next job to execute. This is done by contacting the different OrderAgents and then calculating a score for each order – through a CalculateScore algorithm which calls four subclasses that calculate four scores for, respectively: a CustomerImportanceScore, a CustomerTimeWindowScore, an EmptyMileageScore, and a TrafficJamAvoidanceScore. As a result, the TruckAgent gets an (ordered) array of orders to execute with a list of scores. To avoid (very) local optimisation, the truck agent then takes the highest ranked order and asks for a bid from the other TruckAgents for that specific order. The scoring incorporates the time trucks are still busy, utilizing a truck's ETA, and the place where it will become available again. If there is no other truck that is better capable of executing this particular order, the TruckAgent claims the order, and the truck is instructed to execute this specific order. A TruckAgent can be an initiator, which means that it is actually searching for an order, as described above, or a participant. A participant responds to other initiators, but is not currently searching for an order.

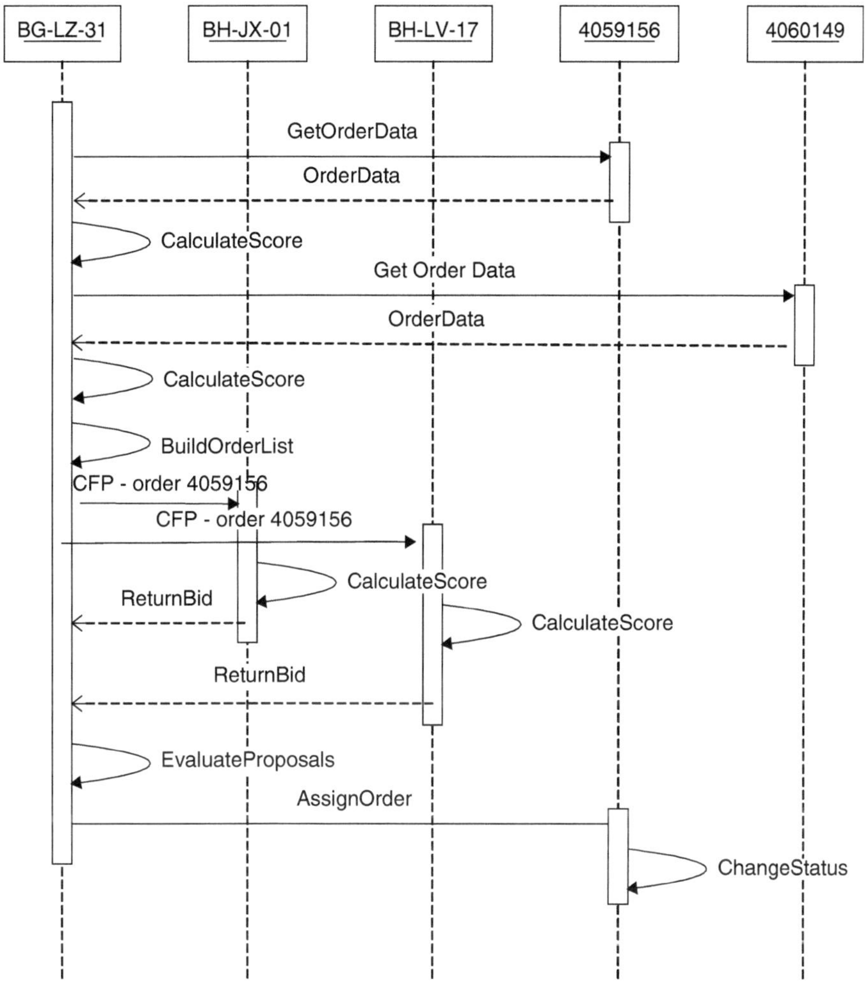

Fig. 8.3 UML Sequence diagram – FindOrder process

The ManagementAgent is a supportive agent that performs several supportive activities. The ManagementAgent is the agent that is among the first to be started in the system; it has functionality to generate for each order an OrderAgent, and a sufficient amount of TruckAgents. In the field-test setting this step is bypassed. In that scenario, the ManagementAgent looks-up a database, and generates the number of trucks (with the proper number plates, used as the ID), as listed in the system for that day. Furthermore, the ManagementAgent keeps track of the amount of orders still to be executed and the amount of trucks still active in the system. It possesses the functionality (in the simulator version) to check whether a day has been completed (that is: all orders executed), in which case it communicates with the SimAgent that it can restart the system and simulate another day.

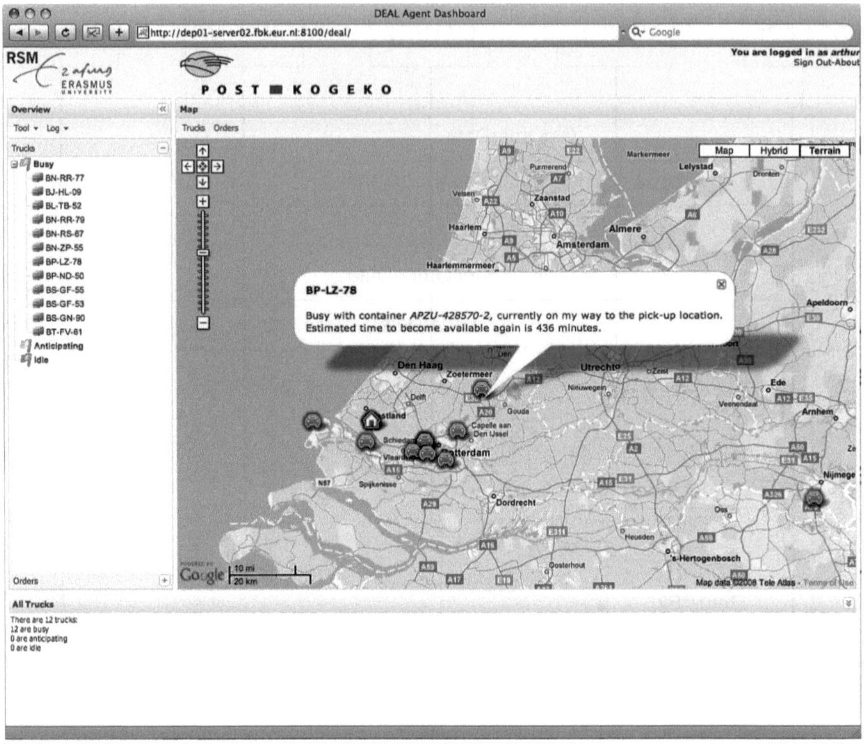

Fig. 8.4 Screenshot interface multi-agent system prototype

In the simulator setting we need additional supportive agents and behaviours; more specifically, the SimAgent, SyncAgent and the TimeAgent. The SimAgent is the agent responsible for starting and executing simulations. In fact, it sets a particular date, starts the simulator server and initialises the agent platform. It then starts the SyncAgent and the TimeAgent, which in turn start the ManagementAgent, which then generate the OrderAgents and the TruckAgents. The SyncAgent takes care of the needed communication with the simulator and syncserver, which are running at a Linux server in the network. The simulator typically simulates another date and time than the current system-time. Furthermore, it can run at a faster(or slower)-than-normal pace. The TimeAgent has functionalities and behaviours to handle this. Other agents contact the TimeAgent to find out the current time in the simulated world.

The TruckAgents and OrderAgents update their status for display in the GUI in two XML files we utilised in the interface, namely trucks.xml and orders.xml. The GUI interprets these files, and graphically displays them on a map (see Fig. 8.4 for the truck view).

In the "Manual assignment – Real-life version" (see Fig. 8.2) the GUI was used to control the MAS running in parallel to the manual planning system. Through buttons and screens in the GUI the user could put the agents to work, overwrite decisions, and get back performance information from the system, mainly on operational data such as KM's driven (empty/full), and hours worked for the trucks, and details on order hours and order availability.

8.5 Evaluation of the Design

8.5.1 Four Different Evaluation Methods

Important in design research are proper (prototype) evaluation steps. There are many different evaluation methods possible. Prototyping can take place for different reasons, as Fitzgerald (1998) explains: for a technical design try-out, or a try-out of novel concepts. Documenting the development of an interactive web application, Levi and Conrad (1996) show that prototyping can be a useful methodology. As such, a prototype helps to get acquainted with new technologies and approaches, to learn from these experiences, and is an ideal tool to gather (end-) user feedback. "*Evaluation means assessing the performance or value of a system, process (technique, procedure, ...), product, or policy. As such, evaluation is accepted as a critical necessity in science, technology, and many other areas, including social applications*" (Saracevic 1995).

Overseeing the diversity of the domain and the many different factors that play a role in implementation of systems, as well as adoption of agent systems, we recognize that one can never evaluate a system on solely one factor, nor is it possible to utilize a single method. Van Hillegersberg (1997) studied Object Orientation (OO) in information systems development. He concluded that, in order to properly study all of the diverse aspects that came with OO, a multi-method approach was needed. Considering this and the ideas by Saracevic (1995), Vokurka et al. (1996), and Kaplan and Duchon (1988) – we recognize the need for a multi-method prototype evaluation approach.

The design and prototyping process as such are already an important evaluation approach, following Nunamaker and Chen (1990) – and therewith our first evaluation method (see Sect. 8.5.2). We chose three additional evaluation approaches, with different levels of evaluation, levels of control and different rigour/relevance balances. These approaches are: simulation (Sect. 8.5.3), expert evaluation (Sect. 8.5.4), and an in-company field test/case study (Sect. 8.5.5), to study behaviour in the intended user environment – see also (Hevner et al. 2004). For details on the methods utilized see Table 8.2. For a longer list of evaluation methods see, Chap. 4 in Moonen (2009).

8.5.2 Evaluation I: Development and Prototyping

Few programmers are gifted enough to construct faultless software code from scratch. Although integrated development environments (IDE), such as Eclipse,

Table 8.2 Methods for evaluation of the multi-agent system prototype

#	Method	Level of evaluation	Level of control	Rigor/relevance	Short description
I	Prototype as design and feedback instrument	Engineering, processing, use or user, and social level	Low	Rigour low Relevance high	A continuous evaluation throughout the design and build phase. Ex-ante evaluation leads to new insights, which will be fed, into a new version of the prototype
II	Simulation	Processing level	High	Rigour high Relevance low	Evaluate the performance of the prototype in a controlled manner – generally, in comparison with other mechanisms
III	Expert opinions	Engineering, input, processing, output, use or user, and social level	Low	Rigour medium Relevance high	An evaluation method in which a group of experts is used to discuss and validate a prototype. This is an accepted method to gather meaning, experiences and insights from (domain) experts
IV	In field case study/ experiment	Input, processing, output, use or user, and social level	Medium	Rigour low Relevance high	A try-out of the prototype in the field. Does the targeted system achieve what was envisioned? Generally leads to suggestions for improvements

help in writing compiler ready code, bugs and design problems tend still to be present. This is either due to faults in the coding, or unforeseen processes or circumstances, but can also be caused by a different programming paradigm, as we found out through the process of prototyping a multi-agent system. The development of a multi-agent system requires a mental switch for classically schooled developers.

Running, tracing and solving bugs and problems, and along that line, rethinking (smarter) mechanisms are therefore part of the construction process of the prototype. The prototype has been worked on by two developers: a main developer, who did most of the programming, and a functional designer (the first author of this chapter) who assisted in the programming. The frequent and sometimes very intense discussions between the developers benefited the prototype enormously, as did the contact with outsiders. Throughout the development process, continuous testing of the code took place, for which a test set distilled from historical execution data from Post-Kogeko was utilized. Two rather simplified days were used, 1 with only 12 orders to be executed by 5 trucks, and 1 with 52 orders to be executed by 26 trucks. A normal day in practice generally has a larger amount of orders and trucks. For testing purposes these simplified days made life easier – due to a reduced setup time for the creation of agents, and easier insight in agent-to-agent communication lines and process flow.

An important decision made relatively late in the process was not mentioned before: the introduction of the OrderAgent. Although present from the beginning in our initial design, we first aimed for a solution in which we only had TruckAgents and Order Objects (along with the supportive agents as described before). The order information was obtained from the QFreight database each time a truck initiated a FindOrder event. The ManagementAgent performed an availability check with the terminal, and updated the order data in the QFreight database. Although this solution worked in principal, it resulted in a large amount of database calls at each FindOrder event, and it complicated the creation of smart behaviours for orders. It would be more logical, and more in line with agent principles, to construct an OrderAgent that has its own behaviours: such as checking and updating its availability, its estimated execution time (the duration of the trip) and communicating its details to a TruckAgent when requested. It also constitutes a basis for future intelligent extensions. OrderAgents contacted the order database just once, only at the setup to read all required order details. In the past, it sometimes happened that – due to the fact that we were dealing with literally tens of thousands of database transactions (and connections) – the system sometimes failed for hard-to-trace reasons despite the static and synchronized methods applied.

8.5.3 Evaluation II: Simulation

Within the context of the same project, other researchers have been working on different aspects of multi-agent systems. Mahr et al. (2008) have done extensive research into multi-agent system algorithmic design, into the performance of MAS, and into the comparison of MAS algorithms with more traditional Operations Research (OR) techniques. They report on a series of simulations. It is shown that in a context with relative high dynamism, their MAS approach chosen performs similar to the online optimization.

Although our prototype was never designed to solve the exact same problem they have been working on, we decided to compare our approach with theirs, nevertheless. It gives insight into how our agents perform, and delivers insights for redesign. We do not explain details of the competing prototypes here, but refer the reader to Mahr et al. (2008). The dataset used for simulation is the same one, and it is based on transaction data from Post-Kogeko.

When comparing our results with the results reported by Mahr et al. (2008), we see several important differences. Their results have very high "idle times", though those are close-to-non-existent/minimal in our approach, but they have less "empty hours". Another difference concerns the job rejections, which is something they observe in their experiments, and we do not. The largest difference however, lies in the amount of "on time" orders which is disappointingly low in our approach. These differences all have to do with the design of the agents. The TruckAgents in the system always try to find a new order, and, when doing so, they select the highest scoring order. However, with deliveries spread over the day, at a certain point the orders that have to be delivered early have been, or are being, served by other trucks already, and the next TruckAgent selects an order which is going to be served "too early". TruckAgents only wait when orders are not yet physically present at the terminal, but not for orders that are going to be delivered (a little bit) too early. This design decision was made in the design phase together with Post-Kogeko planners – they do not work with as strict time windows.

Mahr et al. (2008) have already made critical remarks concerning the dynamism of the simulation setting. The only dynamic aspect in these simulation scenarios was the percentage of order release information known at the start of operations. Terminal and customer processing times are constants, driving speeds are constants and no accidents such as breakdowns occur. Simulation is always an abstraction, but this was too abstract. Especially for a prototype that has been built from the idea that the world changes every minute, and that real-time information makes a difference. Hence, if there is nothing to react upon in real-time, why should one plan or assign in real-time?

The simulations revealed two important findings. First, a serious design issue in our design was discovered by the fact that in the largest part of our simulation runs, a double delivery of orders was observed. A TruckAgent selects a particular order, releases the initiator lock, the OrderAgent is signalled by the TruckAgent, and accordingly updates it status. However, it sometimes happened that the next initiator TruckAgent was quicker in selecting a list of potential OrderAgents than that the OrderAgent that was claimed by the previous TruckAgent had updated its status, despite the delay in the generation of TruckAgents that have been built in as a safety mechanism. This implies the need for another mechanism to synchronize activities between agents. Due to time limitations, we were not able to integrate this into our prototype and rerun the experiments and field-test (although it was not observed there). It is however, an important lesson for further work.

Second, we observed that running at six times normal speed, the agents are still idle most of the time. This could be noticed observing the system performance monitor tool built into the Windows 2003 server. In fact, this means that there is a possibility to put agents to work during the time they are idle; there is a chance for them to do more "intelligent stuff" in the time they are idling, for example preparing future decisions, or doing re-optimization.

8.5.4 Evaluation III: Expert Evaluation

Early 2008, we organized a 1-day event in which workshops were organized with a total of 45 experts participating. Most participants came directly from the logistics sector; a category that includes shippers, 3PLs, and port operators. The other categories are ICT, Consultancy, Policy Makers and Research Institutes/ Universities.

The event consisted of four parts. The entire group of participants first were involved in an introductory session, after which the group was split in two groups. One workshop concentrated on the application of multi-agent system technology within road planning – topic of this chapter – the other on multi-agent application to plan barge rotations (see Douma 2008 and Moonen 2009). With respect to the Post-Kogeko prototype two questions were asked to the experts: (1) What advantages and disadvantages of the shown multi-agent system do you see for road transport (in general)? (2) How should the multi-agent system support the planner in his/her activities?

The answers (written on response forms, followed by a verbal group discussion) can be roughly split in two parts: One, feedback was received concerning the prototype – participants identified weaknesses, and gave suggestions for further improvement. Two, feedback was gathered on the concepts that underlie the prototype demonstrated, and its wider potential for future applications. The largest part of the feedback concerned feedback in the second category.

Despite the perceptual nature of the feedback received, we think that it provides useful insights. A large and diverse group of experts participated. The experts had different backgrounds, and all had experience with either the design and implementation of logistic information systems, the inner-workings of actual operations and processes within logistics, or managerial aspects. Furthermore, some researchers participated that have been working on similar or related concepts and systems. The answers received on the forms were grouped and clustered together, and frequencies of occurrence were counted. For details we refer to Moonen (2008, 2009).

Several participants showed their appreciation for the prototype. They appreciated the underlying MAS principles of having a system composed of autonomous agents that derive a solution through communication and negotiation with other agents rather than, as one participant formulated it, "*uninformed optimization*". Someone else mentioned that MAS is "*well connected to the manual way of working, with local decision autonomy*". A third participant formulated it this way: "*I like this very much; human planners cannot handle the dynamics and complexity of the (current) reality*".

Several critical comments were made. Someone remarked that it is solely a limited prototype, and far from a real system. A list of missing aspects in the current prototype was created. Mentioned were the integration of smarter algorithms in the system; the inclusion of opening times of terminals and customers in the decision-making process; and the need for a structured way to integrate knowledge of human planners in the MAS. Someone else mentioned that the prototype has a highly operational/executional nature: "*How does this prototype connect with the strategic and tactical levels of planning?*" Someone else mentioned that real advantages are only to be realized when companies start collaborating; "*Despite the fact that the shown technology might be a platform for this, the ease of implementation is questionable.*" This implied that it is an organizational behavioural issue rather than purely technical.

As concrete extensions for this prototype, several participants mentioned extensions within the supply chain: such a system should make it possible to connect with terminals and customers, and dynamically negotiate timeslots for pickup and delivery. Another extension mentioned was a connection to electronic marketplaces, where agents (trucks/drivers) can automatically find orders. A third possible extension was to include a driver-agent in the system: currently it is the truck-agent who decides, and the driver lacks autonomy. Fourth, the system should calculate and compare several decision scenarios, which it presents the planner, rather than making an autonomous choice. Fifth, although the system does include a multi-attribute decision-making process, human planners include still many other factors, too.

8.5.5 Evaluation IV: In Field Case Study

A fourth evaluation method we utilized was a real-life confrontation with the environment the prototype was developed for. Together with Post-Kogeko, we decided to test the prototype in the daily practice of container planning, and analyze its workings. Testing a new technology within a company is a useful idea, however, it is not evident how to do it, and what to measure. We decided to aim for an evaluation session, in which we connect live to the Post-Kogeko systems and let the multi-agent system run parallel with the normal planning process. In order to do so, the simulator-based version of the system had to be rebuilt into a version that was able to run parallel to the real-life QFreight and CarrierWeb systems. Also, the agents lose part of their autonomy, since the planner keeps control over the final decision. As such, human interaction with the agents also became an issue.

Sitting down with the planners, we utilized the Think-Aloud technique to gather evaluation data. The Think-aloud technique is pretty much what it sounds like. Someone is asked to do a task, and to think aloud about what he/she is doing. This method makes it possible to acquire insights and feedback that is difficult or even impossible to reach through other methods (Nielsen et al. 2002). Wright and Monk (1990) have proved that the think-aloud methodology not only is effective as such, but also is a useful method to be used by the developers of a system or prototype with their intended users. Developers have turned out to be inaccurate in predicting what problems they will observe in the evaluation. As such, using this evaluation method is a useful instrument in a design cycle, even when used by researchers involved in the development. A day like this generates many results across several categories.

First of all, such a test is an instrument to find bugs and identify missing features in the prototype. Second, and more important from the perspective of our research, is the question of whether the prototype and its concepts as developed hold in real practice, and whether the planners who have to work with it "buy it". Third, it is a moment to discuss future extensions to the prototype and its underlying concepts.

During the tests the two developers of the system were present. Notes were made by both, and shared and compared afterwards. The user interaction (of the planner) with the system, the plan experiences, and interaction about pros and cons of the system were all documented. Two planners participated in the test: a senior planner in the container unit, with 21+ years of experience, and a planner with 8+ years of experience (of which only a couple of months spent in container planning).

During the tests, a couple of bugs and a longer list of missing features were collected. The feedback received on the working of the prototype was very positive. The main conclusions from the tests were:

- The planners do not really care if it is a multi-agent system or not. They want a system that comes with solutions for their daily problems, by giving assistance to the daily job, automating routine work, and providing assistance in the planning tasks.
- The prototype as tested did come with some minor bugs, and it was not feature complete. The session, as such, resulted in a long list of suggestions for additional features. The planners evaluated the features that were present, independent of missing features, and tried to solely consider underlying technologies and concepts.
- The concept of a smart system that runs parallel to the manual processes, and comes autonomously with suggestions for assignments was very much welcomed.
- The multi-criteria order assignment mechanism, as was implemented deliberately, resulted in reactions such as, "*Oh yes, that would also have been an interesting option*"
- In daily practice, multiple decision criteria exist, however, be aware that there are, for example, no fixed narrow time windows, or pertinent rules that some customers are always served faster. Most constraints are pretty flexible.
- The largest troubles currently exist at the chain level: late customer changes, little information from (and interaction with) the terminals, long queues. This prototype could be a basis for a further integration with the up- and downstream supply chains, and help in automatic checking, updating and perhaps negotiating. This would be a real relief.
- From a technical perspective, the test was a success: all agents kept working properly, and the UI (the part the planners interfaced with) made it easy to interact with them.
- From a research perspective, this test was also very interesting, however, it should not stop here. The interesting challenge remaining is to make the next step towards real implementation.

The field-test was followed by a workshop with Post-Kogeko and its supply chain partners. Representatives from the two largest container terminals in the Port of Rotterdam were present: ECT and APM terminals. Furthermore, a representative from CoolControl, Post-Kogeko's number-one container-customer, participated. Also present was someone from PortInfolink. From Post-Kogeko itself, four people were present, and three researchers from Erasmus University and the University of Twente.

The workshop's main conclusion was that the chain as a whole would thrive after information exchange and coordination at multiple planning levels, and a multi-agent system approach would be a useful instrument in this. Several weeks before the actual arrival of the containership, an initial exchange of information could take place: identifying the customer for a specific container, the expected modality, and expected LSP. When the actual pickup approaches more detailed coordination – on container availability, customs handling, and eventually an announcement of a specific visit – should take place. The latter should also be in multiple steps, the last step, for example, 15 min before actual arrival at the loading dock, so that the terminal could already start container handling. The current way of working results in many last-minute operations, leaving no space for any optimization.

In conclusion, we can state that this research project that began with the development of a multi-agent system prototype for a single-enterprise planning environment, eventually triggered discussion on the application of this technology in the wider supply chain. The prototype and its real-world test became an instrument to discuss future application for coordinated road planning in the port.

8.6 Conclusion and Discussion

8.6.1 Summary

This chapter described an applied research project we worked on over the past years. A design and prototype multi-agent system for the real-time planning of container trucks at Post-Kogeko was made, focussing on real-time coordination of activities. Post-Kogeko was involved in the design trajectory. Prototyping the system provided hands-on experience in not only the construction of the system, but also the conceptually different thinking behind multi-agent systems. Several versions of the prototype were developed; most importantly, a fully autonomous simulator version, and a human planner-controlled real-life version. Unfortunately, time did not allow us to construct a true cross-enterprise application in which we could deploy TerminalAgents and CustomerAgents. Furthermore, the research did not result in a concrete implementation (yet).

The prototype has been evaluated and validated through four methods. The combination of different methods with another balance between rigour, relevance and control proved useful in getting a balanced insight into the potential of MAS for transportation. System development provided insight into the complexities of designing and developing a MAS: everything becomes a process flow. Simulation was useful to test the concepts before the actual field test; the comparison with a simulation study from fellow researchers proved the fact that one should thoroughly design one's simulation environment as well – something we did not do due to limited time. The simulation setting used turned out to be too artificial. Expert evaluation was an instrument to gather (subjective) feedback and to discuss future extensions and eventual implementation. The in-company field-test was the most realistic evaluation, closest to an eventual implementation. It provided direct prototype feedback and enabled us to identify a list of bugs, design issues, and missing features. Furthermore, it made it possible to realistically compare the multi-agent system developed to the manual way of working, and discuss future implementation.

8.6.2 Discussion

Our interaction with practioners showed that industry professionals are intrigued by the idea of having information systems that find solutions by utilizing real-time information, and coordination with other (internal or external) systems. Bold and Olsson (2005) identified chain collaboration as the main source for further cost savings for logistic service providers; our research revealed that MAS might be an instrument to realize this, by enabling (real-time) coordination of activities with up- and downstream supply chain partners. Furthermore, we found that end-users of planning tools, or logistic professionals, are not per se interested in multi-agent systems as a technology, rather in its functionality and potential. Krauth (2008) found that users are influenced by the type of feedback they get on the inner-workings of a planning system, when the system performs its calculations. We cannot confirm nor falsify this. Rather we have ground to believe that end-users, who are no technicians, are relatively quickly impressed by new technologies and concepts behind a certain system. A user-friendly user interface can easily give them the impression of a state-of-art system.

It is hard to generalize our findings, as with any (design) case-study (Eisenhardt 1989; Yin 2003). Nevertheless, this chapter showed that multi-agent systems are an interesting instrument to approach real-time and inter-organizational coordination problems in transportation. MAS make it possible to switch to a different planning and control paradigm, focussed on coordination through communication and negotiation rather than an isolated (single-tier) optimization. This can be done in (semi-) real-time, and both intra- or inter-organizations (see also the list of requirements by Sierra 2004). It makes it possible to utilize real-time sensor data in decision-making, such as, for example, GPS or RFID information. One of the important comments received from a series of expert workshops is that "*the inter-organizational domain is [perceived to be] the application area with the largest potential for multi-agent systems*". It turned out that MAS are especially useful in logistic situations that require coordination, last-minute decision-making, and face several – sometimes partially conflicting – objectives. From an information systems design perspective, MAS are a different approach to establishing systems. MAS make it easier to include perspectives of (multiple) stakeholders. Lea et al. (2005) list potential benefits multi-agent systems bring enterprise systems. The authors are not very critical, and it is unclear where the claimed benefits are derived from. Our field research confirms the claimed benefits of "*effective decisions through real-time information sharing*", "*less need for BPR*", "*customization capability*", and to a certain extent also "*employee training*" and "*technology readiness*". However, with respect to implementation – specifically "*implementation time*" and "*implementation cost*" – we doubt whether their statements hold. Consulting firms and enterprise software vendors have large groups of implementation consultants with strong experience in ERP implementations. Custom software development or modular implementation can be expected to take more time, and require other skills.

Hybrid MAS architectures that integrate existing legacy, which and are not of a fully decentralized nature, are the most likely (first) implementations of MAS in supply chains. This statement combines two essential observations. First, few implementations will be green field implementations. Companies generally have existing information systems in place, and a MAS system needs to become part of the larger information systems infrastructure within or between enterprises. Second, MAS designs will be either part of, or have to integrate with, multiple hierarchical control layers with different planning processes depending upon the planning horizon. A MAS that solely performs real-time assignment as we piloted at Post-Kogeko is of limited value. One of the experts formulated it as follows: "*This (...) only shows a limited application: it is highly operational. A future real-life system should include also longer-term planning (tactical/strategic) functionality.*" Hybrid system design does not necessarily interfere with MAS principles. In fact, it might be the only realistic way to get such systems implemented in practice.

MAS might be an interesting answer as the founding principles of supply chain management have been, up until now, difficult to realize through (traditional) information systems (Sharman 2003). Let's consider a couple of examples, partly also researched within the Transumo program. First, the rules of city distribution and logistics are changing (Quak 2008). Local governments impose more and more restrictions, collaboration and coordination between parties might be one of the essential instruments to make a difference. MAS can play an essential role here, as it involves large dynamics. Second, the stream of work presented in Agatz (2009) adds an interesting perspective. It is shown that consumers are highly price sensitive, and that revenue management techniques can make a difference also in logistics operations – whereas this is until now primarily used in more expensive purchases, such as airline tickets, hotel rooms, and holiday trips. Revenue management as a technique can play an important role in future logistic solutions, as it is an instrument to streamline operations driven from the demand side. Intelligent IT and capability to interact and adjust in real-time are essential instruments here; hence the role for MAS. Third, the concept of network orchestration – see the case of Li and Fung as described by Margretta (1998) as an example – requires other IT architectures better capable of handling real-time dynamics and leveraging changes in the network to the fullest extend. As such, innovative IT, and the corresponding innovative mindset still do matter (Ordanini 2005) – opposed to the message of Carr (2003).

8.6.3 *Sustainability*

Getting back to the theme of sustainability. Sustainability deals with the potential for long-term maintenance of wellbeing of humans, which in turn depends on the wellbeing of the natural world and the responsible use of natural resources. There is nowadays abundant scientific evidence that humanity is living unsustainably. Returning human use of natural resources to within sustainable limits will require a major collective effort (Hartmann 2001; Friedman 2008). At the other hand, the quest for sustainability offers many challenging and promising foresights. Nidumolu et al. (2009) come to the conclusion that the only answer to become sustainable means a pure focus on innovation.

Our research has shown the potential for better coordination of activities in road transport – which can lead to less idling of trucks (that generally keep their engines running), smarter routes, and better combinations. The research in this chapter has led to the conclusion that multi-agent systems are a possible instrument to help construct logistic planning systems of a next generation that put real-time information processing and negotiation and coordination at their core. As such multi-agent systems can be a valuable instrument not only in the planning of logistic activities, but might be of good use in many more domains (including smart vehicles, smart electricity grids, smart datacenters, and so on). See also the developments around the upcoming Internet-of-Things (Chui et al. 2010). MAS architectures come in handy in such environments that deal with distributed information, distributed intelligence (e.g. smart devices), and multiple parties with diverse backend systems. Also connecting to higher level cloud services, thus combining local intelligence with aggregated services in the cloud, is a logical extension to any multi-agent system design. Our world, and especially our way of living, can only become really sustainable if our systems and we become much smarter. Influencing consumer behaviour through revenue management techniques (Agatz 2009) might be, as discussed before, interesting to steer and influence operations. MAS can contribute its share, but it is important that we start making real steps. Let us go out, implement, and change.

References

Adler JL, Blue VJ (2002) A cooperative multi-agent transportation management and route guidance system. Transp Res C 10(5–6):433–454

Agatz NAH (2009) Demand management in e-fulfillment, Erasmus University Rotterdam, EPS-2009-163-LIS, ISBN: 978-90-5892-200-7

Bellifemine FL, Caire G, Greenwood D (2007) Developing multi-agent systems with JADE. Wiley, Newyork

Bold A, Olsson J (2005) What it costs to manage collaborative logistics. EyeForTransport report, London

Caridi M, Cavalieri S (2004) Multi-agent systems in production planning and control: an overview. Prod Plan Control 15(2):106–118

Carr NG (2003) IT doesn't matter. Harv Bus Rev 81(5):5–12

Chmiel K, Gawinecki M, Kacmarek P, Szymczak M, Paprzycki M (2005) Efficiency of JADE agent platform. Sci Program 13(2):159–172

Chui M, Löffler M, Roberts R (2010) The internet of things. McKinsey Q 2:70–79

Davenport TH, Brooks JD (2004) Enterprise systems and the supply chain. J Enterprise Inf Manage 17(1):8

Davidsson P, Henesey L, Ramstedt L, Tornquist J, Wernstedt F (2005) An analysis of agent-based approaches to transport logistics. Transp Res C Emerg Technol 13(4):255–271

Douma AM (2008) Aligning the operations of barges and terminals through distributed planning. BETA research school for operations management and logistics. PhD thesis, University of Twente, Enschede

Eisenhardt KM (1989) Building theories from case study research. Acad Manage Rev 14 (4):532–550

Fischer K, Muller JP, Pischel M (1996) Cooperative transportation scheduling: an application domain for DAI. Appl Artif Intell 10(1):1–33

Fitzgerald G (1998) Evaluating information systems projects: a multidimensional approach. J Inform Technol 13(1):15–27

Friedman T (2008) "Hot, flat and crowded" farrar, straus and giroux. Earthscan, London. ISBN 0374166854

Hartmann T (2001) The last hours of ancient sunlight: waking up to personal and global transformation. Three Rivers Press, New York. ISBN 0609805290

Hevner AR, March ST, Park J, Ram S (2004) Design science in information systems research. MIS Q 28(1):75–105

Kaplan B, Duchon D (1988) Combining qualitative and quantitative methods in information systems research: a case study. MIS Q 12(4):571–586

Krauth E (2008) Real-time planning support – a task-technology fit perspective. ERIM PhD series research in management, PhD thesis, Rotterdam Erasmus University, Rotterdam

Lea BR, Gupta MC, Yu WB (2005) A prototype multi-agent ERP system: an integrated architecture and a conceptual framework. Technovation 25(4):433–441

Levi MD, Conrad FG (1996) A heuristic evaluation of a world wide web prototype. Interactions 3(4):50–61

Lewis I, Talalayevsky A (2004) Improving the interorganizational supply chain through optimization of information flows. J Enterprise Inf Manage 17(3):229–237

Lima RM, Sousa RM, Martins PJ (2006) Distributed production planning and control agent-based system. Int J Prod Res 44(18–19):3693–3709

Luck M, McBurney P, Preist C (2004) A manifesto for agent technology: towards next generation computing. Auton Agents Multi-Agent Syst 9:203–252

Mahr T, J Srour, M de Weerdt, R Zuidwijk (2008) Agent performance in vehicle routing when the only thing certain is uncertainty. In: Proceedings of 7th International Conference on autonomous agents and multiagent systems (AAMAS 2008), Estoril, Portugal

Margretta J (1998) Fast, global, and entrepreneurial: supply chain management, Hong-Kong style. Harv Bus Rev 76:102–114

Marik V, McFarlane D (2005) Industrial adoption of agent-based technologies. IEEE Intell Syst 20(1):27–35

Moonen H (2009) Multi-agent systems for transportation planning and coordination. ERIM PhD series research in management. PhD thesis, Rotterdam Erasmus University, Rotterdam

Moonen H, Douma AM, Krauth E, van Hillegersberg J (2008) Obstacles to multi-agent systems implementation – expert opinions confronted with literature. In: Blecker T, Kersten W, Gertz C (eds) Management in logistics networks and nodes. Erich Schmidt Verlag, Berlin, pp 269–290
Moyaux T, Chaib-draa B, D'Amours S (2006) Supply chain management and multiagent systems: an overview. In: Chaib-draa B, Müller JP (eds) Multiagent-based supply chain management. Springer, Berlin
Nidumolu R, Prahalad CK, Rangaswami MR (2009) Why sustainability is now the key driver of innovation. Harv Bus Rev 87:57–64
Nielsen J, Clemmensen T, Yssing C (2002) Getting access to what goes on in people's heads?: reflections on the think-aloud technique. In: Proceedings of the second Nordic conference on human–computer interaction, ACM Press, New York
Nunamaker JF, M Chen (1990) Systems development in information systems research. In: Proceedings of the 23rd Annual Hawaii International Conference on System Sciences, Hawaii
Oink A (2005) Agent technology in het containervervoer. School of Economics, MSc thesis, Erasmus University Rotterdam, Rotterdam
Ordanini A (2005) The effects of participation on B2B exchanges: a resource-based view. Calif Manage Rev 47(2):97–113
Quak HJ (2008) Sustainability of urban freight transport: retail distribution and local regulation in cities. Erasmus University, Rotterdam. ISBN 978-90-5892-154-3
Rudowsky IS (2004) Intelligent agents. Commun Assoc Inf Syst 14:275–290
Saracevic T (1995) Evaluation of evaluation in information retrieval. In: Proceedings of the 18th annual international ACM SIGIR conference on Research and development in information retrieval, ACM, New York, pp 138–146
Schleiffer R (2005) An intelligent agent model. Eur J Oper Res 166:666–693
Sharman G (2003) e-Supply chain management – venturing beyond e-commerce. Business briefing: global purchasing and supply chain strategies. pp 17–24
Sierra C (2004) Agent-mediated electronic commerce. Auton Agents Multi-Agent Syst 9:285–301
Singh N, Lai KH, Cheng TCE (2007) Intra-organizational perspectives on IT-enabled supply chains. Commun ACM 50(1):59–65
Trappey AJC, Trappey CV, Hou JL, Chen BJG (2004) Mobile agent technology and application for online global logistic services. Ind Manage Data System 104(1–2):169–183
Van Hillegersberg J (1997) Metamodelling-based integration of object-oriented systems development. Proefschrift Erasmus Universiteit Rotterdam, Rotterdam
Van Laarhoven P, M Damen, J Fransoo, T Huges, J Lintsen, S van Loon, A Olijslager, C Paauwe, F van Schaik, M Leijnse (2006) Naar een vitalere supply chain door krachtige innovatie (Eindrapportage Commissie Van Laarhoven), Hoofddorp
Van Rijswijck H, Davydenko I (2007) Intelligent agents in transportation planning. TNO Built Environment and Geosciences, Delft, pp 1–49
Vokurka RJ, Choobineh J et al (1996) A prototype expert system for the evaluation and selection of potential suppliers. Int J Oper Prod Manage 16(12):106–127
Wareham J, Zheng JG, Straub D (2005) Critical themes in electronic commerce research: a meta-analysis. J Inf Technol 20(1):1–19
Wooldridge M, Jennings NR (1995) Intelligent agents: theory and practice. Knowledge Manage Rev 1995(January):1–62
Wright PC, Monk AF (1990) The use of think-aloud evaluation methods in design. SIGCHI Bull 23(1):55–57
Yin RK (2003) Case study research: design and methods. Sage, Thousand Oaks

Chapter 9
Demand Management in Transportation and Logistics

Niels Agatz and Jo van Nunen

9.1 Introduction

Demand management, or revenue management, is commonplace in many industries. In order to enhance revenues, revenue management aims to exploit differences in product preferences between customers by prioritizing service to customers with a higher willingness-to-pay. The key lesson from revenue management is that a company should try to use its scarce capacity for its most valuable customers. Instead of accepting demand first-come, first-serve, it may be beneficial to reserve capacity for more valuable customers that may still arrive in the future. There is a huge body of literature devoted to quantity control policies and dynamic pricing in revenue management (for a review, see Chiang et al. 2007), Talluri and Van Ryzin (2004) and Boyd and Bilegan (2003). Quantity-based control manages the availability of product classes, while price-based control is concerned with the price of products. Note that pricing refers to the whole range of incentives that are available to manage customer demand, e.g. financial rewards for peak travel avoidance (Knockaert et al., Chap. 6). Airlines, hotels and rental car industries represent the most successful applications of revenue management (Chiang et al. 2007). These industries all share some similar business characteristics. In particular, their products are perishable, the availability of capacity is relatively inflexible in the short run, and the variable costs operating costs are small, relative to the fixed costs.

Yet, modern ICT technology and Internet retailing make revenue management applications available beyond these traditional sectors (Quante et al. 2009, Agatz et al. 2008c). In transportation and logistics, however, the variable operating costs often play an important role and demand management has to take both revenues and costs into account. Here, the vehicle assignment and the sequence of stops is often

N. Agatz (✉) • J. van Nunen
Rotterdam School of Management, Erasmus University, PO Box 1738, 3000 DR Rotterdam, The Netherlands
e-mail: nagatz@rsm.nl

J.A.E.E. van Nunen et al. (eds.), *Transitions Towards Sustainable Mobility*,
DOI 10.1007/978-3-642-21192-8_9, © Springer-Verlag Berlin Heidelberg 2011

determined after the order-intake, which connects demand management to transportation-optimization, a huge field of academic study with modelling and algorithmic contributions abound (see, e.g., Golden et al. 2008, and Toth and Vigo 2001). Transportation-optimization typically aims at satisfying given customer demand while increasing cost-efficiency. A classic combinatorial optimization problem that often occurs in transportation is the Vehicle Routing Problem with Delivery Time Windows. This problem considers the construction of the most cost-efficient vehicle routes satisfying demand where the stops must occur within some specified time-window (Braysy and Gendreau 2005a, b). Delivery time windows and locations are key input parameters for the optimization, thus determining the efficiency of the resulting solutions. Instead of taking demand (i.e. time windows) as a given, the Internet enables companies to dynamically manage time windows and their corresponding prices in order to increase revenues and cost-efficiency (see, for example, Campbell and Savelsbergh 2005, 2006).

Demand management may focus on other criteria than profitability alone. Global environmental concern has increased the interest in more sustainable ways to do business. Transportation and logistics activities have a direct impact on environmental and social performance criteria, such as CO_2 emissions, pollution and traffic congestion. Transportation requests may differ in terms of profitability, price and service costs, but also in terms of emissions. Demand management can provide a powerful tool to increase a firm's triple bottom performance; people, planet and profit. Transportation service providers could, for instance, prioritize service to 'environmentally friendly' customers. Moreover, demand management enables companies to seduce customers to place more sustainable requests, e.g. for delivery outside rush hour or in a time period together with a neighbouring customer. Note that this links demand management to traffic management. UK-based Internet grocer Ocado, for example, is appealing to the customers' environmental concerns by indicating which delivery time would minimize fuel consumption. The company uses a 'green van' to indicate that a delivery van is already in the customer's neighbourhood at a certain time (see Fig. 9.1).

In this chapter, we introduce several research projects that consider the application of demand management ideas in transportation and logistics, including the home delivery of groceries, automotive logistics and the supply of retailers in the city. All projects have been part of Transumo and are carried out in close collaboration with the business community.

9.2 Demand Management at Albert.nl

Albert.nl is the Internet channel of Albert Heijn, the Netherlands' largest supermarket chain and a subsidiary of Royal Ahold, the retail multinational. Albert.nl offers about 9,000 Stock Keeping Units (SKUs), including fresh groceries such as meat, milk, and fruit, similar to a mid-sized Dutch supermarket. The product prices are identical to those in the conventional Albert Heijn stores, plus a time-dependent

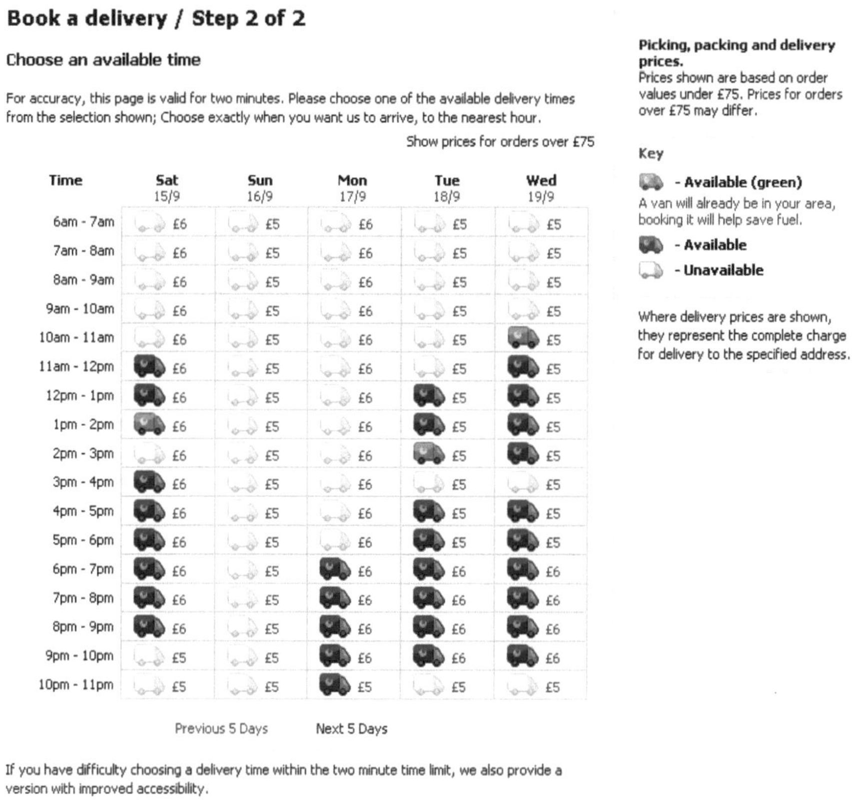

Book a delivery / Step 2 of 2

Choose an available time

For accuracy, this page is valid for two minutes. Please choose one of the available delivery times from the selection shown; Choose exactly when you want us to arrive, to the nearest hour.

Show prices for orders over £75

Time	Sat 15/9	Sun 16/9	Mon 17/9	Tue 18/9	Wed 19/9
6am - 7am	£6	£5	£6	£5	£5
7am - 8am	£6	£5	£6	£5	£5
8am - 9am	£6	£5	£6	£5	£5
9am - 10am	£6	£5	£6	£5	£5
10am - 11am	£6	£5	£6	£5	£5
11am - 12pm	£6	£5	£6	£5	£5
12pm - 1pm	£6	£5	£6	£5	£5
1pm - 2pm	£6	£5	£6	£5	£5
2pm - 3pm	£6	£5	£6	£5	£5
3pm - 4pm	£6	£5	£6	£5	£5
4pm - 5pm	£6	£5	£6	£5	£5
5pm - 6pm	£6	£5	£6	£5	£5
6pm - 7pm	£6	£5	£6	£6	£6
7pm - 8pm	£6	£5	£6	£6	£6
8pm - 9pm	£6	£5	£6	£6	£6
9pm - 10pm	£5	£5	£6	£6	£6
10pm - 11pm	£5	£5	£5	£5	£5

Previous 5 Days   Next 5 Days

If you have difficulty choosing a delivery time within the two minute time limit, we also provide a version with improved accessibility.

Picking, packing and delivery prices.
Prices shown are based on order values under £75. Prices for orders over £75 may differ.

Key

- Available (green)
A van will already be in your area, booking it will help save fuel.

- Available

- Unavailable

Where delivery prices are shown, they represent the complete charge for delivery to the specified address.

Fig. 9.1 Delivery time menu Ocado

delivery fee. Albert.nl has organized its warehouse and delivery operations in two shifts per day. Currently, the company offers its attended home delivery service in all major urban areas in the Netherlands. Albert.nl offers attended home delivery in 2-h delivery windows, which is typical for e-grocery (see Boyer et al. 2003, Boyer and Hult 2005, de Koster 2002, and Yrjola 2001). The booking deadline is about 16 h before the actual delivery. After that deadline, when all the orders for the given shift are known, the company plans the corresponding delivery routes. Subsequently, the orders are picked in the warehouse and grouped by vehicle before actually being delivered. A typical delivery route visits between 10 and 20 customers.

9.2.1 Product and Demand

The core product in e-grocery consists of the physical groceries and the service involved with getting the products delivered to the customer's home. The perceived convenience of the fulfilment service is dependent on various service elements including the lead-time, the length and timing of the delivery window and delivery fee. Internet shopping is appealing to a wide variety of costumers, for various reasons, e.g. a busy lifestyle or a physical disability (Hays et al. 2004). Similar to the airline setting, these customers differ in terms of preferences and willingness-to-pay. For example, consider a busy two income household and an elderly person living alone. Most likely, these two segments differ considerably in their price sensitivity and time flexibility. Albert charges a delivery fee to cover for the additional fulfilment service component. Hence, the revenues in e-fulfilment are made up of the margins on the physical products and the delivery fee. Product margins might differ considerably between different orders. The size of the margin typically relates to the order size and the product characteristics. On the e-grocer's website, the customer reserves a time slot before developing an order list, which means that the total revenues are only known after completion of the order.

9.2.2 Demand Management Levers

In line with the distinction between quantity- and price-based control often used in revenue management (Talluri and Van Ryzin 2004), we distinguish between slot-based control and price-based control. The chosen control type (i.e. slotting or pricing) has a great impact on the way related issues are modelled. Capacity-based control is basically an accept-reject decision. For each time slot, one has to decide if it is available to a certain customer or not. Consequently, rejecting a customer in a certain time slot does not mean that the customer is actually rejected after choosing the time slot. It simply means that the time slot is not available to this specific customer at a given time.

The main levers to manage customer demand in such an environment are the offered time slots and the corresponding delivery fees. The Internet retailer may apply both of these options, slotting and pricing, at different moments in the sales process, either off-line prior to the actual order intake or real-time as demand unfolds.

9.2.3 Research and Results

The research in collaboration with Albert.nl resulted in several papers (Agatz et al. 2008a, c, 2011) and a PhD thesis (Agatz 2009). Agatz et al. (2011) address the problem of assigning specific time slots to zip codes, given a set of service requirements, the Time Slot Management Problem (TSMP). The assignment needs to facilitate cost-effective routing of delivery vehicles. The goal is to choose the delivery options offered to the market so as to maximize expected profit, considering revenues (R) and fulfilment costs (C).

9.2.3.1 Decision Variables

Service offering by region, consisting of timc-window + price,
s_i for $i = 1,\ldots,$ # zip code regions

9.2.3.2 Objective Function

Maximize expected profit per period

$$\max_{s_i} E[R - K|\{s_i\}]$$

9.2.3.3 Constraints

Minimum service requirements

Difficulty: estimate objective value for given service offering, i.e. scenario analysis already difficult, even without any optimization.

Decomposing the objective function into key building blocks:

$$E[R - K|\{s_i\}] = \sum_d p(d|\{s_i\})(R(d) - K(d)),$$

where *d* denotes a demand realization (i.e. set of orders with specific locations and delivery windows) and p(.) is the probability distribution of the demand realizations for a given service offering.

9.2.3.4 Building Blocks

$$p(d|\{s_i\})$$

Modelling dependent on marketing data;
Estimating entire distribution may be infeasible, given availablc data;
Possibly use rough-cut indications instead

$$R(d) = r|d| + delivery\,fee(\{s_i\}, d),$$

Assuming that order volumes are homogeneous across customers; all in all, revenues seem to be the easiest part of the model

$$K(d) = VRPTW(d),$$

i.e. vehicle routing problem with time windows for given set of orders;
N.B. can be decomposed into a separate VRPTW for each shift and

To facilitate further analysis, two fundamental assumptions are made: (1) the total demand is known for each zip code, and (2) the total demand is divided evenly over the set of offered time slots, irrespective of the number of time slots offered. Historical data support the validity of these assumptions. Two different modelling approaches are presented: *continuous approximation* and *integer programming*. *Continuous approximation* relies on simple formulas to approximate routing distances based on problem characteristics, such as vehicle capacity and demand density. Daganzo (2005) approximates the distance between two consecutive stops of a route through a region with a slowly varying demand density δ by $k/\sqrt{\delta}$ where k is a dimensionless constant that is independent of the region shape.

We use similar concepts to estimate the expected total distance travelled in a day for a given time slot schedule. The approach does not rely on detailed data of individual customer orders, but on concise summaries of "local" data.

For example, the expected distance travelled per zip code for an offered time slot is estimated based on the density of adjacent zip codes that also offer that time slot. The expected total distance travelled is then approximated by aggregating over all zip codes and offered time slots. The key assumption of the continuous approximation approach is that the demand density is slowly varying over time and space. The original continuous approximation approach divides the delivery route into two components: (1) the stem distance to the delivery region and (2) the distribution distance between consecutive stops in the delivery region. In our setting, we distinguish between four components of a delivery route:

- Distance between stops within the same zip code within the same time slot;
- Distance between stops in different zip codes within the same time slot;
- Distance between stops in two consecutive time slots
- Distance between the delivery region and the depot.

Given the evaluation of a time slot schedule, local search is used to improve the schedules.

The *integer programming* approach is based on a combination of two cost approximations. Consider a delivery vehicle. The cost incurred by that delivery vehicle is viewed as consisting of two parts. The first part consists of the costs incurred during a particular time slot, which is determined by the 'cluster' of zip codes visited during the time slot. The second part consists of the costs incurred by moving from one time slot to the next. The former costs are approximated by identifying a 'seed' zip code for the cluster and considering the distance of each zip code in the cluster to the seed zip code. The latter costs are approximated by considering the distance between the seed zip codes of the clusters visited in subsequent time slots.

The computational studies on real-life data demonstrate the viability and the merits of these methods. The results show that a more dynamic and differentiated demand management approach can lead to considerable cost savings. The reduction of vehicle-miles per order corresponds with considerable environmental benefits.

9.3 Demand Management at Broekman Automotive

The new-car supply chain encompasses manufacturing, distribution and sales (Holweg and Miemczyk 2003). For the distribution of Asian cars to Europe, the relatively large distances, together with the inflexibility of sea-transportation, make it difficult to match customer demand effectively while controlling distribution costs. Because of the long lead-times, accurate demand forecasts, i.e. number of cars, types, colours, is critical. Car importers typically outsource the distribution of new vehicles to a third-party logistics service provider. Broekman Automotive is such a logistics service provider, that is based in the Netherlands.

Broekman Automotive is the automotive division of the Broekman Group (www.broekman-group.nl), an international shipping and transportation group. The company organizes the transportation and distribution of cars from their arrival at the port of Rotterdam to the delivery at the retailer. The port of Rotterdam serves as the main gate of transport into Europe, from where cars are transported by ship, river barge, train or road. The company owns a fleet of 16 trucks that can handle up to eight cars for road transportation. The automotive division operates an independent car terminal in the port of Rotterdam, which is specialized in the handling of cars and other cargo, that is driven off and on to a vessel. Adjacent to the terminal is the technical car processing centre, Rotterdam Car Centre, with a storage capacity of about 30,000 cars, including multi-storey warehouses with capacities of 5,000–7,500 cars. On a yearly basis, the terminal handles more than 300,000 cars, of which a third requires additional services before being transported to the individual retailers, such as pre-delivery inspections, storage or value added service. The pre-delivery inspection is carried out as a quality check to ensure that all cars are fully working and not damaged during shipment. If necessary, the company also offers reparation, cleaning and reconditioning.

9.3.1 *Product and Demand*

The service offered by Broekman Automotive consists of the logistic handling of incoming cars. Car handling consists of receiving, storage, value-added services and distribution. The demand for this service is coordinated by several car importers. The importer is a car trading company, which buys cars from the manufacturer and sells them to car-dealers. Broekman Automotive delivers new cars to approximately 200 dealers located in 160 cities in the Netherlands. The delivery of cars takes place during weekdays and working-hours. There is no direct communication between the receiver of the car (i.e. the car dealer) and Broekman Automotive. The importer's supply to the dealers is partly on-demand and partly supply-driven. The dealer can request cars to the importer, based on expected sales, or an actual end-customer order. Moreover, the importer pushes slow movers into the dealer stock, to get the cars closer to the end-customers.

9.3.2 Demand Management Levers

Broekman Automotive can manage demand by determining the quantity of service capacity, that is made available to a specific importer (brand) or dealer. The service capacity consists of physical truck capacity and pre-delivery inspection capacity (staff and space). Moreover, the company may use the price of its service to differentiate between different customers or lead-times.

9.3.3 Research and Results

As part of a master thesis project (Van der Zwaluw 2009), we investigated the demand management opportunities at Broekman Automotive. In particular, we studied the differentiation of the service offering in terms of the delivery lead-time and corresponding prices. Currently, all delivery orders have an identical lead-time requirement of 5 days. However, from a customer-service perspective, the actual lead-time requirement may vary from car to car. Price discounts for longer lead-times may motivate the importer to provide more detailed information on the desired lead-time of each car, with respect to promises that are made to the end-consumer. This gives rise to a tradeoff between service (and corresponding revenues) and cost. Given the lead-time requirements of the customer, we developed a simple decision support model that helps to assign cars to delivery trucks at the right time. The results demonstrate that we may substantially increase the number of priority cars that are delivered on-time. That is, the results show a potential increase of customer service and production utility and a decrease in vehicle-miles (and corresponding environmental impact).

9.4 Demand Management in Urban Distribution

Urban freight distribution involves the supply of retailers in urban areas which involves different stakeholders including distributers, retailers, (local) authorities and the people that live, shop and/or work in the urban area. These different stakeholders all have their own goals and considerations with respect to the urban freight distribution issue. While governmental organizations are typically concerned about accessibility, traffic congestion and the reduction of environmental impacts, the shippers, carriers and receivers are usually interested in the costs-aspects of transportation.

Binnenstadservice.nl, established in April 2008 in Nijmegen, is a private initiative to improve the sustainability of urban distribution (see also Quak and Tavasszy, Chap. 9). The goal of the company is to reduce the transport movements in the city centre, which potentially leads to social, economical and environmental benefits.

They currently operate a warehouse outside the centre of Nijmegen to receive and consolidate freight supplies of the retailer shops located in the city. From the warehouse, Binnenstadservice.nl transports the freight directly to the shops, or stores it for later transportation. This decreases the number of trucks that need to enter the city centre, reducing pollution, hindrance and transportation costs, and increases the city's accessibility. The concept can also contribute to an overall reduction of the number of required delivery trucks by eliminating the inefficiencies caused by city centre restrictions such as limited time-window access and vehicle limitations. Besides deliveries, Binnenstadservice.nl also offers services such as collecting packaging materials, home delivery to individual end-customers and providing storage space.

9.4.1 Product and Demand

The main stakeholders in the urban logistics supply chain in which Binnenstadservice.nl operates are suppliers (shipper), transport companies (carrier) and receivers (retailer).

9.4.2 Demand Management Levers

The most important demand management lever is the price charged to the stakeholders for the provided service. Currently, receiving, collecting and delivering the goods to the retailers in the city centre is free of charge to encourage companies to join and create a critical mass.

9.4.3 Research and Results

Currently, the retail shops, although they are the main receivers of supply, usually have no idea of the actual transport costs of delivery. Moreover, they have limited impact on the transportation process. The lack of cost transparency and communication between stakeholders results in a limited visibility of the problems for each stakeholder individually. In his master thesis, Blom (2009) identifies and quantifies the value of the Binnenstadservice.nl solution for the different stakeholders, in particular the transport operators, retailers and governments. The author concludes that all stakeholders may achieve substantial benefits from cooperation with Binnenstadservice.nl. Yet, only transport companies gain direct financial benefits on the short term. The benefits for the carriers and national governments will increase in the future when the idea is expanded to cover a broader range of Dutch urban areas.

9.5 Conclusions

This chapter has shown that the potential of demand management goes beyond the traditional revenue management applications in the airline and hotel business. There are many opportunities to apply demand management in sectors where marginal costs do play an important role. Here, demand management can enhance profitability by influencing both revenues and costs. Besides profitability criteria, social and environmental criteria may be taken into account.

While both sustainability (e.g. emissions, congestion) and cost criteria (e.g. fuel, time) are roughly proportional to travel distance, corporate objectives of demand management in transportation are generally in line with environmental objectives. Demand management allows transporters to reduce costs by providing customer incentives that promote cost-efficient behaviour, aligning the customer's objectives with the system objectives (see also Immers and Van der Knaap, Chap. 14). This implies that demand management facilitates a top-down transition towards more sustainable transportation.

References

Agatz NAH (2009) Demand management in E-fulfillment. ERIM PhD series research in management, Rotterdam. http://hdl.handle.net/1765/15425

Agatz NAH, Campbell AM, Fleischmann M, Savelsbergh M, van Nunen J (2008a) Demand management opportunities in E-fulfillment – what internet retailers can learn from revenue management. Working paper, Rotterdam School of Management, Erasmus University, Rotterdam

Agatz NAH, Campbell AM, Fleischmann M, Savelsbergh M (2011) Time slot management in attended home delivery. Transp Sci (Forthcoming)

Agatz NAH, Fleischmann M, van Nunen JAEE (2008c) E-fulfillment and multi-channel distribution – a review. Eur J Oper Res 187(2):339–356

Blom F (2009) Determining the value of Binnenstadservice.nl for their customers. MSc thesis, Rotterdam School of Management Erasmus University, Rotterdam

Boyd EA, Bilegan IC (2003) Revenue management and e-commerce. Manage Sci 49 (10):1363–1386

Boyer KK, Hult GTM (2005) Extending the supply chain: integrating operations and marketing in the online grocery industry. J Oper Manage 23(6):642–661

Boyer KK, Tomas Hult G, Frohlich M (2003) An exploratory analysis of extended grocery supply chain operations and home delivery. Integr Manuf Syst 14(8):652

Braysy I, Gendreau M (2005a) Vehicle routing problem with time windows, part I: route construction and local search algorithms. Transp Sci 39(1):104–118

Braysy I, Gendreau M (2005b) Vehicle routing problem with time windows, part II: metaheuristics. Transp Sci 39(1):119–139

Campbell AM, Savelsbergh MWP (2005) Decision support for consumer direct grocery initiatives. Transp Sci 39(3):313–327

Campbell AM, Savelsbergh M (2006) Incentive schemes for attended home delivery services. Transp Sci 40(3):327–341

Chiang W, Cheng JCH, Xu X (2007) An overview of research on revenue management: current issues and future research. Int J Revenue Manage 1(1):97–128

Daganzo CF (2005) Logistics systems analysis, 4th edn. Springer, Berlin/Heidelberg

De Koster MBM (2002) The logistics behind the enter click. In: Klose A, Van Wassenhove LN (eds) Quantitative approaches to distribution logistics and supply chain management. Springer, Berlin

Golden B, Raghavan S, Wasil E (eds) (2008) The vehicle routing problem: latest advances and new challenges. Springer, Berlin

Hays T, Keskinocak P, de VM Lopez (2004) Strategies and challenges of internet grocery retailing logistics. In: Guenes J, Akcaki E, Pardalos PM, Romeijn HE, Shen ZJ (eds) Applications of supply chain management and e-commerce research in industry. Kluwer, Dordrecht

Holweg M, Miemczyk J (2003) Delivering the '3-day car'–the strategic implications for automotive logistics operations. J Purch Supply Manage 9(2):63–71

Quante R, Meyr H, Fleischmann M (2009) Revenue management and demand fulfillment: matching applications, models, and software. OR Spectr 31(1):31–62

Talluri KT, Van Ryzin GJ (2004) The theory and practice of revenue management. Springer, New York

Toth P, Vigo D (eds) (2001) The vehicle routing problem. Society for Industrial and Applied Mathematics, Philadelphia

van der Zwaluw M (2009) Improving customer service through order intake control case: new car logistics. MSc thesis, Rotterdam School of Management Erasmus University, Rotterdam

Yrjola H (2001) Physical distribution considerations for electronic grocery shopping. Int J Phys Distrib Logistics Manage 31(9/10):746

Part C
Towards Reliable Transport Systems

Chapter 10
Beyond Punctuality: Appropriate Measures for Unreliability in Rail Passenger Transport

Martijn Brons and Piet Rietveld

10.1 Introduction

Increasing levels of congestion, a growing awareness of climate change, and the notion of peak oil constitute some of the most important global challenges today. European policy making views the promotion of sustainable mobility as one of the key objectives of transport policy. Railway is the natural backbone of any sustainable transport system, offering efficient transport built on social equity, low carbon emissions, low environmental impacts and positive economic growth. Hence, improving the position of the railways is one of the pillars of the transition towards sustainable mobility. Maintaining rail service quality is safeguarded by policy makers through concessions in which railway operators are typically held accountable for measurable indicators of quality aspects, such as punctuality. At the same time, the ambitions of European rail operators, including the Dutch Railways, as reflected by company mission and media statements, aim to develop towards a more customer-oriented focus. As the choice for rail versus other transport is ultimately the traveller's choice, the transition towards a customer-oriented approach seems to provide more potential for improving the position of the railways than a pure process-oriented focus and should therefore be adopted and supported by policymakers. Using customer satisfaction data from the Dutch Railways, Brons

The views expressed are purely those of the author and may not in any circumstances be regarded as stating an official position of the European Commission.

M. Brons (✉)
European Commission, Joint Research Centre (JRC), Institute for Prospective Technological Studies (IPTS), c/Inca Garcilaso 3, Seville 41092, Spain
e-mail: martijn.brons@ec.europa.eu

P. Rietveld
Department of Spatial Economics, VU University Amsterdam, De Boelelaan 1105, Amsterdam 1081 HV, The Netherlands
e-mail: p.rietveld@vu.nl

J.A.E.E. van Nunen et al. (eds.), *Transitions Towards Sustainable Mobility*,
DOI 10.1007/978-3-642-21192-8_10, © Springer-Verlag Berlin Heidelberg 2011

and Rietveld (2008) analyze the relative importance of ten dimensions of the door-to-door rail journey, based on derived importance regression techniques and conclude that travel time unreliability is the second key dimension, just behind travel comfort. However, unlike travel comfort, travel time unreliability receives a low average satisfaction score. Following the marketing literature on customer satisfaction (e.g. Hawes and Rao 1985; Kristensen et al. 1992; Slack 1994; Bacon 2003), the combination of high importance and low satisfaction classifies travel time unreliability as a 'problem area' where improvements are required in order to increase the satisfaction with the door-to-door rail journey. The question remains to what extent improvements in the actual travel time reliability translate into an increase in the travel time reliability as perceived by the rail passenger. A crucial point in this context is how travel time reliability is measured.

In the Netherlands, the Dutch Railways are being held accountable by the Ministry of Transport for the so-called 'punctuality' of trains, measured at 34 important rail interchange points in the Netherlands (Dutch Railways 2006). A train is considered to be punctual if it arrives within 3 min of delay.[1] It is questionable whether such a process-oriented approach of reliability corresponds very well with the customer-oriented ambitions of the Dutch Railways. Brons and Rietveld (2007) formulate a number of criticisms of the use of punctuality as a reliability indicator, including the following. First, apart from the question whether or not the (arbitrary) punctuality margin of 3 min is met, no particular weight is attached to the size of the delay. One could argue that for the traveller it does matter if a train has 3 min of delay or 30. Second, no particular weight is given to the variation in arrival times of trains. One could argue that the passenger's perception of unreliability would include elements of unpredictability rather than only adherence (or lack thereof) to time tables. Third, negative consequences of delays on departure are not captured. Extra waiting time caused by a delayed departure results in a loss of utility, even if the train arrives in time at the final destination. Furthermore, departing late may result in missed connections and hence to even more substantial time losses than late arrivals. These criticisms raise the question whether the punctuality indicator fully captures the actual disutility of the rail passengers caused by travel time unreliability, or if certain alternative indicators of travel time unreliability may perform better in this respect. In the present paper we focus on the key notion of reliability in the context of railway trips. This notion has a clear relationship with the concept of *sustainability*, which is the unifying element of this volume. The main dimensions of sustainability are *people, profit* and *planet*. The *people* dimension is at the core of the present paper, since we focus on how reliability contributes to traveller satisfaction. As people get more wealthy, quality dimensions become increasingly important in their travel behaviour and as reliability of services is an important quality dimension, railway companies cannot ignore this issue. From customer satisfaction it is only one step towards *profit,* since an improved reliability leading

[1]Until 1999, the Ministry of Transport adhered to the international standard of a margin of 5 min.

to higher satisfaction levels leads to a higher willingness to pay for the transport services and also to an increase in the number of passengers. This provides a link with the *planet* dimension: when quality improvement leads to a larger number of travellers by train, this may imply a reduction in travel by car or air, and this will have a beneficial effect on pollution in the transport sector.

From a *transition* viewpoint, the present paper addresses a major change taking place in the railway sector during the current times, i.e. the transition from a supply-driven strategy, where the emphasis is on sticking to fixed time tables, towards a demand-driven strategy, where customer satisfaction gets priority. The challenge is to link the operational processes aiming at keeping trains running according to schedule with the needs and desires of travellers who may face delays.

The main contribution of this paper concerns the broad treatment of reliability in terms of a comparative analysis of a wide range of indicators. Most studies on this subject just consider only one particular way of measuring this important concept, for example, by just looking at only the probability of a delay of say 5 min or by only considering the standard deviation in travel times. Another innovative step made in this paper is that a link is provided between objective measures of reliability and subjective measures, as reflected by the customer satisfaction. This is a very promising route to take, since in the end, the issue on what is the most adequate way of measuring reliability, depends on customer preferences.

This paper is organized as follows. Section 10.2 provides an overview of the data and introduces the different travel time indicators used in the analysis. Section 10.3 describes the results of a series of analyses, i.e., a descriptive analysis, a correlation analysis and a regression analysis on the determinants of travel time unreliability, in which we explore and compare the different travel time unreliability (hereafter abbreviated as TTU) indicators. Section 10.4 discusses the approach and results of an analysis based on regression and correlation estimations of the statistical relationship between different TTU indicators and specifications on the customer satisfaction with TTU. The conclusions are presented in Sect. 10.5.

10.2 Data

For the analysis in this study, we used two databases: customer satisfaction data from the Dutch Railways and data on TTU from ProRail. We obtained data on customer satisfaction from a survey which is conducted on an ongoing basis by the Dutch rail operator NS. Currently, the survey consists of 70,000 forms per year (Schreurs 2005). The survey contains inter alia 37 questions on the satisfaction with different elements of the journey, including the satisfaction with the travel time reliability. The satisfaction scale used is from 1 ("cannot be worse") to 10 ("excellent"). Furthermore, this survey contains data on individual characteristics of the interviewees.

Data on TTU with respect to both arrival time and departure time were obtained from ProRail, the organization in charge of the management of the rail network infrastructure (ProRail 2007). This database covers the period between June 2004 and December 2005 and contains data at the train station level on a monthly basis (19 months). For each of the 346 stations in the database we have the following information: (1) the number of trains with respectively <3, 3–5, 5–7, 7–9 and >9 min of delay on arrival (departure), (2) the total number of arriving (departing) trains, (3) the total number of minutes of delay on arrival (departure); the total number of minutes of delay on arrival (departure) for trains which arrive (depart) with more than 3 min of delay. The data is separately available for different parts of the day (morning peak, evening peak or off-peak hours) and different parts of the week (weekends or weekdays).

Based on the available TTU data, we derived for each train station six different TTU indicators: two indicators that are based on percentages of delayed trains, i.e. (1) the percentage of trains delayed with more than 3 min (3MIN),[2] and (2) the percentage delayed with more than 9 min (9MIN); two indicators that are based on the size of delays, i.e., (3) the average delay in minutes (AVMIN), and (4) the average delay of trains with a delay of more than 3 min (AVMIND); and, finally, two indicators that are based on travel time variation, i.e., (5) the 80–50th percentile (PERC) and (6) the standard deviation (STDEV). The data on 3MIN, 9MIN, AVMIN and AVMIND are directly calculated from the source data. The indicators based on travel time variation, i.e., PERC and STDEV, are estimated based on the available data and a number of assumptions on travel time distributions. For an explanation of the estimation procedure, we refer to Annex A. For all indicators, both arrival- and departure-based specifications are calculated.

10.3 Explorative Analysis of Different TTU-Indicators

In this section, a number of exploratory analyses are carried out: (1) a descriptive analysis of the TTU indicators, (2) an analysis of the correlation patterns among indicators and (3) an exploratory regression analysis explaining the variation in TTU among railway stations.

10.3.1 Descriptive Analysis of TTU-Indicators

Table 10.1 shows the mean and standard deviation of each of the TTU-indicators over the 346 train stations in the database. The results are weighted for the number of passenger arrivals and departures on each station. The mean value of 3MIN on arrival is 15.9%. This corresponds with a punctuality of 84.1%, with a standard

[2]The 3MIN indicator corresponds to the punctuality measure used by the Dutch Railways, except for the fact that it is measured as the percentage of delayed rather than undelayed arrivals (departures), in order to facilitate comparison with the other indicators.

Table 10.1 Descriptive statistics with respect to TTU per station on arrival and on departure for six different TTU-indicators

	On arrival	On departure
3MIN (%)	15.9 (5.5)	14.3 (6.4)
9MIN (%)	3.6 (1.6)	3.0 (1.6)
AVMIN (minutes)	1.40 (0.67)	1.63 (0.66)
AVMIND (minutes)	7.53 (1.26)	7.08 (1.18)
PERC (minutes)	2.09 (0.45)	1.71 (0.44)
STDEV (minutes)	3.64 (0.77)	3.07 (0.76)
N	346	346

deviation of 5.5. 3MIN of departing trains is slightly lower with a mean value of 14.3%. For the other indicators, it also holds that the arrival-based specification has slightly higher values than their departure-based counterparts, the only exception being the average delay in minutes, which is 1.40 for arrivals and 1.63 min for departures.

Based on the results in Table 10.1, we can draw two general conclusions. First, arrival-based and departure-based TTU indicators have rather different values. Second, despite the fact that the average delay on arrival is smaller than that on departure, both the variation in arrival times and the arrival-based dispunctuality are higher than their departure-based counterparts. This paradox may be explained by the occurrence of a small number of early arrivals, which would indeed result in higher variation and a lower average delay, but would not necessarily reduce the dispunctuality. The occurrence of early departures, on the other hand, is negligible.

10.3.2 Correlation Among TTU-Indicators

We carried out a correlation analysis, in order to assess the degree to which the different TTU-indicators do indeed measure different underlying effects. Correlation coefficients between TTU-indicator pairs are given in Table 10.2. The pattern of correlation among TTU-indicators is similar for TTU on arrival (the values above the diagonal) and TTU on departure (the values below the diagonal) in the sense that the set of indicator pairs with a correlation of 0.500 or higher are the same. Both on arrival and departure, 3MIN shows the strongest correlation with AVMIN, and is only weakly correlated to AVMIND and the two indicators based on travel time variation.

The results suggest two clusters of indicators: A cluster with indicators that do not attach specific value to extreme results (3MIN and AVMIN), and a cluster with indicators that do (9MIN, AVMIND, PERC and STDEV). In general, the values of the correlation coefficients indicate that the alternative TTU-indicators measure different underlying effects than 3MIN. This suggests that it may be good practice to include more than one indicator in statistical analyses on TTU.

Table 10.2 Correlation among different indicators of TTU on arrival (above diagonal) and on departure (below diagonal)

	3MIN	9MIN	AVMIN	AVMIND	PERC	STDEV
3MIN	–	0.667	0.815	0.105	0.349	0.356
9MIN	0.716	–	0.692	0.531	0.666	0.746
AVMIN	0.748	0.696	–	0.233	0.169	0.343
AVMIND	0.200	0.552	0.411	–	0.338	0.798
PERC	0.392	0.604	0.080	0.176	–	0.641
STDEV	0.489	0.798	0.402	0.709	0.616	–

All coefficients are significant at the 0.01-level (two-tailed). N = 26,296 (For each of the 346 stations we have unreliability data for each of four periods of the week (weekend, morning peak, evening peak and off-peak hours on weekdays) for each of the 19 months in our dataset. This results in total sample of 26,296 observations.)

Table 10.3 Correlation between TTU on arrival and TTU on departure for different indicators

3MIN	9MIN	AVMIN	AVMIND	PERC	STDEV
0.845	0.840	0.795	0.760	0.800	0.806

All coefficients are significant at the 0.01-level (two-tailed). N = 26,296

Table 10.3 shows the correlation between indicators of TTU on arrival and indicators of TTU on departure. While the correlation coefficients are higher than in the previous table, one might still argue that indicators of TTU on arrival and of TTU on departure measure different underlying effects.

10.3.3 Explaining the Variation in TTU Among Train Stations

In this section, we aim to explain the differences in TTU among train stations from differences in various station- and time-related variables. In order to do so we carry out a correlation analysis and a series of regression estimations, each time using a different TTU-indicator as the dependent variable, while the set of explanatory variables (see Table 10.4) remains unchanged. We use a weighted estimation procedure, in which we weighted according to the numbers of passenger arrival and departures per station.

The estimation results for TTU on arrival are summarized in Table 10.5. As only dummy variables were used as explanatory variables, all estimated coefficients show the difference in TTU between the variable concerned and the reference category, as indicated in Table 10.4.

Table 10.5 shows that 3MIN is higher on weekdays, than in weekends, and lower during the morning and the evening peak, than during off-peak hours. Furthermore, we see that 3MIN is lower in the Randstad region than outside of the Randstad, and lower on Intercity stations than on other stations. As for seasonal differences, the results show that 3MIN is about three percentage point higher in the winter and

Table 10.4 Overview of explanatory variables used

Variable	Categories
Part of the week	Weekdays[a]; Weekend
Part of the day	Off-peak hours[a]; Morning peak; Evening peak
Region	Randstad[a]; outside of Randstad
Type of station	Intercity-station; Other station[a]
Season	Spring[a]; Summer; Autumn; Winter

[a]Reference category

Table 10.5 Results of the regression estimation of TTU on arrival

	TTU-indicator											
	3MIN		9MIN		AVMIN		AVMIND		PERC		STDEV	
(Constant)	0.158	**	0.033	**	1.571	**	7.079	**	1.954	**	3.322	**
Weekend	−0.054	**	−0.016	**	−0.587	**	−0.549	**	−0.108	**	−0.596	**
Morning peak	0.013	**	−0.005	**	0.093	**	−0.809	**	−0.027	*	−0.452	**
Evening peak	0.030	**	0.007	**	0.288	**	−0.110	**	0.132	**	0.072	**
Randstad	−0.002	**	0.000		−0.002		0.106	**	−0.099	**	−0.007	
Intercity station	−0.003	**	0.006	**	−0.269	**	1.034	**	0.242	**	0.670	**
Summer	−0.011	**	0.000		−0.090	**	0.191	**	0.028	**	0.068	**
Autumn	0.029	**	0.004	**	0.261	**	−0.260	**	0.080	**	0.038	*
Winter	0.033	**	0.005	**	0.302	**	−0.204	**	0.089	**	0.056	**
R^2-adjusted	0.252		0.173		0.215		0.086		0.061		0.124	
N	34,272		34,272		34,272		34,272		34,272		34,272	

* = significant at the 0.05 level
** = significant at the 0.01 level

autumn then in the summer and spring, which may be due to weather effects and leaves on the rails.

Columns 2–6 show the impact of the determinant characteristics on the other five TTU-indicators. We limit ourselves to the discussion of a few general observations. The direction of the impact of the set of explanatory variables on 3MIN and on AVMIN are the same. All TTU-indicators are lower in the weekend. All TTU-indicators, except AVMIND, are higher in the autumn and winter. All indicators, except AVMIND are higher during the evening peak. For the morning peak, this only holds for 3MIN and AVMIN.

Table 10.6 shows the estimation results of the regression analysis of TTU on departure. For 3MIN, the direction of the impact of the explanatory variables corresponds with the direction of the impact on TTU on arrival (except for the impact of IC station status). However, the absolute coefficient values, and thus, the impact of station- and temporal variables, is generally lower. An explanation may be that control over departure times is higher than over arrival times. Whenever a train arrives with delay or arrives early, it may be possible to halt the train in the station shorter or longer than planned, in order to improve the TTU on departure. The difference between a train's arrival- and departure time functions as a buffer, by which low TTU on arrival can be absorbed.

Table 10.6 Results of the regression estimation of TTU on departure

	TTU-indicator											
	3MIN		9MIN		AVMIN		AVMIND		PERC		STDEV	
(Constant)	0.156	**	0.031	**	1.688	**	6.802	**	1.841	**	3.120	**
Weekend	−0.045	**	−0.013	**	−0.397	**	−0.512	**	−0.102	**	−0.509	**
Morning peak	0.009	**	−0.003	**	0.028	*	−0.644	**	0.016		−0.313	**
Evening peak	0.029	**	0.006	**	0.246	**	−0.058		0.125	**	0.117	**
Randstad	0.001		0.001	**	0.028	**	0.202	**	−0.108	**	0.012	
Intercity station	−0.025	**	−0.001	**	−0.096	**	0.544	**	−0.165	**	0.026	*
Summer	−0.008	**	0.000		−0.044	**	0.151	**	0.018	*	0.052	**
Autumn	0.022	**	0.003	**	0.151	**	−0.148	**	0.071	**	0.030	
Winter	0.025	**	0.004	**	0.179	**	−0.097	**	0.086	**	0.070	**
R^2-adjusted	0.196		0.123		0.140		0.040		0.049		0.052	
N	34,261		34,261		34,261		34,261		34,261		34,261	

* = significant at the 0.05 level
** = significant at the 0.01 level

Regarding the other TTU-indicators (columns 2–6), there are also differences between the impact of arrival-based and departure-based TTU. First, for all indicators, the difference between TTU on weekdays and in the weekend is lower for departure-based indicators. As mentioned before, the reason for this may be the notion, that the time between arrival and departure time of a train can function as a buffer. Departure-based indicators are, in general, higher on stations in the Randstad area than outside this area. This may indicate that the use of the previously mentioned buffer between arrival and departure time is lower in the Randstad area, possibly due to the higher service frequencies and more complex time table schedule, which may limit the possibilities to halt trains shorter or longer than planned in stations.

Based on the statistical results presented throughout this section in Tables 10.1–10.6, we recommend, that a thorough rail passenger-oriented analysis of TTU should not be limited to TTU, as it is currently measured by the Dutch Railways (and in many other countries). The inclusion of alternative TTU-indicators, based on both the size of delays and the travel time variation, may lead to insights which would not have been gained based on the sole use of punctuality-based indicators.

10.4 The Statistical Relationship Between Different TTU-Indicators and Customer Satisfaction with TTU

In this section, we carry out a series of regression and correlation estimations in order to compare the different TTU-indicators in terms of the degree to which they are statistically related to the customer satisfaction with TTU. Higher correlation or impact coefficients are indicative of a more appropriate measure of the TTU as perceived by the rail passengers. Along the same lines, we compare arrival-based and departure-based TTU specifications. Our approach is as follows. From the customer satisfaction survey, we have observations on individual evaluations of TTU, together with individual characteristics of the traveller, and the usual departure station of the traveller.

10.4.1 Assumptions

Assuming that an individual's TTU evaluation is based on his/her own TTU experience, for each observation the temporal and spatial rail travel pattern has to be determined, i.e., for each passenger we need information on which stations are used, and at which time, day and month trips are made. Although we do not have such detailed data, we do have information on trip characteristics and individual characteristics such as travel date and time, usual departure station, ticket type, travel purpose and travel frequency. Under certain assumptions we can use this information to derive spatial and temporal travel patterns for each traveller. Our assumptions are as follows. We assume that the TTU evaluation is based on TTU on the station indicated by the passenger as the common departure station at the place of residence, i.e. the 'home station'. If the individual travels with a weekdays or weekend student card, the evaluation is based on TTU in the part of the week in question. If the individual indicates to travel mainly during either peak-hours or off-peak hours, the evaluation is based on TTU in the corresponding part of the day. If the individual's travel frequency is less than one rail trip per year, the evaluation is based on the departure TTU of the train series in question. Finally, the evaluation is based to a larger degree on more recent TTU experiences. TTU experiences further in the past receive a lower weight. We refer to Annex B for a discussion of the implementation of this assumption in the model.

Despite these assumptions there are some difficulties in establishing a direct link between an individual's TTU satisfaction score and the actual experienced TTU based on his/her travel pattern. The actual underlying relationship between an individual TTU experience is distorted due to the fact that (1) the TTU experience with specific trains the individual uses is not incorporated, and (2) the TTU experience of certain train services the individual does not make use of, is accounted for. The estimated regression and correlation coefficients in this paper should therefore not be interpreted as indicators of the statistical relationship between satisfaction and TTU. However, given the size of the sample, the robustness of the results, and the fact that they are based on the same underlying data, the coefficients can meaningfully be used to compare the relationship between the TTU indicators and customer satisfaction, and hence the degree to which they capture the rail passenger's TTU perception.

Table 10.7 Results of a regression and correlation analysis on the statistical relation between different specifications of 3MIN and customer satisfaction with TTU

	TTU-specification			
	(1)		(2)	
(Constant)	6.282	**	6.234	**
3MINA	−1.362	**		
3MIND			−1.219	**
Business traveller	0.047		0.039	
Leisure traveller	0.037	*	0.032	*
Car available	0.194	**	0.199	**
Gender is female	−0.027	*	−0.026	*
Frequent traveller	−0.192	**	−0.184	**
Occasional traveller	0.156	**	0.162	**
Peak hours	0.119	**	0.116	**
Off-peak hours	0.264	**	0.267	**
Age below 20	0.003		0.013	
Age over 60	0.279	**	0.285	**
Discount ticket	−0.074	**	−0.078	**
Railcard	−0.096	**	−0.100	**
Randstad area	−0.108	**	−0.102	**
N	57,404		57,407	
Adjusted R^2	0.043		0.042	
Pearson correlation coefficient	−0.084	**	−0.085	**
Partial correlation coefficient	−0.067	**	−0.064	**

* = significant at the 0.05 level
** = significant at the 0.01 level

10.4.2 Estimation Results for Alternative Specifications of Punctuality

Our regression analysis is based on the following regression model

$$S_{TTU} = \alpha + \beta TTU + \gamma_1 D_1 + \cdots + \gamma_K D_K + \varepsilon \tag{10.1}$$

where S_{TTU} represents the satisfaction score and TTU represents travel time unreliability. $D_1 \ldots D_N$ are dummy variables, corresponding to k individual characteristics, which indicate whether or not an individual belongs to a particular passenger subgroup.

Column 1 in Table 10.7 shows the estimation results of the model when *TTU* is specified as 3MIN on arrival ($3MIN_A$), which corresponds with one minus the definition of punctuality used by the Dutch Railways.[3] The estimations are based on the assumptions as described in Sect. 10.4.1. The estimated regression

[3]As such, 3MIN effectively captures the 'dispunctuality'.

coefficient of TTU is −1.327. This means that a 10% point increase in the percentage of delayed trains results in a decrease in the satisfaction score with 0.13. This effect is rather small, which could be explained from the limited information about the travel pattern of the individual passengers.

This is also suggested by the low value of the Pearson and the partial correlation coefficients between TTU and TTU satisfaction, shown at the bottom of the column. As discussed in the previous section, we employ these coefficients mainly as a basis for comparing different TTU indicators and specifications. The coefficients on individual characteristics indicate the difference in satisfaction score between different subgroups of rail passengers and their respective reference category. As we focus on TTU, we will not discuss the results on individual characteristics.

Column 2 shows the results of an analysis with the same specification but with TTU specified as 3MIN on departure ($3MIN_D$). The results indicate that the regression coefficient of dispunctuality on departure is slightly smaller. The same holds for the partial correlation coefficient and the R^2 value. This suggests that the travellers' perception of TTU is more closely linked to experiences with TTU on arrival.

10.4.3 Estimation Results for Alternative TTU Indicators

Next, we performed a correlation analysis and a series of regression estimations in which the statistical relationship between different arrival-based TTU indicators and the customer satisfaction with TTU is estimated. All regression estimations are based on equation (1). The results are shown in Table 10.8. For purposes of comparison, Column 1 shows the results for the MIN3 indicator, while the results for the other indicators are shown in Columns 2–6. Column 3, for example, indicates that an increase in the average size of the delay by 1 min results in a decrease in customer satisfaction by 0.10. As the indicators are based on different units, it is not meaningful to compare the estimated regression coefficients. Therefore, we focus on the comparison of the correlation coefficients en R^2-values. Comparing the estimated correlation coefficients, we find that the correlation with the customer satisfaction score is the highest for 3MIN, followed by AVMIN and 9MIN. The indicators based on travel time variation, PERC and STDEV, show a weaker relationship with the customer satisfaction. The correlation coefficient for AVMIND is the lowest. A similar pattern can be seen from the adjusted R^2 values.

Table 10.9 shows the results for a similar analysis, in which we focused on departure-based rather than on arrival-based RTO-indicators. A comparison of the indicators shows that the order in which they are related to the customer perception of TTU, is the same as for the arrival-base indicators; the 3MIN indicator has the highest correlation coefficients and R^2, followed by AVMIN. However, the differences with the other indicators are smaller. By comparing the results in

Table 10.8 Results of a regression and correlation analysis on the statistical relation between different arrival-based TTU indicators and customer satisfaction with TTU

	TTU-indicator											
	(1)		(2)		(3)		(4)		(5)		(6)	
(Constant)	6.282	**	6.190	**	6.205	**	6.060	**	6.257	**	6.205	**
3MIN	−1.362	**										
9MIN			−3.317	**								
AVMIN					−0.098	**						
AVMIND							0.002					
PERC									−0.086	**		
STDEV											−0.036	**
Business traveller	0.047		0.052	*	0.049	*	0.047		0.049	*	0.052	*
Leisure traveller	0.037	*	0.040	*	0.036	*	0.038	*	0.040	*	0.041	*
Car available	0.194	**	0.190	**	0.196	**	0.193	**	0.189	**	0.189	**
Gender is female	−0.027	*	−0.028	*	−0.027	*	−0.025	*	−0.026	*	−0.026	*
Frequent traveller	−0.192	**	−0.196	**	−0.191	**	−0.194	**	−0.196	**	−0.196	**
Occasional traveller	0.156	**	0.156	**	0.156	**	0.160	**	0.159	**	0.159	**
Peak hours	0.119	**	0.093	**	0.106	**	0.078	**	0.084	**	0.077	**
Off-peak hours	0.264	**	0.268	**	0.267	**	0.272	**	0.270	**	0.272	**
Age below 20	0.003		−0.005		0.007		0.003		−0.003		−0.004	
Age over 60	0.279	**	0.275	**	0.282	**	0.277	**	0.273	**	0.273	**
Discount ticket	−0.074	**	−0.073	**	−0.077	**	−0.078	**	−0.075	**	−0.074	**
Railcard	−0.096	**	−0.095	**	−0.099	**	−0.097	**	−0.094	**	−0.094	**
Randstad area	−0.108	**	−0.120	**	−0.108	**	−0.128	**	−0.131	**	−0.127	**
N	57,404		57,404		57,404		57,404		57,404		57,404	
Adjusted R^2	0.043		0.040		0.041		0.038		0.039		0.039	
Pearson correlation	−0.084	**	−0.056	**	−0.070	**	0.009	**	−0.034	**	−0.023	**
Partial correlation	−0.067	**	−0.046	**	−0.056	**	0.002	**	−0.028	**	−0.022	**

* = significant at the 0.05 level
** = significant at the 0.01 level

Table 10.9 with those in Table 10.8, we see, that this is caused by the fact that the coefficient values for 9MIN, AVMIND, PERC en STDEV are higher, than those for their arrival-based counterparts An explanation may be that these indicators place specific weight on extreme delays. A departure from home with a relatively large delay increases the probability of missing a connection. On arrival at home, this possibility does not apply.

10.5 Conclusion and Policy Implications

This study focusses on the statistical relationship between travel time unreliability (TTU) and customer satisfaction with TTU. In Sect. 10.1, we introduced the topic, discussed how travel time unreliability is measured by the Dutch Railways and criticized some elements of this measuring method, including the exclusive focus of TTU on arrival, the exclusive focus on delays rather than on early arrivals and departures, and the negligence of travel time variation and the size of the delay. In Sect. 10.2, we gave an overview of the data that we used for the analysis. In this section, we also introduced six different TTU-indicators, two based on the probability of a delay, two based on the size of delay in minutes, and two based on the variation in the travel times. In Sect. 10.3, we discussed the results of a series of descriptive statistical analyses of the different TTU-indicators. Based on correlation and regression analyses, we found that the six indicators differ sufficiently from each other in terms of the underlying effect they measure. In Sect. 10.4, we carried out a comparative analysis of the statistical relationship between different TTU-indicators and specifications and customer satisfaction with TTU.

We have shown that reliability has direct links with the central notion of *sustainability* and the underlying dimensions of 'people', 'planet' and 'profit'. In particular, we have included the 'people' dimension in our study by focussing on the perception side of reliability. It is here that profit-oriented railway companies should start, when they want to improve their quality profile, and policymakers should start, in order to attract more passengers, possibly reducing the burden on the environment by reducing the number of trips made by car or by air.

In terms of the *transition* notion, the present study addresses a key issue in the railway sector. Traditionally the planning of railway services was strongly supply driven, with little attention to the customer perspective. Gradually the railway sector is becoming more customer oriented, as can be seen for example on the ample attention given to customer satisfaction and effective policies to improve this. The present paper focuses on reliability from this perspective. By linking objective measures of reliability ('trains being late') to subjective measures of satisfaction by travellers it facilitates the move from supply driven strategies towards demand driven strategies. Another important transition dimension of the study is that it provides inputs to the way contracts between the public sector and operators are formulated. In the case of the Netherlands such contracts are based on a particular way of measuring reliability in terms of probabilities of delays of more than 3 min,

Table 10.9 Results of a regression and correlation analysis on the statistical relation between different departure-based TTU indicators and customer satisfaction with TTU

	TTU-indicator											
	(1)		(2)		(3)		(4)		(5)		(6)	
(Constant)	6.234	**	6.167	**	6.228	**	6.148	**	6.350	**	6.260	**
3MIN	−1.219	**										
9MIN			−3.539	**								
AVMIN					−0.098	**						
AVMIND							−0.010	*				
PERC									−0.165	**		
STDEV											−0.065	**
Business traveller	0.039		0.046		0.044		0.049	*	0.044		0.047	
Leisure traveller	0.032	*	0.037	*	0.034	*	0.039	*	0.037	*	0.039	*
Car available	0.199	**	0.194	**	0.195	**	0.192	**	0.194	**	0.193	**
Gender is female	−0.026	*	−0.027	*	−0.026	*	−0.025	*	−0.027	*	−0.026	*
Frequent traveller	−0.184	**	−0.188	**	−0.188	**	−0.193	**	−0.191	**	−0.188	**
Occasional traveller	0.162	**	0.161	**	0.162	**	0.161	**	0.159	**	0.161	**
Peak hours	0.116	**	0.096	**	0.102	**	0.076	**	0.094	**	0.084	**
Off-peak hours	0.267	**	0.269	**	0.269	**	0.272	**	0.268	**	0.271	**
Age below 20	0.013		0.002		0.007		0.001		0.006		0.001	
Age over 60	0.285	**	0.280	**	0.282	**	0.277	**	0.279	**	0.278	**
Discount ticket	−0.078	**	−0.076	**	−0.077	**	−0.077	**	−0.079	**	−0.077	**
Railcard	−0.100	**	−0.098	**	−0.098	**	−0.097	**	−0.098	**	−0.097	**
Randstad area	−0.102	**	−0.109	**	−0.112	**	−0.126	**	−0.119	**	−0.113	**
N	57,407		57,407		57,407		57,407		57,407		57,407	
Adjusted R^2	0.042		0.040		0.040		0.038		0.040		0.040	
Pearson correlation	−0.085	**	−0.065	**	−0.066	**	−0.014	**	−0.058	**	−0.052	**
Partial correlation	−0.064	**	−0.048	**	−0.047	**	−0.009	**	−0.046	**	−0.038	**

* = significant at the 0.05 level
** = significant at the 0.01 level

and that does not necessarily represent the customer's satisfaction. It is clear that the way in which reliability is measured in the contract will provide incentives to the operator in terms of tactical and operational issues such as the design of time tables and procedures on how to cope with delayed trains. Our contribution sheds light on the issue to what extent the present reliability indicator is reflecting traveller preferences and thus, whether the present contract produces the right incentives.

The results of a correlation analysis of the different TTU-indicators indicate that they exhibit differences in terms of the underlying effect they measure. Based on the pattern of correlation coefficients, two clusters of indicators could be identified. One cluster with indicators that do not attach specific value to extreme results (3MIN and AVMIN) and one cluster with indicators that do (9MIN, AVMIND, PERC and STDEV). The results furthermore suggest that the arrival-based indicators and their departure-based counterparts measure different underlying effects.

Next, we carried out a regression analysis on the impact of various temporal and station-related variables on the TTU-indicators. As for the impact of the temporal variables we found that TTU is higher on weekdays and during peak hours. Furthermore, TTU is higher in the autumn and winter. The impact of station characteristics differs, depending on which TTU indicator is being analysed. 3MIN and AVMIN are higher on intercity stations and on stations in the Randstad area, compared to other stations. The impacts of the set of explanatory factors on the departure-based indicators have the same sign as on the arrival-based indicators but are generally smaller. The reason could be that departure times could be controlled to a larger degree than arrival times. When a train is delayed or arrives early, it could be possible to have it halt longer or shorter so as to avoid delayed or early departure.

Finally, we carried out a correlation analysis and a series of regression estimations, using the customer satisfaction with TTU as the dependent variable. In each regression specification, we included a different TTU indicator as explanatory variable. Due to certain data limitations, we cannot draw any meaningful conclusion about the impact of TTU indicators on customer satisfaction, but we are able to compare the different TTU indicators and specifications in terms of the degree to which they capture the rail passenger's TTU experience. First, we carried out a correlation analysis and two regression estimations comparing 3MIN on arrival with 3MIN on departure in terms of their relationship with the customer satisfaction. The results indicate that the arrival-based specification is more closely linked to the rail passenger's perception of TTU.

Next, we carried out a similar analysis in which we compared the results for the six different TTU indicators. The results showed that both on arrival and on departure, 3MIN is the indicator that is most closely related to the passenger's perception of TTU, followed by AVMIN. Incidentally, these two indicators place no specific weight on extreme delays. The other indicators capture the rail passenger's experience less well, although the departure-based specifications of these indicators perform relatively well. This may be due to the fact that these indicators do place specific weight on extreme delays, since large delays on departure increase the probability of missing connections.

In the introduction of this study, we criticized the use of punctuality by the Dutch Railways to measure TTU, as this indicator may not capture the TTU as experienced by rail passengers. We argued that, due to the arbitrary punctuality margin, trains with a 30-min delay count the same as trains with a 4-min delay, which may not be realistic from the passenger's point of view. In order to investigate this, we included two TTU-indicators which were based on the size of the delay, i.e., AVMIN and AVMIND. The results of our analysis showed that the statistical relationship of the former indicator with customer satisfaction was relatively high, but not higher than that of the punctuality indicator, and the impact of the latter indicator was even lower. This suggests that our criticism does not seem to be a major drawback of the punctuality indicator in practice. Furthermore, we argued that the punctuality indicator is based on arrival times and that unreliability with respect to departure times can also have consequences for passengers. The extra waiting time caused by a delayed departure, may lead to a loss in utility, even if the train arrives in time at the final destination. We found that arrival-based 3MIN and AVMIN had more explanatory power than their departure-based counterparts. However, for some of the alternative indicators, TTU on departure appeared to be more important.

We also pointed out, that the punctuality indicator does not capture the travel time uncertainty as such. In order to address this, we included two TTU-indicators based on travel time variation in the analysis, i.e., PERC and STDEV. These indicators are specified such, that their value increased both as a result of increased numbers and size of delays, and increased numbers of early departures. Our analysis showed that improvements in these two indicators have a smaller impact on customer satisfaction, suggesting that these indicators are worse approximations of the TTU experienced by rail passengers. Hence, one might argue that the exclusive focus on delays is not a major drawback of the indicator used by the Dutch Railways.

Based on the results of this analysis one may be tempted to conclude that, in order to increase the rail share, the attention should remain focussed on decreasing punctuality and, following up on this, the Dutch Railways should continue to be evaluated based on punctuality, perhaps including also some aspects of departure-based reliability. Two remarks can be made in this context. First, it should be taken into consideration that the present study has not incorporated the cost aspect in the analysis. This means that our study does not provide a comparative analysis of cost-efficiency of improvements in the various TTU-indicators. With respect to improving reliability, a useful approach might be a multi-criteria decision analysis, which compares a number of alternative strategies aimed at improving TTU, taking into account both the investment costs of each alternative, and the degree to which it results in improvements in various indicators. Second, the results are based on stated preference data. Whether improvements in TTU result in changes in actual travel behaviour falls outside the scope of this study.

Annex A: Calculation of Indicators of Travel Time Variation

As discussed in Sect. 10.3, we have the following data available with respect to TTU:

- Number of trains with {< 3; 3–5; 5–7; 7–9;>9} minutes of delay on arrival (departure)
- Total number of arriving (departing) trains
- Total number of minutes of delay on arrival (departure)
- Total number of minutes of delay on arrival (departure) for trains which arrive (depart) with more than 3 min of delay.

First, we assume that arrival and departure times are uniformly distributed within each of the five delay intervals. Standard deviation and percentiles can then be calculated based on the centre point of the intervals. The centre points of thee middle intervals are known. The centre point of the last interval can be estimated according to the following equation:

$$\bar{X}^L = \sum_{i=2}^{5} M_i N_i \Leftrightarrow M_5 = \frac{\bar{X}^L - \sum_{i=2}^{4} M_i N_i}{N_5}$$

where $\bar{X}^L$ represents the mean delay in minutes for delayed trains, Mi represents the centre point of interval i, Ni represents the number of trains in category i and$\bar{X}$represents the average delay in minutes. Next, the centre point of the first interval can be calculated as follows:

$$\bar{X} = \sum_{i=1}^{5} M_i N_i \Leftrightarrow M_1 = \frac{\bar{X}^L - \sum_{i=2}^{5} M_i N_i}{N_1}$$

Based on these calculations, the standard deviation can be calculated as follows:

$$SD = \sqrt{\frac{\sum_{i=1}^{5} (M_i - \bar{X})^2 N_i}{\sum_{i=1}^{5} N_i - 1}}$$

The 50th and 80th percentile can be calculated as follows:

$$P^{PERC} = \left(M_1 - \frac{1}{2} R_1\right) + \sum_{i=1}^{k-1} R_i + \frac{\left(PERC - \sum_{i=1}^{k-1} S_i\right)}{S_K} R_k$$

where *PERC* denotes the percentile to be calculated, R_i represents the range of interval *i*, *k* represents the interval within which the percentile is located and S_i represents the percentage of trains in interval *i*.

Annex B: Temporal Weighting of TTU

The value of TTU-indicators for each observation are specified as a weighted average of TTU-values for the 8 months preceding the date of the observation. The weights are estimated once based on the following model.

$$T_R = \alpha + \beta R + \gamma_1 D_1 + \ldots + \gamma_K D_K + \varepsilon$$

$$R = wR_{AH,t} + w^2 R_{AH,t-1} + \ldots + w^7 R_{AH,t-7} + \varepsilon$$

$$w + w^2 + \ldots + w^7 = 1$$

This results in an estimated value for w of 0.37. This indicates that TTU-perception of an individual is based for 63% on TTU-experience in the month and for 37% on TTU-experiences further in the past. The value of 0.37 has subsequently been used to derive the values for all TTU-indicators in the analysis.

References

Bacon DR (2003) A comparison of approaches to importance-performance analysis. Int J Market Res 45:55–71

Brons MRE, Rietveld P (2007) Betrouwbaarheid en klanttevredenheid in de OV-keten: een statistische analyse. Internal research report for the Transumo project Betrouwbaarheid van transportketens. Vrije Universiteit, Amsterdam

Brons MRE, Rietveld P (2008) Customer satisfaction and importance of various dimensions of the door-to-door rail journey. Built Environ 35:30–43

Dutch Railways (2006) Vervoerplan NS 2006 (versie 4.4)

Hawes JM, Rao CP (1985) Using importance-performance analysis to develop health care marketing strategies. J Health Care Mark 5:19–25

Kristensen K, Kanji GK, Dahlgaard JJ (1992) On measurement of customer satisfaction. Total Qual Manage 3:123–128

ProRail (2007) Network Statement 2009 Combined Network based on the Railways Act – version 1.0 dated 14 December 2007. ProRail, Utrecht

Schreurs L (2005) Klanttevredenheidonderzoek Nederlandse spoorwegen. Een onderzoeksmatige toetsing van de kwaliteit en de onafhankelijkheid van het klanttevredenheidonderzoek van NS (in opdracht van Ministerie van Verkeer en Waterstaat, Rijkswaterstaat, Adviesdienst Verkeer en Vervoer). Sartorius OBA Duivendrecht

Slack N (1994) The importance-performance matrix as a determinant of improvement priority. Int J Oper Prod Manage 14:59–75

Chapter 11
Algorithmic Support for Railway Disruption Management

Leo Kroon and Dennis Huisman

11.1 Introduction

Increasing the market share of public transport is considered as one of the solutions for the mobility problems in the Netherlands. Moreover, public transport is seen as a *green* mode of transportation ("Planet"). Thus for achieving more sustainable mobility, travellers will have to be stimulated to use the public transport system instead of their own cars. A higher market share of the public transport system will enable a higher efficiency and profitability of this system ("Profit"). In order to make the public transport system more attractive, an increase in its service quality is needed ("People"). This is especially true for railway systems. Indeed, one of the weak points of railway systems is that disruptions seem to be more or less inevitable, leading to much discomfort for the passengers.

In the Netherlands, relatively large disruptions occur on average about three times per day, each time leading to a temporary and local unavailability of the railway system. A disruption and the involved uncertainty often leads to much more discomfort for the passengers than the few minutes of delay with which they are confronted regularly (Brons 2006). In a disrupted situation, also the lack or incorrectness of travel information may lead to a lot of discomfort. For many people these issues are disqualifiers to use public transport.

In case of a disrupted situation, the disruption management process should quickly provide a modified timetable, rolling stock circulation, and crew duties, so that as much as possible of the service for the passengers can be upheld. However, one of the bottle-necks in the current disruption management process is, that it is carried out completely manually, and that a large number of parties is involved (Jespersen-Groth et al. 2009). This requires a lot of communication

L. Kroon (✉) • D. Huisman
Department of Logistics, Rotterdam School of Management, Erasmus University Rotterdam, Netherlands Railways, 1738, 3000 DR Rotterdam, The Netherlands
e-mail: lkroon@rsm.nl; huisman@ese.eur.nl

J.A.E.E. van Nunen et al. (eds.), *Transitions Towards Sustainable Mobility*,
DOI 10.1007/978-3-642-21192-8_11,

between these parties, leading to slow response times and to solutions that are far from optimal. For example, several trains may have to be cancelled since no appropriate train drivers could be found.

Faster response times and better solutions can be expected by the application of *algorithmic support* in the disruption management process. That is, the modified timetable, rolling stock circulation, and crew duties are generated *automatically*, based on appropriate mathematical models and algorithms for solving these models. Moreover, the application of such models and algorithms will allow to focus in the disruption management process on the passenger flows rather than on the railway system itself. Therefore, such models and algorithms are currently being developed in close cooperation with Netherlands Railways (in Dutch: Nederlandse Spoorwegen, NS). This paper describes these models and algorithms, as well as their potential benefits.

The models and algorithms for real-time disruption management described in this paper build to a large extent on the models and algorithms that have been developed for supporting the planning processes of NS. These models focus on planning the timetable (Kroon et al. 2009), the rolling stock circulation (Fioole et al. 2006), and the crew schedules of NS (Abbink et al. 2005). Based on their application for the development of the railway timetable for 2007, NS was winner of the 2008 Edelman Award of INFORMS.

In March 2009, the advantages of using algorithmic support for rescheduling the crew duties of NS in case of a disruption were clearly demonstrated by the application of an automated crew rescheduling tool after a freight train derailed near station Vleuten. This derailment damaged the railway infrastructure over 5 km, which required the timetable, the rolling stock circulation, and the crew duties to be rescheduled during nearly 7 days. A comparison between the automated rescheduling process for the driver duties with the manual rescheduling process for the conductor duties revealed the advantages of the automated rescheduling process: it leads to better solutions in less time. This case, together with other cases where the manual disruption management process clearly failed (for example, the winter period of December 2009 and January 2010), stimulated the request by the board of NS for the transition from the manual disruption management process to a more agile and algorithmically supported disruption management process.

Algorithmic support will be needed, especially if the plans underlying the railway system are tight. That is, there is just a small amount of slack in the system. This will be the case if the utilization of the railway infrastructure is increased in the near future by higher frequencies and traffic volumes. For example, there are plans to introduce a system with six intercity trains and six regional trains per direction and per hour on several Dutch corridors. At first sight, this increase in frequency is beneficial for the passengers, but it is important to realize that this is only the case if the real-time disruption management process is endowed with the right tools to handle this increased utilization of the railway system in an adequate way.

Conversely, the application of algorithmic support will also allow to increase the efficiency of the railway system. This is relevant since the railway world is becoming more and more competitive. In particular, currently several buffers (in the form of relatively large numbers of stand-by rolling stock units and crew members) are present in the system as a safety net in case of disruptions. However, part of these buffers will become redundant when effective algorithmic support is applied, thereby increasing the railway system's efficiency.

A scientific challenge that needs to be solved for the application of algorithmic support for disruption management is the development of appropriate models and sufficiently powerful algorithms for *quickly* solving these models. This aspect is less important for models and algorithms that are applied for planning purposes. However, in order to be effective in real-time, the computation times of these algorithms need to be short: an algorithm that needs hours to compute a decision that is required more or less instantaneously is useless. Also, dealing in an adequate way with the uncertainty and volatility that are inherent to the disruption management process is still a scientific challenge.

This paper describes the challenges and the potential benefits of the application of algorithmic support for the quality of the railway system. Section 11.2 starts with a general description of disruption management. Section 11.3 describes how the timetable is modified in case of a disruption. Then Sect. 11.4 gives a description of models and algorithms for rolling stock rescheduling that are currently developed. Section 11.5 proceeds with models and algorithms for crew rescheduling. This section also describes the Vleuten case mentioned above. Passenger oriented disruption management is described in Sects. 11.6 and 11.7 concludes the paper with a number of final remarks and subjects for further research.

11.2 Railway Disruption Management

Figure 11.1 gives a high level view of disruption management. Disruption management is an ongoing process that focuses both on the question whether a situation is disrupted or not, as well as on the measures to correct a disrupted situation. For evaluating whether a situation is disrupted, and for reacting effectively in case of a disruption, it is essential to have real-time information on the positions of train units and crews. Furthermore, for upholding as much as possible service for the

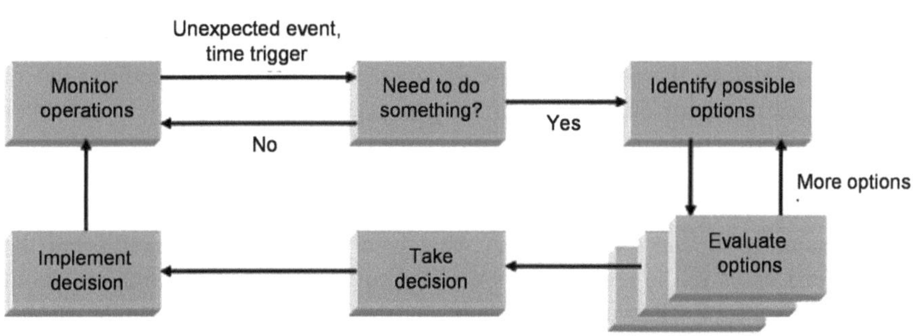

Fig. 11.1 A high level view of disruption management (Source Kohl et al. 2007)

passengers during, it is necessary to have real-time information on the locations and destinations of the passengers. Modern information technology allows this kind of information to be more and more available, although real-time passenger information is still scarce.

A disruption of the railway system is often caused by a blockade of part of the railway infrastructure. Such a blockade may be complete or partial. In the first case no railway traffic is possible at all on the blocked infrastructure, for example, due to malfunctioning power supply. If only part of the available parallel tracks is blocked, as in the case of a broken-down train, then some railway traffic remains possible, but usually a number of trains have to be cancelled.

The modifications in the timetable usually make the rolling stock circulation and the crew duties infeasible as well. Indeed, if some trains are cancelled, then certain train units and crews cannot follow their planned duties. Thus, rescheduling the rolling stock circulation and the crew duties is required. The railway operators are responsible for carrying out this rescheduling process.

A complicating issue in a disrupted situation is the fact that the duration of the disruption is usually not known exactly. As time proceeds, the initial estimate of the duration of the disruption may turn out to be incorrect. As a consequence, the rescheduling process must be carried out several times then. When the disruption is over in the end, an appropriate strategy has to be selected to return to the regular timetable. Going back to the regular timetable *as soon as possible* is not necessarily optimal for many passengers.

An important difference between scheduling in the planning process and rescheduling in the real-time operations is the dynamic environment in which the rescheduling process has to take place. That is, while the rescheduling process is carried out, the status of the railway system is changing at the same time. Thus, apart from the fact that the rescheduled plans are needed as soon as possible, this is another reason for the need for short rescheduling times. Since the rescheduling problems that have to be solved are large and complex, the realization of sufficiently short computation times of the rescheduling algorithms is still a large scientific challenge.

A further difference between planning and operations is the fact that in the operations the existing plans have to be taken into account. This holds in particular when rescheduling the crew duties: the end times of the rescheduled duties should not differ too much from the end times of the original duties. Similarly, the shunting processes related to the rolling stock circulation must not be changed too much, since the feasibility of modified shunting processes is hard to check. For further differences between planning and operations, see Grötschel et al. (2001) and Séguin et al. (1997).

Note that disruption management is different from online scheduling, where events occur completely *unexpectedly*. Conversely, permanently monitoring the railway processes in the real-time operations provides a lot of information about upcoming events. Each event has at least an *expected* event time. Based on this information, one may forecast whether there will be conflicts in the near future due to the timetable, the rolling stock circulation, or the crew duties.

11.3 Timetable Rescheduling

In case of a disruption of the railway system, usually a number of trains cannot be operated. Thus, the timetable is modified by cancelling a number of trips. In the Netherlands, these modifications are usually based on a *disruption scenario*. The disruption scenarios have been prepared by the traffic control organization of the infrastructure manager in cooperation with the railway operators. They describe which trips in the timetable have to be cancelled, which trips have to be rerouted, and in which stations short returns of trains have to be introduced.

The selection of the disruption scenario to be used in case of an actual disruption may require a lot of – time consuming – communication between the infrastructure manager and the railway operators. Moreover, although there may be several hundreds of disruption scenarios, there is usually no scenario that fits exactly with the disrupted situation. Therefore, some fine-tuning of the selected scenario will be needed. For automatically solving this kind of problems, algorithmic support has not been developed yet.

Figure 11.3 shows how the timetable of the 3,000 intercity line of NS may be modified if temporarily no railway traffic is possible between Amsterdam and Utrecht due to malfunctioning railway infrastructure. The 3,000 line provides twice per hour an intercity connection from Den Helder (Hdr) to Nijmegen (Nm) and vice versa, via Alkmaar (Amr), Amsterdam (Asd), Utrecht (Ut), and Arnhem (Ah) (see also Fig. 11.2). The timetable of the 3,000 line is cyclic with a cycle length of 30 min.

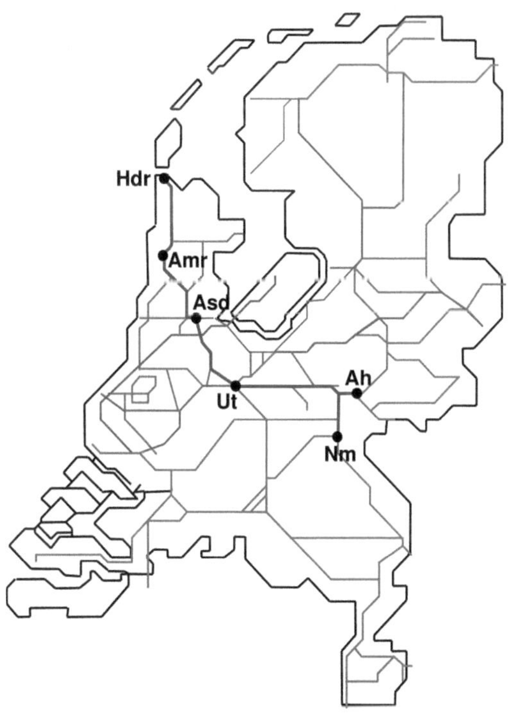

Fig. 11.2 The 3,000 line runs twice per hour in each direction between Den Helder (*Hdr*) and Nijmegen (*Nm*)

The disruption between Amsterdam and Utrecht starts at 8:40 a.m., and has an estimated duration of 2.5 h. A usual scenario for modifying the timetable is to cancel the disrupted trips between Amsterdam and Utrecht, and to introduce short returns of the trains in Amsterdam and Utrecht. That is, a train arriving in Amsterdam from Alkmaar returns in the timetable of the 3,000 line to Alkmaar. Similarly, a train arriving in Utrecht from Arnhem returns to Arnhem. Note that this requires that the routes of these trains in Amsterdam and Utrecht must be modified.

As can be seen in Fig. 11.3, only the first disrupted trains in Amsterdam and Utrecht are put aside at the shunt yards there. After the end of the disruption, these trains are put into operation again. These trains belong to the *grey area* between the regular undisrupted situation and the 'regular' disrupted situation.

As was mentioned earlier, the initial estimate of the duration of the disruption often turns out to be wrong. If this is indeed the case, then the timetable, the rolling stock circulation, and the crew duties must be rescheduled again at the moment that the difference becomes clear.

Due to the described disruption scenario, the services on the 3,000 line outside the disrupted area remain as much as possible the same as usual. In order to compensate for the cancelled trains between Amsterdam and Utrecht, buses may be operated on the disrupted route. Note that also several other train lines operate on the indicated infrastructure. However, in order to keep the figure simple, these have not been shown.

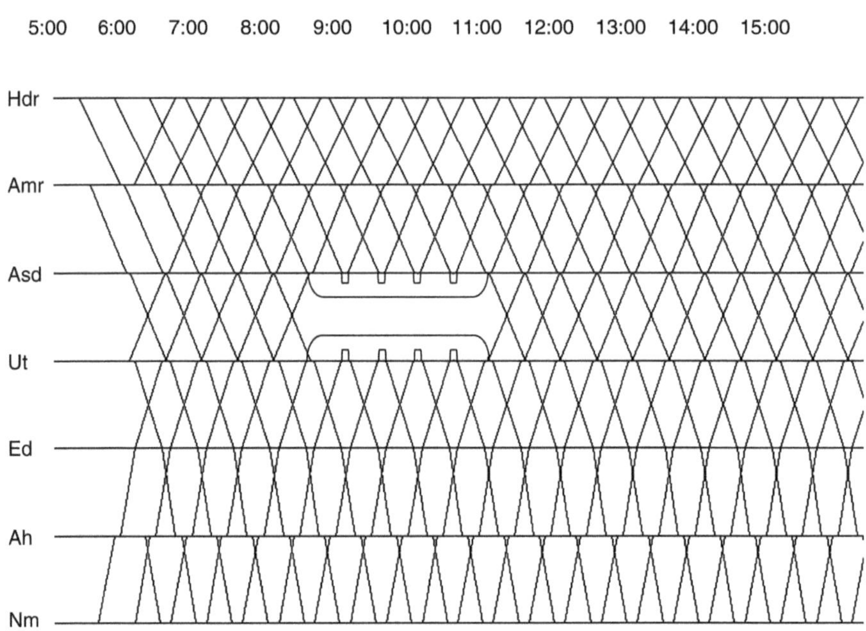

Fig. 11.3 A disruption of the railway traffic between Amsterdam (*Asd*) and Utrecht (*Ut*) starting at 8:40 a.m. with an estimated duration of 2.5 h

11.4 Rolling Stock Rescheduling

11.4.1 Introduction

The rolling stock circulation strongly influences the service of the railway system, and rolling stock costs are a large part of the operational costs of a railway operator. Rolling stock planning aims at allocating an appropriate amount of rolling stock to each train in the given timetable. A rolling stock circulation can be expressed in terms of the rolling stock compositions of the trains, but it can also be expressed in terms of the rolling stock duties. Here, a rolling stock duty is a sequence of tasks to be carried out by a single train unit on a single day. A task for a train unit is a trip in a train from one station to another at a certain time instant in combination with a position in the train.

Relevant papers on rolling stock scheduling and rescheduling are Caprara et al. (2007), Alfieri et al. (2006), Fioole et al. (2006), Peeters and Kroon (2008), Jespersen-Groth et al. (2006), Budai et al. (2010), and Nielsen et al. (2009). In Sect. 11.4.2 we provide some details of the latter paper.

Figure 11.3 illustrates the need for rescheduling the rolling stock circulation in case of a disruption. Indeed, since the compositions of the trains depend on the expected numbers of passengers – which strongly vary over the day and per direction – it is highly improbable that, after a short return of a train in Amsterdam or in Utrecht, its actual composition is exactly the same as its planned one. This difference will propagate to other trains and will lead to mismatches between demand for and supply of seats later on. Furthermore, it will lead to off-balances by the end of the day, i.e. train units ending at the wrong locations. Thus, the rolling stock circulation must be rescheduled.

11.4.2 A Multi-Commodity Flow Model

This section describes a model and an algorithm for rescheduling the rolling stock circulation in case of a disruption of the real-time operations. This description is based on Nielsen et al. (2009). The model is a minimum cost multi-commodity flow model, but it has several additional features.

11.4.2.1 Problem Description

Nielsen et al. (2009) describe a model and an algorithm for the real-time Rolling Rolling Stock Rescheduling Problem (RSRP). Here the timetable and the available rolling stock may change several times in case of a disruption. Real-time RSRP is the problem of updating the current assignment of train units to trips in the timetable whenever the timetable or the rolling stock capacity is changed. The latter may change, for example, due to a breakdown of one or more rolling stock units. An instance of real-time RSRP contains the following elements:

- The original timetable T_0.
- The original rolling stock capacity R_0.
- The original rolling stock circulation C_0.
- A finite list of changes to the timetable and the rolling stock capacity, $< t_1, T_1, R_1 >, < t_2, T_2, R_2 >, \ldots, < t_n, T_n, R_n >$.

Here an element in the list is a triple consisting of a time instant t_i, an updated timetable T_i, and an updated rolling stock capacity R_i. The time instants are assumed to be distinct and sorted such that $t_1 < t_2 < \ldots < t_n$. Each element in the list represents a time instant where a new situation appears, which renders the current rolling stock circulation infeasible. At any point in time t, the changes in the timetable and the rolling stock capacity that will appear after time t are not known yet.

The problem is then to reschedule at time t_i the rolling stock circulation C_{i-1} to serve timetable T_i with rolling stock capacity R_i. The resulting rolling stock circulation is called C_i. At time t_i the rolling stock assigned to trips in T_i departing before time t_i is fixed. The objective of real-time RSRP measures several aspects of the intermediate and the final rolling stock circulations. These aspects are described in Sect. 11.4.2.2.

Note that the foregoing implies a "Wait-and-See" approach to the rescheduling problem. That is, one waits until there is a certain need to update the timetable and the rolling stock circulation, since the existing ones have become infeasible. Otherwise, when rescheduling the timetable and the rolling stock circulation, one might anticipate already on future changes in the environment. Also in practice it is usual to apply a "Wait-and-See" approach.

11.4.2.2 Objective Function

The first objective in real-time RSRP is the feasibility of the new circulation where the limitations on the lengths of the trains are the most challenging ones. In addition, there are several other objectives to be taken into account in the rescheduling process. The following lists several perspectives of real-time rescheduling and the objectives associated with them.

- **The service perspective.** The inconvenience for the passengers should be minimized, which means that cancelling trips due to lack of rolling stock (in addition to the trips that are directly cancelled due to the disruption) should be minimized. Similarly, assigning too little capacity related to the expected number of passengers should be avoided. A complicating issue here is that in a disrupted situation it is hard to forecast the passenger behaviour and hence the passenger demand.
- **The process perspective.** Deviations from the original rolling stock circulation should be communicated to the involved parties. In particular, the feasibility of

the modifications of the shunting plans may be hard to check in detail at short notice. Therefore, the number of such modifications should be minimized.

- **The robustness perspective.** The propagation of the effects of the disruption should be kept local. In particular, the number of off-balances by the end of the day should be minimized, since otherwise the effects of the disruption propagate to the next day.
- **The efficiency perspective.** The number of carriage kilometres driven is closely related to the operational costs of the rolling stock circulation. Unnecessary carriage kilometres should be avoided. Similarly, deadheading trips for solving rolling stock off-balances should be avoided as well.

11.4.2.3 Solution Method

Nielsen et al. (2009) use a model for rolling stock rescheduling that is deduced from the model of Fioole et al. (2006). This model is a minimum cost multi-commodity flow model which also considers the order of the train units in the trains. The concept of a transition graph is used to deal with this aspect. The transition graph describes for each allowed combination of a trip and a train composition the feasible train compositions on the next trip. Then the problem is a minimum cost multi-commodity flow problem, where at the same time for each train a feasible path in the associated transition graph is to be found.

Nielsen et al. (2009) adapt this planning model to the rescheduling context by adding a number of features. First of all, the original rolling stock circulation has to be taken into account. The original timetable is T_0 and the original rolling stock capacity R_0 is assigned to the timetable as described by the original rolling stock circulation C_0. The train compositions prior to the start of the disruption are fixed. The model is also extended with the possibility to assign an empty composition to a trip, i.e. the trip is cancelled.

The model of Nielsen et al. (2009) is applied on a rolling horizon in order to speed up the solution process. That is, rescheduling the rolling stock is only carried out for a fixed time period ahead. This is done whenever the rescheduling horizon has elapsed or at the moment that new information has become available about updates of the timetable or the rolling stock capacity. In order to guide the rolling stock inventories such that the off-balances by the end of the day will be low, the model aims at minimizing the off-balances by the end of each planning horizon. The therefore required intermediate target inventories are deduced from the inventories in the original rolling stock circulation. The weights of the intermediate off-balances increase as time proceeds.

To analyze the rolling horizon solution heuristic, Nielsen et al. (2009) tested it on a set of instances of NS involving a disruption on the so-called Noord-Oost lines. These form the most challenging cases for rolling stock rescheduling at NS. The disruption in the described instances occurs between Utrecht and Amersfoort, implying that no trains can run between these two stations then. The actual duration of the disruption is not known initially, but only an estimated duration is available.

In these experiments it turned out that, given the assumed passenger behaviour, this rescheduling method is able to quickly reschedule the rolling stock circulation in such a way that more service for the passengers is provided than in the case that a straightforward heuristic is applied.

11.5 Crew Rescheduling

11.5.1 Introduction

Each train needs a train driver and one or more conductors. For both types of crew members, a task is related to a trip on a train between two stations where the crew possibly can be changed. A crew *duty* is the set of tasks to be carried out by a single crew member on a single day. Thus, there are duties for drivers and duties for conductors. Initially, the duties are anonymous, i.e. they have not been assigned to real crew members yet. This assignment of duties to crew members is specified by the crew *rosters*.

Crew *scheduling* is the problem of a priori generating the crew duties. In the real-time crew *rescheduling* process, the duties obviously have been assigned to individual crew members already. Thus, one must take into account the existing duties as well as the individual skills of the assigned crew members then. For example, a train driver is allowed to drive a particular train only if he has the appropriate route and rolling stock knowledge.

Since crew scheduling is a highly complex and yet generic problem, a lot of research on models and solution techniques for solving this problem in off-line planning processes has been carried out. Abbink et al. (2005), Fores et al. (2001), Kohl (2003), and Kroon and Fischetti (2001) describe a number of successful applications of these models within various railway companies.

Research on models and solution techniques for crew rescheduling in railway systems is still scarce. First results are provided by Huisman (2007), Rezanova and Ryan (2009), Walker et al. (2005), Abbink et al. (2009), and Potthoff et al. (2010). In Sect. 11.5.2 we present some details of the latter paper. Crew rescheduling for airline systems has received more attention. Relevant papers on airline crew rescheduling are Song et al. (1998), Stoiković et al. (1998), Lettovský et al. (2000), Yu et al. (2003), Clausen et al. (2005), Medard and Sawhney (2006), Nissen and Haase (2006), and Kohl et al. (2007).

Figure 11.3 indicates the need for rescheduling the duties in case of the earlier mentioned disruption between Amsterdam and Utrecht. In this example, it is common practice that there are planned duties for drivers covering the three tasks Amr-Asd, Asd-Ut, and Ut-Ah on one of the disrupted trains. Since the trip Asd-Ut in such a duty is cancelled, the involved driver will not be able to carry out the task Ut-Ah in his duty. So this task must be assigned to another driver. Conversely, in practice the driver will follow the train in its short return in Amsterdam. Thus, he is moving in another direction than prescribed in his original duty. Hence this duty must be rescheduled to get this driver back in his home depot in time, while at the same time carrying out as much as possible tasks.

Although the crew rescheduling process is mainly an internal process, it is one of the recognized bottle-necks in the disruption management process. Indeed, it nearly is impossible to manually reschedule tens of duties in just a couple of minutes. One of the reasons is that for rescheduling the timetable and the rolling stock circulation, dispatchers heavily use the fact that (the basic structures of) these plans are cyclic. Unfortunately, the crew schedule is by definition non-cyclic, for example, because a crew member needs to reach his home depot after a certain amount of time. Moreover, crew rescheduling has to take into account many complex labor constraints. And finally, an important feature is that crews can refuse certain changes in their duties. Currently this happens in practice mainly because crew members are not informed about their completely rescheduled duties, but only about their next tasks. Thus, they do not know if they will arrive back home at a reasonable time.

As a consequence, manually rescheduling one disrupted duty usually requires 5–10 min. Given the fact that it is not unusual that 50–100 duties are hindered by a disruption, it requires a lot of time to reschedule all the crew duties in such a case. This may have a very negative impact on the quality of the railway system. Especially in this process, advanced algorithmic support is badly needed: a train that cannot be provided with an appropriate crew will have to be cancelled with all the negative consequences for the passengers.

11.5.2 A Set Covering Based Model

This section describes a model and an algorithm for rescheduling crew duties in case of a disruption of the real-time operations of NS. This description is based on Potthoff et al. (2010). The model is a Set Covering model, but it has some additional features which allow it to deal with the existing duties.

11.5.2.1 Model Description

It is assumed that the disruption takes place at a certain location, starts at time t_0, and lasts until t_1. The duties that are unfinished at time t_0 are represented by the set Δ. In addition, N is the set of tasks which have not started at the time of rescheduling, and K^δ is the set of all feasible completions for original duty $\delta \in \Delta$. A feasible completion is a sequence of tasks after time t_0 by which the tasks in the original duty are replaced such that the duty still fulfills all constraints at the duty level and ends in the right crew depot at an appropriate time. For every duty $\delta \in \Delta$ and every feasible completion $k \in K^\delta$ we have:

- c_k^δ: the cost of feasible completion k for original duty δ. The cost of a feasible completion is zero if the duty is not modified. Otherwise, the cost is the sum of the cost for changing a duty, the cost for taxis, and the penalties for short connection times and overtime.
- a_{ik}^δ: a binary parameter indicating if task i is covered by feasible completion k for original duty δ or not.

Finally, we define f_i as the cost of cancelling task i. Potthoff et al. (2010) now formulate the crew rescheduling problem, using binary variables x_k^δ corresponding to the feasible completions of duty δ. That is, x_k^δ is 1 if and only if feasible completion $k \in K^\delta$ is used to complete duty $\delta \in \Delta$. Furthermore, binary variables y_i indicate if task i is cancelled ($y_i = 1$) or not ($y_i = 0$).

$$\min \sum_{\delta\in\Delta} \sum_{k\in K^\delta} c_k^\delta x_k^\delta + \sum_{i\in N} f_i y_i \tag{11.1}$$

$$\text{s.t.} \sum_{\delta\in\Delta} \sum_{k\in K^\delta} a_{ik}^\delta x_k^\delta + y_i \geq 1 \quad \forall i \in N \tag{11.2}$$

$$\sum_{k\in K^\delta} x_k^\delta = 1 \quad \forall \delta \in \Delta \tag{11.3}$$

$$x_k^\delta, y_i \in \{0,1\} \quad \forall \delta \in \Delta, \forall k \in K^\delta, \forall i \in N \tag{11.4}$$

The objective function (1) takes into account several aspects, such as the number of uncovered tasks, the number of modified duties, the number of used stand-by duties, and the differences between the durations of the original duties and the rescheduled duties. Constraints (2) guarantee that every task is either covered by a feasible completion or is cancelled. Moreover, constraints (3) ensure that every original duty is assigned to exactly one feasible completion.

11.5.2.2 Solution Method

The crew rescheduling method in Potthoff et al. (2010) uses an algorithm that is based on large neighbourhood search in combination with a column generation heuristic. It can be summarized as follows:

- **Step 1.** Define an initial core problem based on a set of duties to be rescheduled. The set of duties that is considered is the set consisting of the directly disrupted duties and some other duties either on the same route or around the same time on adjacent routes.
- **Step 2.** Compute an initial solution using a Column Generation heuristic. This heuristic is very similar to the method described by Huisman (2007). It uses Lagrangian dual values to construct new columns by solving resource-constrained shortest path problems. Constructive heuristics are used for generating feasible solutions from these columns.

- **Step 3.** Check if there are still uncovered tasks. If all tasks have been covered, then stop.
- **Step 4.** Define a neighbourhood by extending the set of duties to be rescheduled. The additional duties are selected based on the fact (1) that they cover tasks in the neighbourhood of an uncovered task, and (2) that the involved drivers are able to carry out these uncovered tasks. Finally, also a number of additional duties is selected based on their similarity to the duties selected according to (1) and (2).
- **Step 5.** Explore the neighbourhood by a Column Generation heuristic. Here the same comments apply as in Step 2. Then go to Step 3.

Computational results based on realistic instances of NS are reported in Potthoff et al. (2010). These results show that the described rescheduling method usually finds acceptable solutions in a short computation time on a regular PC. Especially in the case that a number of stand-by crews are available, usually no trains have to be cancelled due to lack of a driver or conductor.

11.5.3 Practical Application

The method described in Sect. 11.5.2 was applied by NS for rescheduling the duties of the drivers during a major disruption. As was mentioned in Sect. 11.1, a freight train derailed near station Vleuten (Vtn) on Monday, March 23, 2009. Due to this accident, the railway infrastructure was damaged over 5 km, which blocked the route between Utrecht (Ut) and Woerden (Wd) for nearly a week (see Figs. 11.4 and 11.2). Initially, this route was blocked completely.

On Tuesday, March 24, one track could be opened again, so that limited railway traffic was possible. Therefore, it was decided that the 2,000 line (The Hague (Gvc) – Utrecht) would be operated again on Wednesday. However, in one direction (The Hague – Utrecht) it would use another route, namely via Breukelen (Bkl), where it could turn in the direction of Utrecht. This alternative route was selected to have only trains in the direction Utrecht – The Hague on the disrupted route. As a consequence, the timetable of other trains had to be modified as well. This situation lasted until the evening of Sunday, March 29.

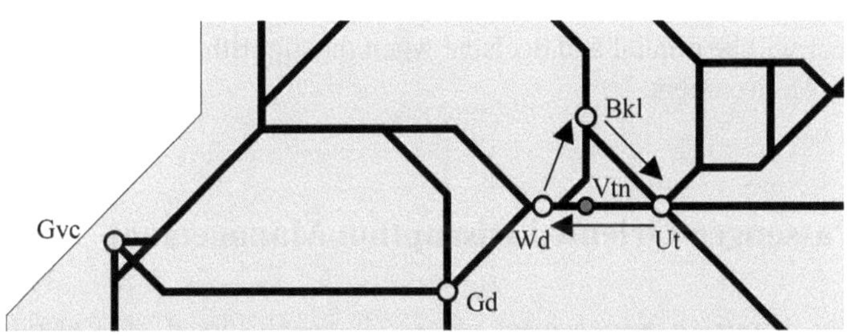

Fig. 11.4 The disruption took place near station Vleuten (*Vtn*) between Utrecht (*Ut*) and Woerden (*Wd*). The 2,000 line from the Hague (*Gvc*) to Utrecht made a detour via Breukelen (*Bkl*)

On Monday and Tuesday of this week, the crew duties were rescheduled completely manually. However, the driver duties for Wednesday and Thursday were rescheduled by the method described in Sect. 11.5.2.2. In fact, only the first three steps had to be carried out: all trips appeared to be covered then already. On each of these 2 days, about 260 driver duties were directly affected by the disruption and had to be rescheduled. The algorithm found a good feasible solution in about 1 h of computation time.

Although the solution approach might have taken into account the individual route and rolling stock knowledge of the drivers, this information was not available at NS in electronic format. Therefore, there were still some conflicts in the driver duties with the actual route and rolling stock knowledge. Fortunately, these problems could be solved relatively easily in the operations.

Unfortunately, the output of the algorithm could not be imported directly into the computer system of the Operations Control Centers of NS. Therefore, two dispatchers typed in all Wednesday's duties during the night before. The same happened during the next night for the Thursday's duties.

The duties for the conductors were still modified manually by the dispatchers. Therefore, we could make a comparison between the algorithmic approach and the current manual process. During the night, four dispatchers could reschedule the tasks in the conductor duties that started until 13:00 on the next day. The remaining part of the conductor duties had to be rescheduled manually during the day, resulting in many duties that did not finish at the regular time and in a lot of communication during the day. Many conductors were not quite happy with their rescheduled duties.

For the last 3 days of the disruption (Friday until Sunday), the CREWS planning system was used to reschedule all the crew duties. This system contains the algorithm described in Huisman (2007) to reschedule the crew duties during planned track maintenance. Of course, such an algorithm also works for an unplanned disruption which is known some time in advance. The CREWS system could not be used for rescheduling the crew duties during the first days of the disruption, since the application of this system has a relatively long lead time. In particular, the process of rescheduling the crew duties for Friday with the CREWS system started on Wednesday already.

Although this Vleuten case does not yet provide an example of algorithmic support for *real-time* disruption management, this case is quite close to it. Anyway, it clearly demonstrates the advantages of algorithmic support for rescheduling the crew duties in the operations: it leads to better solutions in less time. Especially the latter aspect will be crucial and decisive when the algorithmic support is applied in a real-time environment.

11.6 Passenger-Oriented Disruption Management

The current disruption management process is mainly based on a standard set of disruption scenarios, which focus on isolating the disrupted area and on keeping the railway system outside the disrupted area as much as possible as planned originally.

As a consequence, there is no additional railway capacity on detour routes. Service for the passengers is not considered as a target, but is just the result of the taken decisions.

However, as can be seen in the Vleuten case described in the previous section, sometimes more attractive alternatives for the passengers exist. In fact, the railway network should be so dynamic and flexible that its capacity can be adapted quickly to modified situations during and after disruptions. Algorithmic support in the disruption management process will be instrumental in achieving this flex ibility. Examples of alternatives are: temporarily operating another timetable (for example rerouted trains, or shuttle trains), and more or longer trains outside the disrupted area in order to facilitate the rerouting of passengers. Indeed, for the Vleuten case, Louwerse (2009) shows that algorithmically reassigning the rolling stock in the morning peak, can nearly halve the number of passengers without a seat. Since longer trains require more conductors, such a reassignment would not only result in more changes in the rolling stock circulation, but also in more changes in the conductors' duties.

Along the alternative routes for the passengers, passenger transfers from one train to another with short transfer times should be facilitated. For that purpose, trains may have to wait somewhat longer for each other than in the normal situation. This requires permanently monitoring and controlling the delays and connections of the trains, aiming to minimize the travel times of the passengers. The passengers should be informed permanently in an adequate way about their alternative routes. When the disruption is over, returning to the regular timetable should be done in a passenger friendly way, taking into account the stranded passengers at the stations. Returning to the regular timetable *as soon as possible* may not be optimal for many passengers.

To summarize, a much better service to the passengers can be provided during disruptions, but this results in even more complex rescheduling problems than the current ones. Since it is currently already extremely difficult for dispatchers to reschedule the timetable and the rolling stock and crew duties in case of a severe disruption, algorithmic support is obviously even more necessary if NS wants to focus on passenger-oriented disruption management.

11.7 Conclusions and Further Research

In this paper we argued that the application of algorithmic support in the disruption management process will be crucial for increasing the service level of the railway system for the passengers. This is required to increase the railway system's market share in the mobility market. The improved service for the passengers will be beneficial for the People, and the higher market share of the railway system will be beneficial for the Planet and for the Profit. The latter will also be influenced positively by the increased efficiency in the planning stage.

The application of algorithmic support in the disruption management process will help to determine appropriate measures for adapting the timetable in case of a disruption. Moreover, it will help to provide an appropriate capacity per train during and after the disruption, and to rebalance the rolling stock by the end of the day.

Second, it will help to reduce the number of cancelled trains due to missing crew. This is currently one of the bottle-necks in the disruption management process.

The advantages of the application of algorithmic support for the purpose of crew rescheduling was clearly demonstrated by the Vleuten case described in Sect. 11.5.3. Further research into the direction of passenger-oriented disruption management will increase the flexibility of the railway system, so that it will be able to adapt itself to the modified situation in case of a disruption.

The potential benefits of algorithmic support in the disruption management process are currently recognized by the board of NS, both by the inability of the manual rescheduling process to deal with several serious disruptions, and by the successes of the application of such tools in the offline planning processes. In 2008, the latter lead to winning the INFORMS Edelman Award for the application of algorithmic support for the development of the 2007 timetable of NS (Kroon et al. 2009). Now there is a certain eagerness to apply such tools in the disruption management process as well. As a consequence, this is the right time for research in this area, and for getting the results implemented in practice.

As a consequence, algorithmic support for rescheduling rolling stock and crews are currently being developed in close cooperation with NS. The status quo is that the available models and algorithms provide promising results in a laboratory environment: in relatively short computation times appropriate solutions can be generated for the rolling stock circulation and the crew duties. These results were discussed with and approved by the dispatchers in practice.

A further scientific challenge is to solve these resource rescheduling problems in a dynamic and uncertain environment, where the status quo of the system may be changing during the optimization process of the algorithms. This also requires an appropriate model for forecasting the status of the system during the optimization process. Another challenge is to solve the resource rescheduling problems in an integrated way: preferably, the rescheduling problems for the rolling stock and the drivers are solved together. Otherwise, one may end up with a solution where one trip must be cancelled due to missing rolling stock, and another trip must be cancelled due to a missing driver. This solution is obviously infeasible in practice. Also the extension of the models towards passenger-oriented disruption management requires a lot of further research. A final challenge is to test the algorithmic support methods also in a real-life environment. This is not only a challenge from an algorithmic point of view, but also from an information systems point of view. In particular, communicating the rescheduled timetable, rolling stock circulation, and crew schedules to all involved parties, including the passengers, is certainly not an easy task.

References

Abbink E, Fischetti M, Kroon L, Timmer G, Vromans M (2005) Reinventing crew scheduling at Netherlands railways. Interfaces 35(5):393–401

Abbink E, Mobach D, Fioole P, Kroon L, Wijngaards N, Van der Heijden E (2009) Actor-agent application for train driver rescheduling. In: Proceedings of 8th international conference on autonomous agents and multiagent systems (AAMAS 2009)

Alfieri A, Groot R, Kroon L, Schrijver A (2006) Efficient circulation of railway rolling stock. Transp Sci 40:378–391
Brons M (2006) Beleving en waardering van betrouwbaarheid in de ov-keten: een conceptueel kader. Technical report, Free University Amsterdam, TRANSUMO
Budai G, Maróti G, Dekker R, Huisman D, Kroon L (2010) Balancing of railway rolling stock during track maintenance. J Sched 13:281–297
Caprara A, Kroon L, Monaci M, Peeters M, Toth P (2007) Passenger railway optimization. In: Barnhart C, Laporte G (eds) Handbooks in operations research and management science, vol 14. Elsevier, Amsterdam, pp 129–187, chapter 3
Clausen J, Larsen A, Larsen J (2005) Disruption management in the airline industry – concepts, models and methods. Technical report, Technical University of Denmark, Copenhagen
Fioole P, Kroon L, Maróti G, Schrijver A (2006) A rolling stock circulation model for combining and splitting of passenger trains. Eur J Oper Res 174:1281–1297
Fores S, Proll L, Wren A (2001) Experiences with a flexible driver scheduler. In: Voß S, Daduna J (eds) Computer-aided scheduling of public transport. Springer, Berlin, pp 137–152
Grötschel M, Krumke S, Rambau J (2001) Online optimization of complex transportation systems. In: Grötschel M, Krumke S, Rambau J (eds) Online optimization of large scale systems. Springer, Berlin, pp 705–729
Huisman D (2007) A column generation approach to solve the crew rescheduling problem. Eur J Oper Res 180:163–173
Jespersen-Groth J, Clausen J, Larsen J (2006) Optimal reinsertion of cancelled train lines. Technical report, Technical University of Denmark, Copenhagen
Jespersen-Groth J, Potthoff D, Clausen J, Huisman D, Kroon L, Maróti G, Nielsen M (2009) Disruption management in passenger railway transportation. In: Ahuja R, Möhring R, Zaroliagis C (eds) Robust and online large-scale optimization, vol 5868. Springer, Berlin, pp 399–421, LNCS
Kohl N (2003) Solving the world's largest crew scheduling problem. ORBIT Extra, pp 8–12
Kohl N, Larsen A, Larsen J, Ross A, Tiourine S (2007) Airline disruption management – perspectives, experiences and outlook. Journal of Air Transport Management 13(3):149–162
Kroon L, Fischetti M (2001) Crew scheduling for Netherlands railways "destination: customer". In: Voß S, Daduna J (eds) Computer-aided scheduling of public transport. Springer, Berlin, pp 181–201
Kroon L, Huisman D, Abbink E, Fioole P, Fischetti M, Maróti G, Schrijver A, Steenbeek A, Ybema R (2009) The new Dutch timetable: the OR revolution. Interfaces 39(1):6–17
Lettovský L, Johnson E, Nemhauser G (2000) Airline crew recovery. Transp Sci 34(4): 337–348
Louwerse I (2009) Adjusting the rolling stock allocation in case of disruptions. Technical report, Bachelor's thesis, Erasmus University Rotterdam
Medard C, Sawhney N (2006) Airline crew scheduling from planning to operations. Eur J Oper Res 183(3):1013–1027
Nielsen L, Kroon L, Maróti G (2009) Capacity oriented rolling stock rescheduling in passenger railways. Technical report, Erasmus University Rotterdam. Submitted to: European Journal of Operational Research
Nissen R, Haase K (2006) Duty-period-based network model for crew rescheduling in European airlines. J Sched 9:255–278
Peeters M, Kroon L (2008) Circulation of railway rolling stock: a branch-and-price approach. Comput Oper Res 35(2):538–556
Potthoff D, Huisman D, Desaulniers G (2010) Column generation with dynamic duty selection for railway crew rescheduling. Transp Sci 44:493–505
Rezanova N, Ryan D (2009) The train driver recovery problem – a set partitioning based model and solution method. Comput Oper Res 37(5):845–856
Séguin R, Potvin J, Gendreau M, Crainic T, Marcotte P (1997) Real-time decision problems: an operational research perspective. J Oper Res Soc 48(2):162–174

Song M, Wei G, Yu G (1998) A decision support framework for crew management during airline irregular operations. In: Yu G (ed) Operations research in the airline industry. Kluwer Academic Publishers, Boston

Stoiković M, Soumis F, Desrosiers J (1998) The operational airline crew scheduling problem. Transp Sci 32(3):232–245

Walker C, Snowdon J, Ryan D (2005) Simultaneous disruption recovey of a train timetable and cre rosters in real-time. Comput Oper Res 32(8):2077–2094

Yu G, Argüello M, Song G, McCowan S, White A (2003) A new era for crew recovery at continental airlines. Interfaces 33(1):5–22

Part D
Sustainable Logistics and Traffic Management

Chapter 12
Customized Solutions for Sustainable City Logistics: The Viability of Urban Freight Consolidation Centres

Hans Quak and Lori Tavasszy

12.1 Introduction

12.1.1 Sustainability: Challenges in Urban Freight Transport

The current way of organizing the urban freight transport system is inefficient and generates an unsound basis for sustainable development. Urban freight transport is widely recognized for its unsustainable impacts on the environment. The common perception is that the current urban freight transport system has negative impacts on all three sustainability P's: people, profit and planet, also known as the social, economic and environmental issues of sustainability. Urban freight transport, or urban goods movement, is known for its unsustainable effects on:

- The planet, such as global pollutant emissions (CO_2 emissions) and local pollutant emissions (e.g., NO_x, PM_{10}).
- People, such as the effects of emissions on public health, consequences of traffic accidents, noise nuisance, visual intrusion, stench and vibration.
- Profit, such as inefficiencies due to regulations, congestion and decreasing city accessibility (see Quak 2008).

Which unsustainable impact is experienced most, depends on the actor, resulting in a variety of problem perceptions in urban freight transport. Thus, urban freight transport problems can be characterized as complex and compound, because a solution for one actor forms the basis of a new problem for another actor (Browne and Allen 1999). We distinguish four main groups of actors, that are involved in urban freight transport (Quak 2008):

H. Quak (✉) • L. Tavasszy
TNO, Bouw en Ondergrond and Delft University of Technology, Van Mourik Broekmanweg 6, 2628 Delft, XE, The Netherlands
e-mail: hans.quak@tno.nl/h.j.quak@tudelft.nl; lori.tavasszy@tno.nl/l.a.tavasszy@tudelft.nl

J.A.E.E. van Nunen et al. (eds.), *Transitions Towards Sustainable Mobility*,
DOI 10.1007/978-3-642-21192-8_12,

- Local authorities are interested in a liveable city, which implies an emphasis on reducing truck traffic and nuisance, and on improving air quality in city centres. The means of local authorities to look after their interests include regulations, such as time-windows, vehicle restrictions and low emission zones.
- Carriers try to organize urban freight transport as efficient as possible. Currently, their efforts are frustrated by local regulations, such as time-windows that force carriers to make their deliveries during a limited time period. Time-windows force most deliveries to take place during the morning hours. As a result, carriers have to travel during the morning peak periods and face vehicle utilization problems during the other periods, resulting in a serious cost-increase (Quak and De Koster 2007).
- Receivers (e.g., shop owners) like an attractive shopping climate, where nuisance by supplying trucks is minimized. But they also want a reliable distribution system, where goods are delivered at the times promised by shippers.
- Residents want a pleasant environment to live in, which includes clean air (as little local pollutant emissions as possible), no noise nuisance or other inconvenience caused by supplying, loading and unloading trucks.

Furthermore, the national government also has an interest, for example, the reduction of congestion and global pollution. The shippers want an urban freight transport system in which goods are supplied to stores in city centres at low cost within reliable times. And finally, the shopping public desires a nice shopping environment in the city centre.

There are many challenges in making urban freight transport truly more sustainable. However, our current urbanized civilization requires urban freight transport to sustain it. Since urbanization implies people living together on one location (i.e., the city), which is distant from sources of food, consumer products and waste disposal opportunities (see Ogden 1992). Next, urban freight transport is viable for economic vitality. So, urban freight transport is both an important source of sustainability and of non-sustainability in urban areas (Quak 2008).

12.1.2 Outline of this Chapter

In this chapter, we first discuss the many sustainability challenges in urban freight transport. We elaborate on past initiatives to improve sustainability and discuss why customized solutions are necessary to make a transition towards a more sustainable urban freight transport system. Next, in the second section, we focus on one specific solution in detail, i.e., a new form of an urban consolidation centre, coined Binnenstadservice. First, we pay attention to lessons learned from previous urban consolidation centre initiatives, after which we explain the business concept of Binnenstadservice. Next, we discuss the local sustainability impacts of this centre after 1 year. Then, we continue with the national impacts in case the concept is scaled up to more Dutch cities. The third section concentrates on the business model for

Binnenstadservice, since establishing a profitable (or cost-neutral) city consolidation centre seems to be one of the most challenging problems in this transition. And a sound business model is the main condition to embed this customized solution in practice. Finally, in the conclusions, we focus on the sustainability impacts and its relationship with other customized solutions for other urban freight transport problems, as well as with other initiatives to make a transition towards sustainable mobility.

12.1.3 Major Issues in Urban Freight Transport

The local authorities have the challenging task of finding a trade-off between the interests of people, planet and profitability. City logistics initiatives usually aim at reducing nuisance caused by freight transport in cities, while supporting social and economic development (Crainic et al. 2009a). In doing so, local authorities currently focus primarily on the local issues, i.e., the 'people' issues and local 'planet' issues. The policy measures that are used most frequently, are time-access windows, vehicle restrictions and environmental zones (The environmental zones (or low emission zones) focus on improving local air quality. This implies that only the local emissions (e.g., PM10 and NO_x) of trucks are of interest in these regulations. Global emissions of trucks, such as CO_2 emissions, are not considered in the regulations on environmental zones.) (see, e.g., OECD 2003). However, the improvement of these local sustainability issues goes at the expense of the other two Ps (mostly on a more regional or national level); it makes efficient urban goods transport quite difficult, and increases the total distance travelled, and thus CO_2 emissions and transportation costs (Quak and De Koster 2007). Carriers and retail chains consider these governmental policies as one of their biggest problems in supplying stores in urban areas efficiently. TNO (2003) estimates that local authorities' time-windows and vehicle restrictions result in a yearly cost increase of over € 400 million for the Dutch retail sector. Another major difficulty in efficient urban freight transportation is the decreasing city accessibility and the increasing congestion. This problem does not only concern urban freight transport: all traffic participants feel the impact of the increasing congestion in the Netherlands. The yearly costs in the Netherlands due to congestion are estimated to increase from about € 700 million in 2000 to € 2 billion in 2020. The share of goods transport therein is estimated at about € 150 million in 2000 to € 550 million in 2020 (Lemstra 2004, based on AVV).

12.1.4 Initiatives to Improve Sustainability

In other words, urban freight transport faces serious problems. It is therefore no surprise, that many initiatives over the past years aimed at improving (parts of) the problems in and with urban freight transport. Quak (2008) describes over 100

Table 12.1 Urban freight transport initiatives (Quak 2008)

Category	Type	Examples/explanation
Policy initiatives	Road pricing	London congestion charge
	Licensing and regulation	Time-windows, vehicle restrictions and low-emission zones
	Parking and unloading	(Reservation of) loading zones
Company-driven initiatives	Carrier cooperation	Cooperation to minimize inner city kilometres (bundle inner city transport)
	Vehicle routing improvement	Improving vehicle routing by taking actual traffic situation into account
	Technical vehicle improvement	Cleaner engines (e.g., EURO 5) or quiet trucks (Piek)
Physical infrastructure initiatives	Urban consolidation centres	Decoupling flows from outside the city and in the city at a consolidation centre (bundle inner city transport)
	Underground logistics system	Supply goods by using a dedicated underground system
	Road infrastructure development	Improve traffic flow
	Standardisation of load-units	The use of a standard box (city-box) to make consolidation easier
Transport reorganizing initiatives	Transport auction	Create a market for urban deliveries (with the idea to bundle deliveries)
	Intermodal freight	Use other modalities to deliver goods in cities

initiatives, that focus on improving the sustainability of urban freight transport (see Table 12.1 for a summary of the different initiatives' categories and types). Most of the initiatives failed in making the transition towards a more sustainable urban freight transport system, or even resulted in other (sustainability) problems for other actors (Quak 2008). The initiatives' categories and types (Table 12.1) are sometimes a bit interweaved: for example, many consolidation centre initiatives contained also local regulations (or the other way around: many governments started a consolidation centre to offer carriers an alternative in case they perceived the restrictions too strict).

12.1.5 Transition Aspects: Customized Solutions to Improve Sustainability in City Logistics

Basically, we distinguish three types of solution directions to improve urban freight sustainability: logistic, technical and policy solutions. Most initiatives only focus on one (or, at most, two) directions. To improve overall city logistics sustainability, a mix of solution methods is necessary. For example, technical solutions will improve air quality in time, and Intelligent Transport Systems (ITS) could be helpful to make the transition towards a more sustainable city logistics in the near future (see Crainic et al. 2009b).

In the Netherlands, we see positive results on transport costs and CO_2 emissions from a combination of all three solution directions; distribution during non-peak hours. In an experiment, full-truck deliveries to supermarkets are allowed to enter the city centre during the early morning hours in spite of time-window restrictions (see Dassen et al. 2008). In these experiments, trucks are made quieter, to minimize nuisance for residents in the neighbourhood in the early hours of the day (technical). Legislation has been changed, i.e., time-window restrictions have been adjusted, so that trucks are allowed to enter cities early in the morning (policy). Next, logistic changes made it possible to deliver early in the morning and to receive the goods at that time (logistic). The results show a decrease in distribution costs and CO_2 emissions, because fewer delivering vehicles had to travel during the morning peak hours. Residents did not perceive an increase in nuisance. This is an example of how a customized solution for a specific problem can have positive effects, if all different solution directions and actors' interests are considered. However, this solution is not applicable for all urban freight deliveries, since it requires goods to be delivered outside the shop's opening hours. Especially for smaller shops that are not part of retail chains, it is inconvenient to receive goods early in the morning. Another difference between the retail chains' stores and the smaller (independent) stores in a city centre is, how the deliveries are organized. Most of the retail chains orchestrate the logistics to deliver goods to the stores themselves; the majority of the volume for the retail chains' stores is bundled at a retail distribution centre (DC) and transported by private or dedicated carriers from the DC to the stores. For the independent retailer, deliveries are usually delivered by for-hire carriers that deliver the goods at the order of the shipper by whom the retailer ordered. The retailer does not receive its goods in one package, but from different suppliers, delivered by different carriers at different times of the day. So, the independent retailer receives several less-than-full truckload (LTL) deliveries per day. Therefore, the supply of the independent retailers results in many truck trips in the city, but only a limited volume is delivered per trip. Since the organization of these deliveries is not centrally managed, a new customized solution is necessary to enable the transition towards a more sustainable urban freight transport system for LTL deliveries. This transition requires a change in behaviour of carriers and the independent retailers.

12.2 Binnenstadservice : A New Type of Urban Consolidation Centre

Binnenstadservice (BSS) could be such a new customized solution. BSS is a new type of urban consolidation centre. In this section, we present the lessons learned from city consolidation centre initiatives in the past. Most of these initiatives failed.

Therefore, BSS has to differ from these initiatives and show that it has learned from earlier failures; otherwise it won't be a sustainable solution in the end. Next, we discuss the business concept used by BSS, after which we discuss the impacts of the concept after 1 year, and the simulated effects in case the BSS-concept would be established in more cities.

12.2.1 Lessons from Previous Urban Consolidation Centre Initiatives

There have been many urban consolidation centre initiatives in city logistics literature for over more than three decades (see, for example, McDermott 1975). The basic idea is, to separate the distribution activities in the city from distribution activities outside the city. In order to do so, transhipment is necessary at the border of the city. Transhipment at the city border makes it possible to efficiently organize both the transport to the city and in the city. This implies that large vehicles can be used for long haul transport outside the city, without the disadvantages of having these large trucks in the cities. An additional advantage is, that the trucks that enter the city can be fully loaded, since they carry the bundled load of multiple other trucks (we elaborate further on this basic business model for city consolidation centres in Sect. 12.3). Theoretically, a city consolidation centre has positive effects for most actors and on most sustainability issues (see Browne et al. 2005 and Quak 2008). However, making the transition from the current situation towards a situation with a city consolidation centre is difficult in practice, since it requires behavioural changes and trust from especially carriers.

In spite of the many (theoretical) advantages of city consolidation centres for the actors involved, only a few city consolidation centres have been established in practice, and were not terminated within a few years (Quak 2008). This conclusion was also confirmed by Browne et al. (2005), who state that of the more than 200 city consolidation schemes that were planned or carried out in Germany alone (in the last decade), five, at the most, are still active. Therefore, in order to prevent BSS from becoming the next failing city consolidation centre initiative, we will first analyze the lessons learned from these initiatives (Quak 2008). In this chapter, we will not deal with specific city consolidation centre initiatives (see for information on these cases Browne et al. 2005 and Quak 2008), but we limit ourselves to presenting the lessons learned from previous initiatives.

First of all, many store deliveries are already consolidated in some form. This is the case for the deliveries from retail chains, that start at a retail chain's DC, but also for most parcel and express deliveries, that start at a consolidation centre of a logistics service provider or express service. Often, over 50 deliveries for one city are included in one trip. Although this way of consolidation might not be optimal from a city perspective, it usually is from the retail chain's or for-hire carrier's perspective (e.g., in case a retailer plans an efficient roundtrip, but delivers only to one store per city, the roundtrip is efficient from the carrier's perspective, but not from the city's perspective, since a large truck enters a city to deliver only a limited part of its truckload). Therefore, these actors do not have an incentive to change the current situation, but they are – in many initiatives – considered to be the most important actor. Thus, carriers usually do not perceive a city consolidation centre as something that they can profit from (on the contrary). Therefore, existing consolidation centres usually depend on subsidy and restricting regulations, or on complicating circumstances (e.g., a medieval city centre with very narrow streets) in order to be able to operate on the longer term and attract sufficient volume from carriers (Quak 2008).

In many initiatives, the carrier-willingness to cooperate in the initiative is estimated to be high when it starts off, but usually only a few carriers are actually going to use the facility. This results in fewer scale advantages (less bundling) and higher costs per delivery, since the costs for the consolidation centre are spread over fewer deliveries than intended. The following statement of Browne et al. (2005) is an explanation for the overestimation of the number of carriers using a consolidation centre: *"some urban consolidation centre trials have been based on intuition rather than a quantified assessment and as a consequence are never likely to be viable*". Another lesson to be learned is that, although many consolidation centres have been set up as an alternative for carriers so that they do not feel bound by restricting policies, the carriers often consider this process to be the other way around. The restrictions are seen as a way to keep the unprofitable consolidation centre alive, which results in a strong dislike to use the facility. So, in many cases, carriers choose not to make use of a consolidation centre, even if there are restricting policies (Quak 2008).

Furthermore, the following lessons can be learned from past consolidation centre initiatives (Quak 2008):

- Delivering vehicles from the consolidation centre should not obstruct other traffic, as this lowers the public acceptance of the centre.
- The location of the centre should be close to a highway and not too far from the city centre (i.e., the location should not just be an available warehouse, but it should be strategically well-located).
- Forcing FTL deliveries to use a consolidation centre usually leads to more vehicle kilometres, since the full truck has to be divided over several smaller trucks. In addition, there are no bundling advantages. Thus, the consolidation centre should focus on LTL deliveries.
- Complex goods, e.g., frozen or high value goods, make operations in the centre complex and cannot be combined easily with other goods in a vehicle.
- Extra services could make the centre more profitable (or less loss-making), e.g., storage as a pickup point for residents, return logistics, etc.
- Focus on customers for whom a centre can add value, and not only on 'customers' that are (or feel) obliged to make use of the centre.

12.2.2 The concept: Adding Value for Shop Owners

In April 2008, a new consolidation centre initiative was established in the Dutch city of Nijmegen, called Binnenstadservice (BSS). Nijmegen, with over 161,000 inhabitants, is one of the oldest cities in the Netherlands, located in the eastern part of the country. The medieval city centre, located at a small hill and with a historical street structure, contains many small, independent retailers. BSS's consolidation centre is located at a distance of about 1.5 km from the city centre. BSS in Nijmegen differs from initiatives in the past. First of all, BSS focuses on receivers, rather than on carriers, in order to make the transition. BSS's clients are small and independent retailers, and they do not have to pay for BSS's basic service, i.e., receiving goods (at the consolidation centre) and delivering these goods to the store at a time preferred by the store-owner. The concept is rather easy: the retailer that wants to use BSS's services, informs its suppliers of a change in delivery address (i.e., changes its address into BSS's address), so that carriers deliver the goods to BSS. BSS deliberately focuses on small and independent retailers, since their deliveries are usually not optimized or bundled, in contrast to those of retail chains. Besides, these retailers force their suppliers to change their deliveries, which makes the transition happen in practice. By bundling the deliveries from multiple suppliers for the store-owner and delivering the goods at the time the retailer wishes, BSS offers a service that saves the small store-owners time. Next to this basic service, the retailers can purchase extra services at BSS:

- Storage (so that retailers no longer have to use their shop to store goods or rent storage space elsewhere).
- Home-deliveries (for example, for large goods, such as fridges and computers)
- Value-added logistics including retour logistics (of for example, clean waste)
- Possibilities for e-tailing in the city of Nijmegen.

BSS does not receive conditioned goods, such as fresh food or frozen products. BSS also offers its services to non-retail stores for money, such as hotels and the local authorities. BSS uses clean transportation to deliver goods from the consolidation centre to the stores in Nijmegen, i.e., an electronic bicycle and a natural gas truck, in order to reduce local emissions. BSS's mission is to provide logistic services to local inner city stores, regional consumers, carriers and the local government. The objective is to minimize the amount of truck trips in the city centre. BSS started with only twenty clients in April 2008. The initiators and staff of BSS have a good relationship with the retailers in Nijmegen, which makes the transition easier. Normally, the retailers had hardly any contact with the carrier delivering the goods. The number of stores that joined BSS increased to 98 after 1 year. With the increase in clients, the volume delivered to and by BSS also increased. BSS received a governmental subsidy for 1year to start business in Nijmegen. The intention of the subsidy is to give BSS time to find enough customers. The idea is that BSS should be profitable in the future, but this is not the case yet. We will discuss this in more detail in Sect. 12.3.

12.2.3 *Local Impacts After One Year Binnenstadservice Nijmegen*

In this section we discuss the local effects of BSS 1 year after BSS became operational in Nijmegen. We use three scenarios to evaluate BSS's impacts in the city centre of Nijmegen:

- Scenario 0, the base scenario – in this scenario there is no BSS and all stores are directly supplied by carriers, corresponding to the actual situation before April 2008.
- Scenario 1, 1 year scenario – in this scenario BSS has 98 clients, corresponding to the actual situation in April 2009, all other stores are directly delivered by the carriers.
- Scenario 2, maximum potential BSS – in this scenario all possible deliveries (e.g., no fresh or conditioned deliveries, no FTL, etc.) are delivered via BSS.

Based on available traffic data (GLV 2007), data on supplying transport (BCI 2005) in Nijmegen, and the data of 1 year BSS operations, we designed a dataset of all relevant delivering traffic for BSS. This relevant delivering traffic contained about 15% of the heavy trucks that were counted on an average day (see GLV 2007). Non-relevant traffic includes service related trips, FTL deliveries, fresh deliveries, municipality services (e.g., waste, public transport, transport for green spaces, etc.), construction transport, money deliveries, etc., since it is not affected by BSS. We simulated the routes and trucks for all three scenarios, using TNO's logistics model RESPONSE™ (see, for more information, Van Rooijen and Quak 2010). Based on these routes, we determined the traffic intensity on the links in the city centre of Nijmegen for an average day. Next, these changes in intensities are processed in the traffic model of the city of Nijmegen (which includes all traffic, so also passenger traffic outside the city centre and that we received from Nijmegen's local authorities). Next, the local impacts (noise and air quality) for the different scenarios are calculated using another TNO-model, viz. Urban Strategy (see Van Rooijen and Quak 2010 for a more in-depth explanation of the methodology of this exercise).

Table 12.2 shows the logistic results for all BSS relevant traffic for 1 day in the city centre of Nijmegen resulting from RESPONSE™. In scenario 1 (the situation after 1 year, i.e., April 2009), the decrease in number of kilometres is limited. Many carriers still have to deliver stores in the city centre of Nijmegen, next to deliveries to BSS for the 98 stores that joined BSS. Because these trucks have to visit both BSS and the stores that did not join BSS, the amount of saved kilometres is

Table 12.2 Logistic results (BSS relevant traffic) for one day

	Scenario 0	**Scenario 1**	**Scenario 2**
Number of truck kilometres	475	451	323
Light (<7.5 t) truck kilometres	270	220	32
Heavy (>7.5 t) truck kilometres	205	193	7
BSS kilometres (natural gas, light truck)	0	38	284

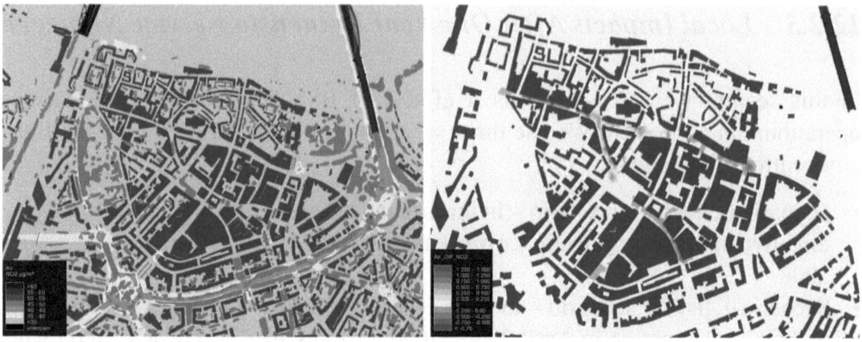

Fig. 12.1 Concentration NO_2 (scenario 0, 1 and 2, left) en differences (right) in concentration between scenario 0 and 2 (in Nijmegen)

relatively low. Note that the number of heavy truck kilometres decreases considerably in scenario 2 (maximum potential BSS). The remaining light and heavy transport in scenario 2 can be explained by the fact that some stores that joined BSS, still receive FTL truckloads directly from the carriers, which is in line with the BSS concept.

Based on these results, one could argue that emissions also decrease, because the number of (heavy) truck kilometres decreases considerably. However, the air quality is determined by the concentration of pollutant emissions in the air, i.e., the concentration NO_2 and PM_{10} (in $\mu g / m^3$). Based on the Urban Strategy calculations, we conclude that there were no air quality problems in the city centre of Nijmegen in scenario 0. The outcomes of the other scenarios hardly show any difference. The concentration in Nijmegen is mainly determined by the other traffic (including passenger traffic) and natural background concentration. The improvement due to BSS (in scenario 1 and 2) is very limited in comparison to these other local emission sources (see Fig. 12.1) (the results for PM_{10} are not shown in this chapter, but these results are comparable to those of NO_2 shown in Fig. 12.1). We calculated the noise levels in the city centre of Nijmegen, using the legal determined method, which implies that we evaluated noise on an average level during parts of the day. Based on this method, we did not find differences between scenarios 0, 1 and 2. However, loading and unloading activities take place at short periods of time, which results in peak levels in noise. Therefore, we also decided to calculate the noise nuisance by loading and unloading activities for residents in the city centre.

The nuisance is determined by the number of residents that experiences a certain number of loading and unloading activities within a distance of 100 m from their homes. Figure 12.2 shows that in scenario 1 and 2, more residents experience fewer loading and unloading activities than before BSS became active.

Based on the decrease in the number of truck kilometres, and especially, the decrease in heavy truck kilometres, we argue that, next to the already presented indicators, also the traffic safety as well as the shopping climate (frequently used indicators for city logistics) has improved in the city centre of Nijmegen due to BSS.

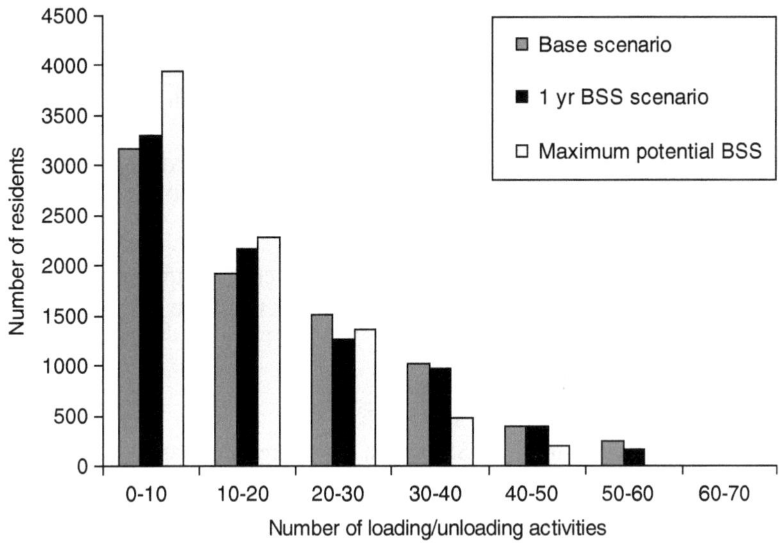

Fig. 12.2 Decrease in the number of experienced loading and unloading activities by residents

12.2.4 Scaling-up: Savings for Carriers

The consolidation centre concept that Binnenstadservice uses in Nijmegen, is also used to set up franchise branches in other Dutch cities:'s-Hertogenbosch (March, 2009), Maastricht (July, 2009) and Arnhem (September, 2009). Other cities in the Netherlands are also interested to start a Binnenstadservice consolidation centre. Eco2city is the national organization that acts as franchiser for local entrepreneurs who want to start a BSS branch in their own city. The clients of this local branch are, similar to the situation in Nijmegen, local shop-owners. The national organization, Eco2city, also concludes contracts with carriers; during the first year of operations in Nijmegen, BSS learned that it added value for carriers. Now, Eco2city offers carriers a contract. This contract states that the carrier will pay Eco2city an agreed amount of money per delivery that is received at a BSS branch. This agreed amount of money differs per carrier, depending on the amount of money a carrier saves due to delivering to BSS, instead of delivering directly to the stores. In this contract, Eco2city offers the carrier to contact all its delivery addresses in every new city, where Eco2city opens a BSS branch, in order to ask them to join the local BSS initiative. As more cities get a BSS branch, Eco2city will become a serious partner for carriers that could offer considerable savings. We continue with this change in the business model in the next section. In this section, we first evaluate the maximum savings a carrier can expect in case more BSS branches open in the Netherlands.

A carrier can expect several advantages from BSS branches, among other things:

- No nuisance due to local regulations (such as cost increasing time-windows, vehicle restrictions and low emission zones, see Quak and De Koster 2007; 2009).
- One contact for all city deliveries (instead of the chaos with different regulations in different cities or neighbourhoods, see, e.g., Dablanc 2007).
- Enough time and space to load and unload the vehicle.

To examine the effects of scaling up the BSS concept to several cities, we designed four scenarios in which the amount of cities that have a BSS branch vary:

- Scenario 0 – no city has a BSS branch.
- Scenario 1 – 6 cities have a BSS branch.
- Scenario 2 – 20 cities have a BSS branch.
- Scenario 3 – 41 cities have a BSS branch (for more information on which cities have a branch in the different scenarios, see Quak and Hendriks 2009).

In these scenarios, we evaluate the maximum savings for carriers as all its delivery addresses join the local BSS branch. This is a maximum; all stores choose individually whether they want to join the local BSS branch or not. In case they do not want to join, the carrier has to deliver that store directly. We calculate the roundtrip planning for two case companies for all four scenarios, based on detailed delivery data for one week with TNO's logistic model RESPONSE™:

- Case 1: *TWI* (market leader in distribution for the travel industry in the Netherlands, i.e., travel brochures, tickets and travel documents to travel agencies).
- Case 2: *Lekkerland* (a company well-known for transporting convenience products).

TWI makes in total 3538 stops at about 1900 addresses during one week with 16 small trucks from one distribution centre (Nieuwveen). TWI normally plans about 25 stops per roundtrip. The average distance from the DC to a delivery address is about 74 km.

In this study we only considered the non-food flows that are delivered from three distribution centres (i.e., Meppel, Son and Waddinxveen) with 118 trucks in 7103 stops during one week. Lekkerland plans on average 14 stops per roundtrip. The average distance from the DC to a delivery address is about 45 km.

Figure 12.3 shows the considerable savings both carriers can achieve if the number of cities with a BSS branch increases (and all their delivery addresses in the city join the local BSS initiative). The fact that all delivery addresses in a city join the local BSS initiative implies, that these results show the maximum savings for carriers. Figure 12.3 shows the total of savings on distribution for carriers (as percentage in comparison to the situation in which no BSS branches exist), kilometres, time and emissions of the local BSS transport are not included in these results.

In cities where a BSS branch is opened, the carriers can make fewer stops. On average, the number of stops can be reduced by 90% in cities that have a BSS

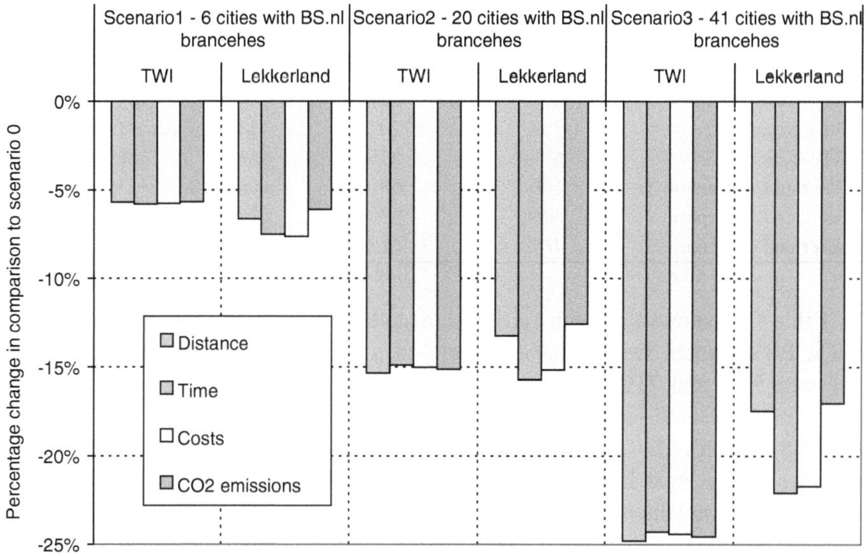

Fig. 12.3 Savings total distance, time, costs and CO_2 emissions based on all roundtrips (in comparison to no BSS branches)

branch, since all delivery orders are bundled in one stop at the local BSS branch. Obviously, this percentage decreases if not all delivery addresses join the local BSS, or if only addresses in the city centre are allowed to join. Most delivery addresses of TWI are located in city centres. Lekkerland also has a considerable amount of delivery addresses outside the city centres.

The carriers show differences in the savings per scenario. However, it is important to note that an increase in BSS branches is for both carriers a considerable money-saver. The differences can be explained by several differences in the logistic organization and types of products delivered between the two carriers. Based on these differences, we conclude that (see also Quak and De Koster 2009):

- In case the length of the roundtrips is restricted by the available time (rather than the vehicle capacity), a carrier can make more savings in distance (and therefore in CO_2 emissions) due to an increase in BSS branches, since it is able to plan more orders in one roundtrip. The number of stops is similar, but the carrier can deliver several orders at one stop at a BSS branch (see case TWI). Considerable savings can be expected, especially, when the distance between the DC and the delivery addresses is large.
- In case the length of the roundtrips is restricted by vehicle capacity (e.g., the case Lekkerland), the savings in distance follow only from fewer kilometres in the city centre with a BSS branch, more efficient roundtrip planning (no city restrictions) and time-savings (bundling several orders in one stop saves stopping time, e.g., parking). These savings are also made by TWI (the case where time restricted the roundtrips).

Table 12.3 Savings per order delivered via BSS branch (in comparison to order delivered directly to delivery address)

	Distance	Time	Costs	CO_2 emissions
TWI – Scenario 1	59%	60%	59%	59%
TWI – Scenario 2	72%	70%	71%	71%
TWI – Scenario 3	69%	67%	68%	68%
Lekkerland – Scenario 1	60%	68%	69%	55%
Lekkerland – Scenario 2	54%	65%	62%	52%
Lekkerland – Scenario 3	48%	61%	60%	47%

Table 12.3 shows that both carriers can save a lot of money per order delivered via a BSS-branch. Delivering an order via a local BSS-branch saves a carrier between 59% and 71% in costs per order, in comparison to the costs per order that is not delivered via a BSS-branch (if all delivery addresses from that city join the BSS-branch). These savings also occur if only the delivery addresses in the city centre join the local BSS-branch; we recalculated scenario 1 for Lekkerland for the situation in which only the delivery addresses in the city centres join the local BSS-branch, instead of all deliveries in the city. The total savings decrease (in comparison to the results in Fig. 12.3) to 1.6% in kilometres and CO_2 emissions and 2% in time and costs. Since the number of orders delivered via a BSS branch decreased from 768 (scenario 1) to 214 (in the scenario with only delivery addresses in the city centre joining), this decrease was to be expected. The savings per order, in case only all addresses in the city centre join, are (in comparison to delivering these addresses directly): 52% in kilometres, 66% in time, 67% in costs and 51% in CO_2 emissions.

In other words, carriers profit considerably from a BSS branch. The positive impacts for carriers increase, as more BSS branches start their local business. The savings per order do not increase, if more cities have a BSS branch, or in case only stores in city centres join the local BSS; these savings are on average about 65% in costs for one order. Although not calculated in this study, these advantages will decrease if fewer delivery addresses join the local BSS branch. In this study we assumed all delivery addresses joined the local BSS initiative.

12.3 Transition Towards a Sustainable Business Model

12.3.1 Basic Business Models for City Distribution

The business case for basic city distribution services, such as an urban consolidation centre (UCC), revolves around the possible savings in transport costs of carriers, if they can avoid the trips through the inner city, by focusing on the first tier task of serving different cities within one tour. City distribution will be outsourced, if these specialised services within cities can be run at lower rates and/or higher service

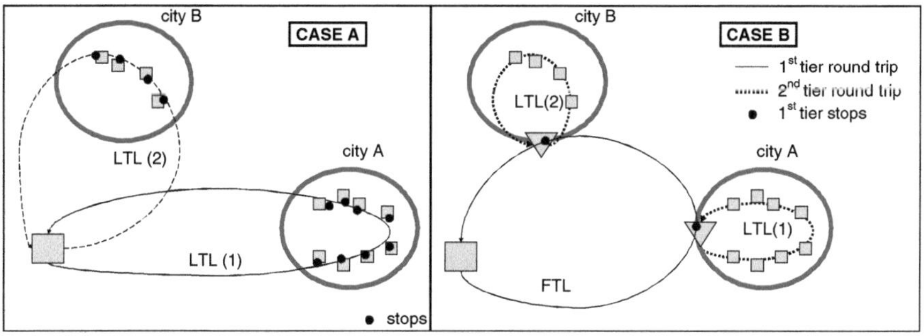

Fig. 12.4 Efficiency improvement in roundtrip planning due to city consolidation centres

levels. The viability of the distribution service depends on at least the following (necessary but not sufficient) conditions:

1. The system viability: is there a benefit to be gained for all parties together?
2. User viability: will each agent gain a benefit from the change?

The step from situation A to situation B (see Fig. 12.4) involves the following changes:

(a) A decrease in costs for the main (1st tier) carrier due to higher productivity (a switch from two LTL to one FTL trip and a decrease in the number of stops).
(b) An increase in costs for the main carrier because of the outsourcing of city tours.

If the net balance is positive, the market will enable a change in the structure of trips by itself. Conditions for change are more favourable when (a) is high and (b) is low, i.e., when

- Initial costs for city distribution are high due to severe congestion or long distances
- External conditions prohibit scale economies to be gained, e.g., with time windows or other access restrictions present
- Purpose built, clean and efficient technologies are applied for city distribution.

Besides the carriers, other agents in the system may incur additional benefits as well. These benefits may include:

- Increased reliability of deliveries (benefit for shop-owners);
- Lower response time for stock replenishment (benefit for visitors);
- Better quality of life (decreasing noise hindrance, improved air quality, safer loading and unloading) in the city (benefit for inhabitants).

These additional benefits provide opportunities to extend the scope of the business model. Firstly, this may involve additional services, like warehouse management, effectively capitalizing on the benefits for shop owners. Secondly, the value of external benefits may be captured and internalized by means of

Table 12.4 Alternative business models for UCC

	Basic services (UCC)	Extended services
No public involvement	• Consolidation centre with own vehicles	• Consolidation centre with extended services (e.g., warehouse management)
	• Carrier market based development (Willingness to pay among shop owners for pure UCC services is limited, see Marcucci and Danielis (2008) and Hofenk et al. (2009))	• Carrier/receiver interaction
	• Level playing field focus	• Possibly compensation scheme required
Public involvement	• Value capturing of external effects	• Value-added service for retail
	• Tax introduction	• External effects of extended services may be limited
	• Recycling of revenues	
	• Concessioning needed?	• Need to separate basic UCC and extended services to prevent cross-subsidization

imposing taxes on shop owners or the visiting public (e.g., through tolls or parking charges) followed by subsequent investments or operating subsidies to the distribution system.

The above leads to a number of alternative business models, that differ by the degree of complexity (i.e., types of services and agents concerned) and the degree of public involvement (Table 12.4). Depending on the type of business model, the introduction and operation of services will require different management processes from private and public stakeholders.

The experience with this range of business models is limited. There is a handful of experiments with UCC's, but none of them have extended their services to value added services such as warehouse management for shop owners (see also Sect. 12.1). Most UCC businesses work with operating subsidies (Browne et al. 2005; Quak 2008). Subsidies are usually provided to cover startup losses, which is also the case with BSS in Nijmegen. However, longer-term sustainability of services is not always an issue during the start. Experience to date seems to indicate that, without structural subsidies, these UCC businesses are not able to be self-supporting (Quak 2008; Van Duin 2009). In these analyses, the positive external benefits are not taken into account, however. Internalizing them would be worthwhile, as they could potentially contribute to a feasible business case. Also the current prices of inner-city movements are still low and quite competitive with the current carriers, while higher prices would allow for the UCC operations to break even (van Duin et al. 2010).

Typically, as long as no structural subsidies are possible, or no limiting conditions exist for regular road transport operations (environmental zoning, time windows or other access limitations) or when congestion is limited, the circumstances to introduce UCC operations as a purely private venture will not be favourable. For a limited number of cities where this combination of circumstances appears, the chances for a UCC are higher. One can compare this situation to the introduction of the subway at the beginning of the twenth century or congestion pricing around the twentyfirst century: the first city where these were introduced was London, where circumstances were pressing. London was the first to find that the level of service of surface transport was low enough to allow a sound business case for innovations in the transport system. Some major cities followed the London example shortly after (Budapest and Paris with the subway, Stockholm with pricing); others took more time or are still not ready.

12.3.2 Development of Binnenstadservice's Business Model

BSS and its national mother company Eco2city experienced with the business model right from the start in April 2008. Marcucci and Danielis (2008) and Hofenk et al. (2009) show that there is hardly or no willingness among shop owners to pay for pure UCC services. Experiences during the first year of operations also showed that earnings from extra services for shop owners did not match the operating costs. In other words, to be self-supporting in time, BSS needs to make changes in its original business model. Carrier-receiver interaction (see also Table 12.4) is limited, which implies that the receiver (i.e., the shop-owner) does not pay lower transport costs to the shipper or carrier, even if the carrier has considerable savings due to BSS (see Sect. 12.2). This imperfection results in the fact, that the receivers are not willing to pay BSS for the basic service. It is important to note that the receivers are necessary in the starting phase of a BSS branch to make the transition possible, since they have to 'force' the carrier to change its behaviour, i.e., delivering the goods to the local BSS, by changing the receiving address. This action is a necessity, because – as was shown earlier in this chapter – carriers are usually unwilling to cooperate in UCC initiatives. Carriers usually fear that the decrease in costs due to higher productivity, is outweighed by an increase in costs because of outsourcing city tours to BSS (see Fig. 12.4). In BSS's current business model, the receivers now force carriers to cooperate with the initiative.

BSS received a subsidy to set up business in Nijmegen and find enough shops to join the initiative. Since especially carriers profit from the services, it is of importance that BSS is able to share in these carriers' profits. If this is not the case, BSS can only use the business model in which there is considerable public involvement (see Table 12.4). Structural subsidies can only be justified by internalizing the positive impacts for society as presented in Sects. 12.2.3 and 12.2.4.

By extending to more cities, BSS becomes a more interesting partner for carriers, that are, after all, usually also operating regionally (or nationally). For carriers it is more interesting to arrange city logistics business with one partner for several cities, than to negotiate with several local UCC managements (In previous UCC initiatives, a UCC was limited to one city. When several cities start their own UCC, a carrier is probably even less willing to negotiate with all the different UCC managers.). Therefore, by scaling the BSS concept, the chances increase for BSS to become a serious partner for carriers. In the autumn of 2009, BSS entered into contracts with the first carriers that were willing to share their savings with BSS. Developments in this direction are inevitable and necessary for the success of the business of BSS and the question whether they will be able to become independent from public involvement in the future.

Next to these gains that the BSS branches will receive from the carriers (via the national organization Eco2city), all local branches have to find other financial gains as well. These local gains differ per branch; examples are gains from extra services, subsidies from local governments (for example, if a local BSS branches solves a local problem, local authorities might be willing to pay for this specific solution), a local branch can (partly) serve as a social workplace, so some (partly-disabled) staff is (partly) subsidized by local authorities. In this way, with different local sources of income, every branch, as well as the national organization, should be able to earn enough gains to be self-supporting. To become financially sustainable in the long term, the business model is adapted to the individual requirements of the different actors. However, it takes a lot of time and energy to actually make the transition happen; i.e., convincing the many different actors to take part in this customized urban freight transport solution. It requires individual contracts with carriers, receivers and local authorities. But if BSS can arrange the financial means for this business model, BSS really becomes a customized solution for several urban freight transport problems.

12.4 Conclusions

Reorganizing LTL deliveries in urban areas, by using a city consolidation centre, but especially by communicating with many actors individually (i.e., shop owners, carriers and local authorities), as was the case in Nijmegen with Binnenstadservice, has positive results on all the sustainability Ps. It is profitable for both carriers and receivers. It reduces the carbon footprint of urban freight deliveries. It also has positive effects on traffic safety and the shopping climate in urban areas. Because of Binnenstadservice, fewer residents experience noise nuisance by loading and unloading vehicles. The concept is already used in other cities in practice. The main challenge is to secure this transition towards more sustainable urban freight mobility, by creating a business model that will be self-supporting in the future. This business model is evolving over time, but some obstacles have to be conquered by communicating to many actors individually. Therefore, we can conclude that it is a very time-consuming exercise to secure this transition towards sustainable mobility for the future.

The serious sustainability issues in urban freight transportation demand customized solutions, tailored to the specific problem at hand. Different actors have different stakes in urban goods movement and perceive different sustainability issues. It is, therefore, necessary to develop a customized solution that takes the specific situation into account. Basically, there are three types of solution directions to improve urban freight transport sustainability, i.e., logistic, technical and policy solutions. To improve sustainability, all three directions should be used, and the different actors should be tempted to be involved in such a solution by offering all of them a number of gains.

One such a solution for LTL deliveries in urban freight transport is Binnenstadservice. In this contribution, we showed that technological solutions (i.e., clean transportation means), logistic solutions (i.e., reorganizing the organization of the final mile in the city), and policy solutions (i.e., the use and enforcement of time-window restrictions and environmental zones) can result in positive sustainability issues.

Binnenstadservice (BSS) differs from urban consolidation centre initiatives from the past: the receivers are the main customers. This resulted in a considerable volume of goods, transported via BSS in Nijmegen after already one operational year. After one year, BSS already shows positive local impacts: fewer large vehicle kilometres in the city centre of Nijmegen, less noise nuisance for residents, and a better shopping climate. Although local pollution decreased as well, air quality – measured in concentration PM_{10} and NO_2 – did not change, because of background concentrations and pollution resulting from remaining transport (e.g., passenger transport).

After 18 months, already three new BSS branches were established in the Netherlands. Carriers can make considerable savings in terms of kilometres, time, costs and CO_2 emissions, in case the number of BSS branches increases in the Netherlands. Depending on the type of carrier and the type of deliveries, a carrier can make savings that range from 5% in distribution costs and CO_2 emissions (in a situation where 6 cities have a BSS branch) to almost 25% (in a situation where 42 cities have a local BSS branch). The savings per order, delivered via a BSS branch instead of directly by a carrier, are huge; ranging from 60 to 70% in distribution costs and CO_2 emissions.

The original business model of BSS aimed at receivers. However, the receivers are not willing to pay for the basic service and do buy sufficient extra services to cover BSS's operating costs. Therefore, the business model evolved over time: on the one hand, a local BSS branch receives money from local activities, such as extra services for receivers. On the other, the national organization of BSS aims at contracting carriers. Carriers save money by using a BSS branch; if the carriers share these savings with BSS, the result is a win-win situation. The carrier saves money and pays a fixed amount per money-saving order to BSS. Supplying all delivery addresses located in the city centre via a BSS branch will lead to the following effects for a carrier:

(a) A decrease in costs for the carrier due to higher productivity (a switch from two LTL to one TL trip, a decrease in the number of stops and a more efficient roundtrip planning).
(b) An increase in costs for the main carrier because of the outsourcing of city tours.

If the net balance is positive, market forces will automatically enable a change in the structure of trips. Conditions for change are more favourable when (a) is high and (b) is low. In practice, convincing every carrier individually turns out to be quite time consuming. However, this is necessary for BSS in order to become self-supporting in the future, since the gains from extra services to receivers and local authorities do not cover the operating costs, and it is not yet possible to internalize the external benefits, such as an improvement in sustainability.

References

BCI – Buck Consultants International (2005) 0- meting "vervoersbewegingen binnenstad nijmegen". BCI, Nijmegen

Browne M, Allen J (1999) The impact of sustainability policies on urban freight transport and logistics systems. In: Meermans H, Van de Voorde E, Winkelmans W (eds) 8th World Conference on Transport Research (WCTR), vol 1, Transport Modes and Systems. Elsevier, Antwerp, pp 505–518

Browne M, Sweet M, Woodburn A, Allen J (2005) Urban freight consolidation centres, final report. University of Westminster, London

Crainic TG, Ricciardi N, Storchi G (2009a) Models for evaluating and planning city logistics schemes. Transp Sci 43(4):432–454

Crainic TG, Gendreau M, Potvin JY (2009b) Intelligent freight-transportation systems: assesment and the contribution of operations research. Transp Res part C 17(6):541–557

Dablanc L (2007) Goods transport in large European cities: difficult to organize, difficult to modernize. Transp Res part A 41(3):280–285

Dassen R, Colon P, Kuipers L, Koekebakker E (2008) Dagrand-distributie supermarkten. BCI, Nijmegen

GLV – Groen Licht Verkeersadviezen (2007) Kentekenonderzoek centrum nijmegen. GLV, Tilburg

Hofenk D, Van Birgelen M, Bloemer J, Semeijn J (2009) Supply chain innovation: a case of sustainable urban freight transport in the Netherlands. 21st NOFOMA conference, Jönköping, pp 11–12

Lemstra W (2004) Stedelijke distributie: samen gaan voor resultaat. Ministerie van Verkeer en Waterstaat, The Hague

Marcucci E, Danielis R (2008) The potential demand for a urban freight consolidation centre. Transportation 35:269–284

McDermott DR (1975) An alternative framework for urban goods distribution: consolidation. Transp J 15(1):29–39

OECD (2003) Delivering the goods – 21st century challenges to urban goods transport. OECD, Paris

Ogden KW (1992) Urban goods movement: a guide to policy and planning. Ashgate, Aldershot

Quak HJ (2008) *Sustainability of urban freight transport – retail distribution and local regulations in cities* (PhD thesis). ERIM, Rotterdam

Quak HJ, De Koster MBM (2007) Exploring retailers' sensitivity to local sustainability policies. J Oper Manage 25(6):1103–1122

Quak HJ, De Koster MBM (2009) Delivering goods in urban areas: how to deal with urban policy restrictions and the environment. Transp Sci 43(2):211–227

Quak HJ, Hendriks BM (2009) De impact van Binnenstadservice – het begin van een nieuw type stadsdistributiecentrum. In: Witlox FJA, Ploos van Amstel W (eds) *Bijdragen Vervoerslogistieke werkdagen 2009* (Transport Logistics Days). Nautilus Academic Press, Zelzate, pp 1–17

TNO (2003) De invloed van venstertijden en voertuigbeperkingen op de distributiekosten in de Nederlandse detailhandel. TNO, Delft

Van Duin R (2009) To be or not to be, a typical City Distribution Centre question. Research on success and failures in ten European CDC-cases. In: Witlox FJA, Ploos van Amstel W (eds) *Bijdragen Vervoerslogistieke werkdagen 2009* (Transport Logistics Days). Nautilus Academic Press, Zelzate, pp 123–145

Van Duin R, Quak H, Muñuzuri J (2010) Still believe! New challenges for urban consolidation centres: the case The Hague. Procedia Soc Behav Sci 2(3):6177–6188

Van Rooijen T, Quak HJ (2010) Local impacts of a new urban consolidation centre – the case of Binnenstadservice. Procedia Soc Behav Sci 2(3):5967–5979

Chapter 13
Closing the Global Supply Chain: The Gateway Towards Sustainability

Erwin van der Laan

13.1 Introduction

The majority of the sustainable supply chain management literature focuses on the trade-off between economic (Profit) and ecological (Planet) impacts. The efficient balancing between those two impacts is called eco-efficiency (see e.g. Quariguasi 2008). Moving towards more sustainable practices is generally bounded by increasing costs, but the implementation of new environmentally-friendly practices could ultimately result in increased market share and profits that cover the additional costs (Wu and Dunn 1995). An important trade-off less often found in supply chain management literature, is between economic and social (People) impacts. According to Murphy and Poist (2002), logistics will only reach its full potential, if economic and social targets go hand in hand. Carter and Jennings (2002) specifically focus on the trade-off between People and Profit, introducing the concept of Logistics Social Responsibility (LSR). LSR comprises activities like sustainable purchasing, sustainable transportation and sustainable warehousing, taking into account factors like ethics, human rights, safety and community explicitly. The authors conclude that organizational culture, top management and governmental regulation are drivers for LSR, but there may be barriers as well: company culture, lack of coordination and lack of resources may prohibit the transition towards effective LSR. For example, Bloemhof et al. (2011) recently found that cultural aspects and financing structures may prohibit the transition to more sustainable transport modes.

Flapper et al. (2005) are one of the first to explicitly relate all three dimensions of sustainability (people, planet and profit) to supply chain management, coining the

E. van der Laan (✉)
Rotterdam School of Management, Erasmus University, PO Box 1738, 3000 Rotterdam, DR, Netherlands
e-mail: elaan@rsm.nl

J.A.E.E. van Nunen et al. (eds.), *Transitions Towards Sustainable Mobility*,
DOI 10.1007/978-3-642-21192-8_13,

term ‘sustainable supply chain management’. Through an extensive literature study Carter and Rogers (2008) state that…

> Firms that strategically undertake SSCM will achieve higher economic performance than firms that pursue only one or two of the three components of the triple bottom line. (Carter and Rogers 2008)

De Brito and van der Laan (2010) argue, though, that there still is a lack of integration of ecological and social sustainability issues in addressing supply chain and operations management problems.

Instead of focussing on sustainability goals in the forward supply chain, a much more effective way of contributing to sustainability is, to substitute sourcing, manufacturing and forward transport operations by take-back, recovery and reuse of products and materials (Hischier et al. 2005), thereby closing the supply chain loop. The management of such closed loops is also referred to as Closed Loop Supply Chain Management (CLSCM, see, e.g., Guide et al. 2003; Flapper et al. 2005). A contribution to environmental sustainability is achieved through the reduction of virgin materials, hazardous materials, energy and emissions, while social sustainability is enhanced through the creation of more jobs (product recovery generally requires more manpower than waste management), welfare and a safe and healthy living environment.

Geyer and Jackson (2004) conjectured that CLSCM is subject to three types of constraints or barriers: lack of resources, lack of recovery capabilities and lack of demand for recovered products and materials. One of the central research questions posed by the TRANSUMO-ECO research project was, to empirically identify the main barriers and facilitators for global (that is cross-border) recovery supply chains as a means to contribute to sustainability. Therefore, we performed a number of case studies, which are presented and analyzed in Sects. 13.2 and 13.3 discusses the main barriers we observed, that may block or delay a transition to sustainable closed loop supply chains. Finally, Sect. 13.4 suggests a number of actions that may remove the identified barriers to set us on a path to true sustainability.

13.2 Barriers for Transition: Case Analysis

Based on 26 in-depth interviews with purchasing, transportation and warehousing managers, Carter and Jennings (2002) identified three possible barriers for Logistics Social Responsibility. A *company culture* that embraces corporate responsibility may be a driver for LSR, but if that culture does not exist or is not supported by top management, it can actually function as a barrier. *Lack of coordination* of activities and objectives may be a barrier if LSR initiatives somewhere in the chain are, for instance, not picked up by other actors, if there are no administrative tools to properly manage, or if there are no consequences for non-compliance. Also *limitation of (technical) resources* is mentioned as a barrier, but this is not discussed in detail.

Table 13.1 Conjectured barriers for effective recovery supply chains

Barrier	Interpretation
Culture	Sustainability not embraced by company or top management
Lack of coordination	Lack of coordination between supply chain partners, lack of administrative tools or protocols
Lack of resources	Lack of products/materials in the right quantity and quality
Lack of recovery capabilities	No access to processes for meaningful recovery
Lack of markets	No access to markets for recovered products and materials

Geyer and Jackson (2004) specifically focus on closed loop supply chain management and conjecture the existence of three barriers ('constraints') that partly overlap with the ones just mentioned. *Limited resources* in terms of reusable products and materials that are of sufficient quality to be reused is the first one. Lack of capabilities to reuse products and materials in a meaningful way is a second. Finally, the lack of markets for reused products and materials prohibits a viable closed loop supply chain. Combining the frameworks of Carter and Jennings (2002) and Geyer and Jackson we propose the barriers as displayed in Table 13.1.

Next, we analyze three recycling chains ('cases') that were investigated by the TRANSUMO-ECO project between 2006 and 2009. The supply chains cover a variety of products (waste paper, electrical and electronic waste, end-of-life automobiles), but have the common denominator that the forward and/or reverse supply chain is border-crossing. After presenting the cases, we provide an overview of the observed barriers for efficient and effective recovery supply chains.

13.2.1 Case 1: The Dutch-Chinese Waste Paper Recycling Chain

This case combines the studies of Van den Broeke (2008) and Sanders (2008).

Due to the imbalance in trade flows between Europe and China, the export of waste paper from Europe to China to be reused as packaging material is important and growing. The main actors in the waste paper chain are the waste paper companies that collect, process and trade waste paper, trading companies that do not actually handle the paper, but are only involved in trading, shipping lines, and terminal owners that deal with the export of sea containers and paper mills that finally turn the waste paper into the final product.

A case study at Ciparo, a waste paper trader with offices in the Netherlands and China, revealed that several factors play an important role in order to successfully adapt to a growing market. First of all, it is crucial to have offices in China and reliable information systems to deal with the elaborate paperwork. The European ordination of waste product transportation (EVOA) regulates the exports of waste materials. Within the EU no special procedures are required for waste paper. Outside of the EU it depends on the receiving country, but for China no special licenses are necessary. Still, the exporter needs to declare the contents and destination of the shipped containers. The receiving party needs to be a recycling company and not some intermediate party. The Dutch ministry of environmental affairs monitors the exports from the Dutch side of the chain, but even then, there is a substantial risk that the Chinese inspection does not accept incoming containers and has them sent back.

Speaking the language and having Chinese intermediate buyers in place is essential, as the Chinese paper mills will not buy directly from European traders. One needs to be familiar with the many peculiarities of the Chinese market to run a successful business. Finally, margins in the business are low, so even when demand for paper increases, small changes in the waste paper price may result in a redirection towards virgin paper. This is very much a trader's market in which there is very little or no interaction between the forward and the reverse chain and between the actors in the reverse chain.

As said, the export of waste paper is an important business, especially for the main port of Rotterdam. Annually, about 70,000 containers with waste paper are shipped from Rotterdam, which amounts to about 3% of total exports and about 11% of all exports to China. A problem with current practice is that the container stack at the port is often used as a cheap stocking location for waste paper that is waiting to be shipped by sea container (Sanders 2008). This misuse of the port's capacity deregulates the port's normal activities, which are already at its limits. The study by Sanders (2008) suggests having a dedicated inland terminal to handle the loading of the containers. As these containers will be transported by barge straight to the quay, instead of by truck, this also is expected to ameliorate current congestions on the A13, the main highway connection to the port, thereby lowering transportation costs, reducing emissions and reducing noise pollution. The study shows that a dedicated inland terminal also provides economic benefits for all parties involved except for the truck transporters. The latter may be a barrier for implementation.

13.2.2 Case 2: The Global Supply Chain of Electrical and Electronic Equipment (EEE)

This case combines the studies of Zuidwijk and Krikke (2008), Zoeteman et al. (2010) and Wang (2008).

The European WEEE (Waste Electrical and Electronics Equipment) directive imposes on all EU member states to implement legislation that enforces companies to collect and recover the products that they introduce on the European markets. Aim is to avoid waste and to promote recycling and reuse through collection and recovery targets. Zoeteman et al. (2010) identify a number of issues that undermine the effectiveness of the WEEE directive:

- It is often administratively challenging to link WEEE to the original manufacturer (OEM). The responsibility that OEMs have for historic waste (that is, prior to the introduction of the directive) is perceived as unfair

- It is often unclear who is responsible for the collection and recovery of WEEE, as it is often unclear when and where the end-of-life stage is reached. This is further complicated when products cross the European border.
- Although OEMs are held responsible for complying with the WEEE directive, the implementation of the directive is left to the individual member states. OEMs thus have to comply with 25 different implementations.
- Much of the efforts are geared towards downcycling, rather than towards high-level product recovery, which significantly lowers the potential for footprint reductions.
- The European ordination of waste product transportation (EVOA) aims to regulate WEEE exports, but cannot currently prevent illegal exports and the unsafe and unhealthy circumstances in which the waste is often processed by developing countries.

According to Zoeteman et al. (2010), the EU25 recycles only 50% of the seven million tons that is generated annually; the rest is incinerated or landfilled (1.6 million tons) or exported (1.9 million tons). China (two million tons) and India (0.9 million tons) are the main importers of WEEE of which most is landfilled. The USA generates about 6.5 million tons annually, of which 80% is landfilled or incinerated domestically. Recycling (0.13 million tons) is minimal. An important threat to social sustainability is the illegal exports of WEEE, which mainly end up in China and India.

The European WEEE and ROHS (Restriction Of Hazardous Substances) directives, although targeted at the European market, have had a major impact on Chinese companies (Wang 2008). Formally, the companies that actually bring the end-products on the market need to comply with the directives, but their manufacturers are often Chinese companies. This means that the compliance ultimately extends to these companies as well.

As Europe is an important importer of Chinese products, the Chinese government has introduced its own version of the ROHS directive, having direct impact on the performance of Chinese manufacturers. A Chinese version of the WEEE directive is also under development, but the main challenge will be the actual enforcement of the compliance. As the first non-compliance scandals have already occurred (for instance, Sony's Playstation in 2001) the pressure from western companies on their Chinese suppliers is considerable. Based on case-study research, it appears that companies apply two strategies to meet legislative requirements: improving internal quality inspection procedures and seeking long-term cooperation with better suppliers.

13.2.3 Case 3: End-of-Life Vehicle Recovery

Driven by environmental concerns about the ever-growing car dump sites, the European End-of-Life Vehicle (ELV) directive was installed in 2000, but prior to that voluntary initiatives had already been developed in several European countries.

Purpose (Gerrard and Kandlikar 2007) is to (1) reduce the use of hazardous substances when designing vehicles, (2) design and produce vehicles that facilitate the dismantling, re-use, recovery and recycling of end-of-life vehicles, (3) increase the use of recycled materials in vehicle manufacture, and (4) ensure that components of vehicles do not contain certain hazardous materials.

The following recovery and recycling targets are enforced at member state level: 85% (including energy recovery) by 2006 and 95% by 2015; 80% (excluding energy recovery) by 2006 and 85% by 2015. Some 7.6 million vehicles are recycled annually in the EU-15 countries of the 11.3 million cars deregistered (ACEA 2007). Auto Recycling Nederland (ARN) coordinates the recycling of decommissioned cars in the Netherlands and given the fact that the EU targets are reached and that the recovery is almost cost efficient, ARN can be seen as a best practice (De Brito et al. 2007). However, as each nation in the EU is free to develop its own implementation of the ELV directive, no standardization of collection and recovery practices exists.

Please note that the recycling targets only apply to those cars that are actually collected for recovery. About 50% of the decommissioned cars are sold to non-EU countries, where no financial structure or recovery capacity is in place to deal with future waste. This makes the effectiveness of the directive half as good as the targets suggest. Actually, the outflow of decommissioned cars has increased during the last couple of years, which threatens the profitability of the recycling effort, as it depends on a large and steady inflow of end-of-life vehicles.

The increasing recycling targets may also threaten profitability as the cost of recovery tends to increase exponentially with the recovery target, while big initial investments in new post shredder technology seem unavoidable in order to be technically able to reach such targets. With respect to the forward chain, most of the efforts are directed towards the production of cars that are safe, comfortable and fuel-efficient; goals that often conflict with possible designs for product recovery at the end of life. As there are hardly any incentives for car manufacturers to adjust the car design for end-of-life recovery, much efforts result in downcycling.

13.3 Framework Validation: Cross Case Comparison

The main barriers for the efficient and effective reuse of materials and products that were identified in Sect. 13.2 are summarized in Table 13.2.

All conjectured barriers where observed in at least two of the three supply chains investigated. Lack of coordination and lack of resources were somehow present in all three. For the waste paper chains most barriers are related to optimizing an already effective recovery chain. More coordination between relevant chain actors may further decrease handling and transportation costs in a business where margins are low.

For the other two chains, it seems that the opportunities for recovery are much higher than the ambition of current legislation. There is no natural culture

Table 13.2 Observed barriers for effective closed loop supply chain management

	Waste paper	WEEE	Automobiles
Culture		– OEMs do not typically design for reuse – Enforcement in China is problematic	OEMs do not typically design for end-of-life recovery
Lack of coordination	– Differences in culture and language challenges opportunities for coordination – No interaction between the forward and reverse chain actors – Mainports are misused as temporary storage space – No coordination between Dutch and Chinese inspection	– No interaction between forward and reverse players (who is responsible for what?) – No coordination of WEEE implementation among member states – EVOA not effective in directing or preventing waste streams	– No coordination of ELV implementation among member states – Lack of standardization of information exchange
Lack of resources	– Lack of capacity of mainports to handle increased waste flows – Small changes in transportation costs or waste paper prices may redirect waste flows	– The collective scheme prohibits the collection of small WEEE and prohibits quality differentiation.	Leakage of decommissioned cars across borders threatens steady volume of resources
Lack of capabilities	– No reliable information systems to handle elaborate paperwork	– The heterogeneity of WEEE makes meaningful recovery challenging from a technical perspective	– No viable technology available to recycle more than 90% of an automobile – Limited or no capabilities in non-EU countries – Limited incentives for high level recovery
Lack of markets	Only suitable for packaging material	Limited markets for high level recovery	Limited markets for recycled material and recovered car parts

of designing for recovery, so legislation seems necessary to provide the right incentives. However, legislation appears to be geared towards waste management instead of value management. As products are not designed for recovery, efficient recovery is challenging and markets for downcycled materials are often lacking. The legislation is not effective in the sense that collection rates are low. Regulations are sometimes unclear and may even conflict.

13.4 Transitions Towards Sustainable Supply Chains

Due to the imbalance in the supply and demand of container loads, a large percentage of containers is shipped empty. This waste of resources can be partly solved through the stimulation of alternative loads that should move in the direction of thc empty container streams. Since in Asia there is typically a large demand for raw materials, and in Europe and (North-) America typically a large availability of end-of-life products and materials, there is a big potential for the bundling of waste streams and successfully integrating these into the forward global supply chain. This integration of forward and reverse flows ('closed loop supply chain') contributes to sustainability in several ways. First of all, separating and bundling waste streams in order to find a useful new purpose for these flows in the forward supply chain reduces the need for virgin materials and energy in the production process and reduces the release of hazardous emissions in the production process. At the same time, making use of the existing empty container capacity does not pose an environmental burden, but instead an economic incentive to reduce empty transport kilometres. Furthermore, the cases presented in this chapter show, that in principle there is ample opportunity for the generation of economic growth through the creation of new markets, products, and services around the practice of product and material recovery, but also that there is a number of barriers (lack of resources, capabilities, markets, coordination) that prohibit these opportunities to fully materialize. Although this is not the focus of the study at hand, we conjecture that most of the barriers are due to the fact that the product recovery phase is not (well) integrated into the product design phase and into the overall business model of the products concerned. For all three cases, the reverse chain is almost completely detached from the forward chain, which provides very few incentives for design for recovery. Furthermore, for all three case regulation and legislation is geared towards *waste* management and not towards *value* management. This again does not provide incentives for design for recovery, but may even lead to lock-in effects, as more investments are directed to 'open loop' waste management and downcycling than 'closed loop' recovery.

Considering the above discussion, for high value recovery networks to succeed, we suggest a transition at three levels:

1. Instead of thinking in terms of waste (a problem), society should start thinking in terms of inputs (a business opportunity).
2. Reuse of products and materials is often organized locally/nationally, where the waste is generated, while cross-border solutions may have much more potential (high volume, low cost). The latter then should be facilitated and stimulated by (inter-) national legislative bodies.

3. Reuse of products and materials often occurs at a very low level of efficiency (downcycling). Higher forms of reuse, such as upcycling and remanufacturing should become the norm. For that, appropriate recovery targets need to be defined.

The case studies conducted in Sect. 13.3 show that there are opportunities to obtain the first level. Unfortunately they also show that the second level of cross-border solutions is currently hindered or even inhibited by (inter-)national legislation. What's more, sometimes there even appear to be conflicts between environmental legislation and import/export legislation. At level 3 it is again legislation that forces businesses to go for downcycling (reuse at the material level, but at a lower quality level than at the original use) rather than higher forms of reuse that maximize ecological and economic value. European legislation on electronic waste (WEEE) and end-of-life vehicles are only successful in the sense that recycling (or rather downcycling) targets are somewhat met, but collection targets are poor.

In line with the barriers of Table 13.2, we propose the following specific actions for a transition towards more efficient and effective recovery supply chains.

Supply of secondary material

- EU Governments need to increase collection rates and global enforcement of regulation.
- Setting up infrastructure for the separate collection of wastes will facilitate high value recovery.

Transport

- For the matching of supply and demand, it is important to achieve transparency of the location of available loads and empty containers, and to distribute the costs and benefits fairly. An independent third party should take the lead in setting up trading sites and portals.
- Logistic service providers should develop new services around reverse logistics.

Recovery

- Quick scans for small- and medium-size enterprises should identify their opportunities for waste reduction (materials, energy and labour) and product reuse.
- Simplified directives would make recovery initiatives more fruitful and economically more viable. Furthermore, they would facilitate enforcement.
- Stimulating investments in processing technology would facilitate recovery initiatives and viability in the long run.

Secondary markets

- We need to create new business models, based on installed base management and long-term customer relations that provide the right incentives for high-quality product returns and the right outlets for those returns.

One could argue that the current path of waste management is not the fastest road to sustainability; there may even be dead-ends due to lock-in effects. Here, instead of the stimulator it should be, legislation may in fact prove to be the biggest obstacle. It seems therefore imperative that legislation is adapted to stimulate and facilitate individual business initiatives for sustainability, rather than investing in collective waste management schemes.

References

ACEA (2007) http://www.acea.be

Bloemhof JM, Van der Laan EA, Beyer C (2011) Sustainable Inland Transportation. Int Jnl Of Business Insights and Transformation 3(3): 121–138

Carter CR, Jennings MM (2002) Logistics social responsibility: an integrative framework. J Bus Logistic 23(1):145–180

Carter CR, Rogers DS (2008) A framework of sustainable supply chain management: moving toward new theory. Int J Phys Distrib Logistics Manage 38(5):360–387

De Brito MP, van der Laan EA (2010) Supply Chain management and sustainability: procrastinating integration in mainstream research. Sustainability 2:859–870

De Brito MP, van der Laan EA, Irion B (2007) Extended producer responsibility in the aviation sector. In: Costa A (ed), Proceedings of the NECTAR conference 2007Faculty of Engineering, University Oporto, Porto Portugal, pp 1–14

Flapper SDP, van Nunen JAEE, Van Wassenhove LN (eds) (2005) Managing closed loop supply chains. Springer, Berlin

Gerrard J, Kandlikar M (2007) Is European end-of-life vehicle legislation living up to expectations? Assessing the impact of the ELV Directive on 'green' innovation and vehicle recovery. J Cleaner Prod 15:17–27

Geyer R, Jackson T (2004) Supply loops and their constraints: the industrial ecology of recycling and reuse. Calif Manage Rev 46(2):55–73

Guide VDR Jr, Jayaraman V, Linton JD (2003) Building contingency planning for closed-loop supply chains with product recovery. J Oper Manage 21:259–279

Hischier R, Wager P, Gauglhofer J (2005) Does WEEE recycling make sense from an environmental perspective? The environmental impacts of the Swiss take-back and recycling systems for waste electrical and electronic equipment (WEEE). Environ Impact Assess Rev 25(5): 525–539

Murphy PR, Poist RF (2002) Socially responsible logistics: an exploratory study. Transp J 41 (4):23–35

Quariguasi Frota Neto J (2008) Eco-efficient supply chains for electrical and electronic products. Dissertation, Rotterdam School of Management, Erasmus University Rotterdam, The Netherlands

Sanders S (2008) Optimalisatie van de oudpapier exportketen in de Rotterdamse haven. Master thesis, Faculty of Technology Management, Technical University Eindhoven, The Netherlands (in Dutch)

Van den Broeke J (2008) Waste paper supply chain between Europe and China: key factors in redesigning business processes of a waste paper trading company. Master thesis, RSM Erasmus University, The Netherlands

Wang W (2008) How do China electronic enterprises receive the impact from EU WEEE legislation? Master thesis, RSM Erasmus University, The Netherlands

Wu HJ, Dunn SC (1995) Environmentally responsible logistics systems. Int J Phys Distrib Logistics Manage 25(2):20–38

Zoeteman BCJ, Venselaar J, Krikke HR (2010) Handling WEEE flows: on the effectiveness of producer responsibility in a globalizing world. Int J Adv Manuf Technol 47(5-8):415–436 (to appear)

Zuidwijk R, Krikke H (2008) Eco-efficiency in WEEE closed-loop supply chains. In: Veenstra A (ed), Proceedings of the international conference on reverse logistics and global closed-loop supply chains, China, pp 95–101

Chapter 14
Transitions Towards Sustainable Dynamic Traffic Management: A Living Systems Approach

Ben Immers and Rien van der Knaap

14.1 Introduction

The Transumo[1] theme 'Transition towards Sustainable Mobility' asks for inspiration and the dare to come with stimulating, new ideas. The sustainability challenge ahead of us will need such input. Our belief is that several paradigm shifts in the field of traffic management are inevitable and necessary. One of them is to recognize that the traffic system needs to be seen and treated as a 'living system'. This has far-reaching implications for our thoughts on how a traffic system should be 'managed and controlled' and might be of fundamental importance in the search for sustainable mobility. In this contribution, we will explore some of these implications, more specifically, those that deal with the relationship between the degree of complexity and the kind of management and control that should apply.

The basic question that is explored in this contribution is, when and how interventions in the traffic system should take place, under what conditions, and in such a way that the quality of the system improves in terms of traffic performance, sustainability, safety, comfort for the end users, etc.

14.1.1 TraDuVem

In the search for sustainable mobility, it is widely recognized that achieving that aim will require major changes and, as a consequence, a transition process is

B. Immers (✉)
Department of Mechanical Engineering, Centre for Industrial Management, University of Leuven, Celestijnenlaan 300A, Heverlee BE-3001, Belgium
e-mail: ben.immers@cib.kuleuven.be; B.Immers@rsTRAIL.nl

R. van der Knaap
OC Mobility Coaching, PO Box 729, Eindhoven 5600 AS, The Netherlands
e-mail: rien.oc@planet.nl

J.A.E.E. van Nunen et al. (eds.), *Transitions Towards Sustainable Mobility*,
DOI 10.1007/978-3-642-21192-8_14,

needed. The transition includes system changes in a variety of fields, including (dynamic) traffic management.

In the project TraDuVem[1] a number of parties[2] joined hands to investigate which paradigm and system changes might be necessary in dynamic traffic management, that would provide a substantial contribution towards the goal of a sustainable mobility system. As a consequence of this ambition, TraDuVem can be seen as a transition arena (Rotmans 2003), in which conceptualizing and networking take place, in order to gain new and groundbreaking insights into an important part of the traffic management society of the Netherlands, like governments, consultants and scientists.

In this chapter much attention will be paid to issues related to transition theory and traffic management. As a consequence, we will highlight one of the more important themes in TraDuVem, i.e. we will investigate how to address the concept of 'living systems' in the framework of traffic management and sustainable mobility. In this investigation, also the relationship between the concept of 'living systems' and the paradigm shifts will be dealt with.

14.1.2 Context

We see that in many countries the application of (sustainable) dynamic traffic management on the road network is not really getting off the ground (van der Knaap and van Wee 2004; Immers and Landman 2009). A stalemate position has been reached at different levels. The introduction of promising new systems has stopped, cooperation between the national government and regional authorities and between the government and the market barely exists, the training of traffic managers shows deficiencies, etc. etc. The situation is even more serious, taking into consideration that the available capacity of the road network is so heavily used, that during long periods of the day one could speak of a 'stress situation'. If we want to break this downward spiral, a fundamental change is necessary in the application and interpretation of dynamic traffic management systems. And this is an international problem, as the next section will make clear.

As said in Staley and Moore (2009), "the major cities of the United States and most of the developed world will die by 2050 from clogged arteries – commercial and private vehicular gridlock – unless we do something now. . ..An inevitable civic fatality is apparent". When impacts on lost productivity, unreliability, cargo delay

[1]TraDuVem: Transition to Sustainable Traffic Management is one of the five cluster projects (Advanced Traffic Management ATMA, Advanced Traffic Monitoring ATMO, intelligent vehicles, IV and Integrated Area Safer Traffic-GIV) under the flag of Transumo be carried out with a new purpose, promoting sustainability developments (innovations – transitions) in the field of traffic management work.

[2]These parties are TNO, Connekt, OC Mobility Coaching, Cap Gemini, Rabobank Netherlands, Siemens Netherlands, Peek Traffic and Safety Traffic Netherlands (VVN).

and safety are considered, the US Department of Transportation's Chief economists think congestion's toll is close to 168 € billion each year (p. 13). The US transportation system and others are in dire need of transformation.

Guiding principles in this fundamentally changed vision on dynamic traffic management are:

- Sustainability asks for an integral and multi-domain and multi-level approach, where several, often conflicting, interests like accessibility, affordability, quality of life, air quality, comfort and safety need to be met all at the same time (Transumo 2004);
- A promising application of sustainable dynamic traffic management has to be cross-border in more than one respect: national and regional, but also public and private;
- The impact of the market (which produces intelligent vehicles) on the traffic-flow will increase in the coming years. The government will face the question what role it should play to ensure proper utilization of road networks;
- The government has the obligation to ensure that the collective interest of the traveller and the public is served at all times;
- Innovations originate in many areas like technology, organization, training, legislation, administration and finance. In traffic management, there is a tendency to focus too much on technology, but technology doesn't solve cross-border issues and is only suitable if it meets traveller demands in a proper way. The Erasmus University Competition and Innovation Monitor, shows, for instance, that success in innovation is determined by technological issues for only 25% (Volberda et al 2005), while new ways of working and organization are responsible for the other 75%! Sustainable traffic management is becoming too complex and it is absolutely inefficient to always circumvent administrative, organizational and legal problems by technological solutions;
- Cooperative systems (technical, organizational, administrative) are capable of reconciling the individual and collective interests, respectively, the public and private interests;
- In addition to improving traffic performance, the proper application of dynamic traffic management can serve other goals, such as improving road safety and improving environmental quality, which are primary conditions for meeting sustainability standards;
- The application of dynamic traffic management calls for a shift in focus from policy formulation to a combination of policy information and implementation. Budgeting of dynamic traffic management activities is often project based, as opposed to structural budgets that are available for the construction and maintenance of infrastructure. A promising application of dynamic traffic management also calls for a structural allocation of budgets. This allocation needs to be based on a long term and shared vision on the application of dynamic traffic management;
- It is important to create and promote an environment in which creative thinking about innovation, change and the implementation of these structural changes is stimulated.

As a precondition for system changes, TraDuVem saw the necessity of addressing and defining different paradigm shifts. Eleven relevant paradigm shifts were indentified (Huisken and van der Knaap 2008; Immers and van der Knaap 2009; Immers et al 2009) as possible contributors to the establishment of a sustainable traffic management regime.

One of the most elementary paradigm shifts is the acknowledgment, that a traffic system needs to be seen as a dynamic 'living system', a system that is changing in time in its character, structure, performance and impacts, and which contains self-organizing properties. The shift consists in abolishing the primacy of hierarchic control in the first place. We need to learn how to give self-organization its proper place, but without leaving the idea of hierarchic control entirely. We need to find out when hierarchic control is necessary and when self-organization can be the dominant force or to find out to which extent the contradictory control situations can be combined in one way or another. In relation to the four other Transumo TM projects, the above analysis applies to all of them, but perhaps most to ATMA (Advanced Traffic Management). The word 'management' is explicitly linked to the control paradigm. This chapter explores and examines the implications of a shift in the control paradigm shift for the future of traffic management. At the end of this contribution, we will discuss the impact of our findings on the four other TM projects.

First, some additional explanation to this paradigm shift. Although the idea of a 'living system' is not beyond discussion (Stacey 2007), the assumption that traffic is a 'living' system, is fundamental in the formulation of the other paradigm shifts. This assumption is directly related to the basic question in this contribution, i.e. when and how, and under what conditions, should we intervene in our traffic system to achieve a higher quality of output and outcome. When we intervene in a system, this will influence its functioning and outcomes, but very often we do not know beforehand in which way. Preferably, we should try to anticipate these effects, resulting in the need for predicting the future or possible futures.

Critics on the concept of living systems (Griffin 2002; Stacey 2007, pp. 228–229) indicate that the suggestion that an organization or system is 'living' is incorrect, especially, if related to innovation, because it suggests a knowable future. The idea of a living system places a greater whole, an entity, "outside the experience of interaction between people, an abstract whole to which they are required to submit if their behaviour is to be judged ethical". It encourages the idea that we are victims of a system, and that we are not responsible for our own actions. Besides, systems never are 'living things' on their own, without human interaction. They are processes of communication and joint actions of people (Stacey 2007), out of which innovation can be explained and stimulated.

In this contribution, we use the idea of 'living systems', however, as a metaphor to describe the fact that the unpredictability of the outcomes of interventions or events leads to problems, when trying to predict the future state of the traffic or mobility system. The unpredictability reveals itself, for instance, in the fact that people very often not behave as policy makers or traffic managers, as we believe they would or should do (Norberg and Cumming 2008, p. 278). The latter too often ignore or misunderstand how people really act and react. A lot of this unpredictability has to do with self- organization, a force that needs to be understood and taken seriously, when policy makers or traffic managers want to intervene in dynamic, self-organizing systems. As a consequence of these conditions, it is important to realise that there should be a match between the characteristics of a system, and the measures taken to influence this system in order to be effective. Doing so means being prepared for unexpected and undesired outcomes by default. We have to make it common practice to 'expect the unexpected' and adjust our measures and interventions to this condition. As will be explained hereafter, this might lead to an alternative paradigm on how to intervene in a complex system in which self-organization of the primary actors plays an important role. This relates primarily to one of the paradigm shifts to be found in Fig. 14.2: the management of unexpected and irregular situations. As a result of this paradigm shift, we will conclude that is it recommendable to change the focus from managing for a desired future to avoid undesired situations, which also relates to pro-activity, societal values, user needs and private responsibility.

14.2 A Systems Approach to Traffic Management

The basic ambition is to create and maintain a well-functioning traffic system. In the case of sustainability that means not an exclusive focus on traffic flow, but attention also for accessibility, affordability, quality of life, air quality, comfort and safety. All these objectives need to be met simultaneously.

When considering road traffic, several parties (actors, stakeholders) with various interests can be identified:

- National traffic centre;
- Regional or local traffic centre;
- Public service (police, fire brigade, ambulance, etc.);
- Private service providers (salvage operator, restaurant, gas station, etc.);
- Road users, travellers;
- Transit operators;
- Freight forwarders, fleet operators, truck drivers;
- Local residents;
- etc.

Which interests should prevail when deciding on the real-time control of traffic? Apart from priorities assigned to each case, three different optimality criterions might be considered:

1. a **systems optimum** where an optimum balance is sought of all collective weighted costs and benefits at the level of society as a whole;
2. a **network optimum** where traffic is to be influenced (by the traffic control centre) in such a way, that a generic target (like the total travel time in the system) is optimized;

3. a **user optimum** in which each user optimizes his own objective function (like his own travel time).

In addition, different priorities can be used, regarding the nature, structure and quality of the traffic flow, where each priority will lead to a different realization of the traffic performance. We might distinguish a focus on:

- Road safety: "double your distance and half your speed";
- Traffic on the highway; access and egress metering of traffic and/or buffers on the underlying network;
- The quality of life: speed reduction on the highway (80 km/h with section control);
- Target groups: construction of target lanes, influencing traffic lights signal settings (e.g. prioritising public or freight transport);
- etc.

It is important to recognize that the interplay between the various actors leads to the observed traffic performance. Road users, service providers, traffic control centres, etc. interact continuously. In the field of Incident Management (IM) for instance, this interplay is summarized by the slogan IM $= (CO)_6$: IM is the result of an intensive interaction between the assisting organizations (the O's), where the C's indicate the type of interaction (Collaboration, Coordination, Communication, Culture, Commitment and Costs).

In an ideal situation, there would be a perfect match between the daily functioning of the system and our ideas about, and models describing, how the system functions. Interventions in a system are meant to lead to a certain response that improves the functioning of this system, but according to complexity theory, this is only likely to happen under certain conditions. It is necessary to understand a system and its responses in order to apply the right interventions. But in practise, the effect of interventions and responses is seldom causal-linear nor predictable, especially when a system has complex properties (a large number of actors, with a large number of interactions, influencing each other continuously in an unpredictable way). To put it briefly, there needs to be a match between the system characteristics and the interventions or (traffic) control system.

In Fig. 14.1, three possible descriptions of the traffic system are shown, all describing practical situations. The difference between the three different regimes can be explained by the nature and extent of the interactions between the components (the users, etc.) belonging to the system, and the level of autonomy that is assigned to the components of the system.

The traffic performance on the road (the traffic process) is considered as the primary **process** of the traffic system. Characteristics of the primary process are the speed of movement, the risk of incidents, the driving comfort, etc. The individual road-users are considered as the primary **components** of the traffic system. In addition, the road authority/traffic regulators and emergency service providers are other key components of the traffic system.

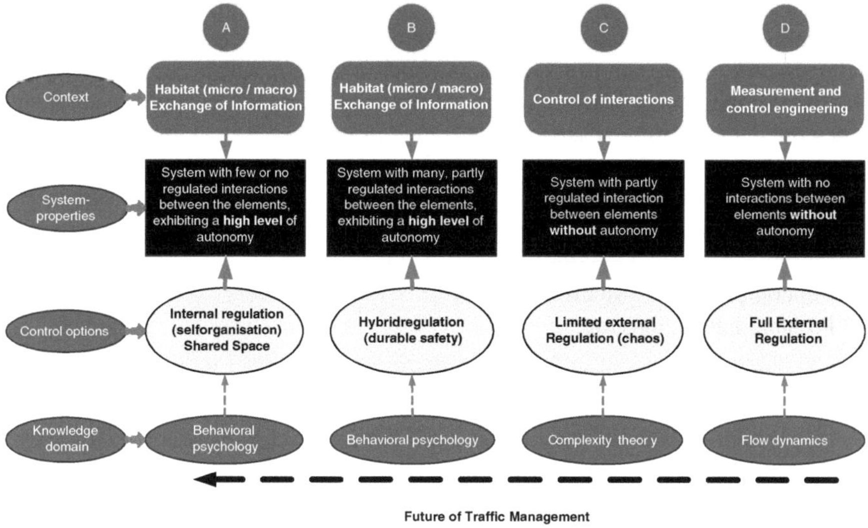

Fig. 14.1 Systematic view of the possibilities and principles for the control of the traffic system in the short term (Immers and Westerman 1995; Immers and Van Koningsbruggen 2001)

The figure shows that the handling of the traffic process is largely determined by the following two characteristics:

1. The degree of interaction between the different system components, and;
2. The autonomy/'intelligence' of the system components.

14.2.1 Interactions Between System Components

The first important characteristic in determining a traffic system is the assessment of its degree of interaction. Interaction means that the state (steady or dynamic) of a system component affects the operation of other system components. A key element is the awareness that this is very often a reciprocal relationship or interdependence (van der Knaap 2006). Interactions and/or interventions can have a different time-frame. An example of a short-term interaction is the driving behaviour of road users, which is influenced by choices of other road-users continuously. These include the choice of travel speed and the decision to overtake. Another example is the traffic jam caused by 'rubbernecking' following an accident. Interactions that occur in the longer term are related to transport mode choice, route choice and departure time choice or even the choice of where to live. When this dimension is of interest, the scope of traffic management needs to be widened to matters such as demand management, the provision of public transport, etc.

If the components of the system to be influenced are 'non-living', that is neither autonomous nor able to choose, it is possible to organize the operation of the system by means of **remote control** (Fig. 14.1, column C). An example is an assembly line with robots in a production plant, or an automated people mover with its own secure infrastructure. Organizing or influencing such a system will be easier the lesser interactions are taking place between the elements/components of the system and when the interactions are easy to describe and/or generate a local impact only. Few or no interactions and no autonomy are characteristic for its well functioning.

When the interactions between the components increase (Fig. 14.1, column B), the traffic process needs to be seen and described as a complex, non-linear process. The myriad of local interactions determines the final overall conduct of the process (the operation of the system).

Possible interactions are:

- Interactions that only occur at short distance (collision);
- Interactions that are 'easy' to describe by laws, applying to all elements;
- 'Neighbour–neighbour' interactions, the elements further away are not involved; there is no 'collective' interaction and no hysteresis;
- Interactions that are independent of the environment or 'habitat'.

In this system there are still non-autonomous components, but their number, and their number of interactions are so large (for example, the interactions occurring in an urban inner city traffic system), that a completely different organization is needed as compared to the remote and hierarchical situation in column C.

An important feature of such complex non-linear processes is that there is little or no relationship between the functioning of the individual subsystems and the functioning of the system as a whole, and this is caused by the lack of autonomy of the individual components. Translated to the traffic process, this means that car drivers on an individual basis optimize their decisions, but the result at a higher level of abstraction is usually a sub-optimal performing transport system. An example of such a system is Delta Container Terminal, Rotterdam Harbour, where automated guided vehicles serve as the transportation link between crane, stack, etc. The operations (transport of containers) on this terminal can be organized in various ways, e.g. based on shortest routes, or via fixed (predetermined) paths, in this way introducing a detour but eliminating interactions/conflicts. Model calculations of the resulting transportation process show, that during busy periods the 'shortest route' approach generates an accumulation of conflicts, resulting in long waiting times. The 'fixed path' approach keeps the number of interactions at a low level thus allowing for smooth operations on the terminal even during busy periods.

Column B represents a completely different situation, despite the fact that these systems also have a high number of (often reciprocal) interactions between the system components. The system in Column B represents our daily, essentially unmanaged and uncontrolled, traffic system. The essential difference between this system and the former system (columns C/D) is that the main components of the system exhibit a high degree of autonomy. This autonomy allows the individual components to formulate objectives, and to set out strategies themselves, thus establishing autonomy on the system component level. Column A represents the most explicit form of complexity, which refers to the Monderman concept

(Monderman 2007) of 'Shared Space' (in which traffic signs, etc.), may be fully absent.

Recognition and acceptance of the characteristics of complex systems may have a significant impact on the future functioning of the system as a whole, and may require completely different or even non-explicit control mechanisms. See, for instance, Vanderbilt (2009), who states that 'dangerous roads may be the safest' (p. 176–210). In the next section, the impact of introducing autonomy on the system component level will be described.

14.2.2 Autonomy of the Components

A second important characteristic is the level of autonomy of the system and the subsequent processes, which could also be described as the extent to which individual components possess intelligence and freedom to choose. At the one extreme (Fig. 14.1, columns B and C) the components are inanimate objects, while in the case of Fig. 14.1, column A, the components represent intelligent creatures.

The current traffic system belongs to the latter category. This characterization of the traffic process as a complex non-linear process, where the components have their own autonomy, will serve as a starting point for the search for suitable instruments.

The behaviour of road users can be characterized as follows:

- It is influenced by information or behaviour of others.
- It is (on the one hand) explorative, because we are taught that active exploration will be rewarded.
- It is (on the other hand) satisfying. Travellers are generally quickly pleased with the choice they have made, they are not constantly optimizing their choices.
- It is retro-rationalizing. With hindsight all actions are rationalized.
- It is supported by experience. There are learning effects (experience, routine behaviour).
- It possesses a certain degree of rationality (with large differences between road users and even per road user, depending on time or mood).
- It is strategy oriented. Travellers often follow a certain strategy (choosing the left lane when there is congestion). Travellers might also change their strategy.
- It is directed at avoiding conflicts. Collisions will be avoided as much as possible.

These characteristics imply that traffic in a network, to a considerable degree, shows the character of a self-regulating system (a 'living system'). Table 14.1 shows the strengths and weaknesses of a self-regulating system.

Essential for the functioning of a 'living system' are the following two aspects:

Table 14.1 Characteristics of self-regulating systems ('Swarm models') ('Out of control – the new biology or machines' [Kelly 1995])

Strong features of self-regulating systems	Weak features of self-regulating systems
Can adapt to the environment	Are not ideal, because of the extensive redundancy and the lack of a control structure
Can evolve over time	Are not controllable because of the lack of authority
Have the ability to recover	Are difficult or not predictable in their behaviour
Can create new structures	Are difficult or not understand, for instance because of their ability to create new structures and new ways to generate solutions
Can generate new solutions for existing or new problems	Show often delayed response to events by the lack of a unified control structure

- The nature, extent and direction of communication between the different system components (the organization of the information exchange between the system components);
- The capability of system components to learn in one way or another, giving the subsystems and, eventually, the whole system the ability to change over time autonomously.

14.2.3 Control Options

The challenge we face with regard to the control (the management) of traffic in a complex and dynamic network, is how to assess, given the self-regulatory nature of traffic – if the traffic system has settled down into a state with a desired quality (steady flow).

Based on the description of the different types of processes (Fig. 14.1) and the characterization of the current traffic process, several options for settlement/ influencing of the traffic process can be distinguished. Essential for the success of the application of control measures is that the people/groups to which control applies, are willing to accept the proposed measures (a possible successful approach could be 'managing on the well-being of people'). The control measures can vary in type and influence the system at various locations.

It is important to avoid treating a complex and highly self-organizing system as if it were a system without any autonomy and with only a few, controllable interactions. This represents a serious challenge, because it is common practise to do so. All too often traffic professionals complain that the road-users did not understand their measures or intentions, while at the same time, they failed to check beforehand if people possibly could or would understand them. Preferably, there is a match between the prevailing autonomy of the system components and the applied control actions; e.g. control actions invite travellers to exhibit specific driving behaviour. It might even be possible (especially in regular situations) that hardly any control actions are required. The travellers are able to deal with such situations without any external intervention; the system organizes itself. Sometimes even (in specific situations) the principle of self-organization is imposed upon a system as the only control mechanism, as is the case in the concept of 'shared space' introduced by Monderman (2007). But even then, the design of the road and its environment needs to be adjusted. It is necessary to influence conditions in and for the traffic system in such a way that it functions according to the desired goals and quality. It is, however, also crucial to take account of the properties of the actors in 'living' self-organizing systems. There are several ways to intervene in these kinds of systems, as we will explain in the sequel.

Many of the paradigm shifts we developed in the TraDuVem project, are related to the insight that a better understanding of human and societal needs in traffic management is essential to create a sustainable traffic system. In Fig. 14.2 the paradigm shifts are visualised.

When we compare this scheme (depicted in Fig. 14.2) to current ITS (Intelligent Transportation Systems) practise, it should be noted that the ITS industry focuses on only a limited number of the issues. Fan et al. (2007) investigated the relation between publications and patents in ITS. They defined nine key fields of interest in ITS (industry clusters): managing transit (1), emergency services (2), archived data (3), maintenance and construction (4), traffic and traffic management (5) and commercial vehicles (6), as well as the provision of driver and traveller services (7), vehicle monitoring and control (8) and electronic payment services (9). In academic research, traffic management (cluster 5) is associated with all eight other ITS clusters (1–4 and 5–9). The analysis of Fan et al. (2007) makes clear that traffic management in the pre-deployment stage of the ITS industry is highly related to only three other clusters: emergency services (cluster 2), driver and traveller

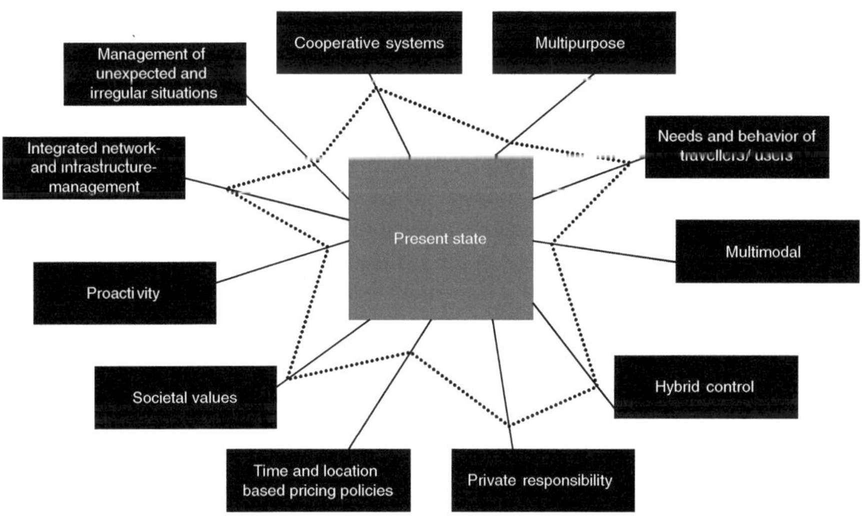

Fig. 14.2 Essential paradigm shifts for realising sustainable traffic management

services (cluster 7) and maintenance and construction management (cluster 4). The authors conclude that there is potential for combining different technologies to develop cohesive and cooperative ITS. This potential needs to be fully developed if we want to bring sustainable traffic management any closer. A closer look at the characteristics of living, self-organizing systems may illustrate this statement.

The ATMA, ATMO, IV and GIV projects (see Note 1 of this chapter) were asked to analyse to which degree they address the various paradigm shifts (see Immers et al. 2009) as developed in the TraDuVem project. When the scores of the four projects are combined, it is easy to see that each issue is addressed in at least one of the projects, except the multimodality concept, which isn't addressed in any of them. Furthermore, they all vary quite significantly in the way they address the ten other issues, although there are similarities as well. One similarity is that they all claim to address at least 5–7 issues of the total of 11, but seldom to its full possible extent. Integrated network and infrastructure management, proactivity and societal values are addressed strongly in three projects, surprisingly the multipurpose issue is only strongly addressed in two projects (ATMA and GIV), and to a certain degree in the two others. This is somewhat surprising, as this issue has the strongest and most clear relationship with the sustainability framework of Transumo.

In a US study of Fan et al. (2007) (mentioned above), the ITS sector is divided into nine clusters. ITS science appears to cover all these fields, while the ITS industry seems to be interested primarily in only three of these clusters (emergency services, driver and traveller services, and maintenance and construction management). If we compare TraDuVeM in the same way with the four other ITS projects in the Transumo programme, it appears that the acknowledged paradigm shifts are even not yet fully covered by ITS science, let alone ITS industry. Although this comparison only refers to four projects (the US study is based on a comprehensive analysis of a large number of projects and sources), this indication seems nevertheless rather valid. Some paradigm shifts like co-operative systems and hybrid control receive a lot of attention in international ITS developments and deployment, but the others rarely get attention, if any.

If 'patents' are taken as a reference, the scientific attention for the various ITS clusters appears to be much broader then the focus of the ITS industry. The analysis of Fan et al. (2007) may suggest that science accepts and adapts new ideas and technologies faster than the industry in the pre-deployment phase. So, if even science hardly picked up attention for sustainable ITS, it seems reasonable to expect that there is still a long way to go in the realisation of sustainable traffic management. For that reason the idea of a transition seems 'fully in place'.

14.2.4 Living, Self-Organizing Systems and Traffic Management

One possibility of control that we wish to discuss implies influencing the behaviour of the components, without changing the characteristics of the process itself.

In Van Koningsbruggen and Immers (2002) three possible forms of self-regulation in traffic are discussed:

- Industrialization: In this coordination principle, a hierarchy applies to the components making up 'traffic'. Components higher in the hierarchy impose objectives on components lower in the hierarchy. As an example, we give a network made up of a ring structure, the ring structure being composed of road sections, and the road sections being composed of intersections and links. Using this coordination principle, the ring imposes an objective through the road sections and then through the links and intersections that will result in a certain division of the capacity among the traffic flows.
- Arbitration: This again involves a hierarchy that applies to the components making up 'traffic'. With arbitration, however, components higher in the hierarchy do not impose objectives on components lower in the hierarchy. Instead, decisions are arrived at by negotiation among the components belonging to the same hierarchical level. In case of conflicts, a decision is forced by means of arbitration by a component from a higher level in the hierarchy.
- Utilitarianism: This coordination principle assumes no hierarchy applying to the components making up 'traffic'. The components negotiate with one another, with the guideline being a single common higher objective (e.g. optimal traffic safety or minimal travelling time), in addition to individual objectives. In case of conflicts, individual objectives yield to the common objective.

The coordination principle to be applied will ultimately form the core of the safe and careful use of the existing road network. For a further elaboration of this approach we refer to van Koningsbruggen and Immers (2002) and Immers and van Koningsbruggen (2001).

14.2.5 Limitation of the Autonomy of the Primary Components

If one does not fully want to hold on to the characteristics of the existing system (self-organizing, living system, column A and B of Fig. 14.1), then other forms of control could be considered. One of the possibilities is the limitation of the autonomy of the primary components (road users). The extent to which autonomy can be taken away can vary (examples are all kinds of 'advanced driver assistance' varying from 'Adaptive cruise control' to 'Autonomous driving'). In the latter case, it is a matter of limited autonomy of the primary component; the system controller has taken over all major driving tasks. Secondary tasks such as monitoring can be held on too.

If, despite of limitation in the autonomy of the components, frequent interactions still do occur between the components themselves, the system still behaves as a complex, non-linear system (Fig. 14.1, column C). However, it will be increasingly possible to control the system by applying global governance and regulatory principles from measurement and control theory. Indeed, by eliminating the autonomy of the components in the system, it might be possible to control the reaction of a component on an event (for example, automatic guided vehicles in the Delta Terminal, Rotterdam Harbour). The end result of the process, however, remains unpredictable, because of the unpredictability of the interactions and their impact on the overall process. In principle, one could say that the laws of complexity apply to these processes.

If the reactions of the components (travellers, vehicles) to events are fully controlled and the process is structured in such a way that activities take place in a fixed sequence, then a system is created that conforms to the principles of measurement and control theory (Fig. 14.1, column D) (for example, fully automated metro systems or assembly lines).

14.2.6 Considering Another Level of Abstraction

In dealing with the traffic system, a level of abstraction is used where each individual component (each with its own autonomy) is treated as a separate entity. If the traffic system is considered from a higher level of abstraction, then all individual components more or less behave in an identical (average) way. In doing so, there is an opportunity to find other, additional guidance and control instruments. At this higher level of abstraction, the traffic system is comparable to standard production and business environments, where other measurement and control principles are applied.

To trace these principles, it is necessary to apply the same level of abstraction. Principles used on a high level of abstraction in manufacturing and business processes are for instance 'Mirroring' or setting up a backup system, the installation of buffers in the process and the use of order acceptance procedures, hierarchic production planning, etc. All of these principles can also be applied to the traffic system (buffers, ramp metering, target line, etc.). The effect of the application of these principles will be greater (or alternatively, we will better be able to assess which of these principles is effective), if the average behaviour of a component shows more resemblance to the individual behaviour.

The above approach not only opens views on new control principles, but also allows us to increase the robustness of the system (the ability of the system to continue operating under adverse circumstances).

14.3 The Urgency of the Traffic Situation

An important aspect of traffic management is that it opens the possibility to resolve emergency situations on the road network (incidents, bad weather conditions, etc.) in a faster or more effective way. However, when dealing with emergency situations, specific conditions may prevail that require strict and rigorous behaviour of both road users and service providers (e.g. traffic managers, police, fire brigade).

Therefore, it may be necessary to change the nature of the regime applicable to the traffic flow conditions and traffic performance in some (critical) situations. At the incident location, a strict form of 'command and control' may apply (everyone should conform exactly to 'Unified Command' rules). This approach may, because of the emergency, be preferred over an approach in which a problem is solved via self-organizing principles.

To guarantee that such required behaviour is well understood by all parties it is important that:

- This behaviour is communicated on a regular basis with the people possibly involved;
- This behaviour is tested and practised by the service providers beforehand.

A possible disadvantage of this rigid approach is that it ignores one of the important features of self-organizing systems; these systems are capable of creating new, innovative solutions for solving critical situations themselves. The difficulty, however, is that there can be no guarantee that a new solution is found quickly. The chaotic approach should preferably be tried out in experiments. Experiments offer the possibility of testing assumptions about the functioning of the system, as well as the opportunity to examine the results in case of extensive self-regulation. The synthesis of these two insights gives a better perspective on effective control of the traffic system (no rules is also a form of control if applied on purpose).

14.4 The Implications of the 'Living System' Paradigm for the Future of Traffic Management

In the past, we assumed that the functionality and operation of systems could be explained on the basis of causal relationships only. Meanwhile, we (at least, some people) now know better. The world is a complex, non-linear system constructed out of subsystems with similar properties. The same applies to the transport system and its subsystems (see Immers and Berghout 2000). We have to deal with living (self-regulatory and learning) systems. Major characteristics of these systems are:

- There is a *reciprocal* relationship between the many elements of the system (Gharajedaghi 1999); and therefore,
- It is difficult to predict how they behave;
- There is a delay in reaction;
- They are difficult to control;
- They do not work optimally;
- The operation of the system is difficult to understand;

Controlling a 'living system', however, is difficult, may not always make sense, and will need different principles than the principles used in the past (causal, command and control), because of a substantial level of self-organization. In this contribution we listed the following principles:

1. Influence the behaviour of actors by highlighting the benefits to them and try to 'steer on well-being' as was done in the project 'Peak Hour Avoidance' (travellers were paid for avoiding the peak period) that was successfully implemented on the A12 between Zoetermeer and the Hague in the Netherlands in 2006 for the first time, and in 'Pay as you Drive' in which insurance costs were linked to driving behaviour of the participants;
2. Change the behaviour of actors by altering the environmental features (change of habitat at different levels, like in the concept of 'Duurzaam Veilig' (sustainable traffic safety; Wegman and Aarts 2006). "In a sustainably safe road traffic system, infrastructure design inherently and drastically reduces crash risk. Should a crash occur, the process that determines crash severity is conditioned in such a way that severe injury is almost excluded". 'Self explaining roads' should make the transport system safer, based on the idea that the lay-out and construction of roads should make clear which behaviour is expected from road-users;
3. Restrict the autonomy of the actors involved (if it works!) by in-car systems (the focus in the TM project Intelligent Vehicles);
4. Restrict the interactions (in nature and number) between the system components (if it works!); and more rigorously;
5. Influence the choices made by actors by introducing new players (e.g. private players introducing smart navigation systems) and/or by changing roles and responsibilities (shift of responsibilities from public to private players);
6. Influence the choices made by actors by changing the structure of the system (e.g. by changing feedback loops or by introducing new feedback loops), which not only applies to road users but also to traffic management centres and their institutional surroundings;
7. In situations where self-organization plays an important role, or is thought to have an important role, the focus should no longer be on providing solutions, but on enabling solutions. This leads to a paradigm shift in the control area, and will force traffic planners to involve road users in the design phase of the planning process, instead of only in the evaluation phase afterwards.

In all cases, traffic management is still a matter of control, but then aimed more at changing or avoiding a situation that we find undesirable, then on the realisation of a situation that we find desirable. Characteristic for change processes in 'living systems' is that it is not yet possible to predict how the system will develop and function in the (further) future. In the past, the (predicted) futures seemed better, but always lead to disappointments. Now we are drowning and defeatism prevails. Soon we will know what we do not want, and life may offer many surprises once again.

This is a very interesting development: a decision-making process in which we do not focus on the desired future but use **the state we want to avoid** as a starting point. Self-organization will do the rest to a high degree.

Within the given restrictions, traffic very often functions properly or properly enough to meet accessibility, reliability or robustness needs. Intervention is primarily needed, when accidents or other unforeseen or foreseen events occur, like big conferences, trade fairs, pop concerts or large numbers of people travelling towards the coast when it is beautiful weather, or just when weather conditions are bad. In general, we want to avoid the consequences of these situations more than striving for an optimal traffic flow or similar conditions.

Of course, the need for being in control is related to certain goals. When, for sustainability reasons, control principles should apply to meet the multipurpose ambition (see Fig. 14.2), a sustainable traffic system should favour the externalities quality of life and air, liveability, accessibility, affordability, safety and comfort, basically, all at the same time. It is presumed that it is not yet possible to meet all these needs at the same time by the present state of technique, knowledge and policy structures. Proof of this 'incompatibility' is to be found in the outcomes of the ATMA analyses. One of the ATMA conclusions is that the optimization efforts (based on modelling) did not lead to a systems optimum for the issues speed, air quality, noise and safety. Speed and air quality had a positive correlation, but a negative correlation showed up when compared to safety and noise.

This analysis is very valuable, as it makes clear the relevance of analyzing the consequences of certain choices on a network level for the various externalities (comparable to the multipurpose issue in Fig. 14.2). Looking at the results from a TraDuVem point of view, however, some important questions remain unanswered. Further research seems therefore a necessity. Drawing further conclusions from this analysis should, therefore, be done carefully.

We believe that future research should also (apart from deciding how to intervene) take into account the characteristic behaviour of a complex system, in which primary actors exhibit quite some autonomy and self-organizing behaviour, and in which learning effects may apply. Perhaps this can be realised in combining the ATMA and ATMO outcomes in further analyses. The ATMO ambition (see Van Lint et al. 2009) is to develop better methods for monitoring traffic and its effects on a real-time basis. Permanent monitoring of traffic management decisions (interventions) and creating feed- forward and feed-back-loops between both disciplines is part of the sustainability challenge. However, it can only be part of the solution. Analysis of complex systems and relevant characteristics teach us that not only the behaviour of travellers is hard to predict, but also that new technologies, other organizational concepts or new services can pop up suddenly and influence the outcomes of the system in an unpredictable way. The ITS development itself is proof for this statement, since hardly anyone could foresee the tremendous impact of in-car systems, GPS and communication technologies on the further evolution of traffic management. Further synthesis and development of the TraDuVem concepts has started in the fields of traffic management, traffic monitoring, intelligent vehicles and sustainable safety, but there is still a long way to go. Taking up this challenge will prove to be inevitable and valuable.

14.5 Conclusions

This contribution had two focal points, viz. discussing the added value of seeing the traffic system as a complex living system with important self-organizing aspects and learning capabilities, and a brief analysis of the way the traffic management projects in TraDuVem dealt with this paradigm.

Concerning the complexity paradigm, the main conclusions are:

- Because of the many interactions between the different system components, the traffic and transport system should be considered as a self-organizing (living) system. The operation of the transport system as a self-regulatory system (and traffic as part of it) may be enhanced by enlarging the learning capacity of the system. Communication between parties plays a crucial role. This communication should not be limited to mutual exchange of information, but should be extended to evaluating situations and giving feedback and feed-forward loops a clear place in the process. The potential for traffic management will have to grow with further developments in the transport system and by developments in society (programme needs, priorities, etc).
- Traffic management and self-organization are sometimes at odds with each other, for example, if a quick solution to a problem must be found. In practice, this means that, depending on the nature of the situation, other traffic management principles may apply. It is proposed that the innovative capacity of a self-organizing system to solve problems in critical situations (e.g. time) is investigated in the form of experiments. In that way, the process of providing solutions can be altered in a process of enabling solutions. This will need an intensive involvement of other disciplines and end-users in the process. The transition literature mentions learning-by-doing and doing via learning. Gained insights and knowledge can play an important role in creating system breakthroughs that may eventually lead to the desired transition towards sustainable mobility.
- Given the characteristics of the system, it is wise to alter the existing paradigm, where we base our actions on a desired future, to a new paradigm. In this new paradigm, we should focus on the features of the current system that we do **not** want and try to start from there, given a global vision on the future and within given constraints. This approach will generate more user-friendly and sustainable solutions, and will lead to a smaller gap between intended and actual outcomes of our interventions in the traffic system.

Concerning the way the traffic management projects in Transumo dealt with the complexity paradigm we conclude that:

- There was a strong focus on technological issues, and there was only limited or no attention for the policy and political environment in which the transition towards sustainable traffic management and mobility should take place.

- Complexity is not yet given enough attention; for this reason mismatches between the traffic system and control efforts may occur that could easily be avoided;
- There is still a long way to go for sustainable traffic management to become reality. Scientific attention seems to be a precondition for the generation of ITS industry patents and for further deployment. When the paradigm shifts of TraDuVem are projected on the other traffic management projects in Transumo (ATMA, ATMO, GIV and IV), it is obvious that the first steps are taken. In the near future, however, a closer co-operation between the themes seems necessary, thus establishing a more systematic approach in making our transport system more sustainable.

References

Fan Y, Khattak AJ, Shay E (2007) Intelligent transportation systems: what do publications and patents tell us? J Intell Transp Syst 11(2):91–103

Gharajedaghi J (1999) Systems thinking, managing chaos and complexity, a platform for designing business architecture. Butterworth-Heinemann, Burlington

Griffin D (2002) The emergence of leadership, linking self-organization and ethics. Routledge, New York

Huisken G, van der Knaap R (2008) A framework for integrated traffic management. In: Proceedings ITS Europe, Geneva

Immers LH, Berghout EA (2000) Autopoiese en beleidsontwikkeling in het verkeers- en vervoersysteem. TNO Inro in opdracht van Ministerie van Verkeer en Waterstaat en Rijkswaterstaat AVV. TNO-rapport Inro-VK/2000-05. Delft, Dutch

Immers LH, Landman R (2009) State of the art TraDuVem. Transumo, Zoetermeer

Immers LH, van der Knaap R (2009) Wanted: new paradigm shifts in dynamic traffic management! In: Proceedings TRB, Washington, DC, January 2010

Immers LH, van Koningsbruggen P (2001) Self-organization in traffic and transport. Paper presented at the first European conference on chaos and complexity in organisations, Lage Vuursche, The Netherlands

Immers LH, Westerman M (1995) Analogieën met verkeer en vervoer met nadruk op dynamisch verkeersmanagement. TNO Inro, december 1996, 95/NV/183, 95/NV/297, 95/NV/311 en 95/NV/310. Dutch

Immers LH, van der Knaap R, Potters P, Kemink M, Muller M, de Vreeze M, Huisken G (2009) Eindrapportage TraDuVem (Final report TraDuVem). Delft en Eindhoven, Dutch

Kelly K (1995) Out of control – the new biology of machines. Addison-Wesley, Reading

Knaap van der R (2006) Simplexiteit als organiserend principe in samenwerking en marketing voor duurzame mobiliteit, balanceren boven chaos in transitienetwerken, Bijdrage aan het Colloquium Vervoersplanologisch Speurwerk 2006, te Amsterdam, Dutch, 23–24 Nov 2006

Knaap van der R, van Wee B (2004) Hoe te komen tot een transitie naar duurzame mobiliteit: een verkenning van theorieën. Paper ten behoeve van het CVS 2004, te Zeist, Dutch, 25–26 Nov 2004

Koningsbruggen van P, Immers LH (2002) Verkeer en Zelforganisatie. In: Verdieping van Chaosdenken: Theorie en Praktijk. Redactie: Frans van Eijnatten, Marian Kuijs & Julien Hafmans. Koninklijke Van Gorcum. Assen, Dutch. ISBN 90 232 3860 5

Monderman H (2007) (mov). Designing shared space. [Video, 57:33]. Urban design London. Masterclass 7. http://www.urbannous.org.uk/udlhm1.htm

Norberg J, Cumming GS (eds) (2008) Complexity theory for a sustainable future. Columbia University Press, New York

Rotmans J (2003) Transitiemanagement, sleutel voor een duurzame samenleving. Koninklijke van Gorcum BV, Assen

Stacey RD (2007) Strategic management and organizational dynamics, the challenge of complexity. Pearson Education, Harlow

Staley S, Moore A (2009) Mobility first, a new vision for transportation in a globally competitive twenty-first century. Rowman & Littlefield, Lanham

Transumo (2004), Projectplan Betere mobiliteit voor morgen en 2010, Transumo, Delft, BSIK voorstel

Lint van JWC, Valkenberg A, van Binsbergen A (2009) Advanced traffic monitoring (atmo) for sustainable traffic management. Experiences and results of 5 years of collaborative research in the Netherlands. In: Proceedings of the 16th ITS world congress, Ertico ITS Europe, Stockholm, pp 1–12

Vanderbilt T (2009) Traffic, why we drive the way we do (and what it says about us). Vintage Books, New York

Volberda HW, van den Bosch FAJ, Jansen J (2005) Slim managen en innovatief organiseren, (results of the Erasmus competition and innovation monitor, Rotterdam, EUR, Dutch. http://www.erasmusinnovatiemonitor.nl/), Jan 2010

Wegman F, Aarts L (2006) Advancing sustainable safety. SWOV, Leidschendam. ISBN ISBN-10: 90-807958-7-9, ISBN-13: 978-90-807958-7-7

Chapter 15
Advanced Traffic Monitoring (ATMO) for Sustainable Traffic Management

Hans van Lint, Albert Valkenberg, and Arjan van Binsbergen

15.1 Overview of the ATMO Project

15.1.1 ATMO Research Scope and Objectives

In the traffic management theme within Transumo, to which the ATMO project belongs, the focus is on *road traffic networks*, which are used for both person and goods movement. Secondly, ATMO focuses on traffic monitoring for (real-time) traffic (and demand) management, resulting in data and information. In turn, these data could also be used for policy evaluation and ex ante research. Figure 15.1 schematically outlines the central role monitoring plays in both demand management (e.g. information provision, pricing) and traffic management (e.g. traffic control). Both must be conceived as dynamic control cycles with a monitoring component, which provides both the input to all sorts of demand and traffic management measures, as well as feedback on the (un)anticipated effects of these measures.

Within ATMO, traffic monitoring systems are defined broadly, and ideally encompass three functional components, these are, (1) measurement of raw data; (2) processing, fusing and interpreting these data; and (3) predicting relevant quantities for sustainable traffic management on the basis of these data. The objective of ATMO lies primarily in the latter two components, that is, to develop accurate and robust methods and models for data processing and traffic state

H. van Lint (✉) • A. Valkenberg
Department of Transport and Planning, Delft University of Technology, Jaffalaan 5, 2628 BX Delft, The Netherlands
e-mail: j.w.c.vanlint@tudelft.nl; a.j.valkenberg@tudelft.nl

A. van Binsbergen
Research School Trail, PO Box 5017, 2600 GA Delft, The Netherlands
e-mail: a.j.vanbinsbergen@rsTRAIL.nl

J.A.E.E. van Nunen et al. (eds.), *Transitions Towards Sustainable Mobility*, DOI 10.1007/978-3-642-21192-8_15,

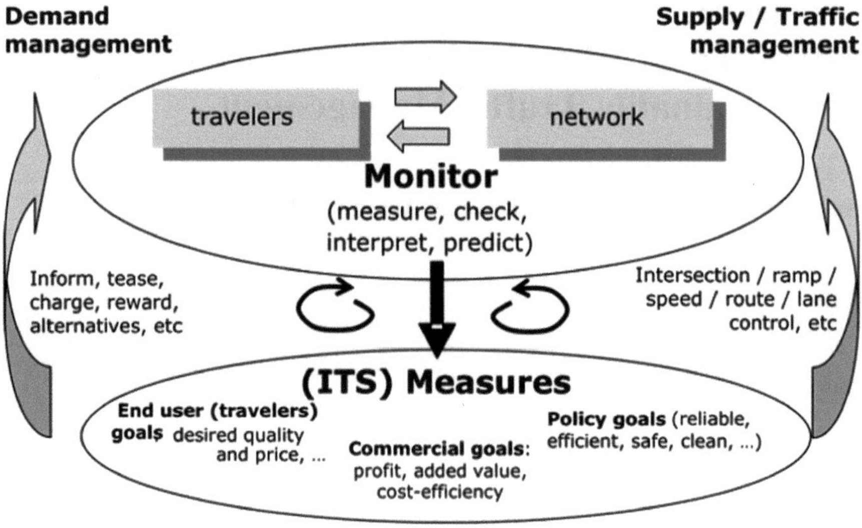

Fig. 15.1 Central place of monitoring in demand and traffic management control cycles

Table 15.1 Classification of raw traffic data with a few examples

	Event-based	Aggregated/averaged
Local data	Vehicle passage, time headway, spot speed	Time mean speed, harmonic mean speed, volume (flow), detector occupancy
Spatial data	Travel time/journey speed, vehicle trajectory	Average travel time/journey speed, space mean speed, speed variance, vehicle fleet composition

estimation and prediction. Below we briefly discuss these three functional components.

1. Measurement and archival of raw data from all sorts of sensors
   Data from traffic sensors come in many forms and qualities, but can essentially be subdivided along two dimensions. The first relates to their spatio-temporal semantics, that is, do the data represent local traffic quantities (flow, time headway(s), etc.) or do the data reflect quantities over space (journey speed, space mean speed, travel time, trajectories). The second dimension relates to the degree of aggregation, where data may represent an aggregate or average over fixed time periods (e.g. 1 min aggregate flows or averaged speeds), or a single event (vehicle passage, travel time, full trajectory). Table 15.1 overviews this classification with a few examples. Note that in the context of sustainability also other (possibly non-traffic related) data are relevant, such as local emissions, weather conditions, etc. Within ATMO, data from all these categories are considered.
2. Data processing (checking, correcting, filtering, fusing) and network-wide state estimation

Data from a multitude of different traffic sensors do not necessarily mount up to consistent, coherent and meaningful information; they are typically characterized by different formats, semantics, temporal and spatial resolution and accuracy, and also differ in availability and reliability both as a function of location, time and circumstances. Both from technical and methodological points of view, the integration of such heterogeneous data into comprehensive and consistent information on the state of traffic in a network (e.g. in terms of speed, flow or density) is a complex and challenging task. Within ATMO, several data fusion and traffic state estimation procedures are developed, on the basis of traffic flow theory and data assimilation techniques (e.g. Kalman filters).

3. Network-wide traffic state prediction and derivation of latent variables. Effective traffic management (and travel information provision) requires *predicting* network-wide traffic conditions. A measure taken at time t on location (or link) A will have effects on time periods $> t$ and on other locations in the network. Within ATMO, combinations of traffic theory based and data driven methods for predicting travel time have been developed. In the context of sustainable traffic management, also variables that cannot be directly measured (e.g. travel time reliability) are required. In ATMO, new methods and models are developed for the derivation of such 'latent' variables.

In sum, the objective of ATMO is the development of methods and models for traffic data processing, state estimation and prediction, and to demonstrate and promote how these intelligent tools can be deployed to achieve more reliable and robust traffic monitoring systems. These advanced monitoring systems, which are both more accurate and broad in their measures, are essential to create a sustainable transport system that meets our access and mobility needs without damaging our environmental, economic, or social well-being.

15.1.2 Structure and Overview of ATMO Research

Broadly speaking, the ATMO project has initiated and sponsored five 4-year PhD projects, several shorter-term R&D projects and pilots, and various educational and knowledge transfer projects. Figure 15.2 schematically shows the timeline from project inception (2004) until project end (fall 2009) and the relationships between the projects. The main rationale of the research structure chosen was to have the short-term projects and pilots follow-up on (spin-off from) the PhD tracks as a means to implement and test the developed ideas, and at the same time, to promote and disseminate the research amongst practitioners (the public and private partners involved in ATMO and Transumo). In the final section of this paper, we will discuss some of the lessons learned during the course of the ATMO project, particularly related to the collaboration and cooperation between academic, public and

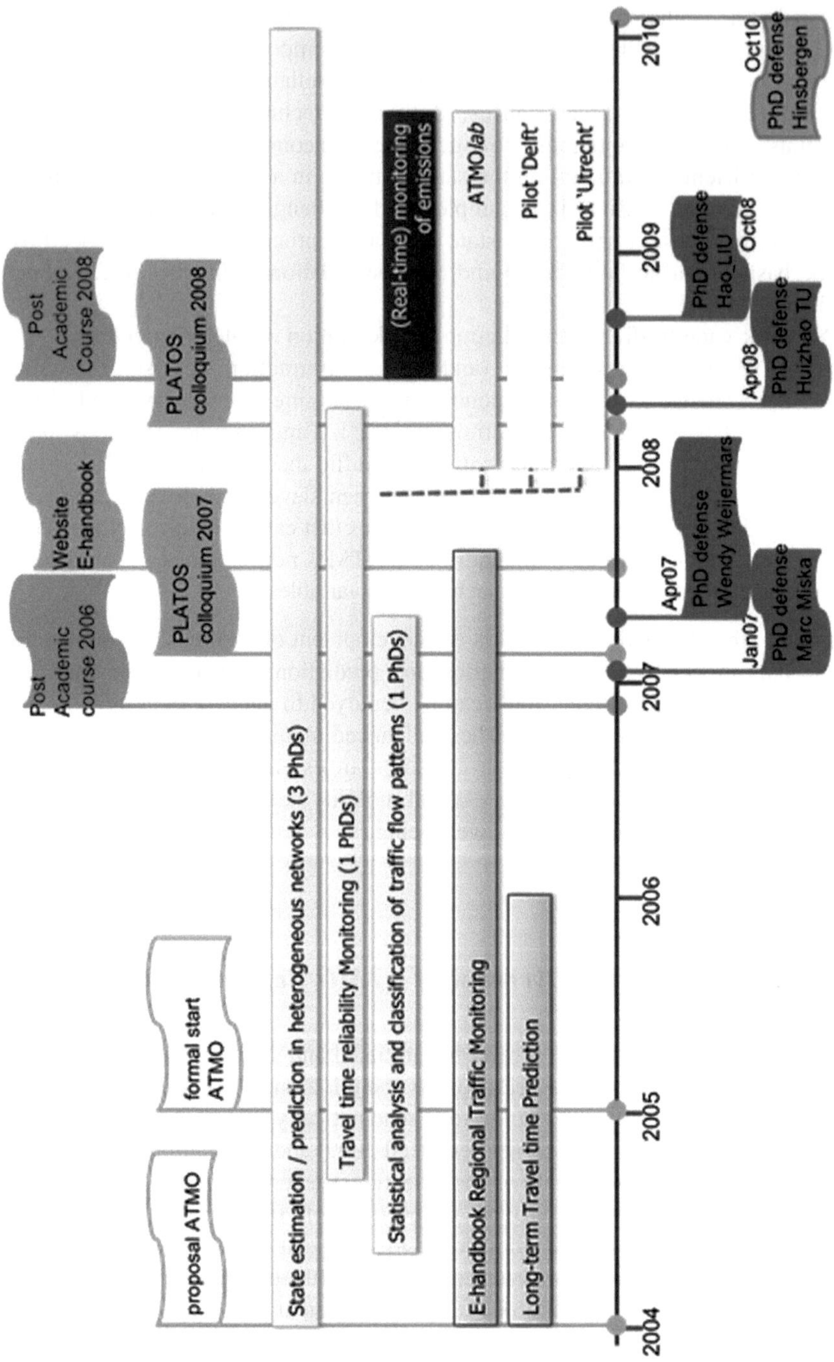

Fig. 15.2 Timeline ATMO project with a selection of subprojects, highlights and results

commercial partners. Below we will first briefly overview the PhD projects and a selection of short-term R&D projects and pilots.

15.1.2.1 Brief Overview of PhD Projects

The five PhD tracks within ATMO all addressed different aspects of the central ATMO theme, that is, translating raw data into usable information for traffic management and traffic information services targeted at sustainable mobility.

In the thesis of Wendy Weijermars (2007), a general cluster method for the determination and analysis of urban traffic patterns is proposed. The research provides insight into within-day and between-day variations in urban traffic flow patterns. The results of this PhD thesis can be used for the determination of typical traffic patterns on the basis of archived flow data, which in turn can be used as a basis for traffic forecasting, traffic management and traffic modelling scenarios. Clearly, in all three cases, a thorough insight into the variability of flows may help to develop new traffic control and management measures targeted, at for example, the improvement of travel time reliability.

Three other PhD projects focused on real-time estimation and prediction of traffic conditions and particularly travel times. In urban networks, both traffic simulation-based (Miska 2006) and data-driven approaches (Liu 2008) were developed. Although promising results were demonstrated on the basis of both synthetic and real data, both projects also emphasized the limits of predictability of urban traffic patterns and travel times. Secondly, these projects also showed that there is no single, most suitable approach to travel time prediction. In a third – and by the time of writing still ongoing – PhD project, a Bayesian ensemble approach is developed which allows the use of an arbitrary number of (data-driven, model-based or any other type) traffic//travel time prediction models. The results obtained so far indicate that this combined model leads to better and more reliable prediction results than those of any of the individual models (Van Hinsbergen and Van Lint 2008).

Whereas (predicted) travel time is a key quantity in real traffic management and information services, travel time reliability has become one of the key performance indicators of transportation networks and corridors. In the fifth PhD project within ATMO a new theoretically and empirically underpinned travel time reliability measure has been developed, which is based on basic concepts of risk analysis (Tu 2008). The key result is that there exists a critical (reliability) flow, which under many different circumstances appears to be much lower (30–40%) than the capacity of any of the road segments constituting a route. This implies that there is a fundamental trade-off between efficiency (maximizing throughput) and travel time reliability. Beyond a 'critical reliability flow' more traffic may be serviced, but at the price of steeply increasing probability of traffic breakdown and a (much) larger uncertainty in the resulting travel times.

15.1.2.2 Overview of Applied Research Projects, Pilots and Knowledge Transfer

To facilitate as well as apply the methods and models developed in the PhD projects a number of shorter-term projects and pilots have been initiated, amongst other things:

- The (Dutch) e-book on Regional Traffic Monitoring (www.verkeersmonitoring.nl). This handbook provides a web-based platform in the Dutch language (in the form of a wiki) to disseminate and share both practical and fundamental knowledge on (regional) traffic monitoring.
- In the city of Utrecht, an urban traffic estimation and travel time prediction pilot (using first order macroscopic traffic flow models and extended Kalman filters) has been set up on the basis of the PhD work of Van Hinsbergen (2010) and Liu (2008).
- In the city of Delft, a pilot was set up in which the original goal was to develop an integrated emissions-based coordinated intersection control algorithm. Although this goal has not yet been achieved the pilot study has revealed a number of important issues related to such a 'sustainable' traffic controller. These will be addressed further below.
- As a final example, the traffic database developed in the Regiolab-Delft project (www.regiolab-delft.nl) has been further extended (in terms of spatial coverage and data heterogeneity) and has been used throughout the ATMO project. Virtually all research in ATMO utilized the Regiolab-Delft data. In the fall of 2009, the front-end web-portal has undergone a major face-lift, thanks to collaboration with the Portland Oregon Regional Transportation Archive Listing (PORTAL) project (portal.its.pdx.edu), initiated by Portland State University, Oregon.

Finally, ATMO has initiated and sponsored several knowledge-transfer projects. We mention here in particular two successful 2-day post-academic courses on regional traffic monitoring in both 2006 and 2008 with over 40 Dutch participants (practitioners, such as regional traffic managers, consultants and public servants), and the 2007 and 2008 editions of the Dutch PLATOS colloquium, a 1-day seminar in which the Dutch 'who's who' in the field of traffic modelling is involved.

15.2 Results of the ATMO Project

In this section we will summarize and discuss three subjects addressed within ATMO. For a detailed treatment we refer to the many publications (reports, journal and conference articles) released in the course of the ATMO project, which are available for download at www.atmo.tudelft.nl.

15.2.1 Travel Time Prediction in Mixed Networks

15.2.1.1 Brief Overview and Taxonomy

There is an increasing need for Advanced Traffic Information Systems (ATIS) that can provide road-users and traffic managers with accurate and reliable real-time traffic information. Whereas many research efforts have been devoted to freeway applications (see e.g. Van Hinsbergen et al. 2007 for an extensive overview), within ATMO the focus was on the prediction of traffic information – and particularly on (departure) travel time – for routes in urban or mixed (freeway/urban) networks. Figure 15.3 provides a taxonomy of travel time prediction models in general (for mixed networks) with a few examples under each category.

Three (overlapping) strands of approaches can be identified:

1. Naïve approaches, where neither model structure nor model parameters are deduced from (real-time) data. The term 'naïve' is rather subjective, but can be interpreted as 'without any model assumption'. Naïve methods are widely applied in practice because of their low computational effort and easy implementation, but the accuracy is usually very low. Examples include instantaneous, measured travel time or a historical average. There are also prediction approaches that combine naïve methods with non-parametric approaches such as regression and/or clustering (Rice and Van Zwet 2004; Nikovski et al. 2005; Huisken and Van Berkum 2003).
2. Parametric (or model-based) approaches employ some fixed mathematical or simulation model (such as microscopic or macroscopic traffic simulation models) with parameters (link-capacities, free speeds or car-following/lane changing parameters) and inputs (inflows, OD flows, turn fractions, etc.) tuned

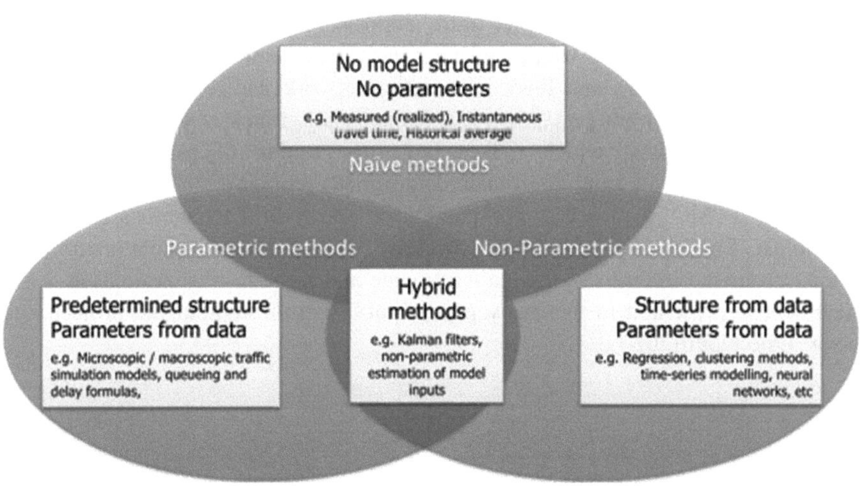

Fig. 15.3 Taxonomy of traffic/travel time prediction models

to real-time data. Also, simpler delay formulas and queuing models fall under this category. Aside from model-parameters and inputs, many parametric approaches have been put forward which 'synchronize' dynamic model variables (densities or other time-varying parameters/inputs) *directly* with data through, for example, Kalman filters (or one of their many variations, see, e.g., Zuurbier and Van Lint 2006; Wang et al. 2006; Van Lint and Hoogendoorn 2007; Antoniou et al. 2005), which can be classified as hybrid approaches that combine both parametric and non-parametric (on-line estimation) techniques.

3. Finally, non-parametric approaches use generic (flexible) mathematical structures with adjustable parameters. Arguably, the largest number of traffic and travel time prediction models fall under this category. Examples include support vector regression approaches (Wu et al. 2003), generalized linear regression (Sun et al. 2003; Zhang and Rice 2003), nonlinear time-series (Al-Deek et al. 1998), state-space models and Kalman filters (Chien and Kuchipudi 2003; Stathopoulos and Karlaftis 2003), feed forward neural networks (Park et al. 1999; Rilett and Park 2001), and recurrent neural networks (Van Lint 2008), to name a few.

Depending on application and design criteria, each of these approaches has advantages and disadvantages. Naïve methods are fast, scalable and easy to implement, but usually lack prediction accuracy (lag behind and exhibit erratic behaviour). Non-parametric methods are in general more accurate and robust (to data failure) and are better suited to learn the non-linear traffic dynamics from data. On the downside, non-parametric models provide essentially location-specific 'black-box' solutions, that is, they are not easily transferred from one application to another. Moreover, non-parametric approaches can only perform well in situations that are 'visible' in the data with which they were trained. Parametric techniques do incorporate underlying traffic dynamics in their equations and structure and hence are better suited to deal with 'unseen' traffic situations, and can be suited to incorporate, for example, traffic control. Furthermore, traffic simulation models offer *network-wide* solutions, that is, they provide one travel time prediction model for many routes and links in a traffic network. However, the number of adjustable inputs, parameters, and variables is usually much larger than the available (real-time) data, which makes real time tuning of such model-based approaches a complex (and often underdetermined) problem.

Within ATMO, parametric, non-parametric and hybrid techniques have been developed. Below, two different approaches (non-parametric vs. parametric) are briefly discussed in terms of the main rationale and some results. A more in-depth treatment is presented in the many papers published throughout the project (see www.atmo.tudelft.nl).

15.2.1.2 State Space Neural Networks for Freeway and Urban Travel Time Prediction

The SSNN Model

The underlying idea in both the work of Van Lint (2006, 2008) and Liu et al. (2006, 2007) is the development of a generic non-parametric model that combines a powerful non-linear and dynamic machine learning technique (a so-called state-space neural network – SSNN) with a mathematical structure that more or less resembles a (physical) traffic network (Fig. 15.4a illustrates and explains this). The SSNN structure consists of three layers with processing units, that is, a hidden layer, a context layer and an output layer. The hidden layer consists of neurons which each represent a road section. Each hidden neuron *j* receives its previous activation x^j_{k-1}, and input u^j_k (detector data) from detectors on this road section only, and calculates a single scalar output x^j_k. In vector notation the hidden layer output reads as follows

$$\mathbf{x}_k = f(\mathbf{w}_0 + \mathbf{w}^x\mathbf{x}_{k-1} + \mathbf{w}^x\mathbf{u}_k) \tag{15.1}$$

In (15.1) the vectors $\mathbf{w}_0$, $\mathbf{w}^x$ and $\mathbf{w}^u$ contain adjustable parameters or weights, and *f* denotes a nonlinear (sigmoid) function, which squashes the hidden neurons outputs between −1 and 1 (or 0 and 1). The context layer does not contain adjustable parameters and operates as a short-term memory (it stores hidden neuron outputs of a previous time step x_{k-1}) and facilitates learning dynamic patterns (e.g. during congestion build-up and dissolution). The output layer consists of just one neuron, which combines hidden and context layer outputs and calculates the SSNN output (expected travel time)

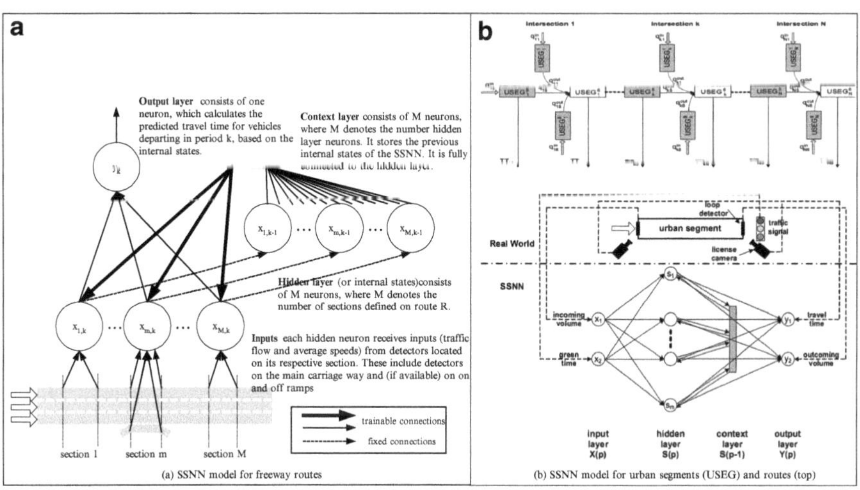

Fig. 15.4 State-space neural network for (**a**) freeway and (**b**) urban travel time prediction (Source: Van Lint 2008 and Liu et al. 2007 [respectively])

$$y_k = h(\mathbf{v}_0 + \mathbf{v}\mathbf{x}_k) \tag{15.2}$$

in which $\mathbf{v}_0$, $\mathbf{v}$ are again adjustable parameters and h represents a nonlinearity (or the identity function). The parameter vectors obviously need to be set such that the SSNN model is able to predict travel time on the basis of new 'unseen' data. This process is called neural network training and is crucial in developing reliable predictors.

Neural Network Training Algorithms Used and Developed Within ATMO

Within ATMO different training methods have been extensively tested, both for urban and freeway applications. In Van Lint (2006) and Van Lint et al. (2005, 2006) the SSNN model is trained with a second order (batch) Bayesian regularized (MacKay 1995) training algorithm. This method aims at minimizing the following cost function:

$$C = \beta \sum_{N_k} (\varepsilon_k)^2 + \alpha \sum_{N_\psi} (\psi_n)^2 \tag{15.3}$$

in which

$$\varepsilon_k = d_k - y_k \tag{15.4}$$

denotes the model error (desired – model prediction), and ψ_n, $n = 1,2,\ldots,N_\psi$ are the elements of weight vector $\boldsymbol{\psi}$ of size N_ψ containing all SSNN weights. In (15.3), β and α are hyper-parameters controlling the contribution of each of the two components in the cost function. This cost function hence balances between minimizing the sum of squared errors (first component) with the sum of squared weights (second component), based on the notion that larger weights make the model more sensitive and increases the risk of over fitting the training data. MacKay (1995) argues that both output errors and weights can be interpreted as Gaussian noise processes with prior variances of $1/\beta$ and $1/\alpha$ respectively, and shows that minimizing cost function (15.3) is equivalent to maximizing the posterior probability density of the weights *given* the training data, hyper parameters and all other assumptions Ω (e.g. model structure), mathematically

$$P(\boldsymbol{\psi}|D, \alpha, \beta, \Omega) = \frac{P(D|\boldsymbol{\psi}, \alpha, \beta, \Omega)P(\boldsymbol{\psi}|\alpha, \beta, \Omega)}{P(D|\alpha, \beta, \Omega)} \tag{15.5}$$

which in turn is equivalent to minimizing the log posterior

$$C^* = -\log(P(\boldsymbol{\psi}|D, \alpha, \beta, \Omega)) \tag{15.6}$$

where D depicts the available training data $\{\mathbf{u}_k, y_k\}$, $k = 1,.., N_k$. The benefit of translating cost function C (15.3) into C* (15.6) is that Bayes rule (used to calculate the posterior) automatically embodies Occam's Razor (MacKay 1995) and that minimizing C^* thus leads to the simplest setting of $\boldsymbol{\psi}$ still warranted by the data D. Within ATMO, various researchers have made extensive use of this important insight. In Van Hinsbergen and Van Lint 2008; and Van Hinsbergen et al. 2009a, b the Bayesian framework for training (and testing) neural networks is further extended such that it allows combining entirely different travel time prediction models, on the basis of the (Bayesian) evidence, which in fact is equal to the denominator in (15.5). This Bayesian framework for model training and comparison enables the analyst to use ensembles of prediction models and provides a principled data driven method of weighting the contribution of each model under different circumstances and with different types of data. For mathematical details on the training algorithms we refer to the articles cited earlier. Another avenue explored within ATMO relates to incremental and online learning algorithms for traffic and travel time prediction models and is treated in detail in Van Lint (2008). Below we will provide the basic rationale.

Alternative Online Learning Algorithms: Online-Delayed and Online-Censored EKF Algorithms

Generally speaking, online learning algorithms are a special class of *incremental* learning algorithms. These incremental learning algorithms adapt the model weights (parameters) $\boldsymbol{\psi}$ after observing a single input, output (target) pattern $\{\mathbf{u}_k, d_k\}$. In contrast, *batch* learning algorithms (which are used to train the SSNN models in Van Lint 2004, 2006; Van Lint et al. 2005) adapt model weights after observing an entire batch of input, output data $\{\mathbf{u}_k, d_k\}$, $k = 1, 2, \ldots$. As a consequence, batch algorithms can only be applied offline. In case at each time instant k both $\mathbf{u}_k$ and d_{k-1} are available, incremental algorithms can be applied online in a so-called one-step-ahead prediction procedure. Roughly, such an online learning algorithm reads as follows, in which $y_k = G(\boldsymbol{\psi}_{k-1}, \mathbf{u}_k)$ depicts an SSNN model with parameters last updated at time k-1:

1. Make a prediction y_k
2. Update model weights $\boldsymbol{\psi}_{k-1}$ with error $\varepsilon_{k-1} = d_{k-1} - y_{k-1}$.
3. Set $k: = k + 1$ and go to step 1

In a travel time prediction context, this one-step ahead procedure is clearly not applicable, since a realized (actually measured) travel time d_{k-1} is not available at time instant $k + 1$ but in fact after $k + d_k$ time periods. The consequence is that no standard online learning procedures (e.g. with 'classic' Box-Jenkins time series models such as AR(I)MA models) can be applied to online travel time prediction. In Van Lint (2008) two alternative incremental training algorithms are proposed.

The rationale behind the online-delayed EKF algorithm is straightforward. A weight update is applied only at time instants k for which realized travel times are available. This inherently delayed learning algorithm reads as follows:

1. At time period p, determine departure time period k = floor(p-d_k) for which the last (arrival) travel time d_k was available.
2. Update weights based on inputs (speeds, flows) and targets (travel time d_k !) available at period k
3. Now predict travel time at time period p with updated weights

Inherently, this delayed learning method will cause the travel time prediction model to lag behind, at least in the early stages of learning. The online-censored algorithm, in contrast, makes use of the fact that in case no travel time measurement is available, one does have a lowerbound estimate of this travel time. Consider that at some time period p the last realized travel time d_m is available from vehicles departing at period m, where $m = p\text{-}d_m$. Although for periods k, $m < k < p$, no realized travel times are available yet, a *censored* observation (in fact a lowerbound value) *is*:

$$d_k > d_k^*(p) = p - k \tag{15.7}$$

Although the true prediction error $\varepsilon_k = d_k - y_k$ (where $y_k = \mathrm{G}(\psi_k, \mathbf{u}_k)$) is not available, again, a *censored* observation of this error *is*, which reads

$$\varepsilon_k^*(p) = d_k^*(p) - y_k \tag{15.8}$$

Due to (15.7), (15.8) represents a monotonically increasing lower bound of the true error ε_k:

$$\varepsilon_k^*(p) < \varepsilon_k,\ m < k < p \tag{15.9}$$

At each time period $p > k$ for which no realized travel time d_k of vehicles departing at k is available, the censored error (15.9) provides an incremental estimate of the model prediction error. Letting

$$\xi_k(p) = \varepsilon_k^*(p) - \varepsilon_k^*(p-1) > 0 \tag{15.10}$$

in which

$$\sum_{p=k+1}^{m+d_m+1} \xi_k(p) = \varepsilon_k$$

implies that for a particular departure time k for which no realized travel time is available, the weights $\boldsymbol{\psi}_k$ can be updated stepwise at each $p > k$. Such an update is retained if this update indeed improves model performance, that is, if

$$d_k^*(p) - G(\mathbf{u}_k, \boldsymbol{\psi}_k) > d_k^*(p) - G(\mathbf{u}_k, \boldsymbol{\psi}_{k+1}) \tag{15.11}$$

which is the case if, and only if

$$G(\mathbf{u}_k, \boldsymbol{\psi}_{k+1}) > G(\mathbf{u}_k, \boldsymbol{\psi}_k) \tag{15.12}$$

In all other cases the update is discarded. The constraint (15.12) implies that if the parameter-update results in a larger predicted travel time than before, it is retained, otherwise it is discarded, in which case $\varepsilon_k^*(p)$ must be reset to zero. Intuitively, this procedure makes sense. For example, in case travel times (of e.g. 10 min) are of an order larger than the unit of discrete time k (of e.g. 1 min), the lower bound of (15.7) will initially (as p is only a few time steps away from k) be much smaller than free-flow travel times. Adapting the weights to these clearly underestimated travel times would not improve learning at all. In situations of congestion build-up, during which travel times tend to increase, it is clear that according to (15.12) updates are retained only if these contribute to the increasing trend. In case of declining congestion, during which travel times tend to decrease, (15.12) has no effect, since in those cases realized travel times will become available increasingly faster.

Finally, note that at any particular time period p, there will be a number of past time periods k for which no realized travel times are available yet. This means that per time period p possibly more than one weight can be applied with censored errors. In this research this is done sequentially, while at each update (15.12) is evaluated with respect to the last weight update, which could also have been applied during p.

Brief Summary of Main Results

Figure 15.5a, b illustrates some prediction results with the SSNN model on the basis of real data on a freeway route (the 10 km 3-lane A13 Motorway between Delft and Rotterdam Airport), and a simulated 4 km urban arterial with three major controlled intersections. In both cases the data for training and testing were obtained from induction loops (Fig. 15.4 schematically outlines how the inputs are connected to the SSNN). From the many results published, a number of main conclusions can be drawn:

- The SSNN models appear to be stable and accurate travel time prediction models with mean average percentage errors between 5% and 10%, depending on application.
- Instrumental in achieving good prediction results is a training procedure which prevents the model from over-fitting the training data. Regularization (as in (15.3)) in combination with the Bayesian framework (Van Hinsbergen and Van Lint 2008; Van Hinsbergen et al. 2009a, b) has throughout the ATMO project consistently led to models which are both accurate and smooth.

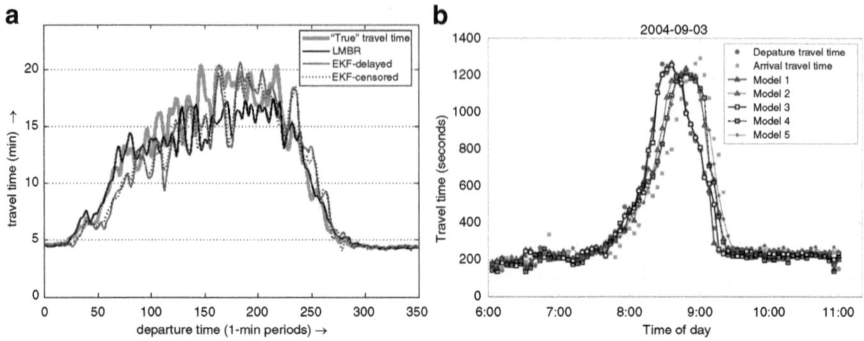

Fig. 15.5 Results of SSNN travel time prediction models on the basis of (**a**) real freeway data and (**b**) simulated urban data (with micro-simulation model VISSIM)

- SSNN (or any non-parametric) travel time prediction models trained off-line (on the basis of a large historical database) outperform models which are trained online (EKF methods in Fig. 15.5a and models 1, 2, 4 and 5 in Fig. 15.5b). Online training takes place each time a new pair of input (flows and speeds) and output data (travel time) becomes available. This is due to the time lag between departure travel time and measured (arrival) travel time, which in fact equals the travel time itself. Although more advanced online learning algorithms have been proposed (see Van Lint 2008), this is a critical drawback of non-parametric travel time prediction models.

15.2.1.3 Travel Time Prediction with Online Macroscopic Simulation

Online traffic simulation models have been the subject of study in recent years (Lebacque 1996; Wang and Papageorgiou 2005; Zuurbier et al. 2006; Van Hinsbergen et al. 2008), for various applications, such as state estimation, state prediction or travel time estimation. However, in order to apply this model on an urban network, extensions are required to the node (intersection) model, since urban intersections are very different from freeway intersections. Within ATMO, three extensions to the node model have been proposed, that is, (15.1) exponentially decreasing turn capacities, (15.2) the separation of low-frequency and high-frequency processes at traffic signals and (15.3) online calibration of turn fractions. Below we will briefly discuss the first two of these.

The number of vehicles that can cross an intersection is reduced by other, conflicting (priority) flows over a node, as illustrated in Fig. 15.6a. As the two flows AC and BC use the same space, for one or both directions the total number of vehicles that can make the move over the node in a certain amount of time, which we label *Turn Capacity* (Γ_r) here, will be reduced. Figure 15.6b illustrates this (exponentially) decreasing turn capacity on the basis of micro simulation data. A simple solution to incorporate this in a macroscopic traffic flow model is to consider

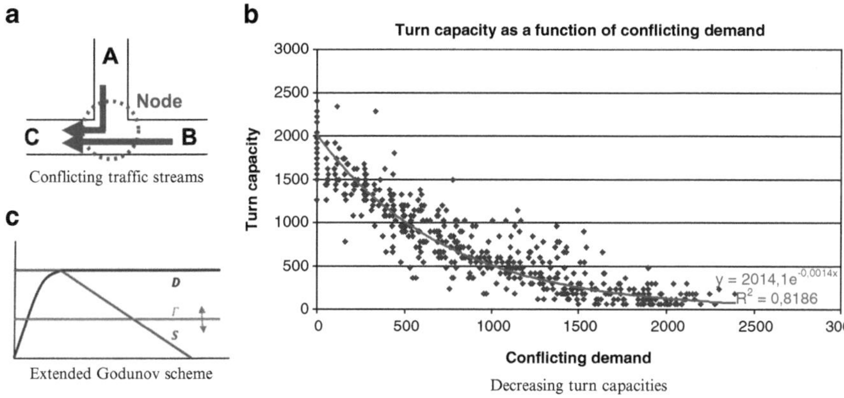

Fig. 15.6 (**a**) Conflicting flows AC and BC cause reduced flow over the node; (**b**) exponentially decreasing turn capacity as function of traffic demand on conflicting (priority) directions (**c**) the Godunov scheme with the turn capacity included. The turn capacity will vary with different intersection layouts and different conflicting demands

the turn capacity as a macroscopic and dynamic variable. The maximum number of vehicles that can make the turn in a given time period Γ_r^{max}, is reduced by conflicting demands D_d as follows

$$\Gamma_r = \Gamma_r^{\max} \cdot f(D_1, \ldots, D_d) \tag{15.13}$$

in which f depicts a parameterized exponential function. The flow over the node is now determined by the minimum of the demand D of the upstream cell, the supply S of the downstream cell and the turn capacity Γ, as schematically outlined in Fig. 15.6c.

In case intersections are controlled by traffic lights, these traffic signals may cause queues upstream of the node, *even in under-saturated conditions*, due to the stochastic arrival of vehicles and possibly time-varying (responsive) traffic control. This phenomenon has a large impact on the resulting travel times (up to 50%). To make macroscopic traffic flow models suitable for travel time prediction, we propose to separate the low frequency flow propagation process (which is adequately modelled by a macroscopic traffic flow model) from the high frequency queuing process under non-saturated conditions (see Fig. 15.7). The Van Zuylen-Viti model (Viti 2006) provides a simple way to predict the length of queues under free-flow conditions, given the current distribution of queue lengths, the average inflow into the queue and the red and green phases. These extensions have been implemented in J-DSMART, a Java implementation of first-order macroscopic (LWR) traffic flow model and tested on the same (simulated) urban arterial as used to obtain the results in Fig. 15.6b. For inputs and parameter calibration, (simulated) loop data at the intersections was used. Figure 15.8 shows the results, and illustrates how the hybrid model performs well in both free flowing and congested conditions.

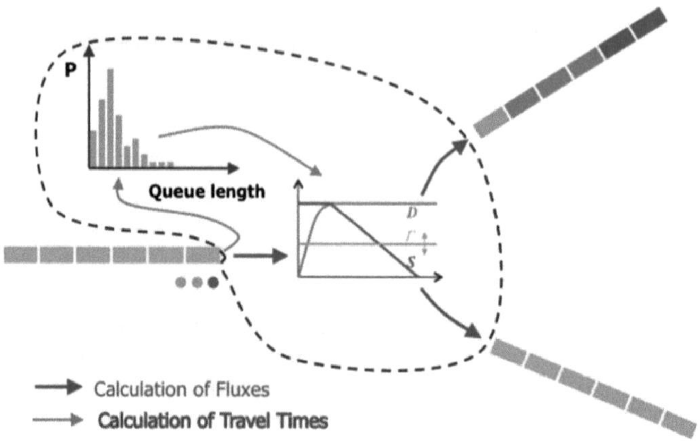

Fig. 15.7 Hybrid first order node model, separating high and low frequency queuing processes

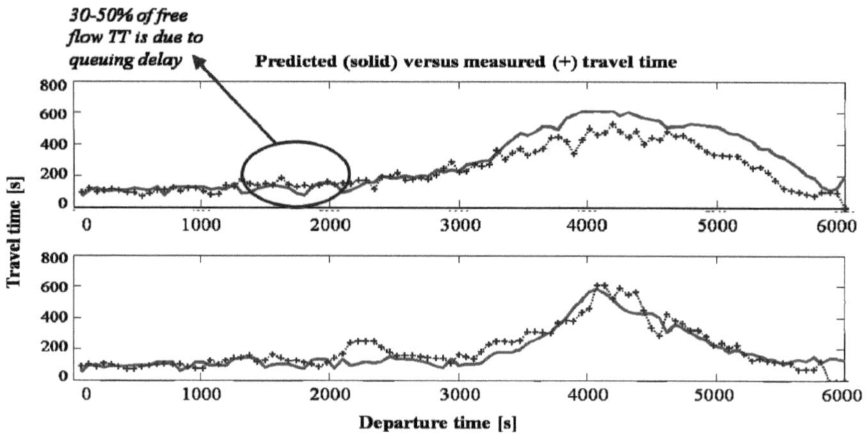

Fig. 15.8 Results urban travel time prediction with the hybrid first order model J-DSMART on a (simulated) 4 km urban arterial with three major intersections

The same model (J-DSMART) is the basic building block of **fileradar.nl**, an initiative by two Transumo researchers (Chris van Hinsbergen (ATMO), Frank Zuurbier (ATMA)) and a direct spin-off of the ATMO project. Fileradar.nl uses J-DSMART in conjunction with advanced data assimilation tools developed in ATMO (and partially in ATMA) to estimate and predict traffic conditions on a network-wide scale. The website www.fileradar.nl and an associated mobile phone application uses this traffic estimation and prediction engine to inform travellers about the past, current and future position of traffic queues on the motorway network. Note that Fileradar.nl was runner up in the 2009 edition of the academic year prize (sponsored by the Dutch national science foundation). Early in 2010, a grant for an extensive feasibility study into the further development of fileradar.nl was awarded by the NSF.

15.2.2 Travel Time Reliability

Whereas (predicted) density, speed and travel time are key quantities in traffic management and information services, travel time reliability has become one of the key policy performance indicators of transportation networks and corridors.

15.2.2.1 Travel Time Reliability a La Carte and the Nota Mobility

Unfortunately, there is no undisputed quantitative measure for travel time (un) reliability which can be deduced from raw data (e.g. travel times, flows). Van Lint et al. (2008) demonstrate that, on a large data set, many of the popular travel time unreliability measures used in practice (e.g. buffer and misery indices and coefficient of variation) are highly inconsistent Fig. 15.9 provides an example scatter plot of the misery index (MI) and the so-called buffer time index (BI), which are commonly defined as follows:

$$\mathrm{BI} = \frac{TT90 - M}{M}; \ \mathrm{MI} = \frac{M|_{TT_i > TT80} - M}{M}$$

in which M denotes the average travel time and $TTXX$ the XXth percentile travel time on a given time-of-day/day-of-the-week period. The buffer time index indicates the percentage extra travel time a traveller should leave earlier than on average, to still arrive on time (in say 90% in the cases) on a given time-of-day/day-of-the-week period. The misery index calculates the relative distance between the mean travel time of the 20% (or 10% or any other percentage) most 'unlucky'

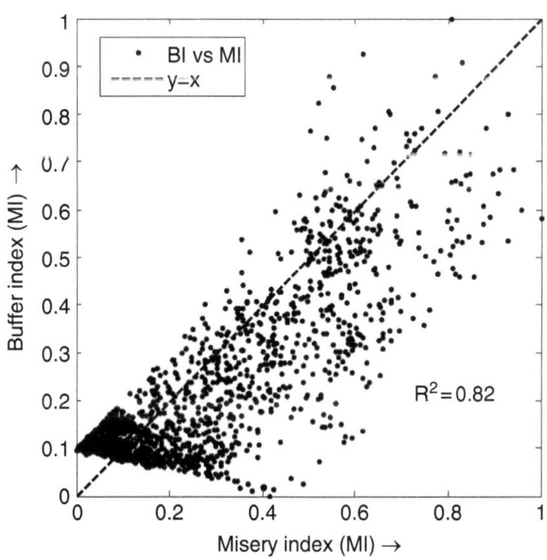

Fig. 15.9 Scatterplot of of two popular measures for travel time unreliability, misery index (*MI*) versus buffer index (*BI*), both normalized to the domain [0.1] (i.e. 0–100% unreliable). Although the R^2 value (*0.82*) suggests a good fit, in reality this only holds for free flowing (reliable) conditions. Under congestion the points are widely scattered and MI and BI provide very different results indeed

travellers and the mean travel time of all travellers on a given time-of-day/day-of-the-week period.

In Van Lint et al. (2008) a more detailed analysis reveals that virtually all used travel time reliability measures are inconsistent, both in terms of numerical value as well as in selectivity. The consequence of the inconsistency between commonly used travel time unreliability measures is that these measures are ambiguous for policy assessment. To put it simply, an analyst could choose the measure which – under the circumstances at hand – provides the most favourable outcome: travel time reliability a la carte.

An example of the arbitrary nature of some of these measures comes from the current Dutch national transport policy document, the 'Nota Mobility' (AVV 2004). In this policy document a number of probabilistic travel time reliability measures is used to express explicit policy goals for the years 2005–2020. For short routes (smaller than 50 km), AVV (2004) states that in at least 95% of all travel times in a certain period should not deviate more than 10 min from the median travel time, while for longer routes 95% of the travel times should stay within a 20% margin around the median. In terms of the probabilistic measures introduced earlier these policy goals can be expressed as

$$\Pr(TT_i \leq 10' + T50|_{TOD,DOW}) > 95\% \text{ for routes} < 50 \text{ km} \tag{15.14}$$

and

$$\Pr(TT \leq 1.2 \cdot T50|_{TOD,DOW}) > 95\% \text{ for routes} > 50 \text{ km} \tag{15.15}$$

In testing these goals against *the current* situation (where we actually used data from the year 2002) on the Dutch highway network, we applied measure (15.14) on a typical short route, the 13 km 3-lane A13 Southbound between The Hague and Rotterdam (The Netherlands) on which the free flow travel time is around 7 min. The second measure (15.15) is applied to a longer stretch of over 40 km. This second route, the A20 from Maassluis to Gouda of more than 40 km contains the one used later on in this article and has a free flow travel time of 22 min.

Figure 15.10 shows the actual (that is, based on data from 2002) and the maximum acceptable travel time reliability according to AVV (2004) on the shorter of the two routes (the A13), that is using (15.14). Clearly, only on Sundays more than 95% of all trips have an acceptable travel time. On weekdays, and particularly on Thursdays, the threshold set by (15.14) is not met during the peak periods, during which less than 90% of all trips are realized within 10 min around median travel time. On Thursdays (Fig. 15.10, bottom) between 16:00 and 18:00 no more than 80% of all trips can be traversed within a 10 min margin around the median. Figure 15.11 shows that on a longer route the situation according to standard (15.15) is even worse. Even on Sundays (Fig. 15.11-top), this criterion is not met during the afternoon peak, while during weekdays (Fig. 15.11-middle and -bottom), in fact travel time reliability drops well below 70% during both morning and afternoon peak hour periods.

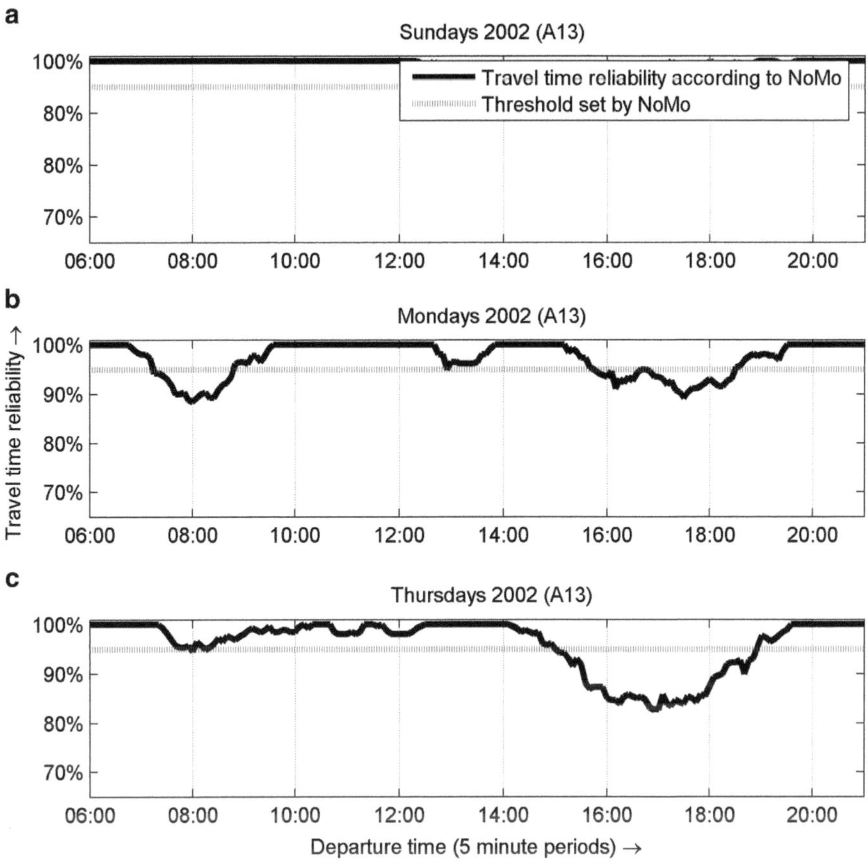

Fig. 15.10 Actual and acceptable travel time reliability on a typical short freeway route (the A13 from the Hague to Rotterdam) according to AVV (2004) for 3 days of the week over 2002

When one considers an expected 20% mobility growth in terms of (person car) kilometres and a 40–80% growth in terms of commercial operations (AVV 2004) and furthermore that

- By increasing motorway capacity in the pace envisaged by (AVV 2004)demand elasticity alone will consume most of this extra capacity, while also a significant amount of induced demand (growth) is to be expected;
- Enabling more travel on motorways also has immediate consequences on travel demand on the connected (non-motorway and urban) networks, for which AVV (2004) does not specifically allocate means nor sets criteria;

It is not very likely that the criteria set in the Nota Mobility (AVV 2004) will be met by 2020. This is further supported by Hilbers et al. (2004) (who, like the Nota Mobility, also use (Schrijver 2004) for their analysis). These authors conclude that travel time reliability – in this case in terms of buffer time indices – "*will most likely*

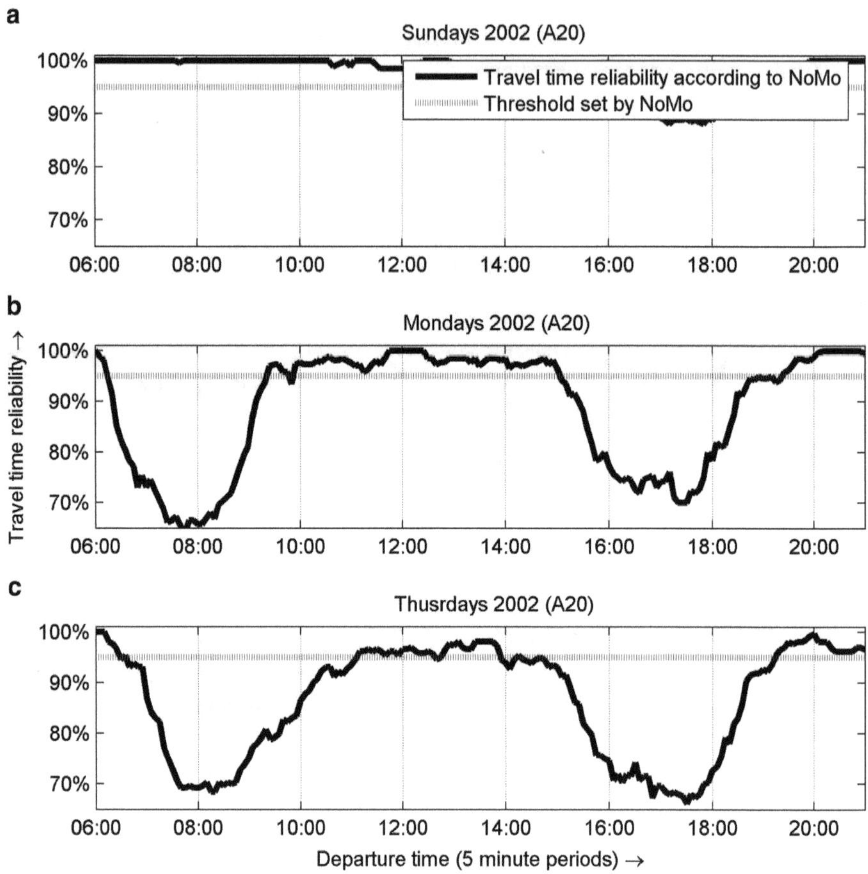

Fig. 15.11 Actual and acceptable travel time reliability on a typical long route (the A20 from Maassluis to Gouda) according to the Nota Mobility [41] for 3 days of the week over 2002

deteriorate in the coming decades and that unreliability will spread both over the day (broader peak periods) as well as over space (increase in the number of unreliable road stretches)". To put it simply, AVV (2004) aims for a quality of travel (expressed in terms of travel time reliability) which is not even met in 2002 on all Sundays, and which – unless miracles (or disasters) occur – is not likely to be met in 20 years from now under the conservative estimate of a 20–40% increase in (total) demand and the expected slowness in upgrading road network capacity.

The underlying point here is to emphasize the arbitrary nature of the measures with which the criteria are quantified and their – in our view – limited value as policy criteria. If, for example, the thresholds (10 min for short routes, 20% for long routes – see (15.14), (15.15)) had been chosen more conservatively, obviously, a very different picture would have emerged. In that case travel time reliability may have looked excellent on most roads during most periods. There is no rationale provided on the basis of which these criteria were set. Secondly, there are some statistical properties of the travel time distribution which are not well represented by current travel time reliability measures such as the ones used in Eqs. 15.14 and 15.15. These properties mainly relate to the skewness of the travel time distribution. Finally and most importantly, none of the travel time unreliability measures proposed in the literature (and/or used in practice) really provides insight into the underlying traffic processes which result in travel time unreliability. As a result, policy analysis on the basis of these measures also does not disclose which policies and measures (e.g. traffic management or road infrastructure design policies) offer the best solutions, i.e. yield to more reliable travel times.

15.2.2.2 A New Theory and a New Measure for Travel Time Unreliability

In the fourth PhD project within ATMO, a new theoretically and empirically underpinned travel time reliability measure has been developed, which is based on notions from risk analysis (Tu 2008). The basic rationale is that travel time reliability on a route r is a function of the probability of traffic breakdown (given a certain demand q_{in}) times the travel time variability (the associated costs) under either free-flowing and/or congested conditions (Tu et al. 2008). Figure 15.12

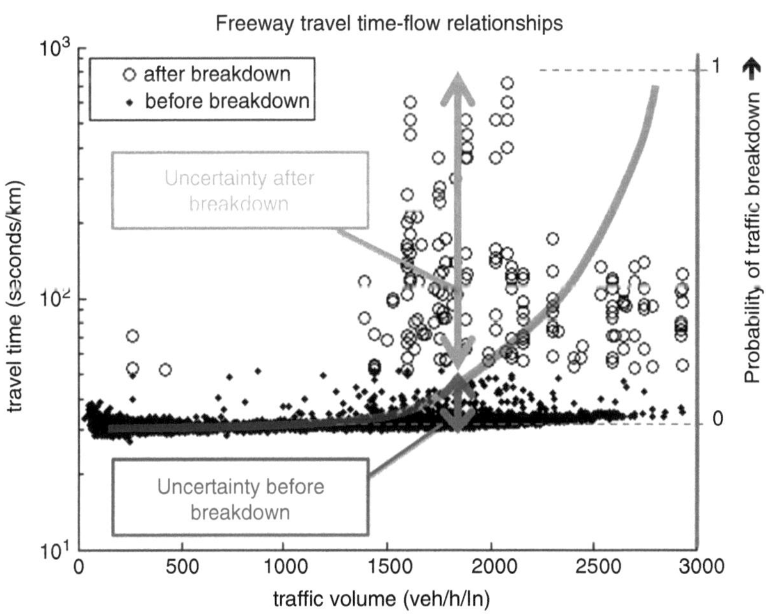

Fig. 15.12 Travel time reliability as a function of travel time uncertainty (variability) and the probability of traffic breakdown

schematically outlines this concept on the basis of a scatter plot of demand versus travel time rate. This concept from risk analysis leads to the following travel time (un)reliability model:

$$TT_{UR}(q_{in}^r) = \left(1 - p_r^{br}(q_{in}^r)\right) \times TT_{VAR}^{free}(q_{in}^r) + p_r^{br}(q_{in}^r) \times TT_{VAR}^{cong}(q_{in}^r) \qquad (15.16)$$

in which:

$TT_{UR}(q_{in}^r)$	Travel Time UnReliability for a given inflow level q_{in} on route r
$TT_{VAR}^{free}(q_{in}^r), TT_{VAR}^{cong}(q_{in}^r)$	Travel Time Variability for a given inflow level q_{in} on route r under respectively free and congested conditions. Within ATMO, TT_{VAR} is defined as the difference between the 90th and 10th percentile travel time (under respectively free flowing and congested conditions).
$p_{br}^r(q_{in}^r)$	Probability of traffic breakdown for a given inflow level q_{in} on route r. Note that this reflects the probability congestion sets in *anywhere* on the route, given that the entire route is still in a free flowing condition.

The travel time reliability measure presented in (15.16) has a straightforward and intuitive interpretation. It equals the expected amount of variation in travel time (distance between the 90th and 10th percentile travel time) as a function of inflow level q_{in}. We assume essentially two contributors to travel time unreliability. The first is the probability of traffic breakdown (which exponentially grows as the flow approaches capacity). The second is the variability in travel time, that is, the spread in delays incurred by drivers under the same circumstances. Since both can be actually measured on the basis of data (or estimated as we will see further below), this travel time reliability performance measure *does* provide insight for actual solutions (policies & measures) which may improve travel time reliability

1. First of all, travel time reliability can be improved by measures which decrease the probabilityof traffic breakdown. These measures may range from simple infrastructure adjustments; speed calming and lane control to advanced vehicle-highway automation.
2. Secondly, measures which aim at reducing the variability of travel time contribute to an increase in reliability, for example travel information services and route guidance. Particularly rerouting (or rescheduling) traffic based on predicted travel time offers opportunities to decrease travel time variability.

Figure 15.13 illustrates that – on the basis of several years of real-data – this new formulation in (15.16) results in a monotonically increasing function for travel time unreliability, which looks very much like the widely used BPR function (Bureau of Public Roads 1964) for *average* travel time.

It is straightforward to fit such a BPR-like cost function on the basis of this empirical relationship between travel time unreliability and inflow (as in Fig. 15.12). This new, so-called TLZ (Tu, van Lint, van Zuylen) function, expresses the travel time unreliability (in units time) on a route of road segments as a function of traffic demand and contains three parameters which can be estimated from data under a variety of circumstances (precipitation, geometry). This TLZ function reads as

$$\widehat{TT}_{UR}(q_{in}) = TT_{UR}^{free}\left(1 + \beta\left(\frac{q_{in}}{\lambda_{ttr}}\right)^{\gamma}\right) \tag{15.17}$$

where:

$\widehat{TT}_{UR}(q_{in})$ = fitted travel time unreliability for a given inflow q_{in}
λ_{ttr} = critical travel time unreliability inflow
TT_{UR}^{free} = free flow travel time unreliability
β, γ = shape parameters

The usefulness of approximating (15.16) with this TLZ function (15.17) is that the TLZ contains – analogously to the widely used BPR function for calculating average travel time from traffic volume – a critical (capacity) flow λ_{ttr}, which in fact is much lower (30–40%) than the capacity (maximum throughput) of any of the road segments constituting the route of interest. This implies that there is a fundamental trade-off between efficiency (maximizing throughput) and travel time reliability. Beyond this 'critical reliability flow' λ_{ttr} more traffic may be serviced, but at the price of a steeply increasing probability of traffic breakdown and a (much) larger uncertainty in the resulting travel times. Figure 15.13 (bottom

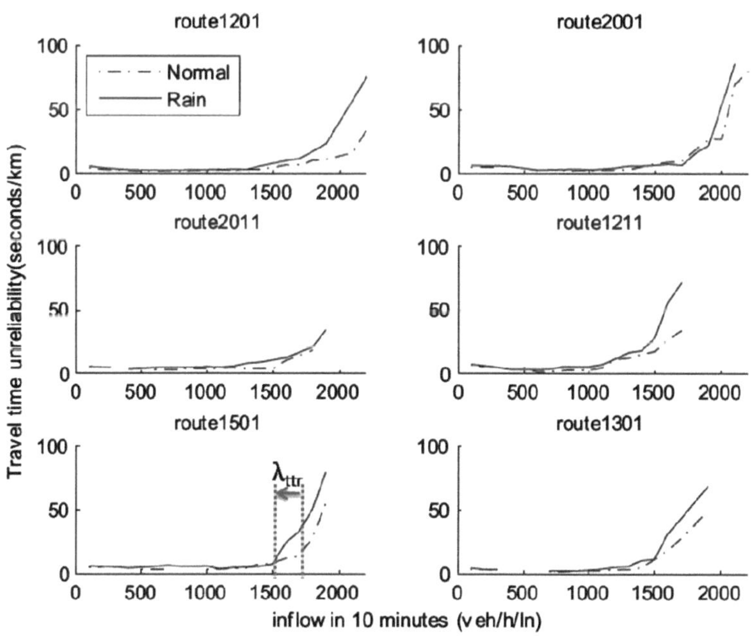

Fig. 15.13 Travel time reliability according to (15.16) on the basis of real data on six freeway routes in the Netherlands under dry (*strip-dotted line*) and rain circumstances (*solid line*)

left) illustrates that λ_{ttr}– like capacity – is a function of amongst other things precipitation (and furthermore of road geometry, traffic control, etc.). The TLZ function in principle could be used for two purposes:

1. The TLZ function can be used as a performance measure in *ex post* evaluation studies on the basis of real data (one needs flows and travel times). In that case, the analysis consists of estimating its parameters, and compare λ_{ttr} between different situations/policies. In much the same way also the original formulation in (15.16) could be used, in which case the probability of traffic breakdown needs to be estimated for different situations/policies – a process which is probably more involved than estimating the 'critical reliability flow' λ_{ttr}. Either way, the resulting travel time unreliability is – just like the standard deviation of travel time for example – expressed in units time and could hence also be coupled to a monetary value.
2. The TLZ function could also be used as a *route* cost function in *ex ante* evaluation studies (dynamic traffic assignment) in much the same way as the BPR function is used as a (link or route) cost function. The main difficulty is that – unlike average travel time – travel time unreliability is not additive over different links which constitute a route. As a result, the TLZ function cannot be used as a link cost function, that is, one cannot simply add link unreliability to calculate the total unreliability over a route. Instead, travel time unreliability can only be calculated for an entire route.

15.2.3 Real-Time Monitoring of Emissions

As a final example of the ATMO research effort, we will briefly discuss a pilot study set up in the city of Delft with the objective to investigate whether it is possible to monitor vehicle emissions in real time. Full detail on this ATMO pilot can be found in Klunder and Wilmink (2009). Real-time monitoring of emissions would enable intersection control targeted at minimizing emissions rather than (or combined with) minimizing vehicle lost time. The key research goal in this pilot study was to assess the possibilities to estimate critical air quality indicators with sufficient accuracy, based on limited sets of traffic data and possibly local air quality measurements, in order to (preferably automatically) activate appropriate control strategies.

In order to study this question, detailed traffic and air quality measurements were carried out on an urban arterial using video-based monitoring, inductive loop detection, and high-resolution air quality and meteorological measurement equipment. Additionally, full-day traffic activity was simulated with the VISSIM microscopic traffic model and input to the VERSIT + microscopic emissions model. The emissions estimates and meteorological data were also input to the HEAVEN Gaussian dispersion model to estimate gaseous concentrations around the intersection. The combined measured and modelled data were used to explore the contribution of

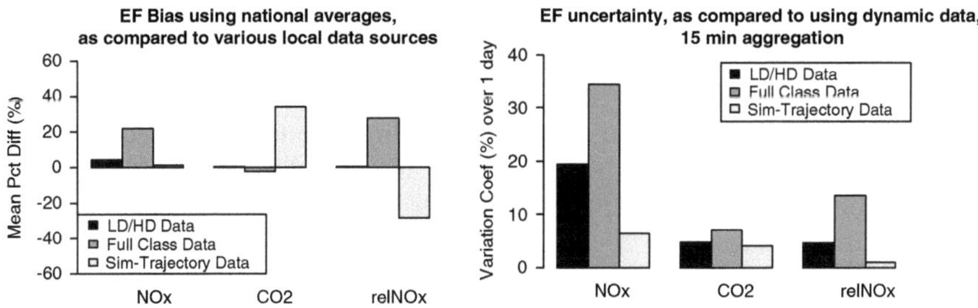

Fig. 15.14 Comparative bias (*left*) and uncertainty (*right*) in emissions factors (*EF*) based on national average traffic data, as opposed to local data, for vehicle class and driving dynamics

various traffic data sources to the accuracy and precision of local emissions and air quality estimates for nitrogen oxides (NO_x) and carbon dioxide (CO_2).

By comparing emissions estimates with measured air quality, this research showed that localized emissions can be estimated on a coarse time scale with sufficient local data. At the location of measurement, relative NO_x emissions (in g NO_x/kg CO_2) were estimated at the hourly level with a mean absolute percent error (MAPE) of 7% over two days. At 15 min aggregation the MAPE rose to 14%, and continued to rise at shorter aggregations, illustrating the challenges of short-term emissions estimates, even with thorough traffic data. For short time periods with fewer passing vehicles, the high uncertainty (un-modelled variance) of on-road emissions from individual vehicles is more apparent, while long aggregations with more vehicles are more easily predicted with mean values.

Figure 15.14 presents in more detail the importance of dynamic local data for emissions factor estimation (in g/km). The left panel shows the bias of using national average emission factors instead of local data at this location for NO_x, CO_2, and relNO_x (relative NO_x: g NO_x/kg CO_2). These are compared for simple light duty/heavy duty (LD/HD) classifications, full vehicle class information from license plate recognition, and speed profiles from simulated trajectories. Full class data provides important local information beyond LD/HD splits (especially for NO_x) due to the addition of fuel and emissions standard data. Local driving dynamics in the form of simulated speed profiles revealed much lower local CO_2 emissions than predicted by national average 'urban' driving.

The right panel in Fig. 15.14 shows the uncertainty of estimated emissions factors due to neglecting dynamic local vehicle fleet and activity data. Again, detailed class information captured much more variance in emissions than simple LD/HD splits. Without heavy congestion at this location, the 15 min activity data was less dynamic over the two days than was the vehicle class data.

In conclusion, dynamic local traffic data provides important information for the accurate estimation of local emissions. The importance of local (and real-time) measurement depends on the uniqueness and variability of the local fleet and local activity. For the purposes of dynamic traffic management (DTM) strategies aimed at reducing local air pollution, real-time local data on the vehicle fleet and driving dynamics (measured or modelled) are needed, as traffic flows alone are not sufficient to make reliable emissions estimates. Still, with the tools currently available, real-time emissions monitoring can only be done on coarse time scales (15 min or more, depending on the required accuracy). This limits emissions-controlled DTM systems to strategies (such as reduced speed limits and class-based routing or prioritization) that are implemented over longer time scales – as opposed to short cycle adaptive management.

As another option, direct measurement of air quality concentrations can be used as a simple trigger for emissions-reducing traffic management, but these measurements alone cannot be used as an adaptive system control because of large disturbances from background concentrations and passing plumes external to the traffic stream. Analyzing roadside air quality measurements did allow estimation of relative emissions factors (with respect to CO_2) for some individual vehicles. While this can be used for direct identification of high-emitting vehicles, the highly turbulent near-field environment prevents sufficient measurements to be used for DTM control.

15.3 Lessons Learned and Further Research

In retrospect, ATMO has succeeded in achieving its main objectives, that is, to link fundamental (PhD) research to practical and applied pilot studies and as such disseminate and popularize research amongst public and private partners. During the course of the ATMO project, however, it became increasingly clear that the jump from PhD research to practical implementation was often too large. Much ‘textbook’ material in the scientific community (e.g. shockwave theory, the difference between instantaneous and departure travel time) was largely unknown or at least not used in practice. Vice versa, many practical issues (e.g. hardware or software limitations) were largely unknown to the researchers. The discrepancy between what is scientifically ‘known’, and what is actually used and incorporated in traffic management (or ITS) practice, has surfaced many times throughout the course of the ATMO project and has been the incentive for, amongst other things, a 2-day post-academic course on traffic monitoring (addressing traffic flow theoretical, methodological and technical aspects), and an e-handbook (in Dutch) on this subject.

The key insight for us (the ATMO project management) was that it is the scientific community who must take (co-) responsibility for, and most importantly, *initiative* in making knowledge accessible and comprehensible for practice, for example in terms of pro-actively explaining or ex post showing why certain measures yield certain effects on traffic processes. The most effective way of doing so is by simply *illustrating* the underlying concepts (e.g. shockwaves, spillback, the capacity drop, variability in flows/travel times, reliability, etc.) on the basis of (large amounts of) archived data.

This implies that, besides the direct and obvious importance of traffic monitoring for traffic management and ITS in both planning and operation, traffic monitoring in the broadest sense (i.e. translating raw data into usable information) also provides the *justification* and the incentive for collaborative research in both traffic management and monitoring. Solving this 'chicken-and-egg' problem (justifying research requires research results) requires entrepreneurial scientists and – inherently – the willingness of public and private partners to invest in public data archiving and mining facilities, tools and methods. The Regiolab-Delft data server and the pilots in Delft and the City of Utrecht are two examples of projects which illustrate that this leads to a win-win situation for both science and practice. Other university-driven data initiatives, such as the Portland Oregon Regional Transportation Archive Listing (PORTAL) initiated by the University of Portland, Oregon (portal.its.pdx.edu), and the international traffic database (ITDb), initiated by Tokyo University (www.trafficdata.info), illustrate that traffic scientists around the globe are successfully taking up this challenge.

There is a broad range of directions for further research into traffic monitoring, many of which are already endeavoured in the Netherlands and world-wide. Let us list a few, which we believe are particularly relevant in the context of sustainability:

- Traffic state estimation (data fusion) and prediction in mixed traffic networks on the basis of heterogeneous traffic data from a combination of different sensors (infrastructure bound and probe vehicle based).
- Real-time estimation and prediction of other quantities relevant for sustainable traffic and travel management such as emission levels and (travel time) reliability.
- Integrated *multi-modal* traffic monitoring, state estimation and prediction (i.e. including bus, rail and slow traffic modes).
- Integrated decision support tools which incorporate the techniques and models developed within ATMO and which enable both ex post and ex ante evaluation and simulation of next generation sustainable traffic management and information services.

References

Al-Deek HM, D'Angelo MP, Wang MC (1998) Travel time prediction with non-linear time series. In: Proceedings of the fifth international conference on applications of advanced technologies in transportation, ASCE, Reston

Antoniou C, Ben-Akiva M, Koutsopoulos HN (2005) On-line calibration of traffic prediction models. In: Transportation research board annual meeting, CD-ROM, National Academies Press, Washington, DC

AVV, Nota Mobility (Dutch: Nota Mobiliteit) (2004) AVV Transport Research Centre, Dutch Ministry of Transport, Public Works and Water Management, The Hague

Bureau of Public Roads, Traffic Assignment Manual (1964) U.S. Dept. of Commerce, Urban Planning Division, Washington, DC

Chien SIJ, Kuchipudi CM (2003) Dynamic travel time prediction with real-time and historic data. J Transp Eng Asce 129(6):608–616

Hilbers H, Eck JRv, Snellen D (2004) Behalve de dagelijkse files. Over betrouwbaarheid van reistijd (Except for recurrent congestion, on travel time reliability – in Dutch). Rotterdam, Ruimtelijk Planbureau, NAi Uitgevers

Huisken G, Berkum ECv (2003) A comparative analysis of short-range travel time prediction methods. In: Transportation research board 82nd annual meeting, CD-ROM, Washington, DC

Klunder GA, Wilmink IR (2009) Real-time monitoring of emissions with traffic data, simulation and air quality measurements. Submitted to the 16th world congress on intelligent transport systems and services, Stockholm

Lebacque JP (1996) The Godunov scheme and what it means for first order traffic flow models. In: Lesort JB (ed), Proceedings of the 13th international symposium of transportation and traffic theory, Lyon, pp 647–677

Liu H (2008) Travel time prediction for urban networks. Trail Dissertation Series T2008/12. Trail Research School, Delft

Liu H, Van Zuylen HJ, Van Lint JWC, Salomons M (2006) Predicting urban arterial travel time with state-space neural networks and Kalman filters. Transp Res Rec J Transp Res Board 1968 (1):99–108

Liu H, van Zuylen HJ, Van Lint JWC (2007) Neural network based traffic flow model for urban arterial travel time prediction. In: Transportation research board annual meeting, CD Rom, National Academies Press, Washington, DC

MacKay DJC (1995) Probable networks and plausible predictions: a review of practical Bayesian methods for supervised neural networks. Netw Comp Neural 6(3):469–505

Miska MP (2006) Microscopic online simulation for real-time traffic management. Trail Thesis Series T2007/1. Trail Research School, Delft

Nikovski D, Nishiuma N, Goto Y, Kumazawa H (2005) Univariate short-term prediction of road travel times. In: Proceedings of the 8th international IEEE conference on intelligent transportation systems, Vienna

Park D, Rilett L, Han G (1999) Spectral basis neural networks for real-time travel time forecasting. J Transp Eng 125(6):515–523

Rice J, van Zwet E (2004) A simple and effective method for predicting travel times on freeways. IEEE Trans Intell Transp Syst 5(3):200–207

Rilett LR, Park D (2001) Direct forecasting of freeway corridor travel times using spectral basis eural networks. Transp Res Rec 1752:140–147

Schrijver JMJ (2004) SMARA calculates travel time reliability (SMARA berekent betrouwbaarheid reistijden). http://www.inro.tno.nl/doc.php?nr=2210. Accessed on October 2005

Stathopoulos A, Karlaftis MG (2003) A multivariate state space approach for urban traffic flow modeling and prediction. Transp Res C Emer 11(2):121–135

Sun H, Liu HX, Xiao H, Ran B (2003) Short-term traffic forecasting using the local linear regression model. In: Transportation research board annual meeting, CD-ROM. National Academies Press, Washington, DC

Tu H (2008) Monitoring travel time reliability on freeways. Trail Thesis Series 2008/7. Trail Research School, Delft

Tu H, van Lint JWC, van Zuylen HJ (2008) Travel time reliability model on freeways. In: Transportation research board 87th annual meeting, Transportation Research Board

Van Hinsbergen CPIJ (2010) Bayesian data assimilation for improved modeling of road traffic. Trail Thesis Series T2010/9. Trail Research School, Delft

Van Hinsbergen CPI, Van Lint JWC (2008) Bayesian combination of travel time prediction models. Transp Res Rec 2064:73–80

Van Hinsbergen CPI, Van Lint JWC, Sanders FM (2007) Short term traffic prediction models. In: ITS world congress, Beijing

Van Hinsbergen CPI, Zuurbier FS, Van Lint JWC, Van Zuylen HJ (2008) Using an LWR model with a cell based extended Kalman filter to estimate travel times. In: third international symposium of transport simulation, Surfers Paradise

Van Hinsbergen CPI, Van Lint JWC, Van Zuylen HJ (2009a) Bayesian committee of neural networks to predict travel times with confidence intervals. Transp res C emer 17(5):498–509

Van Hinsbergen CPI, Van Lint JWC, Van Zuylen HJ (2009b) Bayesian training and committees of state-space neural networks for online travel time prediction. Transp Res Rec 2105:118–126

Van Lint JWC (2004) Reliable travel time prediction for freeways, PhD Thesis. In: Trail Research School, Delft University of Technology, Delft

Van Lint JC (2006) A reliable real-time framework for short-term freeway travel time prediction. J Transp Eng 132(12):921–932

Van Lint JWC (2008) Online learning solutions for freeway travel time predictions. IEEE Trans Intell Transp Syst 9:38–47

Van Lint JWC, Hoogendoorn SP (2007) The technical and economic benefits of data fusion for real-time monitoring of freeway traffic. In: World Congress of Transportation Research, WCTRS, Berkeley

Van Lint JWC, Hoogendoorn SP, Van Zuylen HJ (2005) Accurate travel time prediction with state-space neural networks under missing data. Transp Res C Emer 13(5–6):347–369

Van Lint JWC, Van Zuylen HJ, Tu H (2008) Travel time unreliability on freeways: why measures based on variance tell only half the story. Transp Res A Pol 42(1):258–277

Viti F (2006) The dynamics and the uncertainy of delays at signals. Delft University of Technology, Delft

Wang Y, Papageorgiou M (2005) Real-time freeway state estimation based on extended Kalman filter: a general approach. Transp Res B 39:141–167

Wang Y, Papageorgiou M, Messmer A (2006) A real time freeway network traffic surveillance tool. IEEE Trans Control Syst Technol 14(1):18

Weijermars W (2007) Analysis of urban traffic patterns using clustering. PhD thesis. Faculty of Engineering Technology, department of Civil Engineering, Centre for Transport Studies, Working Paper no. 213. University of Twente, Enschede

Wu CH, Wei CC, Su DC, Chang MH, Ho JM (2003) Travel time prediction with support vector regression. IEEE, Shanghai

Zhang X, Rice JA (2003) Short-term travel time prediction. Transp Res C Emerg Technol 11 (3–4):187–210

Zuurbier FS, Van Lint JWC (2006) Traffic network state estimation using extended Kalman filtering and DSMART. IFAC, Delft

Zuurbier FS, van Lint JWC, Knoop VL (2006) State estimation using an extended Kalman filter and the first order traffic flow model DSMART. In: Eleventh IFAC symposium on control in transportation systems, Delft

Chapter 16
Dynamic Traffic Management Measures to Optimize Air Quality, Climate, Noise, Traffic Safety and Congestion: Effects of a Single Objective Optimization

Luc Wismans, Eric van Berkum, and Michiel Bliemer

16.1 Introduction

Traditionally, traffic problems are treated in isolation in terms of location of the problem and the kind of problem. However, there is a strong correlation between these problems, so clearly solving a traffic problem at one location may result in other problems at other locations. Congestion problems on the main network can, for example, lead to "rat-running" (through-traffic using the secondary road network avoiding these congestion problems) causing liveability problems. Therefore, measures to alleviate traffic problems are nowadays increasingly focussed on the network level. In addition, solutions are sought for the optimization of traffic systems and less emphasis is placed on expanding the infrastructure of the system mainly because of financial considerations and space limitations. This optimization can be achieved using traffic management measures. Traditionally, this type of optimization is focussed on improving accessibility, given particular boundary conditions for traffic safety and liveability (set by law). Yet, the quality of traffic systems is not only a matter of accessibility, but also of externalities such as traffic safety and liveability. Recently, there has been an increase in the attention paid to

L. Wismans (✉)
Department Transport innovation and modelling, Goudappel Coffeng BV, PO Box 161, Deventer 7400 AD, The Netherlands
e-mail: lwismans@goudappel.nl

E. van Berkum
Centre for Transport Studies, University of Twente, PO Box 217, Enschede 7500 AE, The Netherlands
e-mail: e.c.vanberkum@ctw.utwente.nl

M. Bliemer
Department of Transport & Planning, Delft University of Technology, PO Box 5048, Delft 2600 GA, The Netherlands
e-mail: m.c.j.bliemer@tudelft.nl

J.A.E.E. van Nunen et al. (eds.), *Transitions Towards Sustainable Mobility*,
DOI 10.1007/978-3-642-21192-8_16, © Springer-Verlag Berlin Heidelberg 2011

these problems in our society, mainly in the context of climate and air quality, which are of increasing importance when policy decisions are made. This means a need for multi-objective optimization of traffic systems incorporating the externalities (Ministerie Verkeer en Waterstaat 2004; Wismans 1999 and AVV 2002).

16.1.1 Network Design Problem

The optimization of traffic systems by expanding or improving an existing network is often referred to as a Network Design Problem (NDP). This problem is usually formulated as a bi-level programming problem in which the lower level problem describes the responses of road users, optimizing their own objectives, operationalized as solving a deterministic or stochastic user equilibrium problem. The upper level consists of the objective that has to be optimized for solving the NDP. Because of the non-convexity of the problem (Gao et al. 2005; Chiou 2005 and Chiou 2009) several global solution approaches are used, including genetic algorithms and simulated annealing. The optimization of dynamic traffic management (DTM) measures can be seen as a variant of the NDP. There are several studies that formulated multi-objective NDP (MONDP) in which for example the budget-constraint is formulated as a second minimization problem. We refer to Sharma et al. (2009) for more information.

Several studies have been carried out related to the optimization of regional traffic systems using multiple objectives concerning externalities taking traffic dynamics into account. In 1978, Gershwin et al. had already developed a system which could be used to optimize traffic systems by using traffic lights, ramp metering and reserved lanes taking route choice and mode choice into account. The optimization could be travel time, fuel consumption or a combination of the two. More recently Lu et al. 2006 applied a bi-level multi-objective programming model and a genetic algorithm was used as solution algorithm to determine the optimal solution for ramp metering control. Schmöcker et al. (2008) adopt a multi-objective fuzzy logic approach similar to earlier studies of Anderson et al. (1998) and Murat and Kikuchi (2007) to optimize traffic lights, taking into account both emissions and traffic delays. They proved the feasibility of their approach. In Mathew and Sharma (2006) the network design problem is formulated as a bi-level optimization problem in which emission costs and travel time costs are taken into account. They also showed the feasibility of their approach. A grid search algorithm was used in Zuurbier et al. (2007) to determine the optimal application of Variable Message Signs. They used an objective function consisting of a weighted sum of the effects of the air quality and accessibility, and showed that there are different optimal solutions for the individual objectives and for the combined objectives. In Ahn and Rakha (2008) research is done on the effects of route choice in terms of energy use and emissions of pollutants. This research showed that a user equilibrium or system optimum in terms of travel times does not necessarily result in minimizing energy use or emissions.

16.1.2 Aim of This Research

There are more studies related to this subject; however, until now these studies have been limited to considering only a few externalities or are focussed on local optimization. That is why the University of Twente started a research programme to determine how regional traffic systems can be optimized using multiple objectives and traffic management measures taking traffic dynamics into account. This research is about solving the multi-objective NDP in which minimizing the externalities of road traffic using DTM measures are the objectives. This chapter describes the results of research on optimization of the DTM measures of all individual externalities and the effect on other externalities (e.g. what does optimization of traffic safety mean for noise) and research on objectives being opposite or aligned when a traffic system is being optimized using dynamic traffic management measures on the level of objectives of one stakeholder (i.e., road management authority aiming at minimizing all externalities). This knowledge is useful for the multi-objective optimization, because the results can possibly be used to accelerate the multi-objective optimization process in which the Pareto set of solutions, is searched.

16.1.3 Chapter Outline

In the next section the model framework and methodology will be described, in which the model objectives are to optimize congestion, safety, air quality, climate and noise. Then, the solution approach is described and applied in a case study in which (near) optimal settings for DTM measures are determined. The last section concludes with a discussion and directions for further research.

16.2 Model Framework and Methodology

Within this study, the optimization problem is formulated as a bi-level optimization problem. The upper level consists of the optimization of the objectives of the road management authorities concerning congestion, air quality, noise, climate and traffic safety by applying available DTM measures using a genetic algorithm. The lower level consists of the road users optimizing their own objectives (in this case optimization of travel times) operationalized by solving the Dynamic User Equilibrium. In Fig. 16.1 a global overview is given of the framework used.

Fig. 16.1 Framework used

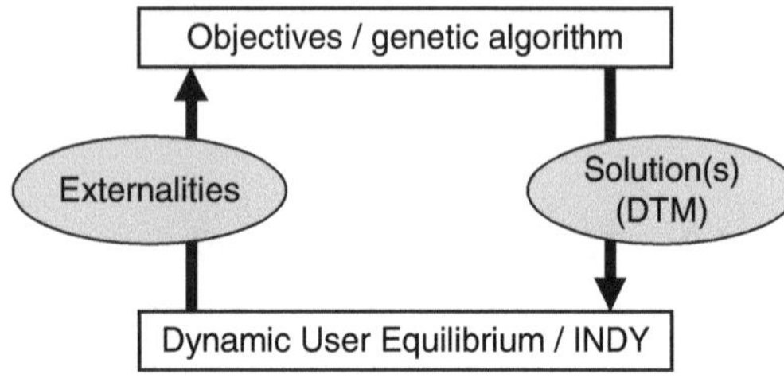

16.2.1 Upper Level

The upper level consists of the calculation of the objective functions and solution approach used, searching for global optima for the single objective functions or a combination of objective functions. Within this section the calculation methods used to assess the externalities and the objective functions are presented.

The optimization is focussed on the optimization of the objectives of one stakeholder, namely the road management authority. However, there are several road management authorities and not just one, and these can have different and possible conflicting objectives. In this study, we assume that there is one road management authority that wants to minimize the externalities of traffic, which means the self-interest of the various road management authorities is not considered. The objective functions used, which all should be minimized, are listed in Table 16.1.

Congestion is represented by the network measure total travel time. The objective function is to minimize the sum of the travel times of all trips. Because fixed demand is assumed, minimizing total travel time is equal to minimizing total vehicle lost hours.

Traffic safety is represented by the measure of the total number of injuries. The calculation method is based on using the relation between exposure (number of vehicle kilometres) and risk per road type (ratio of number of injuries per vehicle kilometre). Important point of attention of this calculation method is that it can only deal with the effect of the dynamics of route choice of road-users (use of different road types) and not with the traffic dynamics on a certain road (speed and speed differences). The objective function is to minimize the total number of injuries. In the literature, there is typically no distinction made in injury risks between vehicle types. Table 16.2 presents some injury risk figures from the Netherlands (Jansen 2005).

The effect of traffic on climate is represented by the measure of total amount of CO_2 emitted by traffic. The calculation method is based on using an average speed based discrete emission function that describes for each vehicle type (passenger cars and trucks) the relation between speed (discrete speed steps of 5 km/h) and the emission factor (emission of CO_2 per vehicle kilometre). The emission function shown in Fig. 16.2 was fitted within Goudappel Coffeng (2007) by using the emission factors estimated in TNO (2001) and a physical calculation of the energy

Table 16.1 Overview of measures and objective functions used

Objective	Measure	Remark
Congestion	Total travel time (h)	Because fixed demand is assumed minimizing total travel time is equal to minimizing vehicle lost hours
$\min Y = \sum_a \sum_t \sum_m \frac{q_{am}(t)\ell_a}{v_{am}(t)}$ (1)		
Traffic safety	Total number of injuries	Calculation based on using the relation between exposure and risk per road type
$\min F = \sum_a \sum_t \sum_m \sum_d q_{am}(t)\delta_{ad}R_{md}\ell_a$ (2)		
Climate	Total amount of CO_2 emissions (g)	Calculation based on average speed based discrete emission functions per vehicle type used within the Dutch study Effects of speed limit enforcement on CO_2 emissions (Goudappel Coffeng 2007)
$\min G = \sum_a \sum_t \sum_m q_{am}(t)E_m^{CO2}(v_{am}(t))\ell_a$ (3)		
Air quality	Weighted total amount of NO_x emissions (g) Weighted total amount of PM_{10} emissions (g)	Calculation based on a traffic situation based emission model using discrete emission functions per level of service, vehicle type and per road type. Emission factors derived from the emission model CAR and the study emissions and congestion (TNO 2001). Two substances NO_x and PM_{10} are assessed
$\min F^s = \sum_a \sum_t \sum_m \sum_d w_a q_{am}(t)\delta_{ad}E_{md}^s(v_{am}(t))\ell_a, \quad s \in \{NO_x, PM_{10}\}$ (4)		
Noise	Weighted average sound power level at the source (dB[A])	Calculation based on the standard calculation method (RMV) used in the Netherlands

$$\min W = 10\log\left(\frac{\sum_a \sum_w \delta_{aw}\ell_a 10^{\frac{\bar{L}_w - \eta_w}{10}}}{\sum_a \sum_w \delta_{aw}\ell_a}\right), \text{ with } \bar{L}_w = 10\log\left(\frac{\sum_a \sum_t \delta_{aw}\ell_a \sum_m 10^{\frac{L_m(v_{am}(t))}{10}}}{\sum_a \delta_{aw}\ell_a}\right) \quad (5)$$

with

Y : objective function congestion (= total travel time) (h)
Z : objective function traffic safety (= number of injuries)
G : objective function climate (= total amount of CO_2 emissions) (g)
F^s : objective function air quality (= weighted total amount of emissions of substance s) (g)
W : objective function noise (= weighted average sound power level at source) (dB[A])
$q_{am}(t)$: vehicle type m inflow to link a at time t (veh)
$v_{am}(t)$: average speed of vehicle type m on link a at time t (km/h)
R_{md} : injury risk of vehicle type m for road type d (injuries/[veh*km])
$E_m^{CO2}(\cdot)$: CO_2 emission factor of vehicle type m, depending on average speed (g/[veh*km])
$E_{md}^s(\cdot)$: emission factor of substance s of vehicle type m on road type d, depending on average speed (g/[veh*km])
$L_m(\cdot)$: average sound power level for vehicle type m, depending on the average speed (dB[A])
$\bar{L}_w$: weighted average sound power level on network part with urbanization level w (dB[A])
ℓ_a : length of link a (km)
δ_{ad} : road type indicator, equals 1 if link a is of road type d, and 0 otherwise
δ_{aw} : urbanization level indicator, equals 1 if link a has urbanization level w, and 0 otherwise
w_a : level of urbanization around link a
η_w : correction factor for urbanization level w (dB[A])

Table 16.2 Overview of used risk figures

Road type (sustainable safe definitions)	Risk (R_{md}) injuries/million vehicle kilometres
Through-road	0.07
Non-urban distributor roads	0.22
Urban distributor roads	1.10
Non-urban access roads	0.43
Urban access roads	0.57

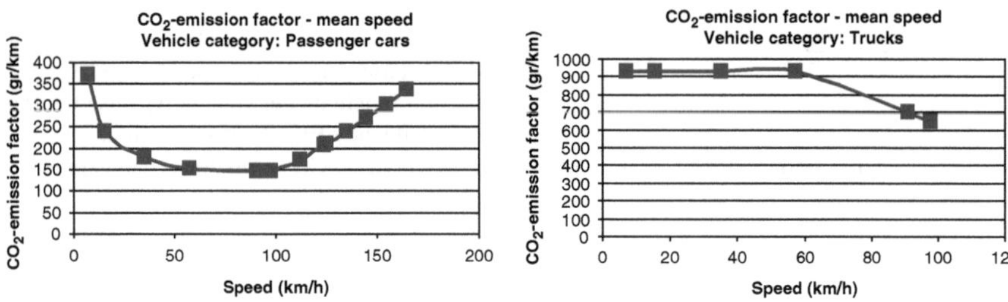

Fig. 16.2 Emission functions CO_2

needed to overcome the rolling, acceleration and air resistances, and the engine's efficiency. One important point of attention is that the emission function is based on the relation between speed and CO_2 emissions that is based on data from highways. The objective function is to minimize the total amount of CO_2 emitted by traffic.

The effect of traffic on air quality is represented by the total amount of NO_x and the total amount of PM_{10} emitted by traffic. Besides NO_x and PM_{10} there are also other pollutants relevant for air quality. However, these two pollutants are the most critical in the Netherlands in relation to the EU limit values. Although, it is straightforward to calculate using the output of the traffic model, the real measure of air quality is the concentration of these substances at certain locations. To determine the concentrations, a lot of extra input is needed, such as weather conditions, type of road surface and the location of screens and buildings to calculate the dispersion. However, it is questionable how best to aggregate concentrations to judge the network performance in terms of air quality; though it is a fact that air quality is related to human health and therefore, it is of importance what concentrations are calculated at particular locations. High concentrations in residential areas are more harmful than high concentrations in rural areas. That is why weighting factors are used per road section dependent of level of urbanization. Within this research three levels of urbanization are distinguished, highly urbanized, urbanized and rural. The weighting factors (w_a, respectively 3, 2 and 1) used are based on the dilution factor that is used in the CAR emission model which depends on the distance and to what extent buildings are present near the road (e.g. street canyons).

The calculation method used to determine the emissions is based on traffic situation based emission factors. The traffic situations are operationalized by using discrete speed intervals (representing the traffic situations) per road type

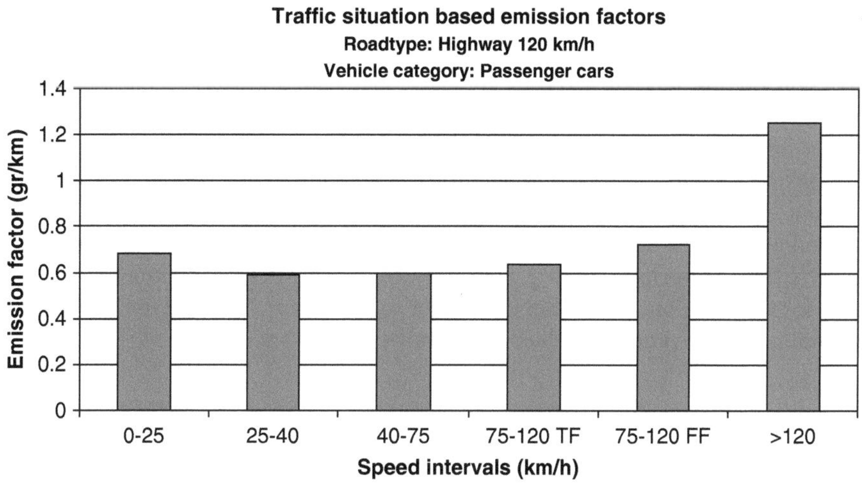

Fig. 16.3 Example of emission factors NO_x

and vehicle type. For highway sections also a distinction is made between traffic force (volume > 1,000 vehicles per lane/h) and free flow traffic conditions (volume < 1,000 vehicles per lane/h). These emission factors are derived from the Dutch emission model CAR and research presented in TNO (2001). An example of the emission factors used for passenger cars on a highway section with a speed limit of 120 km/h is shown in Fig. 16.3. The objective function is to minimize the total weighted NO_x emissions and to minimize the total weighted PM_{10} emissions.

The generation of noise pollution by traffic is represented by the average sound power level (L_m) for each vehicle type at the source. Like air quality, this measure is straightforward to calculate using the output of the traffic model. However, the real measure of noise pollution is the sound power level at particular locations. To determine such sound power levels, many extra inputs are needed, such as type of road surface, the alignment of the road and the location of screens and buildings to calculate the propagation of sound. Again, aggregation of concentrations of noise pollution is not straightforward. Also, for noise pollution it can be stated that high sound power levels in residential areas are more harmful or irritating than high sound power levels in rural areas. That is why correction factors are used dependent on the urbanization level. The same levels of urbanization, w, are used as for air quality, highly urbanized, urbanized and rural. The correction factors (η_w, respectively -7, -10, -13) are based on the distance correction factor used in the RMV method. The calculation method used to calculate the sound emission is the regression function per vehicle category that is estimated within the standard calculation method (RMV). Its function is of the form:

$$L_m(v_{am}(t)) = \alpha_m + \beta_m \log\left(\frac{v_{am}(t)}{v_m^{\text{ref}}}\right) + 10 \log\left(\frac{q_{am}(t)}{v_{am}(t)}\right) \tag{16.6}$$

where α_m and β_m are vehicle type specific parameters, and v_m^{ref} is a vehicle type specific reference speed. Some typical values for these parameters are 80 and 70 km/h for the reference speeds for passenger cars and trucks, and $\alpha_m = 69.4$ (76.0) and $\beta_m = 27.6$ (17.9) for passenger cars (trucks).

An important point of attention of this method is that it is a combination of rolling and propulsion noise and therefore focussed on the rolling noise (which is dominant at higher speeds, typically higher than 40 km/h for passenger cars, depending on road surface) and not on propulsion noise (which is of interest at lower speeds, especially when a vehicle is accelerating). No correction factors are used for acceleration and deceleration or for road surface. The objective function is to minimize the average weighted sound power level at the source.

16.2.2 Lower Level

The lower level consists of the road users optimizing their own objectives (in this case, travel time). The lower level is operationalized by using the INDY traffic model (Bliemer et al. 2004 and Bliemer 2007). The measures are modelled by changing link attributes dynamically using specific controls (e.g. capacity and free speed) resulting in changing traffic propagation and therefore changing route choice of traffic. INDY is a macroscopic DTA model and uses a relative multinomial logit model on a pre-generated route set to model route choice, and the dynamic queuing model to model flow propagation. The output of INDY is used to determine the outcome of the objective functions of the road management authorities using the methods described earlier.

16.3 Solution Approach

The optimization problem is non convex (Gao et al. 2005; Chiou 2005, 2009) and it is also impossible to assess all solutions. The application of DTM measures can be changed continuously in time and in theory often also in application (e.g. green time given to certain turns of a traffic signal) resulting in an infinite number of solutions. We limit the number of design variables by modelling the different measures changing the fundamental diagram used within the flow propagation model (e.g. capacity and free speed) of the links on which these measures apply. We discretize the solution space of the DTM measures in terms of time, by dividing the time horizon into a set of time intervals (e.g., each 15 min the DTM measure application can change), and in terms of applications of DTM measures, by identifying a limited number of applications (e.g., capacities between 500 and 1,500 veh/h using a step size of 100 veh/h). Each combination of a DTM measure application and a time interval is associated with an integer, which means a solution vector of a size that equals the number of DTM measures applications times the number of time intervals. Although the solution space is now finite, it can still be very large. Since each assessment of a solution requires solving a dynamic traffic assignment (DTA) problem, assessing all possible solutions is practically not feasible. Identifying for example 3 measures, each with 11 applications and six time intervals already results in 5.6×10^{18} possible solutions. The solution approach chosen, similar to other related research, is using a heuristic. In our case a genetic algorithm is used. Nevertheless, also these global solution approaches require many function evaluations in order to find an optimum. Therefore, we tested three solution approaches, presented in Fig. 16.4.

Within the first approach, the genetic algorithm searches for optima in the entire feasible solution space. In the second and third approach, the search is divided into two parts. First, an optimal solution is found assuming the application of DTM measures to be constant over time, yielding a 'static' optimal DTM measure. This requires searching in a space of only 1,331 feasible solutions. Secondly, the algorithm determines an optimal application of measures over different time intervals, which means 'dynamic' application of the measures. The outcome of the first 'static' optimization was used to define the starting solutions of the second 'dynamic' optimization. Within the third solution approach, this outcome is also used to reduce the total solution space by assuming that the optimal application of a measure within a certain time interval lies between adjacent applications of the DTM measures. This assumption is made because within a peak period there are no major changes in the relative travel demand of origin destination relations, the

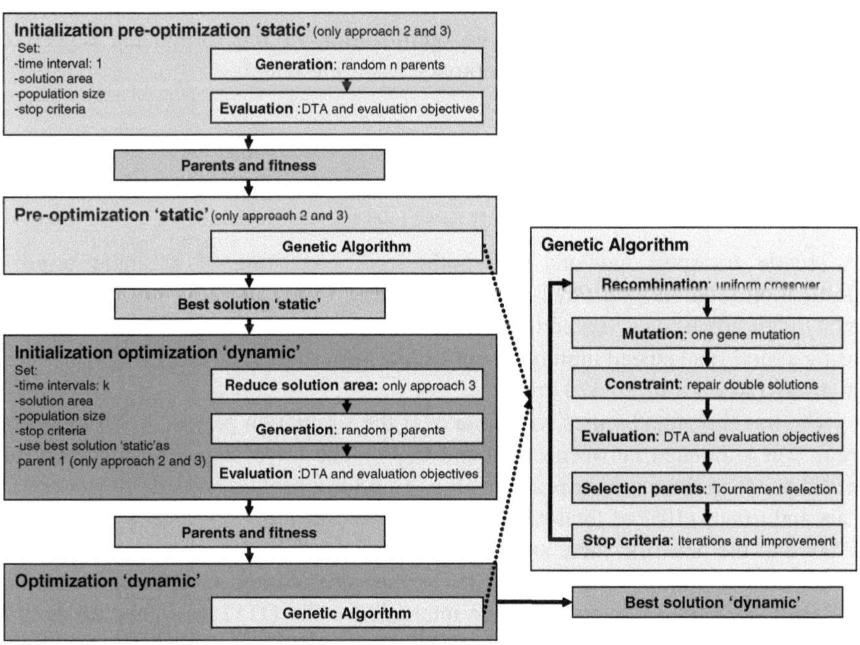

Fig. 16.4 Solution approach

differences between time intervals are mainly the amount of travel demand between an origin and destination. The starting solutions used in the 'dynamic' optimization are the average best performing solution of the 'static' optimization and random selected solutions only using the applications between the two adjacent possibilities per measure. Within the mutation step, the genetic algorithm can also select an application that is two steps away of the average best application. If for example the 'static' optimization concludes that the capacity of a certain DTM measure should be set on 1,000 veh/h for the total evaluation interval, the 'dynamic' optimization randomly varies the capacities of this measure between 900 and 1,100 veh/h in each time interval when the starting solutions are built and can select capacities between 800 and 1,200 veh/h within the mutation step. This approach reduces the total solution area to less than 0.000001% of the original solution area, but in our example still 3.8×10^{12} possible solutions remain. Clearly, the two-stage procedure used in approach 3 is possibly to yield sub-optimal solutions as we rule out a large part of the feasible solution space. However, we envisage to find a near-optimal solution in a reasonable amount of computation time.

16.4 Case Study: Optimization of Externalities

A case study is used to show results when applying the framework, but moreover to show that the different objectives can be aligned or opposite and to compare the solution approaches. After a description is given of the case study, the reference case is shown. Next, results of the optimization of the formulated objective functions and three used solution approaches are presented.

16.4.1 Description

A simple transport network is hypothesized, consisting of a single origin–destination relation with three alternative routes. One route runs straight through a city with urban roads (speed limit of 50 km/h); the second route is via a ring road using a rural road (speed limit of 80 km/h); the third route is an outer ring road via a highway (speed limit of 120 km/h).

The travel demand varies with time over the simulation period. A 3-h morning peak was simulated between 06:00 and 09:00. The travel demand (maximum of 6,300 pcu/h in the morning peak, see Fig. 16.5 for a profile) consists of passenger cars and trucks (10% of total demand).

Within the network, there are three measures available, two traffic lights and a VMS used to change speed limits. These measures can be used to optimize the different objectives. In total six time intervals for the DTM measures are distinguished, equally divided into 30 min slices. The modelling of the traffic signals is done by changing the capacities of the different turns. Capacities can be set between

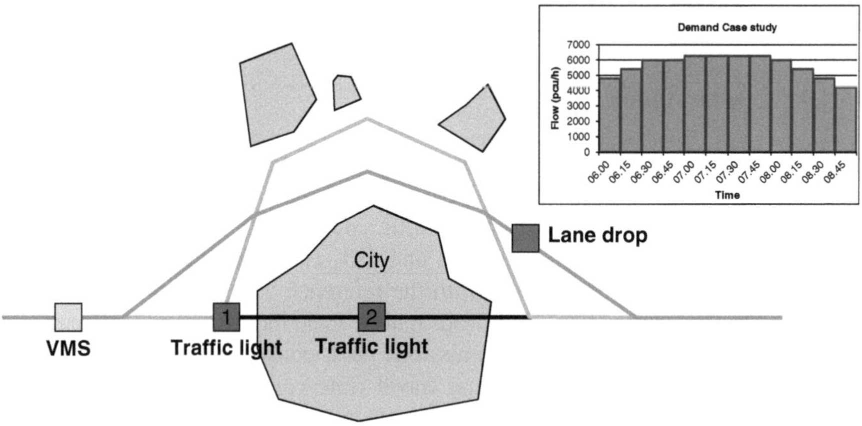

Fig. 16.5 Representation of network

500 and 1,500 pcu/h. The application of traffic signal 1 can be seen as two measures. The first consists of changing the capacity of the route through the city, the second of changing the capacity of the route using the ring road. The modelling of the VMS is done by changing the speed limit on the entire highway. In addition, the capacities were changed in order to take into account the effect of homogenous traffic streams (when the speed limit is lowered). Three different speed limits were considered, namely 120, 100 and 80 km/h. The speed limit of 100 km/h was combined with an increase of the capacity of approximately 2.5% and the speed limit of 80 km/h with an increase of the capacity of approximately 5%. In total 4.0×10^{21} possible solutions exist. Using the proposed framework means that in the 'static' optimization 3,993 solutions exist and after reducing the solution area still 2.8×10^{15} solutions exist in the dynamic optimization. The DTA problem on the lower level is solved using a route choice time interval of 900 s and a flow propagation time step of 5 s.

16.4.2 Reference Case

In the reference case the speed limit of the highway is 120 km/h and the capacity of the traffic signal is 1,000 pcu/h per turn. In free flow conditions route 3 is the fastest route and route 2 the slowest route. In the morning peak, congestion occurs due to a lane drop, resulting in increasing travel times when using this route. Therefore, more traffic uses the other routes through the city and the rural road. In the reference case 78% of the vehicles use the highway route, 9% the rural route and 13% the route through the city within a dynamic user equilibrium (DUE). As a result of more traffic choosing the route through the city or the ring road, there is a queue at traffic signal 1.

16.4.3 Results Case Study

16.4.3.1 Optimization

The results of the optimization are presented in Table 16.3. Each column presents an optimized design for a specific objective and the relative deviation is presented from the minimum found. If for instance traffic safety is optimized, total travel time is 37% higher than the minimum found and CO_2 emissions are 5% higher. The largest improvement in comparison with the reference case is possible for traffic safety. Optimization of traffic safety leads mainly to an increase of travel times, but also emissions. Optimization of emissions and congestion result in similar situations. However, in this case total travel time can be reduced with 3–5%, resulting in 7% more CO_2 emissions and 1% higher weighted NO_x and PM_{10} emissions. The objective which seems most opposite to the other objectives is noise. The deviation of this objective with the optimal solutions of the other objectives is relatively large when noise is optimized. Because most traffic use the roads situated in the rural area, the optimized designs for climate and air quality are almost similar. However, this will not be true in general while in contrast to climate the location of emission is of importance for air quality.

Table 16.3 Results optimization

Optimized designs for each objective

Measure	Min	Reference	Congestion	Traffic safety	Climate	Air quality NO_x	Air quality PM_{10}	Noise
Total travel time (h)	4952.23	2	0	37	3	5	5	60
Total number of injuries	0.0432	20	20	0	20	12	13	13
Total amount of CO_2-emissions (t)	95.5	7	7	5	0	1	1	7
Weighted total amount of NO_x emissions (kg)	779.19	1	1	7	0	0	0	19
Weighted total amount of PM_{10} emissions (kg)	38.65	2	1	5	0	0	0	15
Weighted average L_w at the source (dB[A])	71.66	4	4	2	3	3	3	0

The objectives for congestion, traffic safety, emissions and noise show different optimal solutions, which means there is not a combination of measures resulting in an optimal situation for a combination of all objectives. Optimizing congestion aims at avoiding congestion using full capacity of the three available routes. Maximizing traffic safety aims at maximizing the use of the relatively safe highway route and avoiding use of the urban route. Minimizing emissions aims at avoiding congestion and high speeds and searches for the best trade of between minimizing traffic using the urban roads and the level of congestion on the highway. Minimizing noise aims at lowering the driving speeds as much as possible and avoiding traffic using the urban routes.

In Fig. 16.6 all solutions that are assessed in all 18 optimizations (optimizing six objectives using three approaches) are plotted of the objective congestion related to the other objectives. The efficient frontier or Pareto Set is also shown. If the efficient frontier is large the objectives are mainly opposite. This figure confirms that the objectives congestion and air quality are aligned and that these objectives are opposite to traffic safety and noise. Although not all solutions are calculated, it is possible to draw this conclusion, because if for example noise and congestion were not opposite, both individual searches would not result in this large efficient frontier. In addition, similar results were found in Wismans et al. (2009) in which a

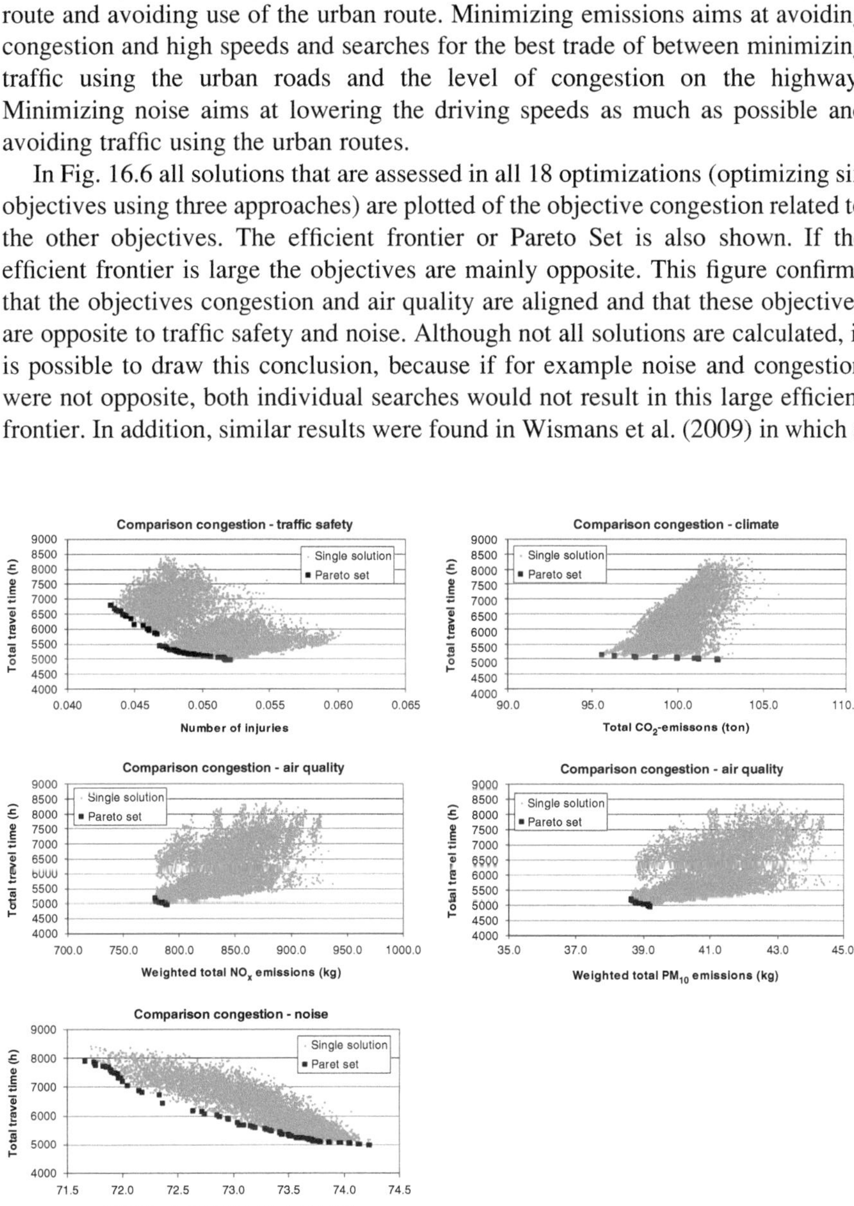

Fig. 16.6 Objective functions solutions related to congestion

grid search was carried out. For climate, it cannot be concluded that the objectives are aligned or opposite.

16.4.3.2 Comparison of Solution Approaches

Next to the used genetic algorithm, a grid search was done for the 'static' optimization to check whether the results of this optimization would yield the optimal solution. The results presented in Table 16.4 show that the static optimization

Table 16.4 Results optimization approaches

Static

		Reference	Grid search		Approach 2		Approach 3	
Objective	*Measure*	Min		–	Min	Iterations	Min	Iterations
Congestion	Total travel time (h)	5,028.43	4,963.95		4,963.95	12	4,963.95	3
Traffic safety	Total number of injuries	0.052	0.044		0.045	6	0.044	10
Climate	Total amount of CO_2-emissions (t)	102.55	95.56		95.56	2	95.56	7
Air quality	Weighted total amount of NO_x emissions (kg)	789.43	781.81		782.04	20	781.81	20
	Weighted total amount of PM_{10} emissions (kg)	39.25	38.80		38.80	8	38.80	14
Noise	Weighted average L_w at the source (dB(A))	74.23	72.17		72.38	13	72.17	19

Dynamic

		Reference	Approach 1		Approach 2		Approach 3	
Objective	Measure		Min	Iterations	Min	Iterations	Min	Iterations
Congestion	Total travel time (h)	5,028.43	4,952.23	75	4,961.20	89	4,963.95	20
Traffic safety	Total number of injuries	0.052	0.046	90	0.045	98	0.043	79
Climate	Total amount of CO_2-emissions (t)	102.55	95.57	93	95.55	25	95.55	78
Air quality	Weighted total amount of NO_x emissions (kg)	789.43	779.19	66	779.68	97	780.66	83
	Weighted total amount of PM_{10} emissions (kg)	39.25	38.71	2	38.65	92	38.67	99
Noise	Weighted average L_w at the source (dB[A])	74.23	71.66	49	71.92	85	71.71	92

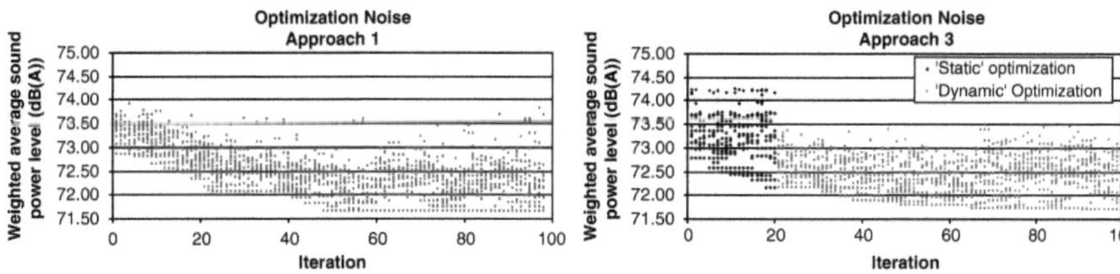

Fig. 16.7 Results optimization process approach 1 and 3

used in approaches 2 and 3 do find the optimal solutions for the static case. The three different approaches within the dynamic optimization find similar results. It can not be concluded that the pre-optimization improves the speed in which optima are found (the 20 iterations of the pre-optimization are included in the number of iterations shown for approaches 2 and 3 for the dynamic optimization). The approach finding the best solution is different for the different objective functions. However, there is no reason to believe that approach 3, in which the solution space is reduced, yields sub-optimal solutions. Especially, because the improvements found in the dynamic optimization are relatively small in comparison with the optimal solutions found in the static optimization. Although tests with approach 1 in which the number of iterations is substantially increased (quadrupled) did not result in major improvements (less than 1%), it remains uncertain if better solutions exists.

In Fig. 16.7 the results per iteration are plotted for approaches 1 and 3 for the objective noise. This figure shows that reducing the solution space does bound the outcome of the objective function. However, within approach 1 the genetic algorithm used results in a similar figure as approach 3. The expected gain in the first iterations by determining the static optimal solution is negligible. This conclusion holds for all investigated objectives. The genetic algorithm used in approach 1 pushes the search relatively fast in the correct direction. The pre-optimization is therefore not accelerating the search.

16.5 Discussion, Conclusions, and Further Research

This research has presented a framework for the optimization of externalities using DTM measures, provides insight into formulating objective functions and showed an application of this framework using three solution approaches. The objectives for congestion, traffic safety, emissions and noise show different optimal solutions, which means there is not a combination of measures resulting in an optimal situation for a combination of all objectives. However, it was found that the objectives concerning emissions and congestion are aligned and that these objectives are opposite to noise and traffic safety. The three solution approaches all using a genetic algorithm differ in the way starting solutions are determined, random or using a pre-optimization, and if the solution space is reduced, using the results of the pre-optimization. The pre-optimization consists of optimizing the application of DTM measures, but assuming the application to be constant over time. The results show that there is no reason to assume that reducing the solution space results in sub-optimal solutions. However, the results also show that using a pre-optimization does not lead in finding better solutions or finding the optimal solutions faster. The genetic algorithm used is effective enough to find the optimal solutions and a pre-optimization is not accelerating the search in our test case. The optimization using the approaches presented needs large computational efforts, which will be increasing when larger networks with more measures are assessed. It is therefore recommended to further improve the solution approaches presented by incorporating knowledge of traffic systems to reduce the solution space more effectively.

This research is part of a research programme to determine how regional traffic systems can be optimized using multiple objectives applying traffic management measures. Our research will proceed on investigating solution approaches that can be used in practice and will be extended by actually performing the multi-objective optimization finding the Pareto set.

References

Ahn K, Rakha H (2008) The effects of route choice decisions on vehicle energy consumption and emissions. Transp Res D 13:151–167

Anderson JM, Sayers TM, Bell MGH (1998) Optimization of a fuzzy logic traffic signal controller by a multiobjective genetic algorithm. In: Proceedings of the 9th international conference road transport information and control, London, pp 186–190

AVV (2002) Werkboek gebiedsgericht benutten. Met de Architectuur voor Verkeersbeheersing. (in Dutch) Rotterdam

Bliemer MCJ (2007) Dynamic queuing and spillback in an analytical multiclass dynamic network loading model. Transp Res Rec 2029:14–21

Bliemer MCJ, Versteegt HH, Castenmiller RJ (2004) INDY: a new analytical multi-class dynamic traffic assignment model. In: TRISTAN V conference proceedings, Guadeloupe, France

Chiou S (2005) Bilevel programming for the continuous transport network design problem. Transp Res B 39:361–383

Chiou S (2009) A subgradient optimization model for continuous road network design problem. Appl Math Model 33:1386–1396

Gao Z, Wu J, Sun H (2005) Solution algorithm for the bi-level discrete network design problem. Transp Res B 39:479–495

Gershwin SB, Ross P, Garner N, Little JDC (1978) Optimization of large traffic systems. Transp Res Rec 682:8–15

Goudappel Coffeng (2007) Effects of speed limit enforcement on CO_2-emissions. Effecten versterkte snelheidshandhaving op CO_2-emissies. Eindrapportage. (In Dutch). Deventer LJJ, Wismans van Beek P, van den Brink RMM

Jansen STMC (2005) De Verkeersveiligheidsverkenner gebruikt in de regio. De rekenmethode en de aannamen daarin (In Dutch). SWOV-rapport R-2005-6, Leidschendam

Lu ZL, Fan BQ, Liu JJ, Zhou YH (2006) Bi-level multi-objective programming model for the ramp control and pollution control on urban expressway networks. Kongzhi yu Juece/Control Decis 21(1):21–35

Mathew TV, Sharma S (2006) Continuous network design with emission pricing as a bi-level optimization problem. Applications of advanced technology in transportation. In: Proceedings of the ninth international conference on applications of advanced technology in transportation, Chicago

Ministerie Verkeer en Waterstaat (2004) Nota mobiliteit. (In Dutch). Den Haag

Murat YS, Kikuchi S (2007) Fuzzy optimization approach: comparison with the classical optimization method using the problem of timing a traffic signal. Transport Res Rec J Transp Res Board 2024:82–91

Schmöcker J-D, Ahuja S, Bell MGH (2008) Multi-objective signal control of urban junctions – framework and a London case study. Transport Res C Emerg 16(4):454–470

Sharma S, Ukkusuri SV, Mathew TA (2009) Pareto optimal multi-objective optimization for the robust transportation network design problem. Presented at the 88th annual meeting of the transportation research board, Washington, DC

TNO (2001) Emissies en files – Bepalen van emissiefactoren. Eindrapportage fase 2. TNO, Delft. Report No. 01.OR.VM.0441/NG (in Dutch)

Wismans LJJ (1999) Optimaliseren verkeersafwikkeling op netwerkniveau. Master thesis, University of Twente (in Dutch), Enschede

Wismans LJJ, Van Berkum EC, Bliemer MCJ (2009) Multi objective optimization of traffic systems using dynamic traffic management measures. In: Proceedings of models and technologies for intelligent transportation systems conference, Rome, 22–23 June 2009

Zuurbier FS, Hoogendoorn SP, Van Lint H, van (2007) Evaluating non trivial objective functions for traffic management by means of optimal prescriptive route guidance. In: 14th world congress on ITS, Beijing Exhibition Center, China

List of Contributors

Niels Agatz Rotterdam School of Management, Erasmus University, PO Box 1738, 3000 DR Rotterdam, The Netherlands, nagatz@rsm.nl

Jessie Bakens Department of Spatial Economics, VU University Amsterdam, De Boelelaan 1105, 1081 HV Amsterdam, The Netherlands, j.bakens@vu.nl

Eric van Berkum Faculty of Engineering Technology Centre for Transport Studies, University of Twente, PO Box 217, 7500 AE Enschede, The Netherlands, e.c.vanberkum@ctw.utwente.nl

Luca Bertolini AMIDSt - Amsterdam institute for Metropolitan and International Development Studies, University of Amsterdam, Nieuwe Prinsengracht 130, 1018 VZ Amsterdam, The Netherlands, L.Bertolini@uva.nl

Arjan van Binsbergen Research School Trail, PO Box 5017, 2600 GA Delft, The Netherlands, a.j.vanbinsbergen@rsTRAIL.nl

Michiel Bliemer Faculty of Civil Engineering and Geosciences Department of Transport & Planning, Delft University of Technology, PO Box 5048, 2600 GA Delft, The Netherlands, m.c.j.bliemer@tudelft.nl

Marco te Brömmelstroet AMIDSt - Amsterdam institute for Metropolitan and International Development Studies, University of Amsterdam, Nieuwe Prinsengracht 130, 1018 VZ Amsterdam, The Netherlands, marco@transport-planning.eu

Martijn Brons Institute for Prospective Technological Studies (IPTS), European Commission, Joint Research Centre (JRC), c/Inca Garcilaso 3, 41092 Seville, Spain, martijn.brons@ec.europa.eu

DOI 10.1007/978-3-642-21192-8,

Said Dabia School of Industrial Engineering, TU/e Eindhoven University of Technology, PO Box 513, 5600 MB Eindhoven, The Netherlands, s.dabia@tue.nl

Ghebreegziabiher Debrezion Department of Spatial Economics, VU University Amsterdam, De Boelelaan 1105, 1081 HV Amsterdam, The Netherlands, g.debrezion@vu.nl

Dick Ettema Faculty of Geosciences Utrecht University, PO Box 80115, 3508 TC Utrecht, The Netherlands, d.ettema@geo.uu.nl

Thomas de Graaff Department of Spatial Economics, VU University Amsterdam, De Boelelaan 1105, 1081 HV Amsterdam, The Netherlands, t.de.graaff@vu.nl

Marcel Hertogh AT Osborne, J.F. Kennedylaan 100, 3741 EH Baarn, The Netherlands, mhe@osborne.nl

Jos van Hillegersberg Department of Information Systems and Change Management, University of Twente, Capitool Building, Room C1-06, PO Box 217, 7500 AE Enschede, The Netherlands, j.vanhillegersberg@utwente.nl

Paul Huijbregts Dutch Institute for Advanced Logistics, Princenhagelaan 13, 4813 DA Breda, The Netherlands, huijbregts@dinalog.nl

Dennis Huisman Erasmus School of Economics, Erasmus University Rotterdam, PO Box 1738, 3000 DR Rotterdam, The Netherlands, huisman@ese.eur.nl

Ben Immers Department of Mechanical Engineering, Centre for Industrial Management, University of Leuven, Celestijnenlaan 300A, BE-3001 Heverlee, Belgium, ben.immers@cib.kuleuven.beB.Immers@rsTRAIL.nl

Rien van der Knaap OC Mobility Coaching, PO Box 729, 5600 AS Eindhoven, The Netherlands, rien.oc@planet.nl

Jasper Knockaert Department of Spatial Economics, VU University Amsterdam, De Boelelaan 1105, 1081 HV Amsterdam, The Netherlands, j.knockaert@vu.nl

Ton de Kok School of Industrial Engineering, TU/e Eindhoven University of Technology, PO Box 513, 5600 MB Eindhoven, The Netherlands, a.g.d.kok@tue.nl

Erwin van der Krabben Department of Spatial Planning, Institute for Management Research, Radboud University Nijmegen, PO Box 9108, 6500 HK Nijmegen, The Netherlands, e.vanderkrabben@fm.ru.nl

Leo Kroon Rotterdam School of Management, Erasmus University, PO Box 1738, 3000 DR Rotterdam, The Netherlands, lkroon@rsm.nl

Erwin van der Laan Rotterdam School of Management, Erasmus University, PO Box 1738, 3000 DR Rotterdam, The Netherlands, elaan@rsm.nl

Hans van Lint Department of Transport and Planning, Delft University of Technology, Jaffalaan 5, 2628 BX Delft, The Netherlands, j.w.c.vanlint@tudelft.nl

Hans Moonen Logica Business Consulting, Postbus 159, 1180 AD Amstelveen, The Netherlands, h.moonen@logica.com

Hans Quak TNO Bouw en Ondergrond, Van Mourik Broekmanweg 6, 2628 XE Delft, The Netherlands, hans.quak@tno.nl

Piet Rietveld Department of Spatial Economics, VU University Amsterdam, De Boelelaan 1105, 1081 HV Amsterdam, The Netherlands, p.rietveld@vu.nl

Ary Samsura Department of Spatial Planning, Institute for Management Research, Radboud University Nijmegen, PO Box 9108, 6500 HK Nijmegen, The Netherlands, d.samsura@fm.ru.nl

Lori Tavasszy TNO Bouw en Ondergrond, Van Mourik Broekmanweg 6, 2628 XE Delft, The Netherlands, lori.tavasszy@tno.nl

Albert Valkenberg Faculty of Mechanical Engineering Delft University of Technology, Jaffalaan 5, 2628 BX Delft, The Netherlands, a.j.valkenberg@tudelft.nl

Erik Verhoef Department of Spatial Economics, VU University Amsterdam, De Boelelaan 1105, 1081 HV Amsterdam, The Netherlands, e.t.verhoef@vu.nl

Eddy Westerveld AT Osborne, J.F. Kennedylaan 100, 3741 EH Baarn, The Netherlands, ewe@osborne.nl

Luc Wismans Department Transport innovation and modelling, Goudappel Coffeng B.V, PO Box 161, 7400 AD Deventer, The Netherlands, lwismans@goudappel.nl

Tom van Woensel School of Industrial Engineering, TU/e Eindhoven University of Technology, PO Box 513, 5600 MB Eindhoven, The Netherlands, t.v.woensel@tue.nl

MIX
Papier aus verantwortungsvollen Quellen
Paper from responsible sources
FSC® C105338

If you have any concerns about our products,
you can contact us on
ProductSafety@springernature.com

In case Publisher is established outside the EU,
the EU authorized representative is:
Springer Nature Customer Service Center GmbH
Europaplatz 3, 69115 Heidelberg, Germany

Printed by Libri Plureos GmbH
in Hamburg, Germany